3/97

HIDDEN CITIES

HIDDEN CITIES

THE DISCOVERY AND LOSS OF ANCIENT NORTH AMERICAN CIVILIZATION

ROGER G. KENNEDY

THE FREE PRESS
A Division of Macmillan, Inc.
NEW YORK

Maxwell Macmillan Canada
TORONTO

Maxwell Macmillan International
NEW YORK   OXFORD   SINGAPORE   SYDNEY

The Free Press
A Division of Macmillan, Inc.
866 Third Avenue, New York, N.Y. 10022

Maxwell Macmillan Canada, Inc.
1200 Eglinton Avenue East
Suite 200
Don Mills, Ontario M3C 3N1

Macmillan, Inc. is part of the Maxwell Communication Group of Companies.

Printed in the United States of America

printing number
1   2   3   4   5   6   7   8   9   10

Library of Congress Cataloging-in-Publication Data

Kennedy, Roger G.
  Hidden cities : the discovery and loss of ancient North American civilization / by Roger Kennedy.
    p.   cm.
  Includes bibliographical references and index.
  ISBN 0–02–917307–8
  1. Indian architecture—United States. 2. Architecture—United States—History. 3. Mound-builders—United States. 4. Indianists—United States—Biography. 5. Archaeologists—United States—Biography. 6. Indians of North America—Antiquities. 7. United States—Antiquities. I. Title.
  E98.A63K46   1994
  720′.97—dc20   94–4390
                                                                              CIP

Endpaper Credit:

Map of Louisiana created by Bartholemy Lafon, surveyor, cartographer, engineer, architect, and part-time pirate, who emigrated from France in 1790. He created the map shortly after the turn of the century; he had already discovered and explored many ancient moundworks (see Chapter 9).

Once again, to Frances

CONTENTS

CITIES AND BUILDINGS

The words *city* and *building* are used in this book in old-fashioned ways: by *city* we mean a place in which a large number of people gather for common purposes; citizens determine cities. By *building* we mean a large three-dimensional construction, whether made of masonry, wood, stone, metal, or earth.

Our English noun *city* comes from the Latin, as does our adjective *urban*, but they arise from quite distinct Latin meanings. The Latin *urbis* and its Germanic counterpart, *burg*, referred more to a place than to an aggregate of persons. The distinction is important because city carries from its demographic root the implication of intention. A city was the consequence of a purpose. Perhaps it is not so much a noun as the outcome of a verb; not a location but phenomenon. A city was where a relatively large number of citizens congregated—the city did not exist without citizens, whereas the urban setting, with its burghers, was, well, just there.

In the Middle Ages, in the British Isles, a city became a place in which a potent religious leader such as a bishop was headquartered. Bishops had, it seems, often located themselves in pious or strategic villages, but as time and travail went on, they found it prudent or pleasant to repair into trading centers.

In these ways, the modern city was formed, but only after the cities discussed in these pages had ceased to be. While they throve these knotted settlements were distinguished by their relatively large size from the hamlets dispersed throughout the countryside and by the intensity of the common purposes of their citizens as demonstrated by the monumental architecture created within their confines manifesting, it is likely, the presence of one or more powerful religious figures.

Build and *building* are also very old words, often used in this text as they were when the English language was being invented, to denote earthen structures.

About 1150, when the word *build* was first employed in English, it referred to the construction of an earthen grave. Three hundred and fifty years later, an early use of the term *to build up* was the description of the process by which King Priam of Troy constructed a "big town of bare earth." So when we refer to the earthworks of the Ohio and Mississippi Valleys as *buildings* no one should be surprised.

COMING OVER
AND INTO THE VALLEY

The trail rises into a meadow where a lightning-burn is healing; on the far side, the land falls away through the spruce. Straight ahead is sky, the sky over the Great Valley.

There is a sweet exhilaration in coming to the summit of a pass where the brightness ahead shines through the last dark band of trees. The weight of a pack sack lightens; the hard part is done; the possible opens before us.

Eighteenth century pioneers passing over the Appalachians into the Ohio Valley wrote often of this feeling of being freed of encumbrances, of fresh beginnings. Judging from what they said, and from what has been said of them subsequently, most of them shared the misconception that they were entering an ample emptiness intended to be theirs alone.

In fact, they carried more baggage than they knew; only a few were able to cast off their preconceptions, and only after much bloodshed. The western vastness was not empty. Several hundred thousand people were already there, and determined to resist invasion. Nor was it without its own history, as the Europeans slowly acknowledged after encountering a profusion of very large ruined buildings. Whatever may have been the edenic expectations of the newcomers, it became obvious that the Indians of the Valley were the survivors of much larger populations.

Even along the headwaters of the Ohio, on the banks of mountain brooks, there were signs of ancient habitation in the form of small burial mounds. As the streams grew larger, so did the buildings on their banks. Below Pittsburgh, at Grave Creek, in what is now West Virginia, a conical mound is still today 2,700 feet (251 meters) in circumference and 70 feet (21 meters) tall. It was built by Indians while Rome was young.

Scores of structures almost equal to its bulk still remain, offering the commentary of the elders upon the coal dumps and slag heaps of the

1

Rust Belt, as the flares of disconsolate gasworks flicker where beacon fires once blazed. In the Ohio and Mississippi valleys, tens of thousands of structures were built between six and sixty-six centuries ago. Some, as large as twenty-five miles in extent, required over three million person-hours of labor.

Sometimes even so late as now, one of us may have an experience as unexpected and full of wonder as those of the first French trappers and British traders when they came among these structures. In the summer of 1991, I was in a cave, searching beneath Indiana for a source of a white mineral called aragonite, which was much favored for sculpture by the Ohio Valley Indians of the third and fourth centuries.

I had passed through a succession of caverns and slippery, narrow passageways. There had been no graffiti for half a mile, and I permitted myself the proud thought that I was the first of my species to come there. Then my head lamp showed on the floor the twisted fibers of the butt end of a torch, and there were sandal-marks in the dust.

I was late by a millennium and a half.

This discovery should not have come as a surprise to me. But though I have been writing American history for nearly fifty years, it was. Others know about that cave, and as the graffiti, some more than a century old, demonstrated, all the knowers were not scholars. But as I talked with friends about the probability that Indians were seeking stone for sculpture in Indiana caves while the Emperor Augustus was losing legions in the German forests, I found that I was not alone in my ignorance of America's ancient past.

This book began with my discovery of the torch and sandal-marks. They led me to learn as much as I could about the people who left them in that cave, and also about why only a few specialists seem to be informed about them.* What did the first European explorers and settlers know about ancient America? Why was that knowledge not passed on, expanded, revised, and made a necessary prelude to American history? The antiquities of Mexico or of Egypt are far better known than those of Indiana, Illinois, or Ohio, and not because they are larger or more ambitious intellectually.

As I have learned, there is as much to say about Euramerican lack of understanding of Indian history as there is to say about the Indians themselves.

The first generation of westering colonizers had little to prepare them for the possibility of ancient cultures as they came into the upper

---

*The curiosity about ignorance probably stems from the second profession which I have plied for many decades, that of security analysis, which has to do with the gap between what is true and what might profitably be learned about the reasons all investors do not agree as to that truth.

reaches of the Ohio Valley between 1770 and 1810. Daniel Boone did not read Spanish, and he knew only what had been learned of the West by the French and by the Charleston traders who had traveled to the Mississippi before he came into Kentucky. The traders had come out of the southern Carolinas, and reached the Mississippi by routes which happened to bypass all the major mound centers. Though the French had been installed around Nashville for decades, in terrain full of ancient ruins, they did not provide forewarning of massive archaeology to their competitors from Carolina or Kentucky. They were mercantile folk; neither by training, inclination, nor the beguilements of leisure were they to be diverted from their goods and ledgers. None of these early merchants was leisured and none seems to have had time for wonder; so, from the 1680s until the 1770s, antiquity slumbered as commerce fretted and scratched overhead.

Antiquity, it is true, had only recently gone to slumber, as time was counted in the Valley. It had been wide awake when in 1539 a Spanish expeditionary force led by Hernando De Soto hacked and burnt its way through active mound-building cultures from the Georgia piedmont to the plains of Texas. But antiquity was silenced soon enough. The would-be conquistadors who emerged into the Appalachian province from Florida left a legacy, though they did not establish colonies. Their legacy was disease. After their microbes thronged to accelerate the destruction already underway by those already loosed by sailors and slavers along the coast upon the Indians, who did not have the appropriate antibodies, an unbroken Indian tradition of many centuries was removed from the scene. It had been destroyed not by force of arms—De Soto's *entrada* was a failure—but by the silent insidious action of European plagues.

De Soto's was the first force of Europeans to enter the watershed of the Ohio, a region the British later called "the Western waters."* And Boone, even had he been fluent in Spanish, would have learned little about what to expect in the West. The Spanish interest in its culture was limited to what pillage might be gotten from its temples and palaces. De Soto's study of its architecture did not go beyond determining the best means to storm its fortifications. So his chroniclers lavished little language upon accounts which might have forewarned the

---

*Traders from Pennsylvania and Virginia had taken their chances beyond the Appalachians since the last decade of the seventeenth century, and had been busy in Ohio and Indiana since the 1730s.

They were mostly Englishmen and Protestant, with an English and Protestant set of preconceptions. Even if Daniel Boone had known the history of his native Virginia he would not have found it easy to admit that the Holy Communion had first been offered on the shores of the Chesapeake by the Jesuits, sixty-eight years before the settling of Jamestown, or to concede that De Soto had led the first Europeans to cross the Appalachians.

English, or the French, or Boone about the ancient buildings of the West. Not until the end of the eighteenth century did some Euramericans begin to show real curiosity in the history of their land and its peoples.

Some of the seekers and invaders who entered under the flags of Spain and Great Britain were pinkish in skin tone, others brownish or blackish. Some were free, some slaves, some indentured servants or slaves for a term. The pinkish ones, masters or servants, discerned themselves as distinguished by skin color from the darker people among them, whether slave or free, and from the people already present in the valley. The races were then said to be White, Black, and Red, though of course not a single person so described was or is, in fact, white, black, or red. The color scheme was artificial, but within it were categorized people of an infinite variety of colors. Rewards and penalties were meted out for no better reason than occupancy of one or another of those artificial categories.* One of our primary themes will be how, in the valley, these people, newcomers and those who had been there for thousands of years, played out their prejudices about each other.

It is true that among the Founding Fathers, the word "African" was virtually a synonym for slave, and "Indian" or "Red Indian" nearly synonymous with "savage."† But not all of them thought this way, and none of them thought so all the time. Many were better and more broadly educated, less prejudiced and more conscious of their opportunities, than they have been said to be by most of their biographers. Especially during the Jim Crow period of American history, from the 1880s through the 1940s, it was conventional to present the views of the Founders on racial matters as shriveled to the crabbed understanding of those who were then writing about them. Probably this was because it was embarrassing to acknowledge that the Founders might have felt obligations and opportunities upon which they failed fully to act. Besides, if, during that unhappy phase in American life, their foiled aspirations were too strongly presented, there was the uncomfortable

---

*I hope those who might think this a plodding way of describing race relations will arrest their impatience a little. I do not find satisfactory the hasty terms now in common currency for the groups of people under discussion. For example, who is an "African American"? Our ancestors came from Africa. No scientist withholds agreement from that proposition. The questions to which all our histories respond are: "When did you come out of Africa? Under what conditions? And, when you came together with others who came to your place by other routes, how did you learn about each other and treat each other?"

†Many of the Blacks who appear, too often silently, in these pages, came into the Valley unwillingly. They made their presence known by attempting to alter the arrangements being made to keep them enslaved. Sometimes they attempted to breach those arrangements by force of arms, sometimes by attempting to escape them.

possibility that the historians' own contemporaries might be induced to be as bold in their thinking as the Founders actually were.

THE NEW ORDER OF THE UNIVERSE

But that acknowledgement is required of us: the Founders had set out to create a "New Order in the Universe"—so they proclaimed on their Great Seal. They had hoped that their new nation might have been freed of the prejudices and superstitions of Europe. But the revolutionary generation was disappointed; the power of old vices was not broken.*

By the end of the patriarchy of George Washington (1789–1797), the Founders, most ruefully President Washington himself, acknowledged that those vices were so ingrained that they were not purged merely by a change of government. Human slavery, for instance, seemed fixed ineradicably within the American system. And though the West offered a second chance, the Founders were not so young as they had been in 1776 when things seemed simpler.

A second theme of this work, extending from the first, is that in the West the Founding Fathers missed a great opportunity. A third is that they knew it. This book has been written because I believe that we, too, have an opportunity and that we must not fail in it. We are likely to do better if we know what some of them attempted, and why they failed. The time has come for another mighty effort to fulfill the highest aspirations of the Founders in the central valley of North America, where they glimpsed the possibility of a work of redemption.

THE OCCASIONS OF GRACE

They had the benefit of a shock of discovery. In few instances in human history has architecture been so important in altering the impression of the nature of one people in the eyes of others. The Founders had not anticipated that they would find, in the West, large, sophisticated, and ancient work, performed by the kind of people still resident there.

That architectural evidence was too obtrusive to be ignored. The new cities of the central valley—Cincinnati, St. Louis, Marietta, Portsmouth, Lexington, Pittsburgh, Natchez, and Nashville—had to be

---

*These sentences are a summary of a diagnosis, offered in the opening chapters of my *Greek Revival America,* of the state of mind of the founding generation, in the aftermath of the first confederacy (1783–1789) and the decay of expectations of what might be achieved under the fatherly guidance of Washington, thereafter.

built by clearing away evidence of older ones. In the countryside there were hundreds of thousands of earthen reminders of prior habitation; there still *are* tens of thousands. The shock of these discoveries forced upon the Founders the possibility that Indians were not all savages.*

Since the Indians were *other,* and yet obviously human, it was not difficult for some of the Founders, especially George Washington and Albert Gallatin, to open their minds to the possibilities presented by the presence of Blacks, also *other* but human. Even Thomas Jefferson's French friends insisted that the Blacks, though enslaved, *were* fully human.

The Founders knew nothing of ancient Africa outside of a little learning about Egypt; had they known something of it at the time they were becoming acquainted with ancient America they might have enlarged their sense of Negro possibility considerably farther—and, by extension, their apprehension of what other darker-skinned people, such as ancient Americans, might have done. But they were neither so fortunate nor so bold. We *are* so fortunate, and we may be so bold. Knowledge of the past may help alter the present.

Fortunately for us, the Founders did not consume all possible salutary surprises about American antiquity. Some startling has been vouchsafed to us. Much has been learned in the late 1980s and early 1990s about our predecessors in the Great Valley, much that still imparts the thrill which encouraged the Founders to make the new beginning they promised themselves and the world.

And we may try again.

---

*Those buildings asserted something new and important about the capabilities of the living descendants of their builders.

This is not to suggest that it was only through Indian architecture that the Founders came to respect Indians, to the extent that they did. The pioneers learned much from the Indians about agriculture, about clothing to be worn in the woods and upon the prairie, about modes of transportation, about pharmacology, and even about how to construct confederations, but little of what they learned seemed to astonish them as the architecture did. None of these other matters received from them the amount of explicit attention and the extensive scientific reporting accorded the mounds.

THE FOUNDERS OF AMERICAN ARCHITECTURE; THE CULTURES THAT NOURISHED THEM, AND THE GREAT DYING

The architecture of the Mississippi watershed is as old as that of Egypt. Though composed of other materials than the sandstone of the pyramids, the monuments of the Mississippi are as large in size and as regular in shape. Indeed, one of the most noteworthy qualities of ancient American architecture is that some of its forms were so regular that they were replicated precisely in locations many miles apart.

The first very large buildings created in North America were constructed about six thousand years ago; most were made by moving earth in baskets woven of vegetable fibers. These baskets, used throughout the valley for architectural work, were as large as the wannigans (wicker pack sacks) many nineteenth and early twentieth century Americans carried on canoe trips—some of us can still recall how heavy they were when filled. Several million baskets were filled with heavy clay for the construction of each of many structures in West Virginia, Louisiana, and Illinois.

Despite so much exertion, the eroded contours of these monuments are not, today, very impressive. After thousands of winters, plows, and pothunters have done their work upon them, they sometimes appear to be little more than discouraged hillocks, about the shape of rain-drenched haystacks. A few, however, remain very grand indeed.

Careful cross-sectional archaeology reveals the layering within these ambiguous shapes: brown earth, and often red clay, earth again, perhaps one or two more tiers or "lenses" of red, black-charred remains of buildings—ritually fired, we may assume—and still more earth, some of it so densely compacted that the fibrous markings of the baskets are still stamped upon it.

The Spanish and French who first saw these hillocks found it difficult to believe them to be the deliberate creations of mankind. They
were so much larger than any work of architecture known to them.
The entire facade of the Palace of the Louvre, in Paris, can fit easily
within the space surrounded by the D-shaped earthen rings at Poverty
Point, Louisiana, built at the same time as Stonehenge. The Papal Basilica of St. Peter in Rome, complete with its plaza and gardens, could
be placed within the circular embankment at Watson Brake, which is
probably at least a thousand years older than Poverty Point.

THE AGE OF THE RINGS

Knowledge of the age of the oldest Indian buildings is only now emerging from carbon and pollen dating. We know about the construction
and occupancy of them from fragments salvaged from embers grown
cold before Gilgamesh or Cheops came to their thrones—the reigns of
these gentlemen are generally thought to have been after 2800 B.C.—
and from microscopic remains of plants left unconsumed in meals prepared at the time cuneiform wedges were first being indented in Meso-
potamian clay.

The Mayan calendar opens with a mythic date of 3372 B.C.; by that
time the people of the Mississippi Valley were already creating monumental architecture. Before anything so ambitious had been built in
Mexico, Central or South America, earthen buildings were arranged in
strict and repeated geometric patterns along the bayous and channels
in what are now the states of Louisiana and Mississippi. In the Mississippi Delta, two of the earliest complexes which can be dated with
much precision lie near Monroe, Louisiana.* The Hedgepeth Mounds
are on the Bayou Darbonne, about twenty miles to the northwest, and
probably were built around 4500 B.C. Above Frenchman's Bend, on the
Bayou Bartholomew, fifteen miles northeast of Monroe, are a row of
mounds whose carbon dates establish them as about a thousand years
younger.[1]

On the campus of Louisiana State University, at Baton Rouge, is the
most ancient evidence of the propensity of humans for architecture to
be found so conveniently to learning anywhere in the world: two coni-

---

*Outsiders conventionally confine the term "delta" rather arbitrarily to a portion of this
vast silty effluvium, that lying on the modern course of the Mississippi below New Orleans.
But ancient rivers draining the upper Mississippi basin have left channels across most of the
present states of Louisiana, Arkansas and Mississippi. Local people begin referring to their
delta, and singing Delta blues, not far south of the suburbs of Memphis, Tennessee, in the
territory through which De Soto's people ravaged their way toward a crossing of the Mississippi itself.

cal mounds, the larger about 130 feet in diameter and 16 feet high, the rich organic soil of which was put in place about 3000 B.C. Six miles north, at Monte Sano, two even earlier conical mounds were destroyed in 1967. They included platforms probably used for cremation, and a structure built on posts about twenty feet square, which may well have been the oldest wooden building of which the plans are clear. A close approximation of what such plans might have been can be derived from the Monte Sano postmolds, where the posts have decayed leaving spaces subsequently filled by earth compacted differently from its surroundings. What a treasure! And it was protected by the compassionate earth until people of our generation saw fit to destroy it.

The story of the five-thousand-year-old mounds at Frenchman's Bend is, so far, happier: a remarkably sympathetic developer recently agreed that its principal building will not become the seventh tee of a golf course.* I recall poignantly the day that concession was made, and how proudly he drove away in his Landrover, more worthy of the best Abercrombie and Fitch could provide than any competitor in the Mississippi Valley. Five mounds are still discernable along the edge of the fairway, the largest a low, haystack-shaped cone about 130 feet in diameter and 10 feet high. The relationship of the five to each other appears erratic, but appearances may not disclose lunar or solar alignments, or some other ordering principle we do not yet understand.

About five thousand years ago, monumental American architecture began to be created in circular or half-circular—D-shaped—forms, the largest of which are so striking that they justify calling the ensuing three millennia in American architectural history the Age of the Rings. Even more precise circles continued to be built thereafter, but they

---

*At Stelly, in south central Louisiana, are mounds which have recently (January 1994) been dated to 2700 B.C.

At Banana Bayou, a small conical mound on the Gulf Coast, and at Avery Island (a salt dome known for its tabasco sauce) on the Gulf Coast, artifacts and carbon dates suggest a date of about 2500 B.C.

As the time scheme settles closer to 2000 B.C. a score or more sites in Louisiana can be added to the list, with complexities increasing until one comes to the full panoply of six mounds and six concentric enclosures at Poverty Point, see below, the most elegant construction since the ten at Watson Brake, not all of which were necessarily as old as that dated to the pre-Poverty Point period.

There are very early sites on the Gulf and Atlantic Coasts, as well. At Claiborne, Mississippi, for example, a half-circular earthwork was placed on top of a midden and topped by another layer of midden (midden is often the refuse of human habitation, and sometimes a deliberate aggregation of human products). Its outside diameter was 700 feet. A small conical mound lay 1100 feet to the east. Carbon dates were found amid the upper midden for about 1100 B.C., 1500 B.C., and 2000 B.C.

There will be further discussion of the Atlantic Coast sites below.

were now accompanied by the first appearance of square, hexagonal and octagonal ground plans on a large scale.*

The first great expression of the Age of the Rings to descend to us in still recognizable condition lies just outside the southwestern sprawl of the little city of Monroe, on the opposite bank of the Ouachita River and eighteen miles south of Frenchman's Bend, at Watson Brake (a "break" is a breech in natural levee of a river, forming a backwater). This oldest monumental circular building yet discovered in North America was probably begun at about the time as the complex at Frenchman's Bend.† Its primary form is a circular embankment three-fifths of a mile long, 820 by 650 feet across and about 3 feet high. The ring is punctuated by ten mounds, one of which rises nearly 28 feet higher. These punctuating mounds of earth atop the platform ring, confronting each other across a flat space or plaza, distinguish the Watson Brake earthworks from thousands of circular mounds of earth or shell across the Gulf Coast and along the rivers of the South and Midwest.‡

---

*There is a large literature of archaeoastronemy for the lower Mississippi Valley, approaching the bulk of that for Stonehenge and for the Anasazi work of the Southwest. We are classifying animals. When we speak of "regular" or "geometric" architecture we usually mean something which fits neatly into one or another of the containers already present in our own psyches. Plato probably was referring to this bottling process when he spoke of thinking like gods, or thinking *along* with, as one *sings* along with, the eternal patterns of the universe.

Carl Jung, the Swiss psychologist and theologian, knew something of American antiquity, but only that of the desert Southwest. It is likely that he would have discussed Louisiana hillocks in Platonic terms had he stopped in Monroe on his way to Santa Fe. Will the time come when it is no more necessary to identify Jung than Plato? In any case, without Plato or Jung to assist us, we tend to dismiss the unfamiliar because it challenges our ability to place it within one of our preexisting categories, sometimes rejecting data delivered to us by our senses only because we have no place to put it. Meanwhile, we must use the language of the familiar in geometry, and write of circles, octagons, and squares, though surely we must be missing other forms which we cannot perceive.

†So far, the requisite carbon for dating has eluded the archaeologists working at Watson Brake, though they have found the baked ceramic cubes characteristic of other structures such as those at Frenchman's Bend and other sites of the same age.

‡Many are probably refuse heaps, left behind as Indians consumed the bivalves within those shells. Some are more stately than that, laid out in large circles empty at the center, so large that they could not have been casually constructed. Sometimes they are very regular in outline, as if drawn first on a template and then built. Many of these can be found on islands along the South Carolina, Georgia, and Florida coasts.

On Sapelo Island, one of the largest is still partly preserved in an ancient forest of oak and cedar. It is about 310 feet in diameter, rising 10 feet from a base about 36 feet wide, forming a total height about 23 feet above a muddy river. It was inhabited (perhaps one should say more cautiously that it was in regular use) between 100 and 1800 B.C.

The presence of pottery fragments at Sapelo confirms that though pottery was not used at Poverty Point, it was within the repertory of Indian crafts five hundred years earlier.

The discipline, prowess in engineering, and regularity in plan presaged at Watson Brake was carried to its fulfillment a thousand years or more closer to our own time and about fifty miles to the east, at Poverty Point. An immense complex of earthen buildings, now known by the name of a plantation which began plowing down that architecture in the 1840s, lies upon Macon Ridge. That it is a ridge is discernable only to people living in very flat country, for it appears only as a modest swelling of alluvial fan deposited perhaps thirty thousand years ago by the Arkansas River as it entered the Mississippi flood plain.

The people of Poverty Point were either successfully organized or (more likely) shared a community of religious interest, for in several extended building campaigns over five centuries they labored upon seven miles of embankments forming six concentric half circles. These embankments are cupped to face the bank of the Bayou Macon (pronounced "mason"), thirty feet below. At the center of the outermost ring, which has a diameter of four fifths of a mile, is an enormous mound, 705 by 656 feet and 70 feet tall.*

Stonehenge, built at about the same time, could be fitted seven times into the enclosure at Poverty Point. Nothing on Salisbury Plain is of the scale of the central mound, thought by some to be an effigy of a falcon, though to more prosaic folk it now seems shaped like an enormous melted chair. There may have been a small platform at the top, and there remains a lower platform 13 feet above the plain.† This two-stage

---

*The terrain of the Delta today is not the landscape seen by the people who first lived there. In 16,000 B.C. the last great glacier, two miles thick in places, had frozen into itself enough of the seas so that the sea level was as much as 350 feet below its current level.

As the ice melted and released the seas, waters rose from the coast to meet glacial waters flooding down the valley from the interior. This did not happen quickly; the emergence of present shorelines took thousands of years, during which humans did the best they could to live in the area, and were confronted with constant change.

Time and time again, works of art and architecture were buried beneath water and silt; there is no knowing what was lost, how many ancestral homes and ceremonial centers relinquished.

Today, one can cruise about the shallow waters of the delta by boat, a few feet above submerged ruins. Our ignorance of this antiquity is, and must be, abysmal. Ancient mounds barely obtrude above low tide; plazas which once held throngs of people are now twenty or thirty feet below channels, across which the motorboats of fishermen make their daily rounds.

Even the surface level of upland sites such as Poverty Point have been lowered by ten or twelve feet by plowing and erosion.

†The notion that this much-eroded and battered mound might initially have been shaped to suggest a falcon with widespread wings is not so fanciful as it sounds. Stone and shell carvings found on the site do take the form of such birds, specific even to the presence of talons. The falcon is a familiar ornamental, or incantory shape, in Indian art in many places in the Mississippi Valley, Mexico, and Central America. Falcon effigies in stone are to be found in Georgia, and in earth along the upper Mississippi.

ascent is one of the unifying forms of these very early mounds.* Ten million basket loads of earth would have been required to complete the work of leveling this plain and then building these structures.[2]

Joe Saunders, an archaeologist who has been working at Watson Brake, Hedgepeth, and Frenchman's Bend, has found that several of the mounds in these complexes also appear to have "aprons" like those of the "falcon mound" at Poverty Point and Motley. All seem to provide for a choreographed movement: coming from the bayou or river one climbed the bank, probably by a graded way, to come out into a plaza. Then, before the great mound, there may have been a court of honor, and above it, on the first level, a place even more restricted. Finally, perhaps beside a pyre or beacon, one might be admitted into the presence of a person of the highest honor.

This use of earth to provide a succession of sacred spaces on ascending platforms persists in American architecture from 3000 B.C. Through the creation of the immense structures of the period between A.D. 1000 and the arrival of the Europeans. The most prominent of these still to be observed today are at Etowah, in Georgia; at Emerald, near Natchez, Mississippi; at Moundville, in Alabama; and at Monks Mound at Cahokia, Illinois. At Cahokia, the sheer size of Monks Mound, with its many ramps and platforms, permits us to visualize easily a graduated ascent to sanctuaries of ever-increasing solemnity—with the sanctum sanctorum at the very top. The great pyramid at Cahokia is greater in extent than that at Gizeh, in Egypt.†‡ Well into the eighteenth century, the Indians—Natchez, Cherokee, Creek, and Caddo—were still building mounds of this sort.

When one comes on foot into the open space at Poverty Point, there is a powerful impulse to seek definition of its huge extent by finding the bounds set by the outer ring, and to get some sense of scale from its hulking mound. But if one approaches Poverty Point from the air, after surveying the archaeology of the Louisiana and Mississippi delta land, it is the *innermost* ring which rivets attention. It is 2,000 feet in diam-

---

*A mile and a half north of the Poverty Point group is the Motley Mound, somewhat smaller but similarly shaped. After severe erosion and the trucking away of most of its "tail" for highway fill, Motley is still more than 49 feet high and what is left of it is the length of a football field.

†To keep things simple, references to locations will be given in contemporary terms, without wearisome repetitions of such modifiers as "within the present-day borders of" or "in modern."

‡Monks Mound is so called in tribute to a Trappist Monastery built on one of its flanks in the eighteenth century.

eter (600 meters), appearing to be a half circle.* This is almost exactly the configuration and the size which the aerial archaeologist can find in at least five other earthworks created in the Mississippi floodplain, all of which may have been built at about the same time. In other words, not only were the Indians of four thousand years ago sufficiently organized to build the huge, even and geometric ring at Poverty Point, but they were also capable of duplicating it across great distances. This was the year in which Priam's Troy fell to the Greeks—if Homer is as reliable as dendrochronology and carbon dating, and if Priam's Troy was that which reached its apogee about 1250 B.C., and was then burnt.[††**]

---

*On closer scrutiny, it has been found to be composed of portions of two circles, drawn from slightly different centers. Its northern and southern segments are drawn from one, and its western side is drawn from another.

[†]In these pages, unless confusion will ensue we will not deploy A.D., C.E., B.C.E., or the convention of modern archaeological writers—B.P. (Before Present). B.C. will appear; the dates falling thereafter will stand as they are presented in general public discourse—such as 1776 and 1992.

[‡]Two of the other 600-meter "half-circles" lie against riverbanks or bluffs, forming D-shaped figures, in the state of Mississippi just west of Yazoo City, about fifty miles east of Poverty Point. They are called Spanish Fort (denominated by archaeologists as 21-N-3) and Leist. A third is at Jaketown, another thirty miles to the northeast.

All these sites have produced archaeological evidence, in the form of points and baked clay, potato-shaped, "Poverty Point objects," indicating that they were occupied at the same time as Poverty Point. Fixing occupancy to construction of earthen architecture is difficult, but coincidences are suggestive.

Little Spanish Fort is near big Spanish Fort; it is, strangely enough, somewhat larger, at 660 meters.

The earthen circle at Marksville, Louisiana, is famous for its much later platform and conical mounds, but it, too, may have been occupied in Poverty Point days, and the outer earthen ring may have been constructed then. It is not as accurately drawn on the earth as two quarter circles as are the constructions listed above. Its form appears from the air to be squashed, but the opening of the "D" is also about 600 meters.

(The numbered references are to Phillips, *Archaeological Survey*, a Harvard publication which established a convention making the naming of these sites less whimsical. The result is a sort of Gray's Botany has emerged for archaeology alongside local names like those given flowers.)

The D-shaped masonry complexes of the Anasazi appeared much later (after 800).

There are also two more "D's" in the delta, outside Poverty Point; their apertures are within a few feet of 2,000, though they are less exactly configured.

**Here are some additional stimuli to further research and controversy among archaeologists:

(1) Some horticulture or agriculture may have been practiced at Poverty Point. Squash seed was recovered in 1978, and both squash and *chenopodia* from the Copes site nearby. But all squash was not domesticated.

Fortunately, Poverty Point, a place of marvels, is accessible to a large public and provided with a good, small museum, where one can find some of the evidence establishing this as the most important center of the art of sculpture of its time in the hemisphere. Around 1500 B.C. and for more than five centuries thereafter, the people of Poverty Point created exquisite small effigies of clams, falcons, and—especially—owls. Their favorite color seems to have been a deep red, the red of the jasper they acquired from the Ozarks or Alabama. Though some of the people with whom they were exchanging their sculpture made use of pottery bowls and cooking pots, the residents of Poverty Point seem to have favored for their baking—at least their ritual baking—vessels of steatite brought all the way from Alabama, Tennessee, and Georgia.

The trade network sending its goods into Louisiana by 1500 B.C. extended for thousands of miles to the north, east, and west. Copper beads from Michigan have been found in Louisiana graves, along with sharks' teeth and shells from both the Atlantic and Gulf coasts. Other minerals, including hematite, galena, and quartz, were brought from the Great Lakes, Ohio, and Tennessee. Bits of obsidian, traceable to the Missouri Valley, probably from Yellowstone National Park, have been found at Poverty Point as well, though in contexts that make it difficult for archaeologists to be certain when they got there.

Until about 1000 B.C., the structures of the Indians had gotten progressively larger and more highly organized as the Poverty Point people produced their beautiful pendants and votive objects, leveled the terraces above their meandering rivers and bayous, and carried millions of baskets full of heavy delta earth to compose their rings and mounds. In the Middle East, this was the time when the Israelites were escaping Egypt for Palestine, and the Age of the Homeric Heroes was giving rise to epic poetry around the shores of the Aegean.

Then, for reasons beyond our ken, virtually all monumental building activity stopped in the Delta; the Poverty Point people ceased their labors, and, we may imagine, dispersed. There was a pause of about

---

(2) There was a plan for the entire work: four of the principal elements of the Poverty Point complex, the Falcon Mound, a small mound 0.4 mile north of the rings called Mound B, and a somewhat larger artificial hillock 1.6 miles to the south called the Jackson Mound are all aligned north and south—along a 352.5 degree alignment.

There are complex spatial relationships as well, which seem to have been based upon a 141 foot unit. These are detailed in Gibson, "Earth Sitting" and "Poverty Point Earthworks."

(3) The firmest radio-carbon dates form two clusters. The first covers a period from 1450 to 1330 B.C., and the data are drawn from areas antedating the construction of the mounds, when, it seems, the terrain was laboriously flattened to form a vast platform. The second cluster is composed of dates from the mounds themselves, and covers only a narrow span of two decades on either side of 1100 B.C.—a long time later (Gibson, "Poverty Point Earthworks," pp. 25–26).

four centuries (800 B.C. until 400 B.C) in the construction of monumental architecture and fine sculpture in the United States.* This was while the classical period was getting underway in Greece, and the *Iliad* and *Odyssey* were placed in written form.

THE AGE OF CONES, PLATFORMS, AND PRISMATIC ENCLOSURES†

In the Ohio Valley, after 400 B.C. there was a resumption of large-scale construction and in the making of fine ceramics and textiles. Indians began burying their dead in tumuli (large earthen structures) of increasing size, some placed directly over circular structures and extending the form of those structures upward to form cones; the cone at Grave Creek was one of these. Apparently burial was important to these Indians, for they placed within the buildings, alongside the dead, pottery, jewelry of copper, silver, beadwork, mica, lead, and obsidian, together with articles of ceremonial use such as pipes for smoking tobacco or other mild hallucinogens. There are thousands of such sites in the upper Ohio Valley above the falls at Louisville. Some of the burial mounds were merely haystack-shaped, but, judging from postmold

---

*An exception may have been an isolated flowering in central Florida, at Fort Center, northwest of Lake Okeechobee. There, construction occurred by cutting into the ground, etching, so to speak, rather than impasto—raising earthen buildings above ground. A ditch was inscribed in the earth forming a nearly perfect circle. It was deep enough (about five feet) to reach the water, which, in this low-lying and saturated everglade terrain, is itself an architectural element as is desert and sand in the Southwest. The people of Fort Center created an aqueous culture, making use of beautifully ornamented dippers of shell, presumably for ritual cleansing, and burying their honored dead in water, after placing them above ponds on platforms raised on stilts, surrounded by wooden sculpture.

The size and date of the Fort Center Circle are intriguing architectural puzzles; it is exactly the same size as two circular embankments in Ohio.

†A prism is a construction, sawn or shaped by human hands, often but not always of glass, whose function is to permit the observation of a reality deliberately altered by the interposition of the prism itself. A prismatic telescope, for instance, bends light and thus makes it easier for us to observe phenomena that would otherwise be invisible. Other prisms concentrate light artificially to permit its qualities to be observed, or, in the opposite case, artificially extend it, so that its attributes, such as colors, may be seen separately.

Many religious symbols and works of architecture function similarly: to make accessible understanding of phenomena that would otherwise defeat the sensory means available to humans. It happens that prisms are often, though not always, bilaterally symmetrical, as are Hopewell earthworks.

I am using the word "prismatic" to describe symbolic architecture with the same intention as the renewed employment of somewhat antique meanings of the words "city" and "building": to encourage renewal of understanding buried beneath subsequent and more banal deployments.

patterns either under them or nearby, nearly all were associated with round, wooden buildings—where, probably, bodies were prepared for ritual burial.[3] During this stage, about the time of Christ, some hilltops in Indiana, Ohio, and Kentucky were set aside separated from the ridges from which they protruded by the erection of walls of stone and earth across the connecting ridges.*

Somewhat later, other Indians in the same general area—often on the same river terraces, as at Marietta, Portsmouth, and north of Chillicothe, Ohio—commenced practicing even more elaborate burial and architectural customs. Elegantly finished sculpture and ceramic vessels were interred in burial mounds, and greater geometric sophistication was deployed in forming ceremonial enclosures. No two archaeologists seem to agree wholly on the precise cultural distinctions to be drawn between these two groups, though there is consensus that the simpler culture preceded the more complex and that the two overlapped for several centuries, after which, from the second century onward, the later group created their refined sculpture out of a wider variety of materials. Their pipes, bearing lively effigies of beavers and birds, as fine as anything accomplished in Europe north of the Alps at the time, are more beautiful to our eyes than any subsequent work done in the Mississippi Valley until the middle of the nineteenth century.

These Indians of the third, fourth and fifth centuries had good eyes for materials from which to make beautiful things. The white aragonite they quarried deep in that Indiana cave turned translucent in the light and open air; the obsidian they obtained from what is now Yellowstone National Park was employed together with copper from Isle Royal or northern Michigan, sharks' teeth from Florida, silver from Ontario, lead from Wisconsin or Missouri, and mica sheets from the Carolinas.

Their architecture is so different from that of the cone builders, that I think it likely that it was created by a cadre of priestly architect/astronomers—geomancers—who brought new ways of building as distinct from the old as the Gothic was from Romanesque. Like the Gothic and Romanesque styles, though, the two ways of reconciling architecture and religion coincided for many years.

These geomoncers vastly enlarged and scrupulously defined the old circular patterns, and added much larger and more precise circular buildings, as well as others: octagons, hexagons, and squares. Some of

---

*The "type site" of these hill forts is Fort Ancient, in Ohio. For a century, until the 1990s, archaeologists generally spoke of a "Fort Ancient period" or even a "Fort Ancient culture," and set its dates much later, after 600. But recent research, to be summarized in Chapter Eleven, makes it clear that the hill top enclosures are as old as many of the cones.

their structures are very large indeed; the Fairgrounds Circle at New-ark, Ohio, is a quarter of a mile across and three stories high. Ameri-cans who know Chaco Canyon or Mesa Verde, built by the Anasazi Indians in the romantic Southwest, seldom have the opportunity to compare Anasazi work to the accomplishments of the Mississippi Val-ley Indians. So it may be worthy of note that the great structure at Pueblo Bonito, in Chaco Canyon*, could be inserted six times inside the Fairgrounds Circle. The most accessible examples of this work are in Ohio, though there are many others in Indiana, Illinois, Iowa, and Kentucky.[†]

In the first three quarters of the twentieth century it was conven-tional for archaeologists (historians were hardly paying attention) to employ the terms "Adena" and "Hopewell" to distinguish these two groups of Indians. These are categories taken from places under cir-cumstances discussed in Chapter Four: Adena is an estate near Chillicothe, Ohio, from which in 1906 archaeologists removed an array of grave goods placed there between 300 B.C. and A.D. 100. Cap-tain Hopewell was a farmer who lived at "the Hopewell place" a few miles away from Adena, from which was obtained an even more ex-travagant treasure of grave goods probably interred a little later, per-haps as late as 400.

But the distinctions between the Hopewell and Adena have been perforated by new evidence, and many scholars are now either aban-doning the terms or saving them only for use to denote differing ways of organizing activity, rather than to mean different people. Physiolog-ically, it is now evident, the Adena and Hopewell were not distinct, nor were their periods of activity. Their architecture is so often juxtaposed so closely that it is possible they shared common ground, as Protes-tants and Catholics have come to do in towns superimposed upon an-cient Indian burial grounds.[‡]

The great days of the cone-makers were over by 200; the geometri-cians seem to have sustained their building over another three or four

---

*Pueblo Bonito is a D-shaped "apartment complex" 310 feet by 154 feet.

[†]These geometrics are the most intriguing buildings created in the Mississippi Valley until Benjamin Henry Latrobe arrived to create a mansion house amid the ancient work at Adena (see Chapter Four) and Bartholomy Lafon introduced piratic neoclassicism in Natchez and New Orleans around 1800 (see Chapter Nine).

[‡]Until the 1970s, it was a staple of archaeological literature that the Adena and Hopewell had differently shaped heads. Recent work, especially that of Paul Sciulli of Ohio State University, puts an effective quietus to that notion. (I am grateful to Bruce Smith for point-ing out Dr. Sciulli's achievement in a personal letter of October, 1993.)

With "Fort Ancient" shriveling as a useful category (see previous note), merging in time with both *Hopewell* and *Adena,* the field is open for the kind of speculation offered in Chapter Eleven.

centuries. I offer some thoughts about why these events may have occurred in a final chapter. The shamanships that brought these Ohio
Valley people together—if my speculations in that final chapter are
correct—were contemporary with King Arthur and Merlin—or, if one
prefers, with the rise and fall of the great city of Teotihuacan, in the
Valley of Mexico, and the early glories of the Zapotecs at Monte
Alban.

THE AGE OF ADJUSTMENT: 500–1100

After the geometricians laid down their instruments, bows and arrows
began to dominate the hunting grounds and battlefields, and corn,
though available for some time, began to dominate the economy. In the
north, architecture on a grand scale ceased. The people of the Lower
Mississippi Valley continued to construct towns, with plazas bounded
by mounds, and toward the end of this period the flattened tops of
those mounds began to be used as platforms for temples and, one may
assume, palaces. The "type-site" for them was Troyville, Louisiana,
which amazed nineteenth century Americans with its huge conical and
platform mounds. In the 1950s, the Louisiana State Highway Department put an end to all that, as we shall see.

This was the period in which the Anasazi cultures of the American
Southwest underwent a series of expansions and contractions, reaching
apogees of their building activity about 800, 1040, 1080, 1200, and
1250. In Europe, the skyline of Byzantium was swelling with the prodigious domes of the Emperor Justinian, though the other capital of the
Roman Empire, Rome itself, fell—repeatedly and ingloriously.* There
ensued the "Middle Ages," producing the Carolingian Renaissance
and the Palatine Chapel of Charlemagne at Aachen (Aix-la-Chapelle)
around 800, as the Anasazi were beginning their grand-scale masonry
campaigns and, in Central America, the Maya built Tikal and Pale-
nque. Islam erupted into Africa and into the extremities of Europe—
Spain on the west and the Balkans on the east. In Cairo, the Mosque of

---

*In Europe, Alaric, the Visigoth, plundered Athens (396) and Rome (410); Rome was pil-
laged again, by the Vandals, in 455, and suffered the ultimate indignity when in 663 a
Roman emperor, Constans II, completed its prostration by sacking it himself. Constans
hauled away to Byzantium even the copper sheeting of the concrete dome of the Pantheon.

That would seem enough to gain for him the distinction as the last emperor of the classical world, but Constans had the misfortune to etch that indignity into architectural history
twice—nine years earlier, before he despoiled the Pantheon, he had been unable to prevent
the Arab conquest of Rhodes and the final destruction of its fallen Colossus. The bronze
fragments went to Edessa upon the backs of 900 camels. It is to John Julius Norwich that I
owe the 900 camels, in his admirable *Byzantium: The Early Centuries*.

Ibn Talun matched the best efforts of the Carolingians, while in Arizona the Hohokam began their larger platform mounds and laid out their plaza "ball courts."

The Maya culture in Belize, Mexico, and the Yucatan was contemporary with that of the platform-and-plaze builders of Louisiana, flourishing mightily from about 300 until about 800. The Maya then declined slowly until the Spaniards put an end to the last Mayan independence in the seventeenth century. What remains to be explained is how the Maya survived the disease vectors which had already reduced the Louisianans to a pitiful few a century earlier.

THE AGE OF PLATFORMS AND PLAZAS: 1000–1347

The year 1000 is one of the true pivot points of European artistic history; when the millenium ended and the world did not, there ensued a great increase of energy. Thousands of large religious buildings were built, first in the Romanesque style and then also in the Gothic.

A similar burst of energy had been underway for a century in the Mississippi Valley from Wisconsin to the Gulf, marked especially by the emergence of the metropolis around St. Louis and Cahokia. Cahokia lies on the east bank of the Mississippi just below its confluence with the Missouri and Mississippi Rivers. This was the American metropolis from the tenth through the fourteenth centuries, a place of many plazas surrounded by large flat-topped (truncated) pyramids serving as bases for temples and palaces.* The contemporary villages of the Dolores Valley in southwestern Colorado and the San Juan Valley in Utah and New Mexico aggregated about as many people (30,000 or so) at their peak, but, unlike Cahokia (using the name broadly to cover a group of communities around Cahokia) they spread across a considerably wider territory.

Their hinterland was a vast plain now called American Bottom, interspersed with lakes and gentle uplands upon which grew urban complexes in crystalline modules, with an array of architecture unprecedented north of Mexico and unrivaled until the nineteenth century. Similar but smaller centers appeared along the Missouri, the lower Mississippi, the Cumberland, Tennessee, Ohio, and their tributaries, in Alabama, along the Tombigbee at and around Moundville, and at centers in Georgia visited with fire and steel by De Soto in 1539.

---

*The Hopewell had a few truncated—flat-topped— pyramids, and so had their contemporaries along the tributaries of the lower Mississippi. But the great age of platform mounds bounding plazas did not commence until after 900.

The year 1300 is as incandescent in American and African history as the year 1000 in European. In Africa, the Cahokian supremacy had been matched by that of the kingdom of Mali. These two cultures, half a world apart, rose together; together they came into decline after 1300. Also about 1300, the great Negro cities of Zimbabwe were emptied, and, at the extreme northern end of North America, the Norse abandoned their settlements. At the same time, building also ceased in Chaco Canyon and in the largest towns in the Four Corners area, including Yellowjacket and Lowry. Their outposts, at Mesa Verde and Canyon de Chellys, were evacuated, and their people emigrated to the Hopi and Zuni villages of Arizona and to the pueblos along the upper Rio Grande. Soon Cahokia and the entire region at the juncture of the Ohio, the Missouri, and the Mississippi were also evacuated, leaving a profound desolation archaeologists call the "Vacant Quarter."*

There is no doubt that a large population disappeared. Part of this mysterious evacuation may have been caused by a mutation of an indigenous disease into a virulent form for which the population had not developed antibodies, or the spreading of such a disease from a previously isolated environment. (This is what possibly happened in Africa when AIDS escaped its previously restricted lair.) Such a possibility in the fourteenth century does not have the political resonance of attributing all evil to the Europeans. And perhaps there was no epidemic to blame: perhaps it was too much growth in population, not too great a decline in population which led to the great evacuation— the resources of densely populated places may have become depleted and the groundwater befouled, so people moved away. That could have happened at any time after the full acceptance of corn culture in the ninth or tenth century and the concentration of corn-consuming, mound-complex-building populations.

THE GREAT DYING

In Europe, during the four years after 1347, the Black Death struck and destabilized medieval society, killing about a third of its population—nearly seventy million people. Long-sustained cultural systems were ruptured, feudalism became a Quixotian joke, the Church lost much of its magic, and the way was open for the rise of capitalism, for the Renaissance and Reformation. The Age of Discovery introduced Europeans and Africans to the Americas, and Americans to those diseases which produced in the New World a Great Dying.

---

*The term "Vacant Quarter" and the concept underlying it is one of the many contributions to historical scholarship by Stephen Williams.

Thirty million Americans or more died of European and African diseases in the first century *after* the invasion of the microbes and the conquistadors, fully *twice* the proportion of the population lost to the Black Death in Europe. This was the great event of American prehistory. Its consequences were far more devastating than those of the Black Death in Europe.

People who have experienced great pain know that after a certain point it is no longer felt, and sometimes is not even remembered. That is what is meant by "shock." Between 1500 and 1700, pain and shock broke the continuities of American culture. A catastrophe occurred which was so great that it is little discussed. Else it would dominate all discourse about the human story in the Western Hemisphere. Plymouth Rock and Pilgrims, Columbus and Captain John Smith would shrink to footnotes. Even the losses of the American Civil War of 1861–1865 were trifling when compared to the Great Dying.

A tragedy on such a scale exceeds our poor powers of thought—we cannot imagine what it was like. In the icy, airless world of the statisticians, however, it can be assessed, and has been during the 1980s. Demographers have studied each region of the continent to determine how much food it had been capable of producing by the methods available before the arrival of Europeans, and how many humans that food might have sustained. These base-line population estimates may then be reduced at the rates known to have depleted other populations exposed to the diseases which struck the North American Indians. These rates may be correlated with historical reports of the pace at which the dying actually occurred. The "net" of all this horror may then be statistically adjusted to population figures actually produced by counting the survivors.[4]

When this computer work is done, it is possible to offer good estimates of the number of people in the New World in 1450. It is probable that nearly seven million people lived in North America *north* of Mexico, twenty-six to thirty million in Mexico and Central America, and another ten million in South America. Within the United States, there had been a total population of three-quarters of a million people on the West Coast, two million on the Atlantic seaboard, including Florida and the Piedmont. More than four million people inhabited the Mississippi Valley.[5]

Eighty percent or more of these people died before the Europeans and their African slaves arrived in the valley; their diseases had preceded them, borne by the conquistadors and the mariners and slaves who had visited the coasts. Many of the cultures present before 1500 were already destroyed. Nothing found in America in 1600 was what it might have been in 1450. There had been too much dying in between.

Loss is the great fact of American prehistory. The densely urbanized population of central Mexico was especially vulnerable to epidemic; cities that had housed millions amid the lakes of in the Valley of Mexico were almost entirely depopulated. Less concentrated nations did not die proportionately. Some enjoyed survival rates as high as a quarter or a third of their numbers, but the million men, women, and children on the island of Hispaniola were wholly exterminated. In the United States, "the entire Timacuan-speaking population . . . and many pueblos . . . became extinct," and the "Lower Mississippi Valley statelets 'disappeared without a trace.'"[6]

Among the survivors, there were few of the elders, few of the frail old people who are custodians of ancestral memories, who keep the sort of "lore" we find in Homer and the Icelandic sagas. All was not lost, surely, but much may have been. The eradication of memories such as these was a catastrophe, leaving the Indians weakened spiritually and prone to spiritual contagion. Despair settled across the land. After despair, among humans, comes infertility, together with high rates of suicide, and the Indian population was slow to renew itself.

The Great Dying underlies everything we say and everything we do. No other continent, no other people, lives in recollection of such an event at the threshold of its modern experience. The Great Dying is recorded by ossuaries (boneyards) covering several acres in places such as Golgotha, in Central Tennessee, and the Dying Grounds of Ohio. The presence and then the departure of large populations was marked by the deserted ruins at Cincinnati, Pittsburgh, St. Louis, Natchez, and Memphis.

The evidence of the rising and falling of ancient cultures, of the alternation of centuries in which there was much building with centuries in which there was little, of migrations and of abandoned settlements during the preceding millennia display the frailty of all human institutions, and the evanescence of the things of this life, leading easily to the conclusion that the human story is more cyclical than progressive. But the irrecoverable, the catastrophic, is also part of that story. And the Great Dying was a catastrophe. In this book, the people who lived after the cataclysm are observed exploring what was left to them by the people who preceded it, seeking to understand those ruins in the light of preconceptions wholly formed in ignorance of the life that produced them. We must, therefore, pay as much heed to the history of prejudice as to the history of archaeology.

aspirations of white Americans as well. This even-handed so-
for all the actors in the drama would justify his primacy in our
but Gallatin deserves that distinction for yet another reason:
he first American statesman to employ the evidence of ancient
rchitecture to justify exertions to redeem the Republic from
ejudice.

A SKETCH

allatin came to the Ohio Valley just after the War of the Amer-
olution. He had been born in Geneva in 1761, emigrated to
ed States in 1780, taught French at Harvard, and learned ca-
1 Maine. He was elected senator from Pennsylvania in 1793,
to Congress in 1795, served as secretary of the treasury under
s Jefferson and Madison, was minister first to France and then
nd, and died just after the Mexican-American War, in 1849.
nic, skeptical, sometimes dry, he was never bitter; he knew
xpress affection, and thus was ready to receive it. Here is one
ters, written in middle age, to his wife:

e and sleep; mind nothing . . . nothing but the hope of seeing you.
hether in the plains or over the hills, whether in the city, or in
, I cannot live without you; . . . I am now good for nothing but
nd good for nothing without you; you will say that anyhow I am
od for much; that may be, but such as I am, you are mine; and you
companion, my joy and the darling of my soul.[1]

ding there must be, for all of us, but married people can hope
ing better than an ending like that of Hannah and Albert Gal-
e died on May 14, 1849, in the room next to his. After only
nths, he followed her—on August 13. They had been together
five years.
in did not package himself well. He would never have made
rman. Though he stood five feet ten or so, he stooped. He was
and his complexion was olive-brown. His eyes, dark hazel
n black, were set in his later years among the kind of wrinkles
after finding life, though often unfair, more amusing than in-
, and his bad teeth gave his every aspect a sardonic cast. His
ns included letting his hair grow too long in the wrong places.
was often soiled; his clothes were fashionable only by Next-
standards. His wife, small in stature, ample in proportion, ele-
urbane, grew to love him after an unsteady beginning of their
. Washington Irving wrote of Hannah Gallatin in 1812 that

CHAPTER TWO

ALBERT GALLATIN
AND THE POSSIBILITY
OF UNDERSTANDING

Albert Gallatin understood the past of the Great Valley as no one else in his time; no one, perhaps, until Abraham Lincoln, so understood its possibilities.

When he arrived in the Ohio Valley at the end of the 1780s, only a few Indians were still there; the Great Dying had done its work. A new multitude began to arrive soon after Gallatin, and, as he observed their arrival, he admonished them to try to live in peace with one another and with the Indians. He was a learned man, convinced that each of the races and nations coming together in that great crucible might generate mutual respect out of a due appreciation of the past achievements of each other. The architecture found in the valley was evidence of the achievement of the Indians.

Amid that architecture in the foothills of the western slope of the Appalachians, Gallatin founded a model community for what he hoped would be a model society. At the highlands, the West for him began, and the garden of America invited new beginnings. Though some of the Founders sensed the opportunity and a few such as Gallatin grasped for it, the West did *not* become a new society in which all three of the great nations of Americans, Black, White, and Red, found a dignified place. The reasons are many and buried deep in prejudices to be examined in subsequent pages. Gallatin did not find many adherents to his view of racial matters, and, admirable as he was, it must be admitted that he might have found more allies if his extraordinary array of skills had included benign demagoguery. But, alas, he was capable of persuasion only of small groups. Though he acted heroically on many occasions, he always contrived to make his heroism appear to be routine. No American of his time took such political and intellectual risks in the interests of both Blacks and Native Americans. Others may have attended one or the other, but he was solicitous of both, and of .

23

the best aspirations of white Americans as well. This even-handed solicitude for all the actors in the drama would justify his primacy in our
account, but Gallatin deserves that distinction for yet another reason:
he was the first American statesman to employ the evidence of ancient
Indian architecture to justify exertions to redeem the Republic from
racial prejudice.

A SKETCH

Albert Gallatin came to the Ohio Valley just after the War of the American Revolution. He had been born in Geneva in 1761, emigrated to
the United States in 1780, taught French at Harvard, and learned canoeing in Maine. He was elected senator from Pennsylvania in 1793,
was sent to Congress in 1795, served as secretary of the treasury under
presidents Jefferson and Madison, was minister first to France and then
to England, and died just after the Mexican-American War, in 1849.

Sardonic, skeptical, sometimes dry, he was never bitter; he knew
how to express affection, and thus was ready to receive it. Here is one
of his letters, written in middle age, to his wife:

> I smoke and sleep; mind nothing . . . nothing but the hope of seeing you.
> . . . Whether in the plains or over the hills, whether in the city, or in
> retreat, I cannot live without you; . . . I am now good for nothing but
> you, and good for nothing without you; you will say that anyhow I am
> not good for much; that may be, but such as I am, you are mine; and you
> are my companion, my joy and the darling of my soul.[1]

An ending there must be, for all of us, but married people can hope
for nothing better than an ending like that of Hannah and Albert Gallatin. She died on May 14, 1849, in the room next to his. After only
three months, he followed her—on August 13. They had been together
for fifty-five years.

Gallatin did not package himself well. He would never have made
an anchorman. Though he stood five feet ten or so, he stooped. He was
balding, and his complexion was olive-brown. His eyes, dark hazel
verging on black, were set in his later years among the kind of wrinkles
acquired after finding life, though often unfair, more amusing than infuriating, and his bad teeth gave his every aspect a sardonic cast. His
derelictions included letting his hair grow too long in the wrong places.
His linen was often soiled; his clothes were fashionable only by Next-
to-New standards. His wife, small in stature, ample in proportion, elegant and urbane, grew to love him after an unsteady beginning of their
marriage. Washington Irving wrote of Hannah Gallatin in 1812 that

she was "the most stylish woman in the drawing room . . . and . . . dressed with more splendor than any other of the noblesse.[2]

Though Gallatin communicated affection without restraint, his morning departure for the Treasury, unkempt and unconcerned, must have been a trial to her. Quite cheerfully, he said of himself that he was a "man without graces," and he never learned the dissembling arts of politics[3] Respected but never popular, his career was marked by abrupt depositions from power. Four times his failure to make himself ingratiating to large numbers caused him to fall from eminences upon which he had been placed by the just estimate of his peers. There were never enough peers.

In 1793, he was forced out of the Senate of the United States, ostensibly because his residency in America had been insufficiently long, but really because he was not British or German and the price of ejecting him was low. In 1798, he was one of the chief targets of the Alien and Sedition Acts, which were aimed at diminishing the political power of recent immigrants. Ten years later, a timorous president, James Madison, found that Gallatin had not raised a sufficiently noisy claque in the Senate to support appointment as secretary of state; his name was never sent forward for confirmation. In 1824, Gallatin became the first vice-presidential candidate to withdraw from a national campaign after nomination by his party. (The next to withdraw under such circumstances was Thomas Eagleton, a century and a half later). Gallatin was also a liability to the ticket because his opponents persuaded the electorate that he was too well informed about the practice of government. That was not how the matter was put, of course—the charge was that he was the choice of "King Caucus." [*]

Gallatin lived at a time in which bellicose ambition was amply rewarded. Military prowess or luck in military matters were surer qualifications for political advancement than a capacity to learn the sober lessons of self-government. He observed "vulgar conquerors" riding through cheering crowds into the White House, and the old statesman called upon his dazzled fellow countrymen to resist "false glory." Muscular celebrity entered the White House with Andrew Jackson, his slaves, and his mementoes of victory over the Indians.[† 4] Gallatin im-

---

[*]In 1992, a return to King Caucus sounds like a good idea. It might be composed of those of the Brotherhood of the Bruised who knew each other by performance rather than by propaganda. In 1992, the cry would be that Gallatin was the candidate of those within the Beltway.

[†]After Jackson came Lewis Cass, Richard Mentor Johnson, Zachary Taylor, Winfield Scott, John C. Fremont, and William Henry Harrison. After the Civil War, the nation had to wait an entire generation to find, in Grover Cleveland, its first nonmilitary president. After Cleveland, only a few years passed before Theodore Roosevelt appeared together with Manifest Destiny.

plored his fellow citizens to forsake military adventures and instead to "improve the state of the world, to be a 'model republic', to show that men are capable of governing themselves, and that this simple and natural form of government is that also which confers most happiness on all . . . above all, that which is attended by the highest standard of private and political virtue and morality."[5] Gallatin took seriously the role of the United States as a model republic.

Gallatin was serious but he was not dour. We are assured by many, even by the unrollicking John Quincy Adams, that he could be funny. Reporting to his diary on the negotiations for an end to the War of 1812, Adams wrote of Gallatin's "pliability of character and . . . playfulness of disposition . . . [which] throws off my heat with a joke." Often, said Adams, when things grew tense, he would, "in a tone of perfect good humor . . . [turn] the edge of the argument into mere jocularity."[6] Gallatin's enemies were as much to his credit as his friends. Those who hated him included the bigots ("fanatics" as he called them), the Indian haters, the slave drivers, and the criers for Manifest Destiny at the expense of "inferior races."

Gallatin had warmth, humor, quick intelligence, and a reliable decency. But he was not an orator. His exposition was consonant with his demeanor, his toilet, and his tailoring. He never mastered the theatrics of exposition, continuing to rely upon uncolored logic. Even when he last appeared in public, at eighty-eight, his style was still that of a neophyte in public discourse, emphasizing his points with a peculiar perpendicular chopping motion which either mesmerized or annoyed his listeners. He seldom raised his voice, and retained unashamed his French-Swiss accent.

He was a wit, but not a witty writer; his state papers, his studies of ethnology and linguistics are models of precision and orderly discourse, but they are heavy. In the Congress, his technique in debate was to hide an edge of satire in a vast pillow of unimpeachable statistical data.* George Dangerfield, the English historian, once rendered a lovely little picture of Gallatin. It ends with Dangerfield's assessment of

---

*In 1800, the Federalists had built up a heavy burden of debt by their military expenditures. One of them who had a fondness for technical terms professed concern that the French would pounce upon the treasury to plunder its "funded capital." Gallatin peered out from his graphs and tables, and observed: "As our funded capital is the same thing as our funded debt, I must confess . . . that I have no objection to give it to the French or to any other nation that will take it." (Walters, Gallatin, p. 121.)

He did not conserve his gift for a quick response for state occasions. Once, in 1794, a crowd of furious farmers, armed with squirrel rifles, pitchforks, and knives, challenged him to say whether or not he thought they had been wrong in burning down the barn of a tax collector. "If you had burned him in it," he replied, "it might have been something; but the barn had done no harm." (Quoted in Walters, Gallatin, p. 73.)

him as a negotiator: "He . . . possessed that rare combination of qualities—a copious intelligence and a sunny temperament . . . substantial but never too solid, firm but flexible." Gallatin began his service to the American Indians by learning their languages and customs. It was characteristic of him that he did so perilously and at the same time prosaically.[7]

GALLATIN AND THE INDIANS

During the summer of 1781, Gallatin learned the rudiments of Abenaki and the management of a birchbark canoe. He also served his adopted country as a militiaman, on its outermost frontier. His canoe was not for wilderness voyaging, or even for ethnological inquiry; he used it to carry rum, tobacco, and sugar in a doubtful trading enterprise to impoverished downeasters in farthest Maine.* The tribes of Maine which had survived European diseases had put up a brave fight against the British but had been driven into the bogs and mountains. Some remnants remained, with no cause to be friendly, but Gallatin took his canoe and sought them out. He saw nothing romantic in this; he was no young Churchill,[†] he merely wished to learn what their lives were like.

By happenstance, while canoeing about the eastern fringes of Maine, Gallatin had his first lesson in the geography of the distant portions of the American North*west* which must also be reached by canoe. He got that lesson at second hand. The French frigate *Amazone* put into the port from which Gallatin did his canoeing. The commander, Admiral La Perouse, was fresh from a campaign in Hudson Bay calculated to distract the British from their activity against Washington's army to the south. Perouse had captured the British outpost of Fort Churchill and dealt the Hudson Bay Company a blow by burning York Factory. Just before setting the torch, however, he extricated from the company's files a prize of war—the manuscript of an account of a voy-

---

*His customers were few, but they included the garrison whose task it was to defend the Bay of Fundy from a British attack which never came. From time to time the officers of the garrison were occupied with higher callings, such as visiting the ladies of Portland; Gallatin, obviously an educated man, was put in charge. Later, when his friends in Congress attempted to tout him as a war hero because he had taken his motley band outside the stockade on a reconnaissance, he refused the honor, observing that he had never met the enemy. Few politicians have been so meticulous.

†Winston Churchill, like Sam Houston and Henry Hastings Sibley (the Minnesota governor, not the Confederate general of that name), took himself off to the frontier, in his case South Africa, for a fling at well-publicized romantic adventure before turning to sober statesmanship.

age down the Slave and Coppermine rivers in northern Canada to the
Arctic Ocean by Samuel Hearne, the first European to cross the Arctic
circle from the mainland of America. Hearne's account, shared by La
Perouse, taught Gallatin much.[8]

There was a gap of a thousand miles of unknown territory to be
filled between the Coppermine and the headwaters of the Ohio, where
Gallatin established himself next; once in New Geneva he went to
work filling the gap with knowledge. By 1804, as the expedition of
Lewis and Clark was being organized, he "suddenly was discovered to
know more about western geography than anyone in government except Jefferson." The President had gotten considerably more with Mr.
Secretary Gallatin than the loyal party lieutenant and financial genius
he had expected.[9] Gallatin supplied maps to Lewis and Clark; they supplied *him* with the information about even larger ruins than those he
had seen in Ohio, for their winter camp had been on American Bottom
near Cahokia. He urged them to look further. Later, he followed with
interest their accounts of ancient architecture along the Missouri River.

After Gallatin left the Treasury in 1817, he was still a power in Washington. When an assemblage of leaders of the southern tribes appeared
in Washington in 1825–26, he urged the War Department to collate
their languages. He had resumed his Indian studies two years earlier,
sending out inquiries to a variety of learned persons. He husbanded
their replies, and, in 1831, was asked by the American Antiquarian
Society if he had anything to add to some short essays he had contributed to a French anthropological atlas. In 1836 he demonstrated that
he *had*—422 pages still eminently worth reading, entitled *A Synopsis
of the Indian Tribes Within the United States East of the Rocky Mountains, and in the British and Russian Possessions in North America.*

The copy of this tome in the library of the Smithsonian Institution is
covered with annotations by intervening owner-readers, embellishing
Gallatin's discussion of eight-one tribes, their physical context, their
prehistory, their relations with Europeans and Africans, and their several cultures. The last half of the book is a detailed analysis of Indian
languages, still useful and astonishingly comprehensive.

Comprehensiveness is a virtue, but a greater is comprehension. Gallatin focused his readers upon the core of all this learning, offering his
opinion that the great mounds of the Great Valley were constructed by
the ancestors of the "real Americans," the Indians, "of a more populous nation than any now existing." Despite the prejudice of his own
day (and our own) to think of all Indians as hunter-gatherers, he correctly surmised that those Indians had been an agricultural—or at least
a horticultural—people.[10]

In 1842, Gallatin founded the American Ethnological Society, serving as its first president, and offering his house as its monthly meeting

place. As president, he contributed another mighty tome, *Notes on the Semi-Civilized Notions of Mexico, Yucataw and Central America,* synthesizing the work of sixteenth century Spanish historians and unpublished work by Hispanic scholars of his own time. It is full of wonderful things. Gallatin underwrote the first volume of the society's *Transactions,* including a new set of taxonomies of Mexican and Central American languages, with many illustrations. When the Smithsonian was organized in 1838, he tilted its emphasis toward Indian studies, making certain that the Smithsonian's initially ample resources were first used to underwrite the *Ancient Monuments of the Mississippi Valley* by Ephraim George Squier and Edwin H. Davis, whom Gallatin had sponsored after they outspent the meager budget of the American Antiquarian Society. When he was eighty-eight, Gallatin went on to publish essays—really books in essay form—on *The Geographical Distribution and Means of Subsistence of the North American Indians at the Time of the Discovery of America,* and *On the Ancient Semi-Civilization of New Mexico and the Great Colorado of the West.*

As a young man, Gallatin assisted George Washington in determining the portage routes between the Potomac and the Ohio; he aided Jefferson in setting the objectives for the Lewis and Clark expedition as well as providing the map consolidating all that was known of their route; his energy animated every important inquiry into the antiquity of the Mississippi Valley. Sixty-three years after he first met Washington south of Pittsburgh, he saw to it that John Charles Fremont published his research into the Indian languages and geography of the Great Basin of Nevada.

Respectfully, thoroughly, and comprehensively, Gallatin scrutinized every scrap of information that could be gleaned about Indian life from the Bay of Fundy to the Gulf of California and the Arctic Circle. Without racial prejudice or racial sentimentality, he launched American comparative philology, with a spirit more important than any system. Beginning in the 1780s, nearly two full centuries before the word "racism" became commonplace among American historians, Gallatin revealed the association of dominance to fear, of fear to hate, and of fear *and* hate to the purposeful disparagement of the accomplishments of others. Gallatin's vision of what might be achieved in the relatively uncluttered opportunity of the West was more ambitious than Jefferson's because his aversion to slavery was deeper, and his grasp both of its specific history and of developmental economics* in general more profound.

---

*Developmental economics are the processes by which resources may be allocated by those seeking to induce a rapid alteration of an economy they deem to be "primitive" to one they might, at the time, describe as "modern."

GALLATIN, THE "MOUND BUILDERS" AND NATIVISM

Many of Gallatin's countrymen had great difficulty "registering," that is, seeing as artifacts *and* as important, even the most conspicuous of the man-made objects they encountered in the West. At first, they insisted that Native American earthen architecture was not, in fact architecture—because it was made of earth. (Some people may still be heard making that assertion.) Then, though admitting it to be architecture, they insisted that the work was not Native American, but, instead, the creation of Hindus, Welsh, Egyptians, the Lost Tribes of Israel, or even the Japanese. A profusion of stories were composed about exotic mound builders, tales diverse in detail but identical in essence: the Indians whose culture was being destroyed in the nineteenth century could not be the same people as those who accomplished such prodigies. Sometimes it was insisted that these savages were the descendants of the barbarians who had swept down upon kindly mound builders. So, this solacing story went, the new Americans, redressing an ancient crime, were agents of delayed retribution. Better than that—theirs was retribution at the hands of a master race. (We return to this topic in Chapter Ten.)

It would be unfair to assert that the American pioneers were unique in embracing a myth of racial superiority to justify self-interest. Such myths have often become the source of political philosophy. They are to be found from Beijing and Tokyo to Madrid, from Baghdad and Zimbabwe to Belfast. They were a primary premise of Inca and Aztec foreign policy before *any* Europeans arrived. But in the 1830s and 1840s, as Gallatin pointed out, genealogical nonsense about a master race (Anglo-Saxons) was triply pernicious for its deployment: (1) to defend slavery, (2) to justify the extermination of Indians, and (3) to further the doctrine of Manifest Destiny. The "destiny" manifested was the imperial expansion of the slave-driven plantation system, first into lands possessed by Native Americans and next into territory torn from Mexico.

"Nativism"* was coming to a boil. The Know-Nothing party was forming. Mobs in the cities burnt out the tenements of recent Irish immigrants. The sweeter side of racism played itself out in the suburbs, as Anglo-Saxon sentimentality produced brisk sales of the novels of Sir Walter Scott, while Gothic Revival villas were erected to look as much as possible like cottages in Old England.

---

*Natives being defined as Whites of European descent born in North America. The Latin American equivalent is "Creole."

Gallatin found stiff resistance to his scholarly reports of monumental accomplishments on the part of the Indian predecessors of the Pilgrim Fathers. The Saxon Race was enjoying itself, but not enough to be completely self-assured; its anxious insistence upon racial superiority might, on occasion, wrap a diffident embrace about other, selected Europeans, but it could not bring itself to credit Indians with a grand history.

Thirty years earlier, Gallatin had been jostled into his first intimation of these complexities by a snob seeking to curry his favor—understandings in public life sometimes come in curious ways. In 1814, while representing his adopted country in the negotiations leading to the Treaty of Ghent, Gallatin was offered what Henry Goulburn, the British emissary, thought to be a compliment. Goulburn commented that Gallatin was still more European than American. Gallatin flared back that the only true Americans were "the Red Indians."[11] Indeed, Indians were the true Americans. And the increasingly smug Anglo-Saxons? Gallatin pronounced the term unscientific. The British in America were as much "Frenchified Normans, Angevins, and Gascons" as Angles and Saxons. He doubted, as well, the virtue of "doubtful descent from men who lived one thousand years ago," who were, he added, a barbaric lot clearly "inferior to Goths."[12] Warming to his subject, Gallatin went on to say that "it is not [to] their Anglo-Saxon descent that the English are indebted for their superior institutions. In the progressive improvement of mankind much more has been due to religious and political institutions than to races."[13]

He hoped that America would drop such notions and embrace all races as co-equal partners. Then "there will be no trace left of the pretended superiority of one of those races above the other . . . the claim is but a pretext for covering and justifying unjust usurpation and unbound ambition."[14]

It would be consoling to be able to report that as the nineteenth century recaptured the evangelistic Christianity which had grown dry in the cold wind of the Enlightenment, religious enthusiasm led Gallatin to reinvigorate his abolitionism and to take up the cause of justice for Indians. But, as we will see in Chapter Ten, the evangelicals were not helpful, and in any case, the religious inclinations of Albert Gallatin were always idiosyncratic—as any true religious convictions must be. He was not even anticlerical in the fatuous and self-congratulatory way of his deist acquaintances. Even in his eighties, when the United States was seized by nativist and anti-Catholic agitation, when the Know-Nothings were invoking what one of them admitted to be "holy horror & unusual zeal against the Roman Catholics," and when *The New York Times* sniffed the air and found that it stank of "the old ineradicable Saxon bigotry, which periodically likes a crusade against

the Pope, Gallatin refused to utter uncritical condemnations of the clergy.[15]

Gallatin was not a scold; he was too practical for that, tackling a series of tasks worth tackling throughout a long public career. During the final forty years of that span, Gallatin offered a series of proposals for the Great Valley: (1) a stable banking system; (2) a vast array of turnpikes and canals; (3) a solicitude for domestic manufactures; (4) an opening of the Mississippi to the agricultural products of the Ohio Valley; (5) preservation of the most important architecture to be found in the region, that of the Native Americans; and (6) resistance to the spread of slavery into the territories.

GALLATIN, MEXICO, AND ARCHITECTURAL CONNECTIONS

Gallatin was practical, yes, but a practical moralist. As the nation filled out, Gallatin hoped, it might also purify itself. For thirty years, sometimes almost alone, he stood against those who distracted his country's attention from reforming itself into imperial adventures beyond the valley. The crowds cheered the Manifest Destiny of Anglo-Saxon Americans to dominate Texas, and, after Texas, Cuba and Mexico. Gallatin insisted instead upon policies growing naturally from "the principle of democracy, which rejects every . . . claim of . . . an hereditary superiority of races."[16]

Gallatin brushed aside "Manifest Destiny," as only one of "these allegations of superiority of race and destiny . . . [which] are but pretenses under which to disguise ambition, cupidity, or silly vanity."[17]

Along the southern and western boundaries of the United States there was plenty of scope for the cupidity which expresses itself in the use of other human beings to do one's labor without pay, and avarice, there, brooked no interference. As soon as the Louisiana Purchase was complete, in 1803, Spanish officers commanding garrisons along its vague western frontier issued invitations to American slaves to find freedom in (Spanish) Texas. To encourage these hemorrhages to the plantation system, they offered the slaves grants of land (anticipating the Freedman's Bureau) and instruction in the Roman Catholic faith.

The American government responded with diplomatic remonstrance and threats of invasion; the Spanish authorities withdrew their offers, but slaves continued to find refuge in Texas. One of the first acts of the Mexican government after independence from Spain in 1820–21 was to declare the abolition of slavery, and though the expression long preceded the performance, Texas became a sump, drawing off slave labor from the American plantations.* The South turned its fury upon Texas, and, beyond Texas, to abolitionist Mexico; fear of slave revolt and avarice for land were powerful propellants.

Texas was acquired in 1845, despite Gallatin's opposition. He wrote that:

> It is too much to ask from us that we should take an active part in permitting the accession of a foreign state, and a foreign slave-holding state, to the union; and that we should consent that new states should again be added to those upon an unequal basis of representation.[18] †

The Mexican War ensued, despite the opposition of Gallatin, John Quincy Adams, Abraham Lincoln, Henry Clay, John C. Calhoun, Frederick Douglass, and Thomas Hart Benton.‡ The president, James K. Polk, was the embodiment of the cool, calculating variety of slave-driving, Indian-hunting, expansionist Tennessee planter. Polk solicited a war, and lost no time in responding to a Mexican raid across the Rio Grande with a full-scale invasion, justified to the public as a war over yet another inferior people.

When Mr. Polk got his war, Gallatin set aside his linguistic studies and his archaeology to engage in the last campaign of his life, in alliance with John Quincy Adams. Despite party differences, the two had always been on good terms. Now they went into battle together, old tellers of truths, full of that kind of idealism which is reduced to its essence by the heat of experience. It was then that the pro-slavery, expansionist party hired an Irish thug, "Mike" Walsh, to heckle Gallatin at public meetings,** and subsidized editors and preachers to expatiate

---

*Spanish Florida had earlier served that function, bringing forth the wrath of Andrew Jackson. He had organized a private invasion and Florida was acquired in 1820, but its swamps had still received refugee Blacks. The Seminole War, fought to close the Florida escape route, flared on the southern horizon for thirty years, reinforcing at once the fears of uprisings in the plantation South and, by a channeling of emotion as twisted as any of the time, an orthodoxy of racial superiority over both Blacks and Indians. The dreaded yet derided "Seminoles" were a mixture of the two.

†Under the voting provisions of the Constitution, Negroes counted as three-fifths of a person for apportioning congressional districts and votes in the electoral college for the presidency. This meant that if a single slaveowner, such as Wade Hampton, had a large plantation comprising an entire congressional district and containing 5,000 slaves, he would, by himself, have voting power equal to that of 3,000 free and independent yeomen in another district.

‡Their reasons, needless to say, were not all the same.

**This was probably the first time in American political history when the cry "Wall Street Bankers" was used in the interest of what later became known as the "paranoid style." In New York in 1846, "nativism" was as rampant as it was in Iowa in 1896.

justifications for expansion. The talk was of the white man's burden. George Wilkins Kendall wrote that Mexicans displayed "few of the instincts which govern other races." A historian, Brantz Mayer, colored in the image: Mexicans were dark, even if they were "Spanish." Though a Mexican might be brave, his could only be berserk bravery, of "Mahomedan fatalism derived . . . from his Moorish kindred." Mexican cavalry were the "Arabs of the American continent."[19]

Gallatin and Adams would have none of this borrowing of antipathy toward Blacks to apply to Mexicans by way of Moors. Were we to find Othello lurking in the ruins of Teotihuacan? The delusion of racial superiority, used all along to justify repression of African Americans and wars against Native Americans, was now determining the conduct of "foreign affairs," meaning relations toward non-Indian nations. The two old patriots were fearless in their candor, infuriating the jingoes. They portrayed the triumphant advance against Chapultepec as slavery's triumph; when the Stars and Stripes was unfurled over the Halls of Montezuma, it was, they said, "Slavery's Flag."

Though the excuse for the Mexican War was that it would give freedom to the Mexican people, its consequence was consigning much of Mexico's territory to the sway of a slave-driving plantocracy. This, insisted Quincy Adams, was merely the latest of hypocrisies. In his book *Slavery and the War,* he tore away the bandage: the American nation, not the Mexican, required redemption. Thereafter he commenced voting against appropriations for the war while offering a stream of abolitionist resolutions. Finally, he took some of the jubilation out of the treaty ending the war and bringing one third of Mexico under the American flag. As the parades blared past the Capital, John Quincy Adams died at his desk in the House of Representatives.

Gallatin's devices were less dramatic. He had produced two of his most forceful essays, asking for peace with Mexico and attacking the aggressive policy of the Polk administration as "unjust aggrandizement by brutal force." Even in the euphoria of victory he ridiculed Polk's assertion that the war had been fought to "enlighten the degraded Mexicans." As for the Indians already within the borders of the United States, Gallatin continued to insist that they, too, be taken seriously as a people capable of great art and architecture.

Dark conspiracies of Wall Streeters have sometimes in fact existed, as I have tried to show in the discussion of the career of Ignatius Donnelley in *Rediscovering America.* But more often than not the slogan was used to distract an audience from debate on economics into a mire of racial antipathy—if not toward Blacks, then toward Jews, if not Jews, then toward "foreigners." However, 1846 was the *last* time that Wall Street Bankers were accused of excessive tenderness towards Blacks and Hispanics.

GALLATIN, ARCHAEOLOGY, AND RACE

The invasion of Mexico in 1846 was America's first foreign war, aside from futile incursions of Canada during the Revolution and the War of 1812. It was also its first media war, and, as an odd consequence, a New World equivalent to Napoleon's invasion of Egypt a half century earlier in drawing public attention to ancient architecture. Photojournalism made its appearance with awkward black boxes, shrouds, tripods, and "hold it!" For the first time, warfare was reported by large numbers of professional war correspondents. Between engagements, after the supply of hometown heroes was exhausted and the humorous possibilities of soldierly cuisine fully dilated, war correspondents must still "file." File they did, with the result that nearly as much ink was spilled on prowess in Mexican archaeology as in prowess on Mexican battlefields.

Archaeologists learned to write eloquently and to be written *about* eloquently by off-duty war correspondents. Everybody wrote and nearly everybody read. The nation was more addicted to books than ever before or since; the 1840s and 1850s were the effulgent decades for publishing. Multitudes bought books, read books, and seemed to form their most intense impressions of reality from books.

Mexico had already received the attention of a series of magnificent writers. As far back as 1804, Baron Alexander von Humboldt was welcomed to Thomas Jefferson's White House on the strength of his account of a year amid the ruins and mysteries of Mexico. Thereafter some became aware of the presence in the New World of architecture on the scale of that of the Valley of the Pharaohs, and some, including Albert Gallatin, understood the application of Humboldt's method to the Great Valley. Humboldt, in turn, understood that Gallatin had information which might link the Mexican to Mississippian nations, so he followed up the White House meeting by urging Gallatin to record what had been learned about the Indians in the West from John Jacob Astor, Pierre Chouteau, and other fur traders. Gallatin's response formed the basis of his later works on ethnology, but it must be admitted that Gallatin was not the man to enrapture a large public on any subject. Livelier models for the use of archaeology to inform history were produced by William Prescott and John Lloyd Stephens. Prescott's account of the world of the Aztecs and its conquest by Cortez, published first in 1843, was still a national best-seller when the Mexican war broke out three years later. Prescott was nearly blind; in compensation for his own disability he provided others with eerily accurate descriptions of pyramids and palaces he, himself, could never see. Drawing upon eight thousand pages of manuscript accounts by others, Prescott depicted archaeological treasures more clearly and beautifully than any writer before or since.

Stephens was already famous for his explorations of Petra and the Egyptian desert when he arrived in New York at the end of the 1830s, and already a virtuoso in literary lionage. Basking in his fame, at Gallatin's urging and encouraged by a generous subscription from his hosts and hostesses, he added Mexico to his list. Stephens coupled archaeology with romantic illustrations by his colleague, Frederick Catherwood, working in the style employed a century earlier by Piranesi to give ghostly grandeur to the ruins of Rome. After arriving in Mexico in 1839, Stephens sprayed the full blast of his charm, energy, and drama upon the remains of the Maya. His first gorgeously presented volume was published in the same year as Prescott's, and his second went out to President Polk's forces as they were occupying Mexico City. Books about Mexican antiquities weighted the saddlebags of officers, filled the knapsacks for enlisted men, arrived by mail, and were used as guides for reconnaissance. Books in translation taught Spanish and English to American and Mexican scholars who assembled in symposia as soon as the powder-smoke cleared to discuss Prescott's *Conquest of Mexico*.

Though prepared by Prescott and Stephens, a new audience for archeology was created by the war correspondents. Astonished Anglo-Saxon voices were heard on the summit of the pyramid of Cholula; how could such prodigies have been achieved by people who were *not* Anglo-Saxon? General Winfield Scott halted his army at Puebla to permit his men to visit its Aztec monuments. "By moonlight . . . these ruined cities . . . [are] an impressive spectacle," wrote one soldier.[20]

There has never been such a literary invasion, not even Napoleon's into Egypt. There were, of course, analogies drawn by Americans between Scott, Napoleon, Mexico, and Egypt; the American armies were modern men coming into the presence of antiquity, an antiquity of pyramids, at that. Prescott had portrayed Cortez as a proto-Napoleon. Now Scott and Zachary Taylor were conquering the conquerors of the Montezumas.

After this excitement washed about for a time, two responses precipitated. The first was to aver that Mexican pyramid shapes and Aztec mummies must necessarily by Egyptian. As usual, some sought to avoid the embarrassment of crediting large accomplishments to Indians. "America," it was said "was another Egypt to antiquaries," bearing witness "that the ancestors of the Montezumas lived on the Nile."[21]

Prescott may have anticipated this response, for he did his best to deter it. The Mexico he painted in indelible and vivid tones was no desert mortuary like Egypt, nor did he depict the Mexicans at the time of the Spanish conquest, in 1519, as Napoleon's Egyptians of 1798—

pathetic, exploited, impoverished people subsisting amid the white bones of antiquity. Prescott's Aztecs were still building temples, palaces, pyramids, and gardens when the Spanish chroniclers arrived.

Those who had read Stephens knew that in 1847 people looking very like those depicted in Maya sculpture were still farming amid the ruins of the Yucatan. Even those who heard only "Anglo-Saxon voices" could not easily deny to the much-abused Mexicans credit for having created the Mexico revealed to American cavalry and infantry. Ten thousand English-speaking witnesses confirmed what Prescott and Stephens had reported. New information poured in as the armies of Taylor and Scott were reinforced by cavalry expeditions sweeping down into Mexico from the northwest, where along the upper Rio Grande Valley and then in Sonora, trained eyes had measured and assessed other Indian buildings. Suddenly, the archaeology of *New* Mexico was added to the American store of knowledge. Some New Mexican buildings in present use bore close similarity to the much larger ones described in Prescott's accounts of the Aztecs and Stephens's of the Maya.

As he approached his ninetieth year, with seven decades of research behind him, Albert Gallatin took up these travelers' accounts, and went to work *On the Ancient Semi-Civilization of New Mexico and the Great Colorado of the West*. In this, his final work, the old man connected the Aztecs to the Pueblo people, and the Pueblos to the Mississippi Valley and all the way to Grave Creek. (Fifty years later, Gallatin's essay served as a stimulus and guide to the explorations of John Wesley Powell into the Gila Valley and the Grand Canyon.)

In 1845 he had already set forth his views in *The Ancient Semi-Civilization:* Mexico and Central America had been civilized by

> several populous agricultural nations . . . with regular forms of government, . . . laws for the punishment of crimes and for the protection and descent of property, a division of labor and of trades, a commercial intercourse, and a currency. They were dressed in cotton cloth, lived in large cities, had erected durable and ornamented temples and palaces, and made great progress, not only in architecture and sculpture, but in jewelry and several other arts. . . .
>
> Was this civilization of domestic or of foreign origin? . . . This . . . most interesting problem . . . involves . . . the presumed inferiority of some races; and whether savage tribes can, of themselves, and without any foreign assistance, emerge from the rudest and lowest social state, and gradually attain even the highest degree of civilization known to us.[22]

Gallatin answered with a resounding "Yes, they can." His patient parsing of the evidence was a prelude to his final assault upon those who could not believe that Indians could create a civilization on their own. Though his subject was Mexico, he could not limit his conclusions to the creation of its monuments. As a self-adopted son of the trans-Appalachian West, he gave his final attention to the Great Valley:

> The monuments left by that race [the mound-building Indians] are principally earthen tumuli or graves, and extensive earthen works apparently intended for defence. To these must be added some remarkable works which could not have been intended for that purpose alone. . . . [such as] Circleville, . . . [and] the quadrilateral mound near the Mississippi [at Cahokia], . . . has some resemblance to the pyramid of Cholulla. [It is three times larger in extent, in fact] . . . [These are] proofs, not only of a more dense and therefore agricultural population, but also of a different social state.
>
> All the modern Indian forts from Florida to Canada . . . were wooden structures defended by palisades, and of a moderate extent. . . . The ancient fortifications, surrounded by earthen ramparts, include occasionally a far greater space than would be necessary to contain, or could be defended by, any modern Indian tribe.[23]

Gallatin specified the earthworks found by Lewis and Clark, the mounds at Cahokia, the circle and square at Circleville, and the cone at Grave Creek, pointing out that "monuments" on this scale are to be found "exclusively in the valley of the Mississippi. . . . Not a single one has ever been found either east of the Allegheny or west of the Rocky Mountains." If they had been built, (as some said) by Egyptians or Hindus or Lost Tribes of Israel, "it seems impossible that . . . they should have left no traces whatever of their existence in the regions where they must have landed."[24]

He concluded that these works were of indigenous creation. Perhaps "their agriculture . . . [was] derived from Mexico," perhaps their builders were "either exterminated or driven away by the savage tribes which surrounded them," but they were Americans. They were of the same stock as the "savages," in the same sense that the classical Greeks were of the same stock as the barbarian tribes that overwhelmed them, and the Romans of the same Indo-European stock as the Goths and Vandals.[25]

It may seem excessive to belabor this point, which seems to obvious to us. But in Gallatin's day, it was by no means settled. Nor was it even settled when the Smithsonian Institution published overwhelming evidence to support Gallatin's position fifty years after his death. Instead, even the most sophisticated of Gallatin's contemporaries were so deeply sunk in social prejudice that they came only reluctantly to accept either Blacks or Indians as capable of art or architecture. This was true despite the accumulations of masses of evidence to the contrary, some of it found under the plows and shovels of the farmers of the Midwest. Though few of Gallatin's countrymen, north or south, were as uncontaminated as he from racial prejudice, and though the absence of slavery was associated for most northerners with the absence of Blacks, he was not utterly alone, and he might have created his own political following beyond the Treasury if he had been only a little more comfortable on stage. The American West was occupied by settlers of European ancestry at a time in which slavery was being questioned by all civilized peoples. It was on its way to abolition nearly everywhere—though it did surge once more in Cuba, Brazil, in the Old South, and because of the influence of southern statesmen in the American West.

Jefferson, Gallatin's political chief, did little to oppose its expansion after 1787, though Gallatin was an avowed abolitionist in the 1790's. It must be admitted that not only did Gallatin himself own household slaves but he also failed to speak out *publicly* against the expansion of the South's peculiar institution until *after* Jefferson's retirement from public office in 1809. But the differences between the two were exceedingly important; Gallatin can best be estimated as an independent figure if his views, which have attracted little attention, are contrasted with those of Jefferson, about which there has been a full bookcase of discussion. We shall come, in Chapters Seven, Eight, and Nine, to a full examination of Jefferson and his prejudices. This fascinating man, clearly the greatest intellect to occupy the American presidency, did, like all of us, have prejudices, and his were very stubborn. With regard to racial matters, they were antithetical to those of his friend and colleague Gallatin, a circumstance which caused them both some discomfort. It has also caused some discomfort among historians, who have confused matters by seeking to arrange things to make Jefferson's preconceptions and his public positions after 1808 appear to have been closer to Gallatin's, or to persuade us that only Jefferson's were possible to "men of their time." This has been a pernicious exercise. It has deprived us of a full sense of the sumptuous diversity of views on race and on ancient architecture which was, in fact, present among the men—and women—of their time.

This book attempts a survey of some of those views. The two subjects—race and ancient architecture—are, as we have already noted, closely related. How people feel about one heavily affects how they feel about the other, as we have seen in the case of Gallatin, and as we shall see in the cases of George Washington and Thomas Jefferson.

CHAPTER THREE

BLOODY YEARS AMID
THE RUINS

Neither Albert Gallatin nor Thomas Jefferson dug much dirt; though in his youth Jefferson supervised the excavation of a Virginia mound, he did not return to fieldwork. Both these statesmen conducted their archaeology at wholesale, encouraging the digging of others, the most important of whom were, it happens, clergymen and generals. After discoveries were made in the field, Jefferson, Gallatin, and the learned societies founded by them interpreted to the world at large what was found.

It is not entirely to be expected that we should look to the annals of evangelism and warfare for the first accounts of systematic archaeology. But that was how it was in the first provinces of the trans-Appalachian region to come to the attention of American statesmanship, for reasons to be explained in the next dozen pages. The reader who wants archaeology straight may wish to skip the politics, but in doing so there maybe some loss of color; the mounds were found amid politics of the most vehement sort. George Washington first campaigned in the Ohio Valley in 1753; forty years later, as president of the United States, he sent Anthony Wayne against the coalition of Indian nations which had until then successfully resisted the efforts of lesser commanders to bring the region under the sway of Europe or Europe's colonists. The story of those years is a bloody one of massacre and rapine, of burned crops and starving people, of viciousness and depredation, of strange, abruptly changing alliances and erratic changes of fortune, and of brilliant glints of the most astonishing decency and philanthropy across a somber scene. Scrupulous scholarship was performed not only in quiet moments but also amid the smoke and surge of battle—sometimes out of necessity, but though that scholarship showed that Indians had been capable of magnificent architecture, too often that truth was lost in the din, and the descendents of the builders treated as savages descended from savages.

The first Genevan intellectual to appear in the Ohio country was not

Gallatin but Colonel Henri Bouquet, a professional soldier of broad learning, who found himself in the summer of 1758 leading the advance guard of a polyglot force of colonials, mercenaries, and Indians through the wilds of western Pennsylvania.* In the rear of the army, Colonel George Washington brought along a contingent of Virginian militia, leading some of them for the third time into this corner of the Laurel Highlands. In 1753, he had conducted a reconnaissance through the French fort system of which Fort Duquesne (Pittsburgh) was the most formidable. It was situated behind swiftly running streams and made use of very large and very ancient Indian earthworks. In 1755, on his second expedition, he had been present as General James Braddock led his red and white coats into an ambush sprung by the French and Indians, having refused the advice of Washington confirming that given earlier by Benjamin Franklin.

Washington was wiser than Braddock; he took account of Indian history as well as of Indian tactics, retreating behind the earthern walls of an ancient Indian ceremonial enclosure with his tattered force, calling the place "Fort Necessity". Bouquet was wiser still, and summoned a superior force before contending with the alliance of Indians and French. Their enemies withdrew, and Bouquet was able to retrieve one after another the four forts Washington had spied out in 1753. All seemed easy; French power in the valley was ebbing.

But the British, with their mercenaries and colonial levies, did not properly assess the will to resist on the part of the Ottawa, Hurons, and other Indian nations allied with France. After the departure of the blue and white uniforms of King Louis in 1762, these confederate nations took matters into their own hands. Striking back into Ohio and Pennsylvania, they reoccupied all the forts the French had lost to Bouquet except Pittsburgh. Along the Great Lakes, the Ottawa war leader, Pontiac, conducted a masterly campaign in which six more British posts were taken and Detroit was put under siege.†

---

*Bouquet was born in 1719 in the little town of Rolle, near Geneva. He learned his trade as a soldier in the armies of Holland and Sardinia, before taking a lieutenant colonel's commission to command a regiment of Germans recruited to fight in North America, in the service of the ruler of Hanover who was also King George III of England.

†At this juncture, the Iroquois abandoned their British alliance. During the previous century, they had several times raided as far as the Mississippi, and after 1740 the Mingo (cousins of the Iroquois) remained in Ohio. In 1762, the New York Iroquois summoned their resources for new western adventures, having relieved their anxieties about what might strike them from behind by turning eastward to destroy the power of the Mohegans. If the British could be beaten back, the Confederacy and its western allies, especially the Ottawa led by Pontiac, might become the dominant powers in the Ohio Valley. So as the French power had receded, many of the Iroquois moved toward resistance to both the British and the Americans. The French had been allied with the Hurons and their Wyandot subsidiaries, traditional enemies of the Iroquois. Though they were less dangerous, now,

The Seneca of the Genessee were the first to take up arms, attacking Fort Venango (near Franklin, Pennsylvania). When they departed, late in June, 1763, none of the garrison were left alive, a lesson heeded by the garrison of Fort Le Boeuf (Waterford, Pennsylvania), which speedily decamped. The fort was burnt, and the Seneca moved on to Fort Presque Isle (Erie, Pennsylvania) where they were joined by a contingent of Ottawa, Ojibway, and Wyandots detached by Pontiac from his western campaign. On June 20, that garrison surrendered.

The attention of the coalition next turned to the fortress at Pittsburgh. A delegation of Delaware were sent to reason with its commander. His options were to suffer the fate of the garrison of Fort Venango, to accept an outcome like that at Fort Presque Isle, or to hold on, like the commander at Detroit, hoping for relief.*

Meanwhile, Bouquet was fighting his way back toward Pittsburgh, through ambushes and August heat. He prevailed after a two-day pitched battle at Bushy Run. Pittsburgh was relieved.[†] [‡]

---

and the British and their colonists were still present, battle-hardened, well-armed, and increasingly bold. Thus after 1763, the Seneca and other members of the Iroquois Confederacy, joined by the Mingo, turned their craft in diplomacy and fury in battle upon those Europeans still in the field.

*The idea that Native American military tactics could not include siege craft is false. They were rare, but they did occur: the French at Fort Rosalie (Natchez) were overwhelmed in the 1720s, and Pontiac kept Detroit invested for six months.

[†]The force led by Bouquet was inferior to that of the Indians and his fate might have been that of Braddock had not the Indians been already weakened by the biological weapons of the British.

A smallpox epidemic had burst out in the fort. Many English immunity systems were strong enough to survive it; the Delaware, Shawnee, and Mingo lacked the necessary antibodies. Their ambassadors were sent away with gifts—blankets from the smallpox hospital, in accordance with a strategy recommended by Lord Jeffrey Amherst, the British commander in chief.

The epidemic that ensued had the desired effect. In Pennsylvania, Kentucky, and Ohio, people died by the thousands. Nothing the Spaniards had done in Mexico or along the route of De Soto in the southeast could match the deliberate and indiscriminate ferocity of this contrived plague.

[‡]Before the impetus of the campaign was lost and winter set in, Bouquet began preparations to carry the war toward the villages of the Ohio nations. His summons went forth to the frontiersmen whose families and farms he had rescued from the Indians.

They were sluggish in responding. Energetic enough in defending their hearths, the "hardy pioneers" were not, as a general rule, disposed toward wars fought beyond the horizon. Bouquet was infuriated by their torpor, and his estimate of American valor was not elevated by dispatches informing him of the massacres of peaceful, Christian Indians who had taken refuge in a jail in central Pennsylvania by the vigilantes of the Paxton district who called themselves "the Paxton Boys." There was some redeeming news: a Philadelphia printer, Benjamin Franklin, had led the Quakers and a few British troops to prevent further vigilante bloodshed, and had written a pamphlet calling the Paxton Boys what they were— murderers, and their work what *it* was—racial crime.

It was not quite Bouquet's last campaign. In 1764, he led a British force in an invasion of Ohio, leaving the river of that name near the present town of East Liverpool, just north of the great assembly of Adena conical mounds which extends from that point southward a hundred fifty miles to the Kentucky border, as the crow flies. Soon he came over the Appalachian foothills of eastern Ohio and entered the gentler terrain which had been the heartland of the Hopewell culture.

PREPARING FOR THE OHIO CAMPAIGN

Twelve centuries had passed since Hopewell times, and a series of plagues of European and African diseases had swept through the region. But the agricultural tradition in which the Hopewell had participated still persisted.* The fertile river-bottoms and terraces of the Licking, Muskingum, and Miami rivers still supported farming villages, though it had been nearly a thousand years since the Indians there had created large earthen or stone buildings. The villagers were now Shawnee and Delaware, who had lived there only for a few decades; they had settled along the Scioto where they might be protected from predators from the east by ridge after ridge of rocky hills.

This central province, rich in ruins, had been regularly visited by Pittsburgh traders in the 1740s, while it was still claimed by France. It was reconnoitered for Bouquet in 1762 by Ensign Thomas Hutchins, a wilderness scout of the intrepidity of Daniel Boone, John Colter, or Jedediah Smith.† In the presence of antiquity, Hutchins negotiated an agreement with the tribes of the heavily settled region along the central

---

Writing to this superiors, Bouquet expressed himself as Franklin did:

After all the noise and bustle of your young men . . . everybody expected that they would have offered their services as soldiers or volunteers . . . as being the fittest men for an expedition against the Indians and as the best way to wipe off the reproaches cast upon them for the violence committed . . . to defenseless Indians. . . . Instead . . . they go as pack horse drivers and wagoners, employs for which a coward is as fit as a brave man. Will people not say they have found it easier to kill Indians in a gaol than to fight them fairly in the woods? . . . I am so much disgusted at the . . . frontier people . . . that I hope this will be the last time I shall venture my reputation and life for their sake. (Bouquet quoted in Van Every, *Forth to the Wilderness*, pp. 204–5.)

*It is possible that the Adena/Hopewell may have consummated the progression from supplementary horticulture to subsistence agriculture. See Chapter Eleven.

†Hutchins had been commissioned to attempt to keep tranquil the Indians living about the Great Lakes while the British finished off the French empire in North America. He did so by setting forth from Pittsburgh, following a beaten trail across northern Ohio to the forks of the Muskingum River and thence to Sandusky, on Lake Erie, and Detroit. After a complete and tranquilizing circumambulation of the Michigan peninsula, he struck off into central Wisconsin, returned to Lake Michigan, and then made his way across Ohio.

Scioto. Their towns were set amidst gentle hills divided by clear and lovely rivers. About their habitations were immense enclosures of earth in the form of circles, squares, and octagons, and around the hilltops above were stone walls several miles long which might be reached by graded pathways.

Thomas Hutchins left these tranquil scenes behind as he hastened back to Pittsburgh, forfeiting the occasion to leave to posterity his impressions of these antiquities of what he called the Lower Shawnee. A pity. But he did provide a map of his travels, which is astonishingly precise. And it was easily followed. Early in the summer, Hutchins led Bouquet's men back across a hundred miles of the hill country of Ohio. In October, on the upper Muskingum, upstream from the mound complex at Marietta and barely thirty miles northeast of the geometric, earthen architecture at Newark, they forced the Shawnee to accept a truce. Captives were liberated, and it appeared that things had quieted enough to justify a return to Fort Pitt (which had replaced Fort Duquesne) for the winter.[1]

After Bouquet's triumph in 1764, the Seneca were persuaded to withdraw from the Indian coalition by Sir William Johnson.* The diplomatic success of Johnson was followed by a reaffirmation, in 1768, of the royal "Proclamation Line" of 1763 and the terms of the truce arranged in central Ohio by Bouquet. Both of these promised to Indians that the British colonials would no longer invade their lands north of the Ohio. Pontiac was removed from the scene by assassination at Vincennes, in April, 1769. The next major Indian leader to appear in the area, John Logan, a Philadelphia-trained Mingo, was massacred by the Virginians in April, 1774, as a prelude to a major Virginian offensive. Four hundred militia under Major Angus McDonald set out from the shadow of the Grave Creek Mound and burnt out four Shawnee towns near the Newark earthworks in August. The Shawnee and Mingo went deep into Kentucky after the murderers of Logan; in response to their response, the British Governor of Virginia, Lord Dunmore, himself led an army to the Ohio. One wing of that force, under Andrew Lewis, fought a bloody battle against the Shawnee and Mingo on the ground settled by George Washington at Point Pleasant, demonstrating to both sides that the cost of further hostilities would be high.

In October, the Indians agreed to another cessation of hostilities, in return for still another affirmation of Bouquet's policy of 1768. At

---

*Johnson was married to a Mohawk woman, and lived between cultures much as his ancestors had lived on the Anglo-Irish frontier of Ulster. Like the marcher-lords of north England and Ireland, the Percys and Fitz Geralds, Johnson and other Irish-American squires sustained the vigor of their stock through intermarriage with the natives. Johnson was the brother-in-law to Aaron Burr's friend, the "King of the Mohawks," Joseph Brant.

Pittsburgh, Dunmore assured them that the people he governed would cease their depredations north of the Ohio, thereby adding yet a further inducement for the expansionary party of Virginia to consider revolution. It cost them little to pretend to another treaty, and another was signed, at Pittsburgh, in October, 1775. Once again, the Indians were assured that the Ohio would be honored as a boundary. When it was not, hostilities began again in Ohio in 1777, as the Tuscarora and Iroquois joined the Shawnee in another coalition against the Americans.

The hero of that war, on the American side, was George Rogers Clark, who had established a beachhead in the conical-mound country near present-day Wheeling. Clark's first campaign in 1778 was intended to keep the British away from the Ohio and to link forces with the Spanish at St. Louis. One of his subordinates, Captain Joseph Bowman, went on from Kaskaskia to establish a base at Cahokia, and was soon able to lead Clark on his first tour of the ruins of that ancient city. Soon thereafter, the French inhabitants of St. Louis, led by Spanish officers, drove off an attack by the British and a thousand Sioux.

Thus secure from a threat to his rear, Clark opened his attack on the Delaware and the British, in Indiana. In August, the Iroquois homelands in New York and Pennsylvania were assaulted by armies under Generals John Sullivan and James Clinton, while Daniel Brodhead of Pennsylvania sacked and burnt twelve Seneca and Delaware villages on the upper Allegheny. The Iroquois answered with expeditions against frontier villages in New York and Pennsylvania.

The 1770s and 1780s were decades of burning and looting of settlements on both sides of the chimerical line along the Ohio drawn by Bouquet, reinforced by the Treaty of Fort Stanwix in 1768, by Dunmore in 1774, and reinstated by the Americans in the second treaty of Pittsburgh in 1775. The damage was greater on the Indian side of the line than on that of the Kentuckians and Pennsylvanians, for the villages of the Shawnee, Mingo, and Delaware were often considerably more prepossessing than those of the Americans. Along the Scioto, Miami, and Muskingum, amid the ruins of ancient settlements, the Indian towns contained scores of houses and warehouses, set amid gardens that had yielded crops—certainly for decades, perhaps for many centuries. These villages were considerably more "civilized" than most of the slatternly settlements from which emerged their adversaries.

There are still writers who depict Indians as hapless victims wandering naked through the forests with bows and arrows, but the Anglo-Americans and Indians were, sociologically, very similar, hunting and practicing agriculture in competition with each other. The competition was very violent. On went the killing: at the head of a force of British Rangers and Indians, Henry Bird went deep into Kentucky in 1780, after which Clark's cannoneers destroyed Bird's bases along the Great Miami—though Bird had the advantage of using Hopewell earthworks as defenses. In 1781, the Pennsylvanians, having cleared the brush from Hutchins's road, repeated Bouquet's invasion of the Muskingum basin. In June of the next year, Washington's agent, William Crawford, now a revolutionary colonel, went even farther, and attacked the Wyandot and Delaware on the upper Sandusky.

THE MORAVIANS AND THE REVEREND JONES

In 1772, a Moravian missionary, David Zeisberger, was in Ohio seeking safe places in which to try once more to create villages for his Delaware and Mohegan converts.* He had seen what happened to those

---

*A paragraph or two of explanation may be useful in explaining how the term "Moravian," which comes from the name of a province of central Europe south of the Carpathians, entered into the tangle of White-Indian relations on the Appalachian side of Ohio.

The Moravian Indians in Ohio were adherents to a missionary sect descended theologically from the followers of Jan Hus, an early Protestant reformer in Moravia in the seventeenth century. Despite the military skill of Hus and other Protestant leaders, the power of Catholic Europe was too great for them, and they were forced to seek shelter on the Saxon estates of Count Nicholas Ludwig Zinzendorf. Zinzendorf might have joined with the other nobility of the region to eradicate them. Instead, he became an advocate for their gentle but bold beliefs.

The Moravians took seriously the love of God for mankind through Christ, so seriously that they sought to bring Christian love to all people, including Negroes and Indians.

Under Zinzendorf's protection, Augustus Gottlieb Spangenberg brought the first Moravian missionaries to Georgia in 1735, hoping to find converts among the Cherokee. Few Indians were convinced, but Spangenberg was remarkably successful among English clergymen. He nudged John Wesley on the road away from High Anglicanism, and so impressed George Whitefield that Whitefield asked Spangenberg to come to Nazareth, near Bethlehem, Pennsylvania, to organize a school for Blacks.

Wesley, like the Edwards, was a steadfast abolitionist. The Convention organizing American Methodism in 1784 took a position close to that of the Quakers on the matter. Later, unlike the Quakers, many southern Methodists backslid from these precepts of their founder.

As Spangenberg was moving his missionary activity northward, Zinzendorf arrived from Saxony; his gospel of love had proved too much for the orthodox Lutherans. It was making the peasantry restive. Together, Zinzendorf and Spangenberg organized many churches in Pennsylvania by 1780. Though the Moravians never became numerous—there were only 8,000 in 1858 and 60,000 in 1965—they were successful in bringing many Indians back into the agricultural, village life from which they had been exploded by the disruptions of the sixteenth and seventeenth centuries.

These endeavors were brought to a bloody end by the "Paxton Boys," vigilante Indian haters who burnt them out of Pennsylvania despite the best efforts of Benjamin Franklin.

who were too accessible to violent neighbors; they could not resist the combination of European diseases, alcohol, and the loss of their traditional means of life. In 1748 he had come upon the remnants of the Tutelo, who, in 1701, had been described as "tall, likely men, having plenty of buffaloes." Now he found the few survivors "a degenerate remnant of thieves and drunkards."*[2]

Finally he found places he thought safe, and founded the villages of Schoenbrunn and Gnadenhutten on the upper Muskingum eighty miles above Marietta. For ten years there was peace for his flock of Christian Indians, but in March, 1782, Colonel David Williamson led the Pennsylvania militia into Ohio and at least ninety peaceful, agricultural, Moravian Delawares and Mohegans paid for their belief in Christ and in sanctuary.†

The barbarities of Williamson's men must not however blind us to the wisdom and love of men such as Zeisberger, as ready to believe Indians capable of great things in ancient days as to take them to be his brothers and sisters in Christ. In 1772, this saintly man was passing through countryside reeking with the smoke of burning villages and stained with the blood of current wars, his mind fixed upon the need to find sanctuary for his people. Suddenly, before him, he found earth-

---

Some of the Moravian Indians were Stockbridges from New England, driven from Massachusetts to the Lehigh Valley, from which the Paxton massacres expelled them once again.

In Ohio, the terrible story was repeated once again. David Williamson's militia took the Paxton Boys' view of Christian Indians. Successful missions for Indians were no more possible on the Ohio frontier than in the Berkshires or in Pennsylvania.

*The cholera epidemics of 1818 and 1833 wiped out so many of the last remaining Tutelo that they ceased to exist as a nation.

†John Heckewelder, one of the Moravians who continued to work among the Ohio Indians even after the massacre of 1782, reported that the angry Shawnee were buzzing about central Ohio like wasps, emerging to attack any voyagers along the Ohio who did not travel in convoys. In the backwaters and marshes below the Portsmouth and Tremper mounds, among the cypresses trailing their "Spanish moss," the Indians lay in ambush for travelers passing without the protection of convoys. These freshwater privateers (they were scarcely to be considered pirates, for they were dealing with people they thought to be enemies) assembled "boats for this purpose . . . two hundred and fifty people have either lost their lives at this place or been taken captive." (Quoted in Henderson, Jobe, and Turnbow, "Indian Occupation," p. 137.)

Things had been quieter in the 1760s, when George Morgan surveyed an abortive settlement at Portsmouth before repairing to New Madrid.

The ecology of the flora at the mouth of the Scioto has been so radically altered by dredging, plowing, and draining that my reference to cypresses is an imaginative extension of their presence in undisturbed swamps considerably farther north on the Wabash, near Vincennes, and along the Ohio in Indiana. These cypress groves are astonishing to those who come upon them, expecting that they would be limited to the bayous of Louisiana. One almost expects to find alligators slithering along fallen logs, and water moccasins imperiling swimmers.

works in the circular and rhomboid shapes Europeans had used to protect their settlements since the bronze age.

Zeisberger had looked into the faces of men and women who had
trusted in him, and in his God, and had suffered for it at the hands of
people who looked like him and spoke his language. Accordingly,
sanctuary was on his mind and sanctuary is what he saw in these
earthen enclosures.

> Traces may be found . . . in . . . many places, where embankments, still to
> be seen were thrown up around a whole town. . . . Near the sites of such
> towns there are mounds, not natural, but made by the hand of man. . . .
> On top of these mounds there was a hollow place, to which the Indians
> brought their wives and children when the enemies approached . . . the
> men ranging themselves round the mound for defensive action. . . .[3]

While he had seen similar earthworks created for religious ceremony
in central Europe and in the British Isles, Zeisberger took those of the
Hopewell to be fortifications. He recorded in his journal the first written report of Hopewell earthworks, which happened to be the relatively simple ones on the upper Muskingum:

> Long ago . . . Indians must have lived here, who fortified themselves
> against the attack of their enemies. The ramparts are still plainly seen.
> We found three forts in a distance of a couple of miles. The whole town
> must have been fortified, but its site is now covered with a thick wood.[40]

Things were not much more peaceful in 1779 and 1780, when
Zeisberger collated his earlier impressions; he still focused upon possible military uses even of the Hopewell geometrics he found on the terraces, as well as the stone-walled citadels on the heights above.

> On the above named hills they always had great blocks lying all about,
> in order that should the enemies attempt to storm the heights these
> might be rolled upon . . . them so as to keep them off. In such attacks
> both sides . . . lost many men, which were often buried in one pit and a
> great mound of earth raised above them.[5]

Those of us who have scrambled to the summits of the bluffs in Kentucky and Ohio where a few of these enclosures remain—beyond the
plow and the ambitions of the tract developer—can only wonder that
Zeisberger's imagination was so energetic as to conceive of anyone
managing to "roll" such immense stones—very big, very heavy, and
rectilinear. Rolling them would be about as easy as rolling the blocks
employed in the construction of Hadrian's Wall across North Britain.

But it is impudent to quibble with a missionary who had the pluck to pause to study these "forts." He was as likely to be butchered by frontiersmen for consorting *with* Indians as to be burnt at the stake *by* Indians mistaking him for a typical frontiersman.

The year 1772 was a good one for observant clergymen in Ohio. Some fifty miles west of the terrain being surveyed at the time by Zeisberger, the Reverend David Jones, exploring the Scioto near Chillicothe and Circleville, was told by a trader, John Irwine, of astonishing concentric circles and an adjacent square at Circleville.* 6

Upon hearing the trader's account, Jones set forth deep into the region occupied by the far from tranquil Shawnee. Though he knew already "from personal acquaintance . . . [that] there are a number of this kind of forts," none was so impressive as that he found when he reached Circleville: "I never saw none [other] so large and complete as this."7

Jones sent along with this account to the *Royal American Magazine* the first map ever published of Hopewell geometrics. The Circleville circle-and-square were identified as "a curious piece of fortification work, found in the Shawanese [Shawnee] country".† 8

As anyone can testify who has attempted to make these observations on the ground, the Hopewell circles and squares are very large; by Jones's time they were covered by brush and trees, making their true extent almost as difficult to ascertain as today, after most of them have been plowed over a hundred times or more.

> North of this town [Chillicothe] are . . . the remains of an old fortification, the area of which may be fifteen acres. It lies near four squares, and appears to have had gates at each corner. . . . From the west middle gate, went a circular entrenchment including about ten acres. . . . This circle included a spring.
>
> Mr. Irwine told that another exactly in this form is to be seen on the river Scioto, the banks of which remain so high as to intercept sight of men on horseback.

---

*Irwine worked out of a base at Pittsburgh; he was a partner of the magnificent George Croghan, who traded in Ohio in the 1740s.

†This is the account which, when it appeared in the magazine in 1775, may have ignited Thomas Jefferson's imagination for the ancient monuments of the Indians.

James Marshall checked the original plat of survey of Circleville in the county courthouse and found that its founders had placed Main Street along the main axis linking the circle and square.

Unlike the Golf Course complex at Newark, and those at Seal (Piketon)—thirty-eight miles down the Scioto from Circleville, and eighteen from Chillicothe—and High Banks—roughly halfway between Chillicothe and Liberty, Circleville had no hyphen to emphasize that axis. Its immediately conjoined circle and square were, instead, like those at Hopeton and at "Old Town," a well-preserved work at Frankfort, fifteen miles up the north branch of Paint Creek from Chillicothe.

Those forts, *or whatever they were designed for* [italics added], are
not all built alike, but some are circular, some in the form of a half
moon, and others square, and contain within the walls from a half to
eight or ten acres.[9]

Surely the Shawnee and Delaware were amused as they stood finger-
ing their muskets, while this clerical gentleman went sweating through
the brush and mosquito-infested prairie marshes trying to measure ancient architecture.*

The earthen circles at Circleville were too formidable to plow out, so
they defined the shape of a little village which grew up within them in
the early nineteenth century. The outermost became the town wall.
After steam equipment facilitated desecration, the wall became a street;
the obliterated inner circle became an alley. By that time it had been
observed that the outer one, with a diameter of 1,200 feet, was the
same size as the Fairgrounds Circle at Newark forty miles away. Residents of Washington, D.C., may get some sense of the scale of these
earthworks by walking laterally across the Mall from the East Wing of
the National Galley to the National Air and Space Museum: they will
have walked the distance across the Fairgrounds Circle.

Later, when scientific measurement was applied to the great half-
circular embankment at Pinson, Tennessee, and to the circle cut into
the earth at Fort Center, northwest of Fort Okeechobee, Florida, it was
found that their diameters were also 1,200 feet. The Newark, Circleville, and Pinson figures were roughly contemporary, while the Florida
circle probably was constructed five hundred years earlier.

Within the outer circle at Circleville is a ditch and then another,
inner circle; its diameter is 1,056 feet. On Moundbuilders Golf Course,
at Newark, across forty miles of open country from Circleville and a
mile from the fairgrounds, is a circle with a diameter of 1,054 feet.
South of Circleville, at High Banks, on the Scioto near Chillicothe, is
one with a diameter of 1,052 feet; eighteen miles downriver, in Piketon
Township at Seal, is a fourth circle, whose diameter is 1,050 feet.[†]

---

*Jones's "old fortification" is the square at Circleville, which measured about 840 feet on a
side, abutting, on the west, two concentric circles. The other figure to which Irwine called
his attention must have been the square and circle at Hopeton, which are joined in the same
way. It is "on the Scioto," though neither its orientation nor the size of its figures precisely
matches those at Circleville—Irwine did not say they did. The *north* middle gate of
Hopeton's "fortification" leads to its circle. The Hopeton circle has a diameter of 960 feet,
and its square has sides of the same dimension. Thus it belongs to the same family as an
obliterated square at Newark, the sides of which were also 960 feet in length.

[†]Circleville and Seal are at the extremities of the Chillicothe group of figures. They are
thirty-six miles apart. Their *circles* are, as we have just noted, close in size; their *squares* are
852 feet by 852 feet and 841 feet by 841 feet.

The geomancers of central Ohio seem to enjoy working with figures on a grand scale and governed by a line roughly 1,050 feet in length. Aside from those *circles* at Newark, Circleville, High Banks, and Seal, there is the *square* at Marietta, which is 1,040' by 1,040', another *square* at Hopewell, which is 1,060' by 1,060'. Along Paint Creek, which flows into the Scioto south of Chillicothe, there were two 1,050 foot squares, one at Frankfort and another at Works East. The *octagon* on Newark's golf course might contain another 1,040-foot *square* drawn to connecting alternate vertices. The larger square at Marietta (1,510' by 1,510') can be composed as by fitting together four 1,040-foot squares and drawing lines from each of their exterior intersections.[10]

If there seems something artificial in the way this Marietta *square* is described, that artificiality is probably the key to understanding how these groups of related figures were generated by the geomancers—as William F. Romain, an avocational archaeologist of immense resourcefulness, demonstrated in the 1990s. Romain discerned, as well, that the Marietta large square would also neatly hold four small circles also to be found along Paint Creek: Works East (760 feet in diameter), Frankfort (720 feet), Seip (750 feet), and Baum (760 feet). And, as readers possessed of compasses and pencils may already have noted, the 1,040- or 1,050-foot circles can be drawn by connecting the centers of these four 720- to 760-foot circles, as they nest in the Marietta square.[11]

Seven hundred fifty is not quite eight hundred, nor is eight hundred quite eight hundred fifty or nine hundred fifty. So we must compose several other families at these intervals. The square at Portsmouth, Ohio, and a maladjusted square at Dunlap, on the Scioto between Chillicothe and Circleville, have 800-foot sides. The squares at Seal and Circleville, and the half-circle at Hopewell, are in the 850 family. The squares at Newark and Hopeton are governed by 960-foot sides, while the circle at Hopeton is 960 feet in diameter.[12]

A glance at the map demonstrates how clearly related are these figures, spread across five thousand square miles of central Ohio.

The person who does not wonder at this will not wonder at anything.

On the ground, the wonder grows. The Ohio composites are considerably larger than any of their components: the octagon taken together with its adjacent circle on the golf course at Newark would occupy the entire southern end of Central Park in New York City from Central Park West to Fifth Avenue and as far north as Sixty-seventh Street. The Circleville and Fairgrounds circles could each easily contain the entire Metropolitan Museum of Art—Temple of Dendur, Rockefeller wing, and all.

The Fairgrounds Circle has remained relatively intact because circles were popular forms for racecourses in the nineteenth century, and because earthen walls made good bleachers. A mortuary mound in the center of the circle, where ancient people prepared their dead for cremation, served until about 1920 as a gathering place for jockeys. The walls of the circle itself are twenty feet high, surrounding a ditch ten feet deep. From the bottom of this ditch, the embankment was as high as a three-story building.*

The Observatory Circle and its accompanying octagon owe their continued availability to archaeology to their presence within Moundbuilders Golf Course.† Despite fairways, sandtraps, and paved cartpaths, they are still there. Though they have been stripped of the sacred ways that once prepared pilgrims to visit them, these ways are clearly depicted in nineteenth century maps, and invite us to inquire as to the extent that these figures were connected physically to their counterparts on the Scioto as well as being associated geomantically.

THE GREAT HOPEWELL ROAD

In 1796, Thomas Hutchins's relatively straight path was used again by Ebenezer Zane. Zane had been commissioned by the Congress to fulfill one of the earliest of the "internal improvements" Gallatin inherited from Alexander Hamilton, by tracing out a national road between Wheeling, in what is now West Virginia, and Limestone (Maysville), Kentucky. He began his "trace" from the Ohio in the area where Adena engineering had reached its apogee in the construction of the Grave Creek Mound, thirty miles south of the entrepot of Bouquet and Hutchins. From the river, Zane's surveyors cut their way westward until they came to a cross-shaped mound called the Tarlton Cross, then a landmark, as it must have been in Hopewell times. There, near what is now the Lancaster, Ohio, airport, they intersected with the route followed by Hutchins, which had continued for some distance toward the Newark earthworks, probably along an ancient route through a heavy forest of enormous trees leaving little undergrowth. Nineteenth century accounts tell us that their crowns were so interconnected by vines and by their own foliage that sunlight filtered only dimly through.

---

*Recent excavation has demonstrated that the final third of the present height was added by WPA "restorers". It now looks from the bottom of the ditch as high as a five story building.

†The ridges or "banks" of a processional way from what seems to have been a settlement site in Newark to the Golf Course figures are noted by streets called "Ridgelawn" and "Fairbanks."

Southwest of Tarlton Cross lies a wet prairie called the Pickaway Plains, skirting the northern fringes of the Chillicothe Hills. The "Plains" were open, boggy prairie and light woods; the "Hills" are outcrops of the Appalachian Plateau denying easy passage southwestward, until one comes close to the Scioto. Finally a pass appears where that eager little river has forced its way through toward its juncture with the Ohio at Portsmouth.[13]

Where the Scioto had done its work of aeons, creating level terraces and floodplains, Zane and his engineers were able easily to turn southward again, passing a mile east of two platform mounds associated with a rectilinear earthwork called Cedar Bank and within a few hundred yards of the earthen circle and square at Hopeton, and descended onto the floodplain to make a crossing to Chillicothe. Zane's turning point beside the Scioto may have been the terminus of the Great Hopewell Road or, instead, that thoroughfare may have gone straight through to Chillicothe, with no "jogs" in between. That is the view of Bradley Lepper, the historian-archaeologist serving as chatelaine for the Fairgrounds Circle and its museum in Newark, who was the first to stitch together many of the clues for the thoroughfare for which he, first, suggested the name "Great Hopewell Road".* [14]

Lepper, a straightforward fellow, acknowledges that such an unjogged trajectory would have had to make its way over the flanks of a conspicuous landmark called Sugarloaf, a projection of the Chillicothe Hills, and that in Hopewell times there was no imperative for anyone to climb mountains to sustain a straight line to Chillicothe. The town did not exist. The Indians in the Southwest did not permit topography to deter linearity, and Lepper points out that the modern town does occupy the centerpoint of more than twenty groups of earthen monuments.[15] These figures spread across a thirty-mile stretch of the Scioto, from Circleville on the north, with its circle and square, to the twins of these figures at Piketon (otherwise known as Seal) on the south. Many of these were, and still are, linked by lines of embankments, like those near Newark. In the Southwest, the counterparts to these earthen parallels are Chacoan lines of stones, curbing, low mounds, and even core-veneered walls.[16] The Hopewell buildings we have described, circles, squares, and octagons, were once connected by roads. There is no doubt of that, and it is likely that the Great Hopewell Road was the most ambitious of those so far rediscovered.

The chief advocate for the "jog" hypothesis (as distinguished from the linear or Chacoan hypothesis) is William F. Romain. Either Lepper's hypothesis or that of Romain may be proven correct by fur-

---

*Cedar Bank is bounded on the west by a bluff, by two of the area's 800-foot sides, and by a 1,400-foot embankment. The Hopeton figures are each more than twenty acres in extent.

ther inquiry on the ground and by the use of aerial sensing devices, but the alternative termini they suggest are only a few miles apart. The principal discovery is the road itself. The evidence on the ground is impressive; and so is the fact that larger portions of it, now destroyed, were still to be seen in the nineteenth century.[17]

The first report of it to be published was that of Caleb Atwater, the postmaster of Circleville, in 1820. Atwater gave an account of the "antiquities" of the area, many of which he had himself visited. From the Newark octagon, he said, "parallel walls . . . extend southward . . . traceable many miles, in the direction of the Hohocking River, at some point north of Lancaster [where they] . . . connected with similar works."[18]

An element particularly arresting to students of the Chacoan road system of the Southwest was added in 1911 by the scholarly superintendent of Newark's schools, J. D. Simkins. Simkins published a map itself referring to "maps and data antedating 1861" and to "parallel walls said to have extended 30 miles southwest" of Newark. In an upland area, just southwest of Newark, Simkins's map showed a small circle, attached by a stem to these parallel walls, located about a half-mile from the golf course, with the annotation that there were others like it farther south. It was labeled "H." "H" was the right letter. A *herradura* is a wayside shrine. There are many along the Chacoan road system in New Mexico.[19]

Radiating from Chaco Canyon itself, the "Great North Road" and "Great Southwest Road" extended for twenty or thirty miles. (In the Chacoan system there were also short stretches of graded ways, introducing individual pueblos, like the half-mile parallel embankments at Hopeton, Dunlap, and Portsmouth.) Both the long and short ways were bordered by low embankments of stones and gravel, with *herradura* every few miles. In Ohio, the way stations southwest of Newark are at intervals of a little over two miles, the same as those which have been noted between the way stations along the ancient Peruvian road systems.[20]

Though tractors and earthmovers ripped and leveled much of central Ohio in the 1920s, that was also the decade in which aerial photography began to offer new means of picking out what was left. The pioneer aviator W. S. Weiant, Jr. reported in 1930 that near his new landing strip being built two and a half miles from Newark, he could see from the air lines of earth along the route of the Great Hopewell Road.[21]

Weiant also added (and photographed), two miles beyond Simkins's "H," another *herradura* he called "the airport circle," at the end of an earthen cul-de-sac. As we are wont to do, Weiant was made nervous by the presence of such things; turning from the abyss of awe, he made a joke of it. Perhaps, he wrote, each of these cul-de-sacs was "a filling station or a hot-dog stand." Perhaps. But it is more likely that they were, instead, like Stations of the Cross in Christian practice. (Weiant's reports were confirmed by aerial photographs taken six years later by Captain Dache M. Reeves of the U.S. Army Air Corps.[22])

In 1991, Bradley Lepper was kind enough to welcome my analogy to Stations of the Cross, and, sixty-one years after Weiant's reference to hot-dog stands, Lepper used the Christian analogy in a discussion with neighbors in Newark. Thereupon, another participant suggested a joint expedition to his backyard, where Simkins's long-lost "H" *herradura* could be discerned clearly in a low circular formation in the grass.[23] With this point established, Lepper was also able to locate nearby a set of the parallel walls barely a foot high, but nearly four hundred feet long, on the route of the Great Road.

If we may be permitted to interpret Ohio archaeology of the Hopewell period in the light of the archaeology of the eleventh century in Chacoan New Mexico and Utah, we may offer some hypotheses about what happened along the Great Hopewell Road. This requires some imagination: we ourselves have little experience with pilgrimage. The route to Compostela has been superseded by an autoroute; Chaucer's road to Canterbury has been lost to the sprawl of south London; devout Muslims disembark from jets to complete their journeys to Mecca. But a visitor to southern Ohio can still find remnants enough of the Hopewell achievement to imagine what it was like for pilgrims to travel among the sacred enclosures along the Scioto and at Newark.

On the Moundbuilders Golf Course at dusk, when the last "birdies" have been scored and silence settles amid the shadows, it is possible undistractedly to follow the processional way. That leads for a hundred yards between embankments tall enough to cut off direct sight of the lights of the neighborhood, between an ancient Hopewell octagon and square, each of more than twenty acres in size. Then one can imagine that long stretches of the sixty-mile length of the Great Hopewell Road were like this, as it linked ceremonial places intended to be experienced in sequence by pilgrims choreographed to move through earthen enclosures.

We can even imagine the sounds they heard along the way, the music of pan-pipes and drums. Many three-tubed copper objects have been found in Hopewell graves, which held pipes of reed—like the instruments still played by the Indians of the Andes to the accompaniment of drums made by stretching hides across the mouths of ceramic vessels. The Hopewell were also expert potters and there were plenty of deer in ancient Ohio.

The Pilgrims might have been refreshed, perhaps in each *herradura*, by a smoke of the dried leaves or stems of native plants (such as strong

Ohio tobacco), thereby mildly altering states of consciousness. Smoking was a ritual act; Hopewell burials contain many pipes upon which totem-animals face the smoker. Finally, at the end of the journey, a traveler could be led through sacred enclosures of increasing solemnity, and then up a ramp to the summit of a platform mound. There, waiting, might be a shaman wearing sheets of glistening mica, suited in thousands of pearl beads sewn upon cloth woven in brightly colored patterns, with spools of copper distending each ear lobe and a copper panel suspended on the chest.

Together with these objects in Hopewell graves, H-shaped instruments of aragonite have been found. Aragonite turns beautifully translucent when brought to the surface. An instrument of aragonite can catch the glint of sun or moon as it is whirled upon a cat's cradle of twisted thongs. I have heard the sound made by a whirling aragonite "H," an eerie keening which may also have been heard in the *herradura* along the Great Hopewell Road—a high moaning, like the north wind.

THE ROUTES TO MOUND CITY

Let us be more specific about the routes taken by those who completed their pilgrimage from Newark along the straight section of the Great Hopewell Road and by Thomas Hutchins and Ebenezer Zane as they approached the Scioto eighteen centuries later. Some, who crossed the Scioto immediately, could have gone forward through a series of liturgical cleansings. First there might be preparation before a great platform mound still standing in the lowlands until the middle part of the nineteenth century; then they might enter the half-mile sacred way, between parallel embankments, which preceded the enclosure at Dunlap (now gone).

Others (after transversing a field now occupied by a drive-in theater) might have been received at Cedar Bank within a rectangular enclosure large enough to contain six football fields and holding another platform mound, before proceeding directly southward a half mile to another earthen platform (gone), and, following the same bearing, into the circle and square at Hopeton.

Though plowed down to a few inches in height, the two enclosures at Hopeton were still discernible in 1993, and with a little more archaeological effort, so was another set of half-mile parallel embankments, probably leading toward another ancient ford. Across the Scioto there was the great mortuary center which is now the Mound City National Monument. (The other half-mile set of parallel walls, which we have noted as leading to the enclosure, led, when seen *from* Dunlap, directly to Hopeton, as those *from* Hopeton pointed to Mound City.)[24]

Other groups of travelers might arrive in this Mound City–Hopeton–Cedar Bank–Dunlap complex from the south, some having passed the ford at Chillicothe used by Zane, now unnoticed beneath railroad and highway bridges, from a complex of many circles underlying the modern town, or from another complex known as "Works East" (two circles interlocked with a square) just on its eastern limits.[25]

A second group of pilgrims coming from the south may have followed the eastern shore of the Scioto, along a narrow, dry platform between the bank of the river and the Chillicothe hills. It led from two other figures, the closest of which to Chillicothe is a surviving octagon and circle at Highbanks. This circle, as we have noted, is a nearly exact twin of that on the Moundbuilders Golf Course, sixty miles away at Newark; the octagon is less than half the forty-four-acre area of that at Newark, but the two distant composite figures are clearly related: their axes are precisely at right angles to each other. (Most modern buildings, even if built to equal dimensions, are not situated in any way that associates them in such a fashion; the great exception, of course, being those mosques which face east.) Beyond Highbanks, in Liberty Township, is a very close counterpart, in shape and size, to the interlocked circles and square at Works East.[26]

These travelers may have come farther, perhaps all the way from a third complex of complexes, fifty-five miles down the Scioto at its intersection with the Ohio, at Portsmouth.[27] Let us retrace their steps to the extent that those steps can still be discerned.

The east shore Chillicothe hills close in again beyond Liberty township, forcing engineers ancient and modern to make some decisions. In the 1830s, the engineers of the Ohio Canal, which led from Chillicothe to Portsmouth, selected a route on the west shore, on a relatively low, flat terrace. Eight miles below Chillicothe, the canal builders were able to sustain their grade because they could make use of an *existing* "cut" for a road through the twenty-foot elevation of Switzer's Point. The passage is a quarter of a mile long; the ancient ones had moved an immense amount of earth.[28]

Switzer's was not the last place on the west shore at which the escarpment comes close to the river. A little farther downstream, the Hopewell builders were forced to make a crossing back to the other side, and built another *herradura* on the east shore. A mile beyond it lie the circle and square of the Seal or Piketon Works. As we noted earlier, they are almost identical in size to those at the other extremity of the Chillicothe complex or complexes, at Circleville.[29]

A mile below Piketon the ancient Indian engineers produced another massive "cut," this time on the east shore terrace. Their work was reused by another set of nineteenth century builders, those constructing the Chillicothe and Portsmouth Turnpike, who could simplify their task by laying their road through a preexisting, two-hundred-foot, graded way graining twenty-two feet in elevation. Thereafter, they followed this route marked by embankments for nearly a half mile.[30]

ARCHITECTURE IN KENTUCKY

Less than twenty miles beyond the turnpike cut on the banks of the Scioto, a mound center now almost obliterated beneath the town of Portsmouth sent forth its own set of parallel embankments to meet this road as it appeared from the north. Portsmouth was another ceremonial center, as extensive as those at Newark and Chillicothe. Early accounts describe its processional ways as extending at least twenty miles and crossing the Ohio twice. At one extremity was a great cone, four hundred ten feet wide at the base, and truncated below its peak to form a platform about twenty feet above ground level, reached by a graded way up its flank. It was approached by four avenues, dividing four concentric earthworks into four precise quadrants.*

From the outermost of the cone's encompassing circles, one set of parallel embankments went toward the Ohio, passing a circle and a figure variously described as an octagon and a hexagon, to descend by a graded way down a fifty-foot bluff.[31]

Crossing a ford, the processional way emerged upon the north shore and proceeded two and a half miles toward—something. All that is left today are segments of two concentric circles, and some strange horseshoe-shaped earthworks. These mark, perhaps, a settlement site, or, perhaps, they were what have been called in Europe lunar crescents. The circles around them were the same size as two of those surrounding the cone across the Ohio. Two processional ways leading into the circles on the Ohio side are at the same intervals as two of those in the Kentucky-side concentrics.[32]

---

*The maps of these now obliterated earthworks are not clear; my totting up of their dimensions differs from that of William Morgan; by his count the outermost had a diameter of 485 meters, or 1,600 feet. That is not how I read Squier and Davis's plates XVII and XVIII. I think they indicate the outermost to be only 1,200 feet; that would put it into the same family as the outer circle at Circleville and the Fairgrounds Circle.

The Tremper burials described below are indisputably Hopewell. The Kentucky-side giant cone, through never carefully excavated, has traditionally been thought to share the shape and therefore the likely provenance of the Adena structures at Grave Creek and along the upper Ohio. I offer the thought that the quadrential circumstructures around it may have been put in place by the Hopewell, for geomantic purposes or for the hegemonic reasons suggested in Chapter Eleven.

From this central area, two more processional ways emerged. One led northwest toward the entrance, four miles away, of the Tremper Mound. This relatively flat structure, about four hundred feet square, contained a mortuary building holding about three hundred seventy-five cremated Hopewell burials, in a chamber supported on a wooden scaffolding of six hundred posts.[33]

Returning from the Tremper Mound toward Portsmouth, one might turn toward the south, away from the "lunar crescents," along another sacred way for two and a half miles to two other concentric circles and, perhaps, another octagon.* After another earth-bounded mile one would once again across the Ohio River. On the other side of the river the embanked roadway resumes and proceeds toward two sets of parallel embankments, each a half mile long, flanking a square.[34]

Fording these rivers had been easily possible, it seems; the gravelly Scioto confused the Ohio; each deposited across the other reefs and banks which became shallow in low water. These reefs seem to have remained stationary long enough to encourage their architectural use. But no longer; the U.S. Corps of Engineers saw to that, responding to the hooting agony of steamboats beached unexpectedly where beaches had no governmental license to be.

Ashore, the destructive capacities of settlers were abated by the limitations of pre-steam technology just long enough to allow the creation of maps of the Portsmouth works. Picks, shovels, and wheelbarrows were not quite competent to obliterate them all before mapmakers made use of an interval of renewed curiosity about them in the 1840s.

Much has been lost to heedless change in Kentucky, as Clay Lancas-

---

*The possible octagon or hexagon on the south, or Kentucky, side of the Ohio River, near the cone, appears in Hempstead, *Antiquities,* p. 12. Bradley Lepper found Hempstead, as well as a more octagonal figure appearing on a map of Portsmouth made after 1848 and reprinted in an article by J. H. Edwards, "Ancient Fortifications," pp. 102–104.

The octagon on the north, or Ohio, side of the river was described as a "fort contained, as I remember, about five acres, . . . an exact octagon, with bastions at the angles, and evidently by a skilled engineer." This account was given by J. E. Wharton, in an old man's memories in 1876 of youth in the 1830s. His report (first appearing in P. P. Cherry, *The Grave Creek Mound,* n.p.) has been cited as recently as a guidebook published in the 1980s, but was dismissed as "certainly spurious" by the most systematic investigator of the area, E. Thomas Hemmings. ("Investigations of the Grave Creek Mound," p. 10.)

"Certainly" is a little emphatic. Though no octagon appears in any other early descriptions, all of which speak of "elliptical forts and circular redoubts" (Winthrop Sargent, 1787, as finally published in 1853) or "square and circular redoubts" (Jonathan Heart, 1791, posthumously published by Imlay), and though Mr. Cherry had lived amid octagons elsewhere and may have blurred memories of them into those of Portsmouth, he was there before the surface evidence of both of these figures was destroyed. In a few more pages we will come to a third much-debated octagon, sixty miles away, on the Elkhorn, near Lexington, Kentucky.

ter demonstrated in his *Vestiges of a Venerable City,* describing the melancholy history of Lexington. The neoclassical town of the early nineteenth century, whose destruction is chronicled by Lancaster, itself replaced architecture of equal interest which had been standing there for a thousand years when neoclassicism made its entrance.

Lexington is the capital of the bluegrass region watered by Elkhorn Creek; the Elkhorn and the bluegrass are appropriate symbols of its history. The grass, like neoclassicism, is exotic, introduced by Europeans. The Spaniards observed southern Kentucky in the 1540s, but they were in such rapacious haste that they did not pause to describe what they saw; in any case they could not have reported bluegrass. The French who appeared a century later thought themselves superior to the natives because they had a written language and the Indians did not. But even these proudly literate intruders failed to record their observations, for their notations were confined to keeping inventory, at posts such as French Lick (now Nashville).

The first written descriptions of the Elkhorn region are in English, composed by latecoming pioneers such as George Rogers Clark and Daniel Boone. It was then a serene landscape, caressed by time into small risings and fallings, without the least jaggedness or abruptness. Its weather as well was and is unusually gentle for the American midlands.* The mean annual temperature in the Bluegrass is 60 degrees Fahrenheit, and in this rare instance in America a mean or average temperature is significant. The mountains lying diagonally eastward from the Bluegrass join in moderating all extremes with the limestone underlayment upon which it lies so comfortably. Limestone is used in stoves to provide an even temperature. Being porous it also holds water, and immense quantities of water are limestone-held under Kentucky, available to seep upward into springs delightful to cultivators of the surface and to animals which, sleek and leisured, await the hunter.

The symbol—one might say the hieroglyph—of this compatible land is composed by the spreading branches of the Elkhorn Creek, flowing through a prairie which is sky blue in June, as miles of thick, fine, lovely, European *poa compressa* open their seedpods to the sun. The bluegrass prairie really is blue.

The most interesting early architecture in Kentucky beyond the southern portion of the Portsmouth complex lies in the Elkhorn valley. This is Kentucky's Canaan, into which entry is made easy by the Kentucky River and the antler-forms of Elkhorn "Lick." This was the

---

*This is true of central Kentucky, though the city in the United States having the widest extremes is St. Louis (Cahokia), not far distant. It must have been a place of immense strategic significance to have drawn so many Mississippians to it for so long. In winter it has recorded 22 degrees below zero and in summer 112 above.

route into Kentucky taken by most pioneers, though the picture of Daniel Boone leading wagons full of hardy pioneers across Cumberland Gap is indelibly graven into American myth.

Chief among the Elkhorn earthworks was an octagon measuring one hundred fifty feet on a side, with three graded entrances.* Each of these was blocked by small interior mounds in the same pattern as the much larger works in Ohio at Newark and on the Scioto. Into this ceremonial space, in the late 1780s, Richard Jonathan Shipp and his wife, Elizabeth Doniphan Shipp, inserted a log cabin, calling both the earthwork and the house "Lovedale."†

FORTS ANCIENT

It is not love that comes to mind when one comes to the hilltop citadels in Ohio and Kentucky. European experience would seem to justify our thinking of these as castles demonstrating a decline into the Dark Ages after some Pax Hopewelliana, a darkness gleaming only fitfully upon Indian Kings Arthur and Charlemagne, with Byzantine-surrogates lurking in the Delta and rough teutonoid tribes ready to swoop in upon Hopewell seigneurs fortifying their villas.

Sad to say, scientific archaeology has forced jettisoning this romance of barbarians and a feudalized Midwest. Radiocarbon dates for these forts are from 100 to 400, while Adena/Hopewell cultures were thriving. Copper breastplates, mica sheets, pearl beads, and effigy pipes shaped as birds or bears or beaver have been found in the hilltop

---

*The nomination form for this earthwork submitted to the National Registry of Historic Places (its site number is 15 WD 1) says that it was "first described by Rafinesque in 1820, and subsequently by Squier and Davis (1848), Collins (1874), Young (1910) and Webb and Funkhouser (1932). Originally described as an octagonal platform or enclosure with three entry ramps and interior conical mounds . . . [now] largely obliterated." Collins would be Richard Collins, *History of Kentucky*, Maysville, 1874; Young would be Bennet H. Young, *The Prehistoric Men of Kentucky*, Filson Club, Louisville, 1910, and the last reference is to William S. Webb and W. D. Funkhouser, *Archaeological Survey of Kentucky*, University of Kentucky, Lexington, 1932. But Berle Clay, of that university tells us in a letter dated June 26, 1992, that in its present state he has "trouble seeing" this figure as an octagon.

Clay also refuses his assent to the proposition offered by the engineer James Marshall that there is another large octagon on the North Elkhorn, in northern Fayette County, surrounding the Peter Earthwork. "I just don't see it."

The best way to see either would be with better aerial sensing data, which is not quite yet available.

†The grandson of Jonathan and Elizabeth Shipp had a racehorse called Sunny Slope, which is the name given the brick house the Shipps' children built on the place by 1820. The house was occupied by the great great grandmother of Harry S. Truman. It is possible that the enigma of that "S." has now been solved—why not "Shipp"?

"forts" of Kentucky and Tennessee—interred, apparently, at roughly the same time as those found amid the geometric earthworks of Ohio.

Do these fortified escarpments, sometimes alone, sometimes seeming to be guardians of the classical octagons, circles, and squares along the Paint, the rivers of Kentucky, and along the Ohio from Cincinnati to Portsmouth, mean that architecture became militant, or perhaps apprehensive? Were these, indeed, fortified settlements, or were they ceremonial spaces bounded by stone? And what are we to make of other, roughly contemporaneous enclosures on the loamy bluffs above the Mississippi?

I think there are answers to be offered to these inquiries, but they are answers of the imagination. They belong, therefore, in Chapter Eleven.

Some of these rock-walled enclosures lie on terrace tops above major waterways; those that do not, guard instead very old trails from waterway to waterway, and then cross-country to the sea. The route over which presides Tennessee's Old Stone Fort apparently began in Ohio, on the Scioto, then crossed into Kentucky on its way to the Nashville basin, and then crossed the Cumberland, to scale and then descend the highlands to the Tennessee River at Bridgeport. From there it made its way across Georgia to the Atlantic coast at or near St. Augustine. When it was mapped in 1684 by the French, as part of an effort to show that La Salle had conquered all this for King Louis, it had been in use for at least one milennium, and probably for two.

The Florida outcome is indicated by the presence in Hopewell burials in Ohio of ornaments made of shark and barracuda teeth from Florida, to which we have already given some attention, of Ohio chert tools in Florida, and, as well, by the evidence of intellectual exchange: the similarities in dimension among the circles incised into the earth at Fort Center, in Florida, and raised as embankments at Newark and Circleville.

The first explorers to come into Kentucky and Tennessee from the British colonies found that many of the hill "forts" had stone pavements projecting from the bottom of their walls—slabs of stone laid against the outside of sloping embankments of rubble and pounded earth, and postholes chinked with stone on the upper surfaces, for palisades. Were digging or "sapping" devices of prehistoric warfare? It appears that sieges did occur; these battered, armored, and palisaded walls were broken at intervals by towers and abutments, from which attackers might be exposed to enfilade fire from *atlatls*. As we recall, bows and arrows arrived on the midwestern scene later, only after 700 or 800, having been used in the Southwest two centuries earlier.

Though the English explorers did, indeed, find many of these fortress towns (the French called those they themselves had built "bastides"), they did not at once associate them with Indians, and for good reason. The Spaniards under De Soto and his successor, Juan De Pardo, and, two centuries later, the English led by James Oglethorpe, proprietor of Georgia, were known to have brought military engineers into the Tennessee Valley. These experts produced their own forts, which, in ruins, looked much like the ruins of the Indian buildings. In the 1680s, Pardo built ruder versions of the Spanish coastal fortresses (of which San Augustin's Castel San Marco is the grandest) along the upper reaches of the Tennessee River—forts San Pedro, San Pablo, and San Juan. (The flooding of these sites by the Tennessee Valley Authority has not helped their archaeology.)

Vaguely aware that the Spaniards had been there ahead of them, the frontiersmen fell into the habit of calling anything resembling sophisticated military architecture "Spanish Fort."* At Lexington, in 1781, Captain John Todd built a square palisade, set on pounded earth embankments and surrounded by a moat, with bastions at the corners. As a good Anglo-American patriot, he may have followed the example set for him by the moldering stockade of Fort Loudon, two hundred miles away on the Tennessee River, built twenty-four years earlier for a British governor by a Franco-Dutch engineer, Willem Gerard de Brahm.†

But Todd had prototypes more conveniently at hand. Two were described in 1784 by John Filson, in the "neighborhood of Lexington . . . furnished with ditches and bastions." Filson took them to be of Spanish origin, and, therefore, at least five hundred years younger than they actually were. Like Fort Loudon, their bastions were of pounded earth, and bore the marks of stockades. Like many hilltop strong points, but

---

*This custom led Benjamin Franklin to refer wryly to the embankments at Marietta as having been made by deserters from De Soto's forces. It was easy in 1780 to confuse Pardo's expeditions to the Tennessee of the 1680s, which did produce forts, with that of De Soto, who passed along the same river banks forty years earlier without leaving any architecture.

†De Brahm is something of a mystery himself. He may have been German, French, or Dutch. See, if you will, Kennedy, *Orders from France*, p. 458.

He entered the region the hard way, through the mountains from the east, after laying out a series of garrison towns in Georgia for Oglethorpe.

On the shores of what is now a TVA lake, De Brahm constructed a rhomboid (stretched triangle) of pounded earth topped by a stockade, with bastions at the corners. The purpose, ostensibly, was to protect friendly Cherokees from the French. As no doubt the Cherokee were aware, it also established a British military presence along the headwaters of the Tennessee.

Near Fort Loudon, at the confluence of the Holton and Little Tennessee rivers, and Town Creek, there was an earlier, probably Mississippian, rhomboid, but without bastions, terminating at a cone with a flattened top about a hundred feet across. It was called Lenoir, and is gone. See William Morgan, *Prehistoric Architecture*, p. 112.

Also destroyed is an even more intriguing ceremonial center in the vicinity, at Dayton, Tennessee, which was known as Hiwassee. It occupied an island at the juncture of the Tennessee and Hiwassee rivers now deep under the TVA's Lake Chicamauga. See Morgan, p. 105.

unlike most Hopewell ceremonial centers of earth on river terraces, the "ditches" were true moats—*outside,* not inside the earthen barriers and stockade.[35]

Mysteries are compounded after 500, as enormous animal effigy mounds began to appear, such as the opossum in Newark, and earthen panthers, birds, and bears in Wisconsin and Iowa. The "Serpent Mound," in southern Ohio, a quarter-mile-long effigy of a serpent holding a globe in its mouth, has now been established to have been constructed rather late in this period, about 1066. The comet with a tail shown in the Bayeux Tapestry celebrating William of Normandy's invasion of England in that year is not wildly dissimilar; such a comet did pass across the heavens of Normandy, Hastings, and Ohio at the time.

So perhaps the serpent effigy is not a serpent, or not only a serpent, after all. Perhaps, like other effigies, it was created in troublous times in an effort to reestablish a harmony with the other creatures of the earth.*

ARCHAEOLOGY IN TENNESSEE

The westernmost provinces of the states of Tennessee and Kentucky occupy a fertile terrace bounded by two large rivers flowing in opposite directions. As the Mississippi presses southward toward the Gulf of Mexico, the Tennessee, a hundred miles away, provides one of the Great Valley's studies in recalcitrance. Its destination is the same, but across two states it proceeds in parallel to the great river but northward, toward the Ohio. The Cumberland takes its cue from the Tennessee, flowing out of the Nashville Basin and then northward to eventuate in the Ohio only a few miles upstream from its colleague.

The Ohio, having swept in from the east, gathers them in and pirouettes in a great half circle before joining all to the Mississippi, which has in the meantime reached agreement with the Missouri.

Cairo, Illinois, and Paducah, Kentucky, are the principal cities observing these leviathan movements and rejoicing in the fertility they have left behind in the central riverine plain of North America, an empire to arouse the envy of any pharaoh. It is a hot empire, like the Nile, but so humid that it would exhaust a bedouin very quickly.

Cairo and Paducah are at the same latitude as Williamsburgh, Virginia. They are considerably hotter in the summer than Roanoke or

---

*The dating of the Serpent Mound was accomplished in the summer of 1992 by a team of researchers whose report has not yet been published, but was reported in a letter from Bradley Lepper.

Lynchburg, and feel as southern as Memphis—the Memphis in Tennessee; it is not so much farther north of Memphis in Egypt as one might think. That Memphis lies only so far away in latitude as the 30th degree, and so does New Orleans. Memphis, Tennessee, was established downstream from Cairo, Illinois, by Andrew Jackson overlooking the delta of the Mississippi; Memphis, in Egypt, was established by the pharoah Menes to preside over his conquest of the delta of the Nile.

Ever since Jackson and his friend John Overton founded Memphis in 1819, intentionally fixing upon it an Egyptian metaphor, antiquity has been in the minds of those who came into the American empire stretching from Memphis to Cairo, an empire to arouse the envy of any pharaoh. The Cumberland, Tennessee, Ohio, and Mississippi course through deep black earth which has amply supported human life for many years, a thriving northern province of a culture which exchanged objects and, one may assume, ideas, with the people of Poverty Point before 1500 B.C., and thereafter produced major works of architecture with a few interruptions for three thousand five hundred years.

THE EQUIVALENCES OF PINSON

Around Pinson, in western Tennessee, the Forked Deer River courses through an array of mounds surrounded by embankments and linked by a design scheme extending for many miles. Pottery analysis and carbon dates place their construction in the period between 50 B.C. and A.D. 300—Adena/Hopewell times. In 1823, a Tennessee antiquarian, John Haywood, reported that at their apparent center he had measured a mound 87 feet tall with a flat top 50 feet square.* Now finally protected within a state park, it has suffered considerable wear and tear, and measures only 72 feet high, though it remains 350 feet in diameter at its base. That is very big: it required more than two million cubic feet of earth (60,000 cubic meters) to construct.

From this artificial hill, sight lines probably had to be cut through the woods to place precisely other mounds marking the extremities of what was probably a walled enclosure. Two of these huge earthen platform-markers still exist, each three-fifths of a mile distant, one at

---

*Haywood's account of the Pinson complex is found in his *Natural and Aboriginal History of Tennessee*, pp. 136–37; his estimate of the height of its largest mound was confirmed in 1870 by Gerard Troost, State Geologist of Tennessee, in 1875 by E. H. Randle, President of McKenzie College, and also by engineers of the Gulf, Mobile and Ohio Railroad (Mainfort, 1986, p. 8). Working in 1963 and in the early 1980s, Dan Morse and Robert Mainfort found it to be only 70 feet tall.

the northeastern corner and another at the southeastern. A third is only at a slightly shorter distance, perched on the edge of the bluff overlooking the floodplain.

Three-fifths of a mile is quite a distance to measure accurately across broken terrain traversed by ravines and brooks. We have come to expect accuracy of measurement of Adena/Hopewell architecture; the Pinson complex is composed by geometry almost as rigorous. A half circle 1,200 feet in diameter contains the northeastern "marking mound." Circles of exactly this size are talismanic, as we noted at Fort Center, Florida, at Newark, Ohio, and at Circleville.*

The Pinson complex has been shabbily treated by agriculture and by erosion. It is impossible to verify today a report of 1875 that it contained two further Hopewellian structures, *a graded way* smoothed and bounded by earthen embankments across a long stretch of countryside, and a *sacred way* leading from the enclosure to the riverbank, "well fortified around about with fortified way to the creek." The Pinson graded way is not so long as the sixty-mile Great Hopewell Road across Ohio, but in the middle of the nineteenth century we are told that in Tennessee "a well beaten and travelled road once led to this city of mounds from the west."[36]

From whence? It is not easy to be certain of its origin after its entire course has been plowed for 160 years, but there are also reports of an embanked and graded way leading *toward* Pinson from the Johnston site, which contains more mounds, less than three miles away and on the same bluff of the Forked Deer River.

> [On the southeastern end of the Johnston site there was a] dirt wall parallel to the river. . . . [There] is another wall of the same size and length, distant one-quarter of a mile . . . The wall next to the river, at a point equidistant from its end, turns to the river; and from the river by another short parallel wall. . . . The two short walls to the river leave an opening of the enclosure, and doubtless was once a covered way.[37]

Doubtless, an Ohioan might echo, "covered" in the sense that like the sacra via at Newark, Marietta and along the Scioto, it was protected by flanking earthworks.[†]

---

*The Pinson figure is precisely circular for only half its circumference; thereafter its abandons precision at a precipice and bends inward to include only about 60 percent of the thirty-acre area it would have comprehended if entire.

†It is one thing to make architecture in abstract shapes, placed indifferently upon the earth. It is another to place those shapes in abstract relationship to stars, moon, or sun. Like the Ohio sites at either end of the Great Hopewell Road, those at Pinson and Johnston are aligned geographically to relate to each other and to the magnetic north.

The largest and apparently defining mound at Johnston, roughly two-hundred feet

The references in these early reports to a "creek" bounding the Pinson and Johnston complexes do not sound very prepossessing, and the U.S. Army Corps of Engineers has turned what there was into a straight and narrow sluiceway. But in 1875 steamboats could reach these architectural complexes from the Mississippi and the Ohio, and surely dugout canoes could have done the same fifteen hundred years earlier.

"Well fortified around"—what could that mean? Colonel Pickford Jones reported that in 1840 he had ridden through the brush for six miles along an outer embankment surrounding its "city of mounds," which may once have held more than thirty buildings.*

The archaeologists who later worked at Pinson were especially struck by the presence of platform mounds in a ceremonial center that was in full use (judging from carbon-dated evidence) from 100 B.C. to about A.D. 500. Its occupants used pottery found elsewhere to have been common in the Adena/Hopewell period.

Since 1978, in large part because of the accumulation of new evidence at Pinson, archaeologists have commenced retesting and rethinking the chronology of platform mounds in general. A consensus has now formed that these structures were built in the central region of North America as early as the time of Christ. This is new: it alters much that had previously been thought about the motivation of American builders in the Adena/Hopewell era, their organization, and their religious life.

Platforms imply hierarchy. It has long been understood that hundreds of thousands of baskets full of earth carried to create rigorous architectural forms imply intense organization. But there had persisted a hypothesis of happy Hopewellian volunteers. The new evidence does not refute this myth, it merely tests it, and asks how long volunteering persists before it becomes obeisance.[†]

---

square and still twenty feet high, is set about 5 degrees east of magnetic north. So is the mound set within the Hopewellian 1,200 foot figure at Pinson. We will return to these matters in Chapter Eleven.

*Mainfort did not find the embankment reported by Colonel Jones, which was also described by William Myer ("an archaeologist affiliated with the Smithsonian Institution"), and concluded that "there is no evidence that the alleged embankments encircling the mound complex ever existed." A good deal of plowing had intervened. (Mainfort, *Pinson Mounds,* p. 4).

†Platform mounds at Marietta, Baum, Ginther, and Cedar Bank, in Ohio, and the small platform mounds within the Newark works, have been tested and found to date from the Hopewell era (see Mainfort, "Pinson Mounds," p. 82, and, for other contemporary platform mounds, see Brose, *Hopewell Archaeology.*)

Intermediate in ambition between these simple two-stage mounds and the four hierarchially arranged spaces on Monks Mound at Cahokia are a number of intriguing stepped

A platform implies something to put upon a platform. What went on top of those platforms? Excavators of truncated pyramids built before 800 or 900 have not found evidence of the kind of wooden buildings found upon similar mounds constructed five or six centuries later—postholes, bits of wattle-and-daub, and textile fragments indicating wallcoverings. The plain fact is that we do not know what use was made of the Adena/Hopewell platforms.

AN ARCHITECTURE OF TURMOIL?

Along the banks of the Forked Deer River, as it wanders northwesterly between the Mississippi and the Tennessee, there are many other mounds of ambiguous date.* The puzzles compound on the bluffs above the great river itself, where there are many hilltop sanctuaries similar to those in Ohio and in eastern Kentucky and Tennessee, but built entirely of earth. The bluffs of the great river do not provide much building stone, so the architects of these buildings used what came to hand, creating linear embankments with bastions cutting off the natural causeways leading to isolated cul-de-sac bluffs. We will see such structures again as we follow Lewis and Clark up the Missouri, and seek to parse out the evidence telling us why and when they were created in Chapter Eleven. Here, in passing, it may be useful to observe that in the middle of the nineteenth century Americans used hilltops such as these to create picturesque scenes centering upon Gothic Revival cottages, implying, as these ancient forts may have implied, continuity and safety, which may too have been among the architectural programs of the Adena/Hopewell. In Newark, Ohio, as on several Kentucky hilltops, one of these symbols of a spurious antiquity is set next

---

mounds arranged as sequences of platforms, in Arkansas, at Sherman, near Osceola, and at Barney, near Helena (lost). Multiple steps, though not ranged as circles, are also to be found at St. Louis; Lenoir, in Tennessee; Angel, in Indiana; Kincaid, in Illinois; Upper Nodena, in Arkansas; and Magee, in Mississippi. See entries for these places in William Morgan.

It is not likely that many archaeologists would agree, but it is even possible that the chair-shaped mounds of the Ouachita and Bayou Macon, dating back three thousand five hundred years, may indicate an even earlier platform-building tradition. On the other hand, they may not have carried structures. Some people can be quite impressive standing all by themselves on a high place.

*One of these smaller centers is at Obion, on private land. It has seven mounds around a rectangular plaza nine hundred by two hundred feet in extent. The buildings seem to have been built later than those at Pinson, but considerably earlier than those at Cahokia. (Garland, *The Obion Site*, especially p. 121).

For an admirable reconstruction of the relationship between Mound Bottom and Obion, see Morgan, pp. 108–9.

to a mound a thousand years older than the invention of the Gothic style, and contemporaneous with classical Greece.

That Gothic cottage in Newark might just as easily have been in the Greek Revival style, but in Marietta it should have been Roman. Marietta was founded by the Cincinnati, soldier-heroes of the Revolutionary War, with whom we will assemble in Chapter Six. Though it has lost its Hopewell squares, it retains its earthen Adena cone, because that mortuary mound lies surrounded by a band of the kind of graves Americans hesitate to destroy, the resting places of our own heroes, the Cincinnati, exemplars of the ideals of the noblest Roman of them all, the Founder of Founders, George Washington.

We will come to their chronicle when we have introduced Albert Gallatin's friend Thomas Worthington, the squire of Adena and primary opponent to the Cincinnati.

CHAPTER FOUR

THE GALLATINIANS: THOMAS WORTHINGTON AND ADENA

The moral force of Albert Gallatin showed some of the leaders of the West how they might look at their rising empire. Moral force was his gift to the imaginative, his window glass went to the literal. From his factory at New Geneva, Gallatin shipped them glass to enable them to look out upon their private empires without undue exertion. Among those who benefited both from his leadership and his glass was Thomas Worthington, senator (1804–1807 and 1811–1814) from and governor (1814–1818) of Ohio.

In 1806, Gallatin glass was inserted into the window frames for Adena, Worthington's villa upon a hilltop overlooking Chillicothe, designed the year before by Benjamin Henry Latrobe and built under his mail-order direction over the ensuing two years. Latrobe was the nation's most celebrated architect, sponsored by President Jefferson and Vice-President Burr, and close friend of Secretary of the Treasury Gallatin. He had given coherence to the United States Capitol, and was providing the famous porticoes to the White House.*

"Called at the time of its erection . . . the most magnificent mansion west of the Alleghenies,"† Worthington's house was set among other

---

*Gallatin and the architect had been friends since 1796, and around 1803, it was probably Gallatin who brought Worthington into Latrobe's circle of clients.

†Adena had a rival and an exact contemporary, Mt. Braddock, not far from Gallatin's Friendship Hill. Adena is not Georgian (that is to say, old-fashioned at the time), but neoclassical (which is to say, modern). Mt. Braddock is the finest Georgian house west of the Blue Ridge. Designed by an English architect, Adam Wilson, for the ironmaster Isaac Meason, it was built in 1802. If it were on the James, it would be a destination for pilgrimage, but it languishes unkempt and unappreciated.

Someday, some rich Pittsburgher may rescue it, and the proud inscription of its completion date in the stonework over its door will once again proclaim the pride of the Pennsylvania frontier. Mt. Braddock lies in an anthology of architecture just south of Pittsburgh. The Meadowcroft Shelter is the earliest, having been hewn a little larger by human hands around 20,000 B.C. Gallatin's Friendship Hill comes next, and after Mt. Braddock comes Frank Lloyd Wright's "Falling Water."

and older magnificences. His estate was at the centerpoint of Ohio's ancient earthen monuments—Hopewell octagons, circles, and squares, and the burial cones of people to whom Worthington inadvertently gave the name by which they are described today. The name "Adena" he found in "a tome on ancient history," describing "places remarkable for the delightfulness of their situations."[1] A visitor who comes to Adena for archaeological, historical, or architectural reasons will see Gallatin's glass at its best at sunset or sunrise, when the diagonal light of the sun strikes the seamless, honey-colored limestone walls of the house, clear of all ornament or projections, and makes of it a tight crystal, as if all of glass. It might be a joint project of Gallatin and Mies van der Rohe.* Of course, any work of Latrobe's reminds one most of all of him, the first architectural genius to work on these shores since 1492. Adena is our best surviving example of what Jefferson called the cubical school of design, its central elongated cube flanked by two smaller elongated cubes, the three enclosing an entry courtyard shaped as an elongated square.[2] The excitement of Adena does not arise, however, from its neat solution of a neoclassical challenge, but from two other causes. The first is the eerie ways in which its form and materials participate in a much older architectural tradition. The second is its place in the history of American race relations.

Worthington could scarcely avoid acknowledging the prowess of the Indians in architecture. It was as if he had settled on the banks of the Nile, or in the precincts of Ankhor, and there were Indians living all about him still, with whom, as a statesman, he had to contend. Some of them actually became his friends.[†]

Worthington, like Gallatin, was a member of the party of Jefferson. Encouraged by Gallatin, he corresponded with Jefferson about the mounds along the Scioto Valley of which he became proprietor on his own estate and agent of the Washington family. It is probable that he also represented Jefferson and Gallatin, both of whom speculated in Ohio real estate.[‡] On June 12, 1808, Worthington wrote to tell Jeffer-

---

*Mies van der Rohe was a twentieth century architect famous for glass boxes tooled in immaculate detail. In the United States, the most famous examples of this work are his Farnsworth House, in Illinois, the Seagram Building in New York, and a series of towers on the waterfront in Chicago.

[†]In the 1790s, both Latrobe and Gallatin had been befriended by Aaron Burr. The three were united in subtle ways: Gallatin had already demonstrated his interest in Indians. Burr's childhood was spent under the guardianship of uncles and a grandfather who were missionaries among the Stockbridge Indians in western Massachusetts. Latrobe was the son of a Moravian missionary, trained in Moravian schools. His mother came from a family of missionaries to the Pennsylvania Indians.

[‡]In what is now Jefferson County, West Virginia, earlier Worthingtons had grown prosperous, building among the estates of the Washingtons and Masons their own somewhat less

son about the earlier uses of the quarries from which the stone for his house had been taken. He had observed limestone walls, some of them several miles in length, surrounding the platformlike hilltops above his landholdings along Paint Creek. Worthington did not profess to know when these enclosures had been created, or their original purpose. Like most of his contemporaries, he thought them to be forts.*

A military assumption was natural enough; a major battle had been fought at Chillicothe as the Indians resisted a Kentuckian assault in September, 1787. The following summer, the Kentuckians repeated David Williamson's barbarities against the trusting Indians of the Moravian towns; this time it was the friendly Piankashaw at Vincennes who were massacred. Worthington's first reconnaissance of this holy ground occurred when the stench of fetid bodies was not yet purged from the embers of burnt-out Indian houses.

The Ohio that Worthington reconnoitered was rich with Indian architecture and European discovery. He was fortunate to have some predecessors of his temperament who led him to observe everything carefully when he arrived.

THE EXPLORATIONS OF CAPTAIN HEART AND THE GENERALS

In 1790, General Josiah Harmar and 1,420 men went up the Maumee against the Shawnee, Miami, and Delaware, and were twice defeated. In November, 1791 Arthur St. Clair barely managed to escape with a

---

stately, but not inconsiderable, stone houses. Two of them were Quarry Bank and (with a note of pretension) The Manor House. The Washingtons, Worthingtons, and Masons had also begun investing in land on both sides of the Ohio as early as the 1760s.

George Washington served as Ohio land-agent for Thomas Worthington's father in 1774; Worthington later performed that same function for the heirs of Washington, keeping an eye on the lands of Bailey Washington along Paint Creek. These Washington properties interested him for several reasons, including the stone fort he described in a letter to Jefferson dated June 12, 1808.

In 1784, Jefferson told James Madison that he did not own any land outside the watershed of the Rivanna River, but later he did join in the speculative fever for Ohio lands. (Jefferson to Madison, Nov. 11, 1784, *Papers,* 4, p. 3.)

---

*Latrobe himself would, I think, have been as unlikely to think first of the military uses of Ohio enclosures as to leap to the conclusion that the colonnades surrounding the piazza of the Basilica of St. Peter in Rome were defensive in nature, had *he* come upon *them* in ruins. His education in architecture was broader than Worthington's. He had explored St. Peter's and visited the ruins of temples built in Italy by Greeks who used the term *temenos* for sanctified areas set apart from the pollution of daily life. The Greeks used rectilinear platforms of stone; the Adena used circles of earth, while the Hopewell employed, in addition, octagons and squares.

third of his command after he was surprised in the same area by the forces of Little Turtle. St. Clair sent his regulars into the woods in bright white and blue uniforms, targets as conspicuous as the scarlet sacrifices presented by Braddock in 1755.

In 1793, the *Transactions of the American Philosophical Society* carried a lengthy, posthumous communication from Major Jonathan Heart, "a youth of the most promising hopes and splendid talents— talents which might have proved ornamental to his country, and useful to mankind," who had gone to his death in St. Clair's debacle. Heart's talents were for archaeology, and he was a great loss. He had already presented a discussion of the Marietta works in 1787, in *Columbian Magazine,* accompanied in his report to the Society by a further discourse on the architecture at Grave Creek, Portsmouth, Marietta, along the Miami, and near Chillicothe. He reported as well an intriguing reconnaissance of the monuments along the lower Mississippi.[3] The author of that obituary for Heart, Gilbert Imlay, while mourning for "my young friend," thought it right to record both Heart's admiration for the past accomplishments of the Native Americans and his own consciousness that those against whom he was at war were no skulking savages, but an "heroic people" with "singular prowess" in battle. Imlay gave benediction to Heart with lines from the *Iliad,* in which two contending heroes meet their doom.[4]

Had Imlay known General Richard Butler as well as Heart, he might have extended his Homeric analogies, for Butler was an even more compelling hero. Born in Dublin, he fought for American independence for seven years, and was brevetted a general in 1783. He then set forth for the frontier, participating in the first scientific archaeology at Marietta, compiling ethnological notes leading to an *Indian Vocabulary,* and negotiating settlements with the objects of his study. Protesting St. Clair's Braddock-like parade-ground tactics, Butler died beside Heart in the ensuing defeat.

If we knew more of Butler's view of Indians, and of his vision of what a good society might be in the West, we might be able to include him within our list of Gallatinians, but he has had no modern biographer, nor even an obituary like Imlay's for his companion. Richard Butler does deserve a place in this tale because he was so moved by the Indian architecture he found that he sought George Washington's views about what he knew his commander had explored more thoroughly than he, and thereby elicited Washington's only recorded comment on the importance of that architecture, which will shortly be reported in its context.

To the accounts of General Butler and Major Heart were added those of other officers who had served under Washington's command, Colonel Winthrop Sargent, and Generals "Mad Anthony" Wayne and

William Henry Harrison. Harrison came upon the earthworks at Cincinnati in 1791, at the age of eighteen, when he was serving as a lieutenant under St. Clair. By August 1793, he knew them well enough to escort Wayne on a tour—or so he said forty years later. It may well be that they were both led by Sargent, who sent the first map of Cincinnati to the American Philosophical Society in 1799, but by the time Harrison got around to his archaeological phase, in the 1820s, Wayne was remembered as a hero worthy to accompany the heroic Harrison, while Sargent was forgotten.[5]

Wayne was assembling two thousand regulars, about the number Washington had led to Yorktown, and a ragtag collection of militia for an assault upon the Ohio nations. But on that summer afternoon he found time to walk the plain to survey the ancient architecture of his opponents, which was "literally covered with low lines of embankments." It appears to have been another Hopewell center; there was at least an implied circle (a typical Hopewell configuration of a precisely drawn segment of a circle with the balance omitted) with a small circle-ellipse attached (830 feet by 730), like those in the Paint Creek complexes.[6] Cincinnati was built on the ruins of a predecessor, an ancient city, but between 1794 and 1830 it grew so much more rapidly than Marietta that it paid little heed to that heritage, and by the time any systematic effort was made to make maps of the monuments of the region little of the past was left.

WORTHINGTON'S SOUTHERN CAVALCADE

By the end of August, 1793, Wayne was ready, and led his forces to a surprise attack upon the Indians at Fallen Timbers where he was victorious. Two years later, Thomas Worthington gingerly reconnoitered the situation in the Scioto Valley. It seemed safe enough, so he returned to Virginia. Just before Christmas, he married a neighboring heiress, Eleanor Swearingen, and in January, 1797, they set forth for an Ohio estate.

They did not go alone into the wilderness; they were prosperous. Worthington's neighbor, Samuel Washington of Harewood, said just before the wedding that he was "the only man in our neighborhood that has money," and the Swearingen—or Van Swearingen—connections brought more than money. The family had come from Holland and had taken happily to the American frontier. Several Van Swearingens married Indians.

In March 1798, there wound through the crinkled hills of western Virginia the familiar pageant of the westering of the gentry of the American South. Readers of southern family histories would expect to see the cavalcade and its entourage turn southwest; if it terminated in the Black Belt, Hampton kinfolk might be remembered in the van; if bound for Natchez there might be Marshalls leading the way; if it turned yet more southerly, toward Louisiana, it might be led by Skipwiths and Randolphs. None, of course, would be expected to go alone into the wilderness; all would be accompanied by shackled coffles trudging on behind.

The chronicle of the westering of the Worthingtons has passages which might be derived from those of the Hamptons, Marshalls, Skipwiths, or Randolphs. It speaks reverently of "their furniture, including two lovely pier glasses inherited by Eleanor from her mother, . . . family silver and linen, farming implements, pots and pans, chickens, fruit trees, shrubbery [we assume pruned well back] and seeds of every kind." There were the usual extensions: two brothers of Mrs. Worthington, their doctor and friend, "Dr. Tiffin and his family, which included his wife, his parents, two brothers, and two sisters," the family miller and his sons, and an entourage of Blacks.[7]

But this was no ordinary southern family, nor was theirs an ordinary destination. Bearing the seeds of European and African culture, this caravan turned north, toward Adena. The difference between the Worthingtons and the others was that they drove no coffle of slaves. Before taking the road to Ohio, Thomas Worthington manumitted all the people he owned.*

In this uncompromising and expensive statement against slavery (manumission was giving away property—to itself), Thomas Worthington demonstrated that he had much in common with the Yankee Cincinnati of Marietta. But he was a Virginian still, and after settling himself into Ohio, he set himself up as the leader of the party of Jefferson and Gallatin. He shared with them an enthusiasm for ancient architecture, and one of the delights of his new situation was that he was

---

*The Worthingtons were already a little "different." They were Quakers who had arrived with the Scotch-Irish migration out of Pennsylvania, rather than Anglicans like their neighbors who had moved *uphill* from the tidewater. By 1800 they had lapsed somewhat from their Quakerism, owning slaves and marrying out of the brotherhood/sisterhood, but the younger members of the family received renewal in their faith from the arrival in the Worthington-Washington enclave of the widow Paine and her two daughters. The Paines came to stay at Harewood, one of the Washington manors, after Lucy Paine married George Steptoe Washington in 1793. A year later, on September 15, James Madison, a forty-three-year-old congressman, married the widow's other daughter, Dolley, in Harewood's Doric-paneled drawing room, before its green marble fireplace.

Though Dolley Paine did not retain her Quaker ties after she married Madison, other members of the family did, and reminded the younger Worthingtons that her father had once lived in Virginia and manumitted his slaves when he moved north. That action on the part of the elder Paine was notorious. Most of the Washingtons and Masons in the region disapproved of it, but it may well have caught the conscience of Thomas Worthington.

in the midst of it. The neighborhood of Chillicothe contained architecture considerably more impressive than the "log cabin but neatly furnished" to which Worthington brought his wife from Virginia.

The emigrant Virginian had written to her that their homesite was near "an Indian mound [which] will afford a lovely situation for a summer house, and commands views of the whole town, having about thirty-five feet perpendicular height." This is a good description of the Adena Mound, which has become perhaps the most famous in the United States. He did not, it turned out, build a summer house on that mound. Instead, as the nineteenth century opened, he began thinking of a better site a half mile away, high on the hill above the town, on which Latrobe created his villa five years later.[8]

In the same letter in which Worthington told his wife about the Adena Mound, he reported that on the previous day he had "attended the funeral of an Indian—the only son of an old man who was much respected for his fine qualities. The Indians made a great lamentation over him."[9] In 1901, archaeologists commenced the investigation of the Adena Mound, disclosing treasures buried two thousand years earlier with those "respected for . . . fine qualities," a hoard of glorious works of art, in copper, pearl, and mica. In 1901, treasure was enough. Archaeology was not in one of its ambitious phases. Having yielded its hoard, the Adena Mound was destroyed. There is nothing left today to mark the site. Householders mow grass and children play "kick the can" where, in the time of Augustus Caesar, people buried their dead with such great ceremony and, one may assume, with "great lamentation."

In one of those telling juxtapositions which ought to have induced reconsideration decades ago of the relationship of these two "cultures," the great mortuary center of the Hopewell was only a mile away, on a compass bearing directly north from the Adena Mound, a bearing, which, continued, leads directly to the enclosure at Dunlap. The Hopewell burial place, now the Mound City National Monument, contains a score of mounds, rebuilt after several occupations and a bulldozing by the United States Army. Each of these tumuli harbored its own store of wonders, rescued by archaeologists barely in time. It is appropriate that the Founding Father with the deepest knowledge of American antiquity, Albert Gallatin, should have had a part in the creation of a house on such a site.

Membership in the party of Gallatin and Jefferson might have been stapled to Thomas Worthington's birth certificate, born as he was during the Revolutionary period among the slave-owning Virginian gentry of the Piedmont. But Worthington was not easily corralled at any time. Orphaned in early childhood, he escaped his guardian, General William Darke, and went to sea. After voyaging to the West Indies and the

Baltic, his ship was hijacked by the British Navy, and he barely escaped a press gang. Thereafter he saw fit to return to the bucolic serenity of western Virginia, remaining, however, only long enough to acquire Revolutionary War land warrants in Ohio from Darke.*

As a United States senator, Worthington voted to exclude slavery from Louisiana, despite Jefferson's pressure to take the opposite view, proposing that all slaves brought into the newly acquired Louisiana Territory be manumitted after one year.[10] He was not popular among the Virginia planters, and in Ohio he also earned the opprobrium of those who believed the only good Indian to be a dead Indian.

A SOIREE AT ADENA

During the War of 1812, Thomas Worthington served briefly as general of the militia. We are told of his reconnaissance of the Indian force besieging Fort Wayne, together "with eight other whites dressed as Indians . . . [and] seven Indian guides," and we may be forgiven for imagining that it might not have been easy for eight portly gentlemen to abandon their cigars and pier glasses, and go skulking about the underbrush.[11]

Though the military experience of General Worthington of the Ohio militia was limited, he did, however, know something about Indian negotiations. In 1807, just as Adena was being completed, he and his partner Duncan Macarthur were sent by the governor of Ohio to one of the Shawnee settlements near Greenville. They were to persuade the war chiefs, Tecumseh among them, to remain neutral when war came again with the British. They felt themselves successful; so pleased were they that they invited the Indian leaders to accompany them back to Chillicothe. The idea commended itself to Tecumseh, Blue Jacket (who had been on particularly good terms with Worthington), Roundhead (a Wyandot), and the Panther (a Delaware).

They not only came, but stayed a week, being feted by the local gentry; Tecumseh took the occasion to provide three hours of spellbinding oratory to the citizens of the town. He made clear his determination to keep his warriors north and west of the Greenville Treaty Line (established in his absence in 1795, after Wayne's victory)—if the Whites remained east and south of it. Tecumseh was probably certain that they would not and was contemplating what he would do, over the next three years, *as* they did not.[†]

---

*Land warrants were often issued as veteran's bonuses.

[†]In 1811, William Henry Harrison had ample occasion to discover that Tecumseh had not been idle. The fierce battles at Tippecanoe and the Thames were just over the horizon.

One cheerful afternoon, the four Indian leaders accepted the invitation of the Worthingtons to attend a soiree at Adena. Some accounts state that they had camped about the house for the whole week, taking their meals in the house. In any case, the story of that afternoon stamped itself upon the memory of Worthington's daughter, though it is not included in his official biography. We must turn, instead, to Bil Gilbert's wonderful biography of Tecumseh.

> Exotic victuals were shipped in from the east [more likely from New Orleans], fancy china and the best silver were brought out, and the whole table was arranged in the intricate pyramid style then thought very fashionable.[12]

Worthington's daughter recalled her briefing: "We were strictly charged to take no notice of their eccentricities." The briefing given by Tecumseh to his colleagues is *not* recorded, but it must have been considerably more subtle. They were there for business, as Gilbert notes: "these four men[who] had between them probably cut down, bashed in the heads, and lifted the scalps of more than a hundred white people." Yet they entered graciously and stood about in one of Latrobe's carefully crafted cubical drawing rooms,

> balancing cups, making small talk with the creme de la creme of the backwoods. . . . Inevitably an accident did occur. . . . When the servants passed around the coffee cups, one of the savages [Gilbert's word] . . . was inadvertently overlooked. Immediately the other three began to gibber excitedly at him and he to respond with growing heat and apparent anger. What was actually happening was that they were making an *unsoma** joke, ribbing him about having a totem animal so slow and stupid that it could not find coffee. Understanding nothing of this, the white guests imagined that they had seriously insulted the chiefs and that soon the pyramid table might be drenched with blood.
>   Thereupon Tekamthi [Tecumseh] displayed his social skills. . . . He explained to the Worthingtons that he and his men were making jokes which were hard to explain to outsiders. Relieved the whites fell all over themselves to keep the cups of the savages filled. . . . Years later, when he came across an account of the dinner at Adena, Gaynwah, the Shaw-

---

Unsoma is a metaphysical concept I will do my best to explain, to the extent that I can understand it. At birth, each Indian male is given by his tribe an association with one of four sets of spirits. That set he must defend against jokes in a social situation, and defend much more fiercely against jibes if the atmosphere is not friendly. He is also expected to make jokes about the spirit-set of his friends: friendly jokes. I am sure there is a great deal more to it than that.

nee historian and great-grandson of Tekamthi, was vastly amused, commenting: "I have no doubt that these quantities of extra coffee were another great joke followed up after they returned to Greenville. I could not help laughing when I read about the chief, knowing what followed."[13]

Blue Jacket was an expert dissembler. He and the other Indian leaders were as well aware as their hosts that nothing except a great plague would keep the Whites from violating the treaty line, like all the treaty lines before and after it. They needed a respite in which to continue gathering supplies and arms. Indeed, Blue Jacket had had to hurry back to Greenville from such a shopping trip among the British at Detroit in order to be present for his earlier meeting with Worthington.

The week of speech making and coffee drinking in Chillicothe was a diplomatic triumph; it bought more time. The coffee joke, it is true, was risky. It might have produced a commotion. They were playing for time; their situation was grim: there were not enough arms and ammunition in the British arsenal to make it possible for 50,000 Indians to stand off the 400,000 Whites already in Kentucky and the 260,000 in Ohio.

There was a story told on the frontier that the real joke was neither the mock fight nor the deluge of coffee, and that the "savage" Blue Jacket was no savage, that he was, in fact, a cousin of Mrs. Worthington, born a Van Swearingen and captured in his youth wearing a blue jacket. The story is exceedingly unlikely to be true, sad to say; the dates just do not work out. None the less, the density of spirits, *unsoma* and otherwise, must have been great in that house during that coffee party. At no time did so many strands of our story come together and weave into each other so deeply as during that evening, in Latrobe's cubical drawing-room.

Worthington was remarkable among the frontier politicians of his day in seeking to treat Indians as fellow humans. He had lived among them much of his life, including the Van Swearingen cousins of his wife. He had kinfolk on both sides of the frontier; that may be one reason why he was skeptical of Harrison's policy of pressing Indians and Whites into a war. He derided Harrison's provocations, and called the narrow victory at Tippecanoe a melancholy affair. Like Washington and Aaron Burr before him, Worthington urged that the United States strive for an accommodation to settle the Indian boundaries without further bloodshed.

But bloodshed was a way to power. Indian fighting was a profession in the West. When successfully plied, it led to presidencies for Andrew Jackson and for Harrison, and led close to the presidency for Lewis

Cass and Richard Mentor Johnson of Kentucky.* The Age of Jackson, and of Harrison, had begun.

That was not a hospitable world for Worthington and Gallatin, allies through life, despite a brief outbreak of rivalry between them in 1824, when they were both candidates for the vice-presidency.† Gallatin was actually nominated by the Republicans-becoming-Democrats, but withdrew when it was discovered how little enthusiasm the country had for this consummate Washington insider. It was "a misfortune grounded in a miscalculation" he said, ruefully.[14] The same might be said of Worthington's effort to return to the United States Senate in that year. He was old, a mere militia general, and ran head on into the rising cult of "regular" military heroes, the most conspicuous of whom were Andrew Jackson and William Henry Harrison. Worthington came in a poor third.

The label "Jeffersonian" would obscure Worthington's profound differences from Jefferson, for he was even more advanced than Gallatin in his actions with regard to slavery. He not only opposed the South's Peculiar Institution in theory; he acted upon his convictions. Virginians of principle led the antislavery forces of the Northwest Territory, in this they were united with the territory's Yankee immigrants. Worthington shared that leadership with Edward Coles of Illinois, another Virginia-born governor of a state hewn from the Northwest Territory.

Illinois does not have a Coles Memorial, but Ohio's Adena could well become a shrine to the conscience of Virginia, where pilgrims might meditate upon the lives of men such as Coles and Worthington.[15] It could also become a place for larger meditations upon American race

---

*Johnson, the only vice president of the United States, so far, to be married to a Black woman, is a large figure, too large to be cramped into a footnote. I have tried to do better for him in an essay in *Rediscovering America.*

He was a westerner, raised to manhood in Kentucky, whose life was full of ambiguity. He was extolled as an Indian killer, "the captain who killed Tecumseh," though he devoted much of his time to the support of a school for Indian children, the Choctaw Academy.

R. David Edmunds has cautioned me in a letter of May 22, 1991, that Johnson's role in the affairs of the Academy was not as spotlessly philanthropic as believed in Scott County, Kentucky, or as I presented the matter in *Rediscovering America.*

Edmunds reports that there is "some good evidence" in the National Archives that Johnson connived with Richard Henderson, the other proprietor of the school, to secure government contracts, and that there are "some questions" about the final destination of profits produced by the products created in this early "normal school." Further, Edmunds's own research of the records of Indian agents in the West suggests that they were prodded to secure enrollment of tribal orphans—all this has left him, as the best scholar on the subject, "suspicious."

†They seem to have survived the occasion without animosity, for Gallatin kept on paying Worthington thirty dollars a year as his agent for Ohio land.

relations, inviting consideration of the achievements of Americans of other than European ancestry. Adena is the finest of the early accomplishments of European neoclassicism west of the Appalachians and it is set amid the sacred precincts of the Indians. Furthermore, Thomas Worthington and Albert Gallatin (whose citizenship was sworn in Virginia) were far ahead of most other Virginians in their view of how American society might comprehend Blacks, Whites, and Indians. But not ahead of the most famous Virginian of them all.

CHAPTER FIVE

GEORGE WASHINGTON: HIS LAND, ITS INHABITANTS, AND THE CINCINNATIAN SOLUTION

George Washington had more firsthand knowledge of the American West and of its inhabitants than any other president of the United States before Andrew Jackson. He owned more important archaeological sites than any other president, any time. Like Albert Gallatin and Thomas Jefferson, he advocated scientific exploration of the ancient architecture of America, though he had less opportunity than they to pursue the subject himself. His policies with regard to living Indians were those of a man who had friends among them, had fought beside them, and respected their ways. Washington advocated neither the obliteration of Indian cultures nor their assimilation, but, instead, the apportionment of the interior of the North American continent into vast reservations, allocated separately to Indians and to non-Indians. In this, he found little support from either Jefferson or Gallatin, but as was always the case, his views were consistent; his regard for the evidence of the Native American past was an aspect of his regard for the Native Americans present.

As a surveyor in 1749, 1750, and 1752, Washington explored the valleys between the Blue Ridge and the rocky highlands marking the continental divide. In 1753, on his first military mission, he went all the way over, into the upper reaches of the Ohio watershed. Serving as a spy and messenger for the governor of Virginia, he delivered an ultimatum to the French, demanding that they and their Indian allies abandon their posts and villages on the upper reaches of the Ohio.

Though he saw many ruins of ancient buildings, he was not able to give them much attention. He was in enemy territory on a mission of provocation; the perils of his position were demonstrated in the following year when he ambushed a French party sent on a mission similar to his own, and killed its leader. The French refused to withdraw, and, in 1754, at Fort Necessity, dealt Washington his first personal military defeat—his worst until the series of disasters in and around the city of New York early in the Revolutionary War. The retreat from Fort Necessity was inglorious, but not so horrifying as the debacle which occurred nearby in the next year, when General Braddock took his force of redcoats into an ambush. Serving under Braddock, Washington was in command of the Virginian militia; though suffering from a high fever, he rallied and rescued the remnants of the army after its proud general died of his wounds.

Three years later, Washington was back in the West, accompanying another English general who went to his death. John Forbes was already ill when, carried in a litter, he followed as his deputy, Bouquet, and Washington led a new army back to the Forks of the Ohio, where, upon the ruins of Fort Duquesne, the city of "Pittsbourgh" was founded.

The defining political event of the formative years of Washington's generation was Britain's conquest of Canada and the Mississippi Valley.* The formal removal of French power from North America in 1763 exceeded the most exuberant expectations of the British colonials, as the collapse of Russian Communism has transcended those of their descendants. Second only to the withdrawal of the threat of France from the frontier was the fact that Americans had a part in the drama—a nobler part than many of those they had been taught to consider their betters. They saw the British in defeat. They knew Braddock's disaster could have been avoided had he taken the advice of Benjamin Franklin and Washington. During Bouquet's successful campaign to redeem that defeat, the Virginians demonstrated that they knew how to fight very well when they had decent leadership. And they were becoming acquainted with the western terrain.

During the Revolutionary conflict that ensued, American forces carried the war to St. Louis and nearly to Detroit. Washington directed that western strategy, and in 1784, soon after the success of his own army at Yorktown, he was back again at the Forks of the Ohio. That was how he first became acquainted with Albert Gallatin.

WASHINGTON AND GALLATIN

Their meeting occurred in a one-room cabin which had been used as the office and sleeping quarters of the chief surveyor for Virginia's interests in a region still contested with Pennsylvania. Gallatin had been occupying the only bed in the place. It was his headquarters as he made

---

*Manila and Havana also fell to the British imperial sweep.

use of his training by the Abenaki to reconnoiter the headwaters of the Ohio by canoe and portage.

Washington already owned much of that landscape. On the afternoon of September 24, 1784, seeking to learn what might be the most convenient routes for settlers across the mountains to his holdings, he was interrogating one after another of an assemblage of local worthies (he was "slow in forming an opinion" said Gallatin later). Then a young stranger broke in—in a Swiss-French accent: "Oh, it is plain enough"—and pointed to the map.[1]

> The good people stared . . . wondering at his boldness. . . . General Washington . . . laid down his pen, raised his eyes from his paper, and cast a stern look at Mr. Gallatin, evidently offended . . . but said not a word. . . . He continued his interrogations for a few minutes longer, when suddenly stopping, he threw down his pen, turned to Mr. Gallatin, and said, "You are right sir."[2]

Washington had a famous temper. He was as habituated to deference as Dwight David Eisenhower, whose cold blue eye I once felt in a somewhat similar situation. And that was in the twentieth century; by 1952, even generals running for the presidency were occasionally interrupted. In 1784, Washington was treated by everyone else like a choleric prince. That very day he had noted in his diary "an apology made me" because the backwoods gentry had failed to make an appropriate "address . . . as they found my horses saddled and myself on the move." But like Eisenhower, Washington was also accustomed to deploying whatever talents, however meager, came to hand, and Gallatin was a real talent. The general took his measure in that wilderness log cabin, and the impudent surveyor was invited to dine with him.[3] Thereafter, Washington expressed a desire to occupy the cabin until morning. There was no question who would get the cot; Gallatin wrapped himself in his blanket and spent the night on the floor.

WASHINGTON, GALLATIN AND ARCHAEOLOGY

Washington and Gallatin were never friends, but they did understand each other; that understanding began on the September night in 1784 when Gallatin relinquished his cot to Washington; less than a year had passed since word was received of the end of the War for American Independence.

Washington was fifty-two; as the most eminent man in the United States, he had a right to the bed. He was also almost certainly the *tall-*

est man present—by his own account "six feet high and proportionately made; if anything rather slender than thick for a person of that height with pretty long arms and thighs." None of his shirts have survived, but curators at the Smithsonian who measured his uniform concluded that he would wear a modern 38 or 40 long, with a 34-inch waist, a 36–38-inch chest, and a 33-inch sleeve.[4]

He was a Virginia squire, conservative to the marrow of his bones, but, like many a squire of his time and like Gallatin, he was a speculator. That does not mean that he squandered time upon theoretical inquiry; it means that he was a true believer that real estate will be worth more tomorrow than today. Accordingly, Washington had accumulated huge holdings of river-bottom land in Pennsylvania, western Virginia, and Ohio, many of them important to archaeology.[5]

One of these was near the meeting place of Washington and Gallatin, on the Monongahela; it included an earthwork enclosing a large interior court. Though it had probably been a ceremonial center, the first Europeans to come upon it characteristically took it to be a defensive work. After 1770 it was known as the "Old Fort at Redstone."*

With their elegant sense of propriety, some New Englanders preparing an invasion of Indian territory in 1788 made use of this ancient Indian liturgical center to mobilize their forces. Within its walls they assembled a second *Mayflower;*† from it they set forth downstream. To complete their symbolic journey they disembarked and commenced a colony within its first important counterpart on the north shore of the Ohio, at the place they called Marietta.

Before these emigrants descending the river came to Marietta, they passed the Grave Creek Mound. When Washington camped there in 1770 he observed, on its summit, trees bearing graffiti of Europeans, one dated 1735; it was already a favorite way station of tourists. The scientist William Barton later described it as a "stupendous eminence . . . composed of huge quantities of earth. . . . One of the most august monuments of remote antiquity."[6]

In 1803, the Grave Creek Mound moved the Reverend Thaddeus M. Harris to verse:

> Behind me rise huge a reverend pile
> Sole in this desert heath, a place of tombs.
> Waste, Desolate; where Ruin dreary dwell,
> Brooding o'er sightless skulls and crumbling bones.[7]

---

*The Old Fort is now lost beneath the town of Brownsville.

†The original name of the craft was *Adventure Galley*. It was later changed to *Mayflower*.
   The first party to set forth for Marietta, in April, 1788, embarked at Samrill's Ferry, now West Newton, Pennsylvania, on the Youghiogheny.

The reverend pile is still there, still "huge"; it was the largest building along the upper Ohio, looming over a region where the Appalachian rivers gather themselves for a rush southwesterly toward the Mississippi, where the names of Braddock and Washington, Bouquet and Gist, Duquesne and Legardeur de Saint-Pierre, Pontiac and Tecumseh, Logan, Queen Allaqippa, Little Turtle and Cornstalk were entered upon the pages of American history. The steel and glass bank buildings of Pittsburgh laid up in the 1960s, 1970s, and 1980s are taller, but not more impressive, especially when one considers the three million baskets full of earth required to create an earthen cone of the size of Barton's "stupendous evidence" before the age of steam.[8]

NATURAL HISTORY

Like the first Europeans to come into the Ohio watershed, those under the command of De Soto, the French explorer, Robert Cavelier, sieur de La Salle, did not leave us their impressions of its landscape or its animals.* George Washington was more forthcoming. A meticulous reporter and naturalist, Washington described the upper reaches of the Ohio in 1770 as they were before they became the rust belt. Pittsburgh was still Fort Pitt; and its principal landmark was still that great mound which was only removed in the 1840s, to make room for a Greek Revival bank.

Washington was not prone to literary effulgence, but he was moved to adjectives such as "remarkable" and "extraordinary" by the opulence and fecundity of the Great Valley. Deer and wild turkeys delighted him, and pigeons in their sky-darkening flocks. On the floodplain of the Kanawha, a tributary of the Ohio, he measured two of his sycamores: one was forty-five feet in circumference and the other thirty-one. A catfish came to his hook his companions said to be small for the waters of the Ohio, but it was larger than anything he had seen before.

The word "abounds" recurs constantly in Washington's Ohio River diaries: the shore of the river "abounds in wild geese and several kinds of ducks . . . many shallow ponds, the sides of which abounding in grass, invited innumerable quantities of wild fowl among which I saw a couple of birds in size between a swan and a goose; and in color somewhat between the two; being darker than the young swan and of a more sutty color: the cry of these was as unusual as the bird itself, as I never heard a noise resembling it before." It was probably a blue heron. In a few minutes he shot "five wild turkeys" for food.

---

*La Salle did not choose to inform posterity whether or not he actually penetrated to the Ohio Valley itself, during his mysterious absence in the winter of 1669–70, though some say he did.

A few days later, he wrote that "this country abounds in buffalo and wild game of all kinds as also in all kinds of wild fowl, there being in the bottoms a great many small grassy ponds or lakes which are full of swans, geese and ducks."[9]

Buffalo were as new to the Ohio Valley as Navajo were to the Southwest. Both may have been drawn out of the plains between the Rocky Mountains and the Mississippi, though in opposite directions, by the disruptions of the sixteenth century, possibly caused by the Great Dying. As we have noted, the population of the Ohio Valley dropped sharply between 1500 and 1550; among those who died were hunters, and in their absence, plains animals such as buffalo were free to invade areas previously too dangerous for them.

In the light of their rather sudden appearance in large numbers, the references to "buffalo," to "bull" and "calf," in Washington's accounts, carry shadows.

The presence of the animals so observed did not betoken a sweet domesticity but instead, disaster. The editors of Washington's diary have noted that they found it "curious" that "the Indians with him did not seem to know of the now famous mounds . . . which were a short distance from the river at this point; but in all probability, the unusual formation did not attract the savages' notice." This was not *very* curious: when Washington was there, in 1770, those Indians were still making reverent use of those mounds to bury their dead.* "Notice" was paid by the grave-goods they placed beside those they loved and lost. It is probable that they had no intention of "attracting the notice" of a stranger to sites they held sacred and secret, containing structures which could never have been built by "savages."†[10]

WASHINGTON AND PATRIMONY

Washington's patrimony was in land, though not much nor very good land. He inherited little from his ironmaster father. Only upon the deaths of other senior members of his family did he acquire the 2,500-acre "Little Hunting Creek Tract," which became the Mount Vernon estate. And his more ample holdings only came to him with his marriage to the land-rich widow Martha Custis, long after he had become capable of assessing the kind of land he wanted. That resulted from his

---

*These are what archaeologists sometimes call "intrusive burials."

†We will have considerably more to say about this matter. As these words are set in print, another site of this kind, which also contains one of the most important geometric earthworks in the Ohio Valley, was obliterated by the bulldozers of a gravel company. Who are the "savages" now?

own explorations and from a thorough acquaintance with painful lessons being learned by his neighbors, the Fairfaxes. They were heirs to the Culpeppers, who, by dint of service to the Crown in the English civil broils of the seventeenth century, had been provided 5,282,000 undefined acres of Virginia—a princely gesture from the Merry Monarch they soberly served.

Before the barons Fairfax arrived in Virginia to watch over their interests, a new sort of gentry was getting rich there, some through assiduous self-serving while acting as agents of the Fairfaxes. Chief among these was Robert Carter, called "King" Carter for the regal estate he acquired, including several hundred thousand of the choicest acres formerly possessed by his employers. By George Washington's time, this "king" and his sons had grown richer than the merely baronial Fairfaxes, who had too long remained absentee and absentminded.

Washington's experience of the West grew cumulatively, steadily, and deeply. In 1748, when he was sixteen, he began a survey of the Fairfax properties along the tributaries forming the upper Potomac.*

He already had heard much of the West, for after the death of his father, Washington became the ward of his older brothers Lawrence and Augustine, two of the organizers of the Ohio Land Company, which had 200,000 acres in the West, and Lawrence travelled to England in 1749 to secure 500,000 acres more. Conversation in their households was enlivened by tales of mountain passes and upland meadows and rivers rushing westward toward the Ohio.

With money saved from his surveying fees, Washington made his first western acquisition, 453 acres known as "Dutch George's"† on the upper Potomac. Further purchases followed, until, by the time he was twenty, he owned a total of 4,200 acres.

In his second and third surveying seasons, Washington crept closer to the mound country, but did not enter it until he made his celebrated reconnaissance of the French forts around Pittsburgh in 1753. This foray marked his entry into the Ohio Valley and thereby into watershed of the Mississippi, "the new empire" of the West.[11]

His next experiences beyond the Appalachians were not happy—his own campaign of 1754 and Braddock's defeat. As Washington marched back to the Ohio with the finally triumphant Bouquet, his eye was peeled for real estate, and his pen was busy urging that military roads be built to connect that real estate to Virginia. Not long after-

---

*Two years earlier, Peter Jefferson surveyed the southern extremities of the same holdings (his three-year-old son Thomas was left at home).

†The name was not a disrespectful implication that Washington was of German ancestry, but alluded to George Van Swearingen, of the frontier family into which Thomas Worthington married.

ward, he bought Great Meadows, the site of his capture by the French in 1754—for development. His defensive position there had been within "two natural entrenchments" which could be turned to a square by filling in the ends with wagons or a (new) palisade and "clearing the bushes." At the Forks of the Ohio, just north and west of the French earth-and-palisade fort, there loomed a larger earthwork about fifteen hundred years older, called the McKees Rocks Mounds, where Washington proposed a new fort be built.[12]

* * *

In a letter which might serve as the charter of American westering, Washington wrote to his neighbor, Captain John Posey, of "fortunes . . . made . . . by taking up and purchasing at very low rates the rich back lands which were thought nothing of in those days, but are now the most valuable lands we possess." Then came a hymn tune to the beat of which has marched every subsequent generation of Americans:

> I would . . . ask whether it would be better to labor under a load of debt, where you are, which must inevitably keep you in continual anxiety, and dread of your creditors . . . or to pluck up resolution . . . and disengage yourself from these encumbrances and vexations . . . to remove . . . where there is a moral certainty of laying the foundations of good estates to your children.[13]

Washington did not await the cessation of hostilities to resume his campaign for a western estate. In 1760 he met with a Captain Bullet in Alexandria to discuss an acquisition on the Ohio, and in 1763 joined with the Mississippi Company in petitioning the Crown for two and a half million acres at the intersection of the Ohio, Mississippi, and Tennessee Rivers. Their prospectus sang of "soil uncommonly fertile," "the fitness of the climate," and of equal or greater importance, "the goodness of the navigation." Washington wrote in his diary that the "climate [was] exceedingly fine, the soil remarkably good; the lands well watered with good streams, and full level enough for any kind of cultivation. . . . Game which is so plenty as not only to render the transportation of provisions there (bread only excepted) altogether unnecessary, but to enrich the adventurers with the peltry."[14] As we shall see, this was also good country in which to prospect for ancient Indian sculptures. It lay not far north of Obion.

INDIAN GEOPOLITICS

There were, of course, the Indians to contend with. Washington's Indian policies altered during the course of his career as his role among them enlarged from that of a scout to that of a statesman. He had much to learn from them. At first it had been forest lore and the maneuvering of a canoe. Later, the Iroquois, in particular, gave training in a broader kind of survival, how a small nation may maneuver among Great Powers and thus learn coalition politics.

In the 1750s, it was necessary for the Virginia frontiersman to become acquainted with the Balkan intricacies of Ohio Valley politics. The Iroquois Confederacy of nations, though based in western New York and central Pennsylvania, was influential as far as the Mississippi, where their war parties encountered those of the powerful, numerous, and sophisticated Cherokee of the southern Appalachians. Some of the smaller tribes were powerful as well. Among these were the Shawnee, who were reoccupying the area after a century of disease and warfare had left it as devastated as portions of Germany after the Thirty Years War.

These Indian nations had already been much reduced in numbers by the Great Dying. Their wars of the seventeenth century, made the more lethal by European weapons, further diminished them. No more than sixty to seventy thousand remained in the entire region from the Finger Lakes to Duluth where once dwelt a half million or more, but those sixty to seventy thousand had their own ideas about the future.

The agreements they won from Bouquet and Dunmore appeared to install a great reservation system north of the Ohio and east of the Mississippi. It was a triumph for Iroquois diplomacy, which bartered away the lands of the others, hoping to turn the European advance toward the south and west. The Iroquois themselves were left in possession of the upper Susquehanna Valley and their traditional lands around the Finger Lakes of New York.

Though Iroquois and Cherokee had demonstrated that the heartland and its eastern margins were one, from the perspective of Whitehall the Appalachians were still a significant geopolitical boundary. British imperial policy regarded the West Indies as of first importance, the coastal colonies of North America as secondary, and the Great Valley as a bore. Certainly it was not worth the continuous vexations stirred by taxation to finance Western military adventures. American auxiliaries did not take well to discipline, and by 1760 the gentlemen of England had concluded that it was not desirable that such unruly colonials spread themselves further. Asserting an intent to mollify the Indians, a royal proclamation was issued forbidding the Americans to continue invading the valleys of the Ohio and Tennessee, until the king's "future pleasure be known." Thus was established the famous "Proclamation Line."

The Virginians were furious; after a pause, they became ingenious. The King of England had drawn a line. The imperatives of geography drew *them* irresistibly to transgress it. The West called, as the moon once upon a time called the tide to flood the toes of Canute. Washington refused to be bound by the "pleasure" of King George, and ordered William Crawford to go beyond the proclamation line, instructing him to neglect no "present opportunity of hunting out good lands." Washington did, however, entreat Crawford to "keep this whole matter a profound secret," and to pretend that he was hunting animals, instead.[15]

Five years later the Proclamation Line was withdrawn, permitting Washington to do his work in the light of day. He sought to pick up what he could of the two hundred thousand acres Governor Dunmore had promised him and the other Virginian militiamen who had gone west to fight the French and Indians; he pursued the hope that the Crown itself might perform upon another promise to grant land to militia officers; and finally he expected the king to create negotiable land claims as payment to traders who had suffered from the raids of Pontiac's forces.

After 1770, Washington found himself once again in the West, pursuing these opportunities. Crawford made their tactics explicit: "the man that is strong and able to make others afraid of him seems to have the best chance." Washington has sometimes been described as unimaginative. But with regard to the West, he was capable of feats of speculative thought. At the end of the 1760s his ambitions reached the lower Mississippi, where the climate might be even more benign than Ohio, and navigation to European markets made easy by way of the Gulf.

In 1775, on the brink of his revolutionary service, Washington planned another real estate campaign on the Ohio, and in 1784 wrote of a desire to travel the Great Lakes as far west as Detroit and then down the great river to New Orleans, passing through the heart of the new empire. "I shall not rest contented," he said, "till I have explored the western country."[16]

During the Revolutionary War, General Washington learned much about symbolic gestures, especially how certain truths are associated with certain colors. In 1784, facing fourteen squatters who had occupied his property in defiance of his title, he pulled from his sleeve a handkerchief the color of blood. Holding it by the corner, he said: "Gentlemen, I will have this land just as surely as I now have this handkerchief." He got the land.[17] Whether in search of land or in its defense, he was a hard man. He wrote an old companion in arms who had become his custodian in the West that despite "the friendship that has long subsisted between us," he would brook neither distraction nor lassitude in acquisition. "Every day or hour misapplied, is a loss to me. . . . [No] part of your time [may be spent] to other business; or to amusements. . . . [You are] a man who has engaged his time and service to conduct and manage my interest on the Ohio. . . ."[18]

In the 1950s and 1960s, historians delighted themselves with accounts of Washington's overreaching, dissembling, and strong-arm tactics during his campaign to build a western estate. There was truth in their stories, and truth, too in their insistence that he sometimes cloaked interest in principle. When his lower Mississippi speculations were aborted by the *British* governor, Washington generalized the action as "proof of [their] . . . malignant disposition toward Americans." When other *Americans,* in this case the state legislature of Pennsylvania, attempted to regulate him out of large tracts of prime land, he requested that an old comrade in the record office circumvent those regulations "if the matter can be so managed on your entry book." Closer to home, the royal Governor of Virginia frustrated his Ohio plans by issuing a regulation against block-buying of large tracts. Washington responded by instructing his younger brother Charles to buy under his own name, and to cover the subterfuge by denying to anyone "any part of this letter, so that you can be drawn into no trouble."[19]

Washington's speculations reached their climax when he sent a letter to a fellow veteran of the French campaign stating what is transparently a falsehood, that he had *not* used his position as their former colonel to select out of that allotted to all his comrades the best land along the Ohio for himself.

Those who complain against that sort of thing in the real estate business call it "cherry picking"; in 1770, the complainers against Washington had not themselves troubled to go to the West to do the picking. That is how he saw the matter, it seems. He left the shelter of a more famous cherry tree to utter these words:

> No country ever was, or ever will be settled without some indulgence; What inducements have men to explore uninhabited wilds, but the prospect of getting good lands? Would any man waste his time, expose his fortune, nay life, in such a search, if he was to share the good and the bad with those that come after him?[20]

THE HEAD AND THE HEART—
LOVE FOR A CONTINENT

Washington's proclamation might have been penned by Cortez or Pizzaro, by Strongbow in Ireland or by Roger I upon the shores of Sicily. Yet it is not a complete statement of what the West was to Washington. Washington is the despair of psychobiographers because he revealed so little of himself except in action. He did not ruminate, or, if he did, he did not tell us about it. He wrote excellent natural history; that was safe enough; his letters and diaries he took to be the legitimate business of posterity; therefore they were intended to reveal only what he wanted us to know. Matters he thought private, though not in the least discreditable to him, were only implied or left in silence. We know that Washington's West was a place of wonder or enchantment, in its profusion of animals, its strange people, and magnificent ruins. He gave avid descriptions of these western peoples, animals, and scenery, he reported conversations with Indians, and wrote to them letters and addresses which, as he adjusted them *in his own hand,* reveal how his own feelings about them differed from those of his draftsmen. But he left no *Notes on Virginia* or *Notes on the Ohio* beyond those in his journals; his self-image was as different from the scholar-statesman Jefferson as his images of Blacks and Indians from Jefferson's.

Washington left us enough to know this about him: he was respectful of Indian religion and Indian ways of life-ways. He did not insist that the only good Indian was either dead or assimilated. He extended his interest in contemporary Indian life to ancient Indian architecture, and at the end of his life expressed regret that he lacked time to pursue those interests. And, in the same final years, he took a most un-Jeffersonian view of the slavery question and its relationship to the politics of Virginia.

Even then, it is true, he was prone to those acquisitive frenzies with which all Americans addicted to real estate may sympathize. After his presidency, in 1797, as in the 1780s after the Revolution, he was forced to sell western land. Dreams of future gain were yielding to the painful necessities of the present. Divestiture was becoming urgent, goaded by disappointed pride, a disappointment of special poignancy because administered by his creditors. Totting up his gains and losses in western real estate, Washington was led into alliteration, as we often are when moved: "I have found that landed property at a distance from the Proprietor, is attended with more plague than profit."* [21]

There is more in this wry admission than cool economic judgment— there always is more in George Washington's stately prose than its bare meaning. In the best of the multivolume biographies of Washington, James Thomas Flexner offered a suggestion as to Washington's

---

*Albert Gallatin came to a like pass, thirty-six years later, and seconded the motion. In a letter to his son James about his Ohio Valley lands he wrote: "It is a troublesome and unproductive property, that has plagued me all my life. I could not have invested my patrimony in a more unprofitable manner." (January 13, 1827, quoted in Adams, *Gallatin*, pp. 621–3.)

character that has drawn derision from those made uncomfortable by
biographers who sympathize with their subjects:

> In no other direction did Washington demonstrate such acquisitiveness
> as in his quest for the ownership of land. . . . The yearning of a childless
> man for tens of thousands of acres, many of which could easily prove
> financial drains throughout his own lifetime, might well have been an
> expression of love, a form of worship for the vast American continent.[22]

Flexner was careful with his words; he meant "love." Love is not always generous. Though Washington demonstrated a remarkable absence of jealousy in his love of women (one woman, to be precise, and
she associated with the West—as we shall see), as to Western lands he
was a fiercely jealous lover. And the "new and rising empire of the
West" comprised for Washington lands situated upon navigable rivers;
rich in soil, promising an abundance of crops." More than that, however, it was a presence, a gravitational force in his psyche, drawing him
into the Great Valley.

That gravitational power had been reinforced by experience: there
are many kinds of love. Washington first went westward in the company of the friend most important to him during his young manhood,
George William Fairfax of Belvoir, the mulatto son of Colonel William
Fairfax of Belvoir.[23] Washington and Fairfax were united in youthful,
heroic adventures during that phase in life in which young men go
forth into the forest to contend with dragons and make their fortune.
In Washington's psychic story, that archetypally driven experience occurred in the West.

These relationships do not evaporate; they form crystals of character, setting the context for future experience. In Washington's case, it
has become conventional to place George William Fairfax in the
shadow of his wife, Sally. It is said with a smirk that she was the primary reason for Washington's regular visits to Belvoir. But Washington made no effort to deny either to Fairfax or, later, to his own wife,
that he fell in love with Sally. When your dearest friend marries an
attractive woman you have two reasons to come under their rooftree.
There is not a wisp of evidence that Washington ever betrayed his
friendship with George Williams Fairfax, a friendship grounded in
their adventures in the West.

After heroic companionship came initiation into battle—the whistle
of bullets, the rattle of drums, the skirl of the pipes, the abyss of disgrace and the redemption of victory, the first thrill of command and
success. Graven upon George Washington's memory were these excite-
ments, and with them, the West itself—an open scene with boon com-

panions of all classes, coming to a respect—at first rueful and then affectionate—for the Indians who lived there.

WASHINGTON AND SLAVERY

In his old age, Washington, always searching for companionship, attempted to induce David Humphreys, his former military aide, to leave his post as minister to Spain and come to Mount Vernon, there to become "a companion in my latter days." Humphreys replied that he was getting married, to which Washington responded that the news "annihilated every hope" since he had resolved never to have "two women in my house when I am there myself."[24]

It was at once an admission of loneliness for friendship and an avuncular joke. Washington understood that Humphreys was right to have other interests, now, than tending even so eminent an old man as he, so he allowed himself a flash of his ancient humor. Humphreys had been his confidant. Their correspondence reveals something about the character of Washington and about the evolution of his ideas. He confided to Humphreys his first full and public expression on the matter of slavery:

> The unfortunate condition of the persons whose labors I . . . employed has been the only unavoidable subject of regret. . . . [To] lay a foundation to prepare the rising generation for a destiny different from that in which they were born, affords some satisfaction to my mind, and could not, I hoped, be displeasing to the justice of the creator.[25]

Washington had been coming slowly toward this way of thinking. In 1774, he described the rule of plantation owners over slaves as "arbitrary." As he took command of the Continental Army in 1776, he left his Virginia behind. Though he had traveled outside the Old Dominion before, even his western explorations had been brief, and he had never lived for more than a few weeks in the North. Now he found himself beyond the Mason-Dixon Line in the company of idealistic young officers, both French and American, to whom slavery was abominable.

Lafayette, Alexander Hamilton, and John Laurens became Washington's sons by adoption. Within their circle, he reflected upon the matter of race; it seems probable that they reawakened in him doubts about the truth of the view of Blacks conventional among his Virginia peers. Those doubts could not have been wholly quiet during his friendship with their predecessor in his affections, George William Fairfax. Fairfax was a living reminder to Washington that black people, or partly black people, might be worthy of his respect and affection.

Over the next two years, Washington observed the bravery of free Blacks in a series of New England campaigns. Even before Hamilton and Laurens sought his support for the creation of a Black Corps, he endorsed the desegregation of the troops provided by Rhode Island, and, after 1782, recruitment of free Blacks in the South as well.

After the war, as president, he found himself for the first time a city dweller living amid Blacks who were both free and skilled as artisans. Philadelphia was the capital of the United States until the city named after Washington was ready for occupancy by his successor, John Adams. Philadelphia was also the center of abolitionist agitation. Wartime experiences had changed Washington's views somewhat, and he had permitted himself to treat free Blacks as citizens, but his racial views were still evolving. His first response to abolitionist Philadelphia was to send his household slaves back to Mount Vernon to avoid the automatic freedom required by the laws of Pennsylvania.

By September, 1793, however, he had reached the conclusion that he wished to "liberate a certain species of property which I possess very repugnantly to my feelings." This plan, revealed only to his secretary and stripped from the documents kept in his public records, was to sell Mount Vernon to British investors with the slaves attached. They would be hired by the new owners "as they would any other laborers." Washington would continue to bear the cost of bringing up the children of his former slaves until they, too, could support themselves.[26] To his chagrin he found no takers among the English; they were still unwilling to deal with the leader of so recent a rebellion, and the laws of Virginia were not hospitable to manumission, however disguised.

When Washington left the presidency and Philadelphia, in 1797, he reversed his previous response to the laws of Pennsylvania. Instead of sneaking his household salves *away,* he sneaked them *out* of his household *into* freedom, where their escape could not be detected by the Virginians.* Once back at Mount Vernon, surrounded by implacable hostility to manumission on the part of all but a few of his neighbors,

---

*So secretive was he that he was only found out (by Flexner) in the 1980s. Michael Zuckerman admonishes that these paragraphs are too generous to Washington's quiet liberation of his slaves. "Even when he does conclude to free his slaves, finally, he does it . . . in darkest secrecy, so that the public impact of his change of convictions is nil. No bully pulpit for George on this matter." (Letter of November 27, 1992.) I think the action is important, none the less, as a statement of his own views. He was still President; if he had made a public expression of his antipathy to slavery he might have brought to an end the fragile experiment of which he was in charge. Perhaps he should have done so; it can be argued that it would have been better if he had. But that is an argument other than one that would be appropriate to discussion of the actions of a private citizen.

he encouraged his slaves to marry, lest they be separated. In his will he required that his executors support the old and infirm among his slaves and provide to the young the same education received by Whites until they were twenty-five and ready for employment. By then, he hoped, the world would be ready for them. Finally, they were all to be set free at the death of his wife. Since many of them had come to the family from her, and since she would otherwise have been left with no one to tend her in her last years, this seemed a reasonable provision.

A gulf had opened between Washington and other planters. By the end of the 1790s, he rendered his judgment on the Peculiar Institution to a visitor, John Bernard: "Nothing but the rooting out of slavery can perpetuate the existence of our union by consolidating it in a common bond of principle."[27] One might expect such language from Abraham Lincoln in 1864, or from John Quincy Adams in 1840, but not from an elderly Virginia planter in 1797.

By then, Washington was full of surprises: he told Edmund Randolph, who had been his attorney general, that should the Union separate north from south, he had made up his mind "to move and be of the northern."[28]

WASHINGTON'S WESTERN COLONY

By the 1790s, Virginia's thin red soil was nearing exhaustion. Entire townships were being abandoned to broom-sedge and briars, as blood-red rivulets carried their topsoil to become mud flats in the Chesapeake. Farmers looked enviously at "the . . . immense . . . fertile Country between the Blue Ridge and the Allegheny Mountains"—Washington's words—and beyond. In the Shenandoah Valley a Washington-Mason-Worthington investment program commenced which soon lapped over into the Ohio watershed. "How trifling" even the Shenandoah seemed "when viewed upon that immeasurable scale, which is inviting our attention" beyond the Alleghenies.[29]

For fifty years, Washington lavished his surplus cash upon the purchase and development of lands in the West and devoted his not inconsiderable imagination to schemes for settling thereupon indentured servants from the Rhineland, dispirited Irish, Highland Scots, and Dutch refugees from the revolutionary broils of their own country. He sent to "the Kanawhas" (the two valleys of the Kanawha Rivers in what is now West Virginia) expeditions of slaves and indentured servants from his own lands in Virginia, though often the ranks of colonists were depleted by Indian skirmishes and the defections of both slaves and servants. He sought to buy all the buffalo calves he could find on the market, asking his managers to tame them if possible, so they might be sent forth to the Kanawhas to breed, multiply, and make him a herd.

On his expeditions into the upper Ohio Valley, Washington searched out its most fertile and sheltered river terraces. Their value as farmland determined his choices, the reason his search was of such great assistance to archaeology was that his criteria were those of the unmechanized farming of his time, which matched quite closely those of other searchers, two thousand years earlier. The Adena/Hopewell people had been farmers, too, though they practiced a form of agriculture even simpler than Washington's, working only with hoes, without plows and without growing much corn. Like all frontier farmers, they supplemented with game the diet they cultivated on their farms, but the soil and the sun remained the most important factors in their selection of homesteads.

If an archaeologist were today to seek out the architecture created by such a people, there would be no better plan of campaign than to follow the tracks of Washington, especially his survey in 1770. Trained in agriculture, and with an eye for terrain convenient to river transportation, he moved with the sureness of purpose made possible by ready cash.

So did Gallatin, in the 1780s, thanks to his remittances from Geneva; he came bounding along after Washington, following the marks of his surveying expedition of 1757, of his map-making of 1770, and of the real estate survey which had brought the Great Personage back to the banks of the Cheat River in 1784.

WASHINGTON'S MOUNDS

In 1770, Washington's inadvertent but systematic archaeological survey commenced at the point at which the first, large mounds appear on the portage trails between the tributaries of the Potomac and the uppermost reaches of the Ohio. Thence, his explorations took him down the Monongahela to the Ohio, along the Ohio all the way to the Great Kanawha, and up the Kanawha's lower reaches. By 1794, he owned "on the Ohio and Great Kanawha about 33,000 Acres in eight surveys." His survey map is a guide to what Cyrus Thomas of the Smithsonian described in 1894 as "the most extensive and interesting ancient works to be found in the state of West Virginia." "Washington Bottom" is especially dense with prehistoric mounds.[30]

Thomas's map of the Kanawha earthworks and today's Geological Survey maps of the area show Washington's footprints: brooks flowing into the river are still called "Washington Creek," "Cabell Creek" (named for one of Washington's partners) and, as if to remind us of his role as Cincinnatus, "Tiber Creek."

Washington could hardly ignore the mounds; these earthen buildings were by far the largest architecture he had ever seen or ever would see.

On November 1, 1770, he camped near the base of the McCullogh Mound, three hundred feet in circumference and prominent upon a hilltop; on the 8th he disembarked and walked upon the shore of the river. He could have seen from his tent the "sacra via" and mounds at Marietta, had it not been raining so hard.

From the 11th through the 19th he worked his way slowly upstream, past dense concentrations of earthworks. He spent three days inspecting the terrain around Half Moon Mound and the great earthen cone at Grave Creek. He was at the mounds at "Indian Town" on the 15th, and around the mound centers at Beech Bottom on the 16th.

THE INVENTORY

Neither Washington nor Gallatin limited themselves to the western provinces claimed by Virginia, which extended to the doors of the slatternly cluster of cabins becoming Pittsburgh. Washington plunged heavily in Ohio, Kentucky, Indiana, and Pennsylvania lands—an aggregate of about 60,000 acres. Gallatin used the money sent by his relatives in Geneva to acquire 184,786 acres in what is now West Virginia, and then continued to speculate elsewhere, especially in Ohio. Next to "Washington land" there came to be "Gallatin land." Next to "Washington Bottom" on the Ohio, Gallatin and his partners built their own outpost.*

In a letter to the Marquis de Lafayette, Washington had made much of his desire to return from the Revolutionary army as "a private citizen on the banks of the Potomac . . . [and to repose] under the shadow of my own vine and my own fig-tree, free from the bustle of a camp and the busy scenes of public life." But the shadow of his own vine and fig tree did not solace him for long, nor did he "move gently down the stream of life." He paddled up the Potomac and busied himself once again with his western interests.[31]

He set out his program in another sort of letter, written to his agent for western lands; having "closed all my transactions with the public,

---

*Washington's purchases north of the Ohio were on Indian lands, in violation of treaties. But, so far as I have been able to determine, they were not made after he entered the presidency.

it now behooves me to look into my own private business, no part of which," he said, "seems to call louder for my attention, than my concerns with you."[32]

Washington told others, and probably himself, that when he went to the West in 1784 it was to divest himself of his holdings. Instead, he did what speculators often do. He "traded up." That required him to organize land into units for sale, to drive off squatters, and to find out how to reach his properties with turnpikes and canals. By the time of his death he had *added* 3,051 acres in Ohio on the Great Miami River and 5,000 more in Kentucky to the 4,675 acres he owned in Pennsylvania, 9,744 along the Ohio, and 43,466 along the Kanawhas. In 1789, he even parted with his prize stallion "Magnolia" in exchange for 5,000 acres along a creek in Kentucky.

The West, the Great West, was always present for Washington, beckoning beyond Wildcat Mountain, beyond the Blue Ridge, the Massanutten, and the Laurel Highlands. Even at Mount Vernon it was there, undeniable, drawing energy away from the house itself, away from the Atlantic world.

MOUNDS AT MOUNT VERNON

The Mount Vernon estate is laid out in three parts, the Potomac shore, the house and buildings, and the West. The famous portico looks out toward the broad tidal estuary upon which, in Washington's day, ships passed regularly from his port at Alexandria to the West Indian market.

Sitting in its shade in his favored chair, Washington could close his eyes in satisfaction, envisaging Caribbean customers for his wheat. Their sugar plantations needed food, which he supplied at prices sustaining him in comfort while his tobacco-growing neighbors languished. He never forgot the importance of that southward aspect, retaining his brother's name for the house, Mount Vernon, in commemoration of the Caribbean triumphs of Admiral Vernon, under whom that brother had served. Washington's only sea voyage was to Barbados, accompanying that brother in hopes of restoring his fragile health.

If one prunes away that famous West Indian portico, the house is English. Washington remodeled it constantly; the final changes provided elegant Adamesque interior plasterwork to render the dining room fashionable, as the Fairfax's Belvoir, next door, had been fashionable in Washington's youth. Architecturally, Mount Vernon remained part of the old empire.

The western outlook of the estate was set toward the new empire rising beyond the sunset. On this side, Washington surrounded his English house, gardens, and lawn with a casually planted "wilderness." "Wildernesses" were common enough in Italian, English, and French garden design, having been created first as transition zones between his close-cropped, neat formal gardens and his farming operations.* But Washington's was a wilderness with an American difference. It swept in two broad curves to reveal, at the end, "an open and full view of the distant woods." He was emphatic about the importance of this invitation to the west, remonstrating with Samuel Vaughn, who had made a drawing of the estate, that Vaughn had erred in omitting that opening—"you have closed the prospect." Vaughn made an even greater error, however: he failed to emphasize that the view was framed by two artificial earthen mounds.[33]

Washington commenced the construction of those mounds soon after the earth was warm in March, 1787. It is said that he took the idea for them from Batty Langley's *New Principles of Gardening*. However, Langley's handbook merely suggested that while a *new* house was under construction, the earth taken from digging out its foundations be moved a little into the garden "for raising of mounts, from which, fine views may be seen." Washington was not disposing of earth from digging a foundation nor were his mounds nearby. They were built of earth dug and transported for the purpose, and at a considerable distance from an old house.[34] Furthermore, he planned that the mounds not be looked *from* but be looked *at*. Why? Merely "in order to plant weeping willow thereon?" A great fuss—and two large piles of earth—if that were all. The best clue to his intentions is that he told Vaughn he was staging a view to the west: "The trees terminate with two mounds of earth on each side of which grow weeping willows leaving an open and full view of the distant woods. The mounds are at sixty yards apart."[35]

Washington's open, U-shaped design for the Mount Vernon estate, set next to that drawn by the unfortunate Vaughn, suggests two other plans. One might be a template for a horseshoe magnet, open to the West. The other might be Jefferson's plan for the hilltop at Monticello. All have the same orientation, the same closure at the east open to the powerful attraction of the great valley of the west.†

---

*In Italy, nearly all of those Renaissance wildernesses have disappeared along with the farms, creating the impression that Italian gardens were entirely severe and tame.

†Most landscape historians would probably derive Washington's mounds from British "mounts," or Thames-side follies, or Langley's instruction. But most landscape historians have never been to Grave Creek.

WASHINGTON AND WESTERN ARCHITECTURE

After George Washington's death, the pages covering the 6th through the 16th of November in the diary of his Ohio exploration of 1770 were so chewed by rodents as to be intelligible only in patches. One of the unchewed sections permits us to place him in the rain opposite the Marietta mounds. His subsequent camps can only be located because they are listed on a separate page; we have lost his observations on what he saw as he passed hundreds of ancient Indian buildings along the Ohio River and its tributaries, Grapevine, Capeening, and Grave creeks, and many villages still occupied by Indians. On pages still surviving, Washington noted that he frequently met parties of Iroquois and Shawnee on the river, led by people who recognized him from his campaign of 1757–58, when they were all allied together against the French.

The first entry in his diary that can be fully redeemed from the rodents, after that for Marietta, is apparently that for November the 16th. Its tone is different from that prevailing through the 5th. The sequence of cool, businesslike reports on soil conditions, trees, and ease of navigation has been broken. The language has become almost domestic in feeling, encouraged by the emergence of a character who had previously seemed unimportant. "Here it was for the first time the old Indian spoke of a fine piece of land and beautiful place for a house, and in order to give me a more lively idea of it, chalked out the situation upon his deer skin."

The architectural sketch of "the old Indian" seems to have remained in Washington's mind, together with its setting. "The old Indian" had a name, which can be translated as "The Pheasant." He was a sagacious old bird, discerning his listener's nature, and addressing that nature with sureness of aim: "The spot he recommends for a house lies very high, commanding a prospect of a great deal of level land below on the creek, the ground about it very rich and a fine spring in the middle of it, about which many buffaloes use and have made great roads."[36]

The creek, wrote Washington, was named for the buffalo, "Bull Creek." It may well be that today called "Buffalo Creek," which lies about five miles east of Washington's campsite near the Beech Bottom Mounds, running, as he said it did, "parallel with the long reach in the Ohio . . . having fine bottoms which widen as it extends in to the country, and towards the head of it is large bodies of level rich land."[37]

The site proposed by The Pheasant for Washington's house in the

West was not only beautiful, it was provisioned with a variety of sources of fresh protein. In the lowlands were "many shallows . . . abounding in . . . wild fowl . . . buffalo and wild game of all kinds." And it might be conveniently served without paddling all the way up the creek by disembarking from the Ohio at a gradual landing, where a storehouse might be situated. Such an easy entrepot would be "very necessary as a stage or lodgement, in coming up the river."[38]

In 1773, Washington wrote Thomas Lewis that he would dispose of any of his holdings except the Round Bottom, which still awaited the "lodgement." Washington informed Lewis that this was "the only piece of land I had upon the Ohio, between Fort Pitt and the Kanawhas." But that was not the case. He owned thousands of acres along that stretch of the river, with a multitude of other choices. It seems that he felt it unnecessary to give Lewis a more sentimental reason—an architectural suggestion from an Indian.* [39]

On October 24th, 1770, Washington had camped at a more obvious choice for a house, on a broad terrace at the mouth of the Great Kanawha River, a place already hallowed by the ruins a large ancient Indian settlement. His descendants made use of it during the nineteenth century, calling it Point Pleasant. It had been his chief experimental station in western colonization, where potatoes, turnips, and corn were to be raised amid the two thousand peach trees he caused to be planted.

But in 1774, Point Pleasant was stained by the blood of Indians and Virginians in a needless slaughter, and polluted by the memory of a deliberate humiliation of Washington himself at the hands of Lord Dunmore, the last colonial governor of Virginia. Dunmore took the colonial militia into a war as much against the western aspirations of his competitors, the Penn family, proprietors of Pennsylvania, as against Cornstalk, leader of the Shawnee.

Dunmore was engaged in a parade of force along the Ohio when Cornstalk surprised a detachment of Dunmore's force at Point Pleasant, and in a long day of confused skirmishing, knifing, and scalping,

---

*Here is a summary of Washington's lands along the Ohio and its tributaries, compiled from his own records and secondary sources:

    3,051 acres at the mouth of the Little Miami

    23,216 acres on the Great Kanawha, above its junction with the Ohio, and 209 acres at Burning Spring, on that river near Charleston

    4,470 acres at Big Bent, just above the Great Kanawha

    2,448 acres 16 miles below the Little Kanawha

    2,343 acres at the junction of the Little Kanawha and the Ohio

    1,293 acres at Round Bottom, just south of Wheeling

    2,813 acres at Miller's Run, west of Pittsburgh

    1,656 acres at Simpson's (Perryopolis) south of Pittsburgh

    236 acres at Great Meadows

each side lost 150 men. Washington was in Philadelphia at the time, busy with revolution—one might say, from a British point of view, with sedition. Dunmore sent Washington's colonists packing, decreeing that his claim to the ground was void on a technicality.

By the time Washington received his next report on his colony, the fields were deserted, the cabins burnt. Where he had planned an exemplary and profitable settlement, desolation reigned. The Washingtons never found a purchaser for this cursed spot. As late as the 1830s, the general's nephew, Samuel Washington, was still eking out a living there, tending the general's "Battle Sword" until it found its way to the Smithsonian.

Dunmore's gesture of disdain toward Washington personally would have been enough, but the royal governor infuriated him on broader grounds: he made known his determination to prevent further settlements north of the Ohio. Some of Washington's comrades from the 1758 campaign were already there, and more were on the way. On November 5, 1774, they delivered the famous "Fort Gower Address" declaring that they would no longer serve either the Crown or its appointed governors. They would go into battle only for the honor of America and Virginia. The Revolution had begun.*

During the feverish period between Washington's retirement as commander-in-chief of the Continental Army, at the end of 1783, and the beginning of his presidency in 1789, he was engaged in business in the Ohio Valley rather than rumination about it. By 1788, his desire to bring his inventory of land to market had become frenetic; all else gave way to it. He refused to be distracted even by subjects which he acknowledged were of importance and which might, in other circumstances, have elicited his views. As a result, we have been deprived of the last two occasions on which he might have told us how he felt about the Native American architecture he had seen in the West.

Though he gave his gardeners instructions for the mounds at Mount Vernon, he did not pause to inform posterity why he did so, nor did he allow himself to enter into an exchange of views on mound builders. General Richard Butler, an old companion now exploring the West, sent him an "Indian Vocabulary," with the marginal note that he had compiled it after traveling extensively in the West. Washington acknowledged that Butler had been noble to have "exerted . . . [himself] to throw light upon the original history of this country, to gratify the curiosity of the philosopher." Noble, he seemed to be saying, if one had time, as he did not, for philosophy. He admitted that he had al-

---

*We will have occasion to observe that when Washington himself had the responsibility for a governmental policy toward Indians and Indian lands, he took precisely the position which he had earlier detested at the hands of Dunmore.

lowed himself to give thought "respecting the different tribes of Indians inhabiting the Western Country [and] the traditions which prevail among them," and allowed that Butler's research might prove to be "very valuable and may lead to some useful discoveries [about] those works which are found upon the Ohio and other traces of the country's having been once inhabited by a race of people more ingenious, at least, if not more civilized than those who at present dwell there. . . . Any clue . . . which can lead to a knowledge of these must be gratefully received."[40]

But at the moment "clues" of a different sort would have a *more* grateful reception. Butler "had opportunities of gaining extensive . . . information respecting the western territory . . . its rivers, and the face of the country," and Washington could use such information to interest potential purchasers. Leaving philosophy aside, he fired off a barrage of inquiries about "direct, practicable, and easy communication" between Lake Erie, the Ohio, and the Potomac, especially questions as to the routing of canals. And that was that.[41]

The third opening had closed.

AN ARCHITECTURAL SKETCH FOR A WESTERN HOME: WHAT SORT OF HOUSE MIGHT IT HAVE BEEN?

Washington might have been content with a good tavern, a store, or a fort on the Ohio, with a country seat on the Bull Creek site. Even today, amid the Rust Belt, it is a "fine piece of land." There he might have recalled the lines he copied while learning penmanship as a boy:

> These are the things, which once possess'd
> Will make a life that's truly bless'd:
> A good estate on healthy soil,
> Not Got by Vice nor yet by toil . . .[42]

For George Washington, one of the things to be enjoyed upon a good estate was good architecture. He was a man of settled views on this, as on many matters, ordaining that his western tenants build log structures harmoniously proportioned in sixteen-by-eighteen-foot modules. He conducted his own building campaigns on the mansion at Mount Vernon, with Batty Langley's patterns in hand, and drew the elevation and plan for his parish church at Pohick.

The house at Mount Vernon had not been truly his. He inherited it.

The best he could do was to remodel it with a result the ungainliness of which has only been redeemed by its familiarity.

What might he have done for himself from the ground up? Washington might have set aside the showy Palladianism of Mount Vernon, recalling the greatest Western house he had seen as a young man, Greenway Court, Lord Fairfax's hunting lodge in the Shenandoah, where he and George William Fairfax rested often on their way to the West.*

We have come back to the Fairfaxes, and to Washington's friendships in the West. The most poignant demonstration of Washington's desire to rekindle in a companionable old age the recollected joys of his youth was a letter sent to Sally Fairfax not long before his death. She was now an elderly widow, living in England.[†]

The Belvoir estate had fallen into desuetude. Some Virginia superpatriots were seeking to treat all Fairfaxes as enemy aliens. But the grand old man of American independence, married and in the full glare of public scrutiny of his every action, wrote a woman he had loved in their youth, as he had loved her husband, asking her to return to Belvoir and to "spend the evening of your life" as a neighbor.[43]

[None of the] many important events [that had intervened] nor all of them together have been able to eradicate from my mind the recollection of those happy moments, the happiest in my life, which I have enjoyed in your company. . . . It is a matter of sore regret, when I cast my eyes

---

*Greenway Court had an additional distinction, of which we have only become aware in the twentieth century. It is near the Thunderbird Site, where about nine thousand years earlier there had been built the earliest building which archaeology has found in the United States so far. In the earth at Thunderbird were left the marks of a central structure, and, if we read them right, an additional row of post-holes to support an amenity of the sort Washington called a "piazza" at Mt. Vernon. Virginia not only possesses the most famous veranda in America, but, it seems, the oldest, as well.

(Joe Saunders informs me in a letter dated August 11, 1992, that at Monte Sano, Louisiana, a layer of charcoal covers a rectangular post-hole pattern. The carbon dates for the charcoal are about 5000 B.C.)

There are other sites of ancient human habitation in the Ohio Valley, including one in Medina County, Ohio, but so far as I know none show evidence of earlier evidence of architecture than Thunderbird.

†The younger Fairfaxes had returned to England in 1773. Lord Thomas, sixth Baron Fairfax, bachelor uncle to George William, remained quietly at Greenway Court throughout the Revolution, still vigorous enough at eighty-four to bring "a negro wench" to bed. He appears to have shared a preference for women of African descent with his cousin, the father of George. He is generally described as "the bachelor lord," or as a person who disliked women. But his account book shows that until very late in life he sustained an interest in them if they were black. (See Brown, *Virginia Baron*, p. 230.)

Fairfax sank into his final coma as the bells were being rung to celebrate Washington's victory at Yorktown.

toward Belvoir which I often do, to reflect that the former inhabitants of it, with whom we lived in such harmony and friendship, no longer reside there, and that the ruins can only be viewed as the memento of former pleasures.

She did not choose to come. Perhaps she was deterred by the condition of Belvoir, or by consorting with the leader of a revolution, or by the feelings of that leader's wife.

CHAPTER SIX

THE CINCINNATI

Thirteen years after they dined together beside the Cheat in 1784, Washington and Gallatin dined again, at the White House. Judging from what Gallatin wrote to his wife of *that* occasion, not much had changed in their relationship. "He [the president] looked, I thought, more than usually grave, cool and reserved. Mrs. W. inquired about you, so that you may suppose yourself still in the good graces of our most gracious queen, who, by the by, continues to be a very good-natured and amiable woman. Not so her husband . . . but that between you and me, for I hate treason. . . . "[1]

The final reference was to the most celebrated contention between Gallatin and Washington during the intervening years. In 1794, Gallatin was at the head of those Democratic Societies whose petitions on behalf of the whiskey-distilling frontiersmen of Pennsylvania were thought by President Washington to transgress beyond impertinence toward treason. The president was bedeviled by insurrections and threats of secession across the West, and exhausted from days in the saddle. As he drilled an army to be sent against the "Whiskey Rebellion" in Maryland and Pennsylvania, Washington sent an address to Congress on November 19, 1794, using the most intemperate words of his presidential career. He implied treasonous intent on the part of "certain self-created societies," which he said, had "fomented combinations of men who, careless of consequences . . . have disseminated . . . suspicions, jealousies and accusations of the whole government." His government.[2]

Thomas Jefferson responded with his own hyperbole, describing Washington's splenetic as "an attack on the freedom of discussion, the freedom of writing, printing, and publishing." Washington had not, in fact, proposed repression of the societies, though he was exasperated at threats to a hard-won union, especially when other gentlemen pandered to the rabble. He knew that his secretary of state (Edmond Randolph) was forming policy in consultation with the representative of France. He may have also known that his secretary of the treasury (Hamilton) was conspiring with the British. And he knew that the value of his own western lands was being reduced to distressed merchandise because the government he headed could neither assure land titles, collect taxes, nor enforce the law in the West.

Washington raised the largest army ever seen on American soil—larger than any force he assembled during the war for independence—to put down a rebellion in the western hills. That army, and the elaborate pageantry with which he assumed its leadership, had intended to achieve more than collecting taxes and preventing further tar-and-feathering of tax collectors. With Alexander Hamilton breathing fire at its head, it was to redeem the honor of the Republic, and to hold the Ohio Valley within the Union.[3]

The causes and consequences of the ensuing campaign amid the tributaries of the Ohio River are buried deep in the compost of inconspicuous experience. There are no trumpet calls in its history, no famous names, no din of celebrated battles. Nor are there easy dates to remember. None the less, the Whiskey Rebellion of 1794–95 emerges from obscurity into prominence in the American chronicle because of the fervor with which it was repressed by Washington and Hamilton. They were not stupid or lacking in breadth of vision. On the contrary, they made a correct assessment of the threat posed by the rebellion. It was possible that the Union would, in fact, come apart. Washington's presidency was focused upon preventing that outcome.

Rulers do not generally take office to preside over the liquidation of the empires or republics over which they are given rule, but Washington's determination was more than a spastic seizure upon the status quo. It arose from a love for the West—precisely that, a love—which like all loves projected upon the loved the aspirations of the lover. The West must be held because it might become better than the East. It offered not only riches but also redemption. This is the primary theme of this chapter: Washington and those who shared his vision of the West aspired to make in it a new and better society. They did not aspire to inventing polities; that was the Jeffersonian game. They were conservatives, with a due regard for continuities, for experience, and for hierarchy. So their new society was to have been built on traditional lines, purged of the recent accretions they felt to be hasty, dishonorable, or, as they might say, unseemly.

Therefore these Federalists, and their general-president, have appeared as somewhat foolish in the annals of liberal history; the Western Cincinnati have scarcely appeared in those annals at all.* During the nineteenth century, their romantic conservatism was laughed to scorn by admirers of other causes, such as those of Thomas Jefferson.

---

*The Washingtonian founders can conveniently be grouped as Cincinnati, though not all were members of the Society itself, which was open only to his officer corps and its male descendents.

But part of the Federalists' deference toward tradition was a more general deference to history. They carried into the West a watchful acknowledgment of what might already be there, upon the land itself. They were ready to learn from the evidence of the past.

In this they differed from the heedless, insistent, grid-making, expansionist, arrogant advocates of manifest destiny and restless innovation who swept their hopes aside and much else, as well.

Yet, though they failed in the end, it remains true that the officer corps formed and disciplined by Washington led the post-war expansion into the Great Valley, and discovered much of its ancient work. What was for Washington an unconsumated curiosity about the monumental architecture of the West became for many of his lieutenants a determination to preserve it. The nation's first Historic Preservation Ordinance was passed by the Cincinnati at Marietta in the 1780s.

Preservation was the first step, taken out of respect for what was present on their arrival, upon the ground. There was a second: respect for who was present, which was coupled with a willingness to acknowledge that those Indians still there, however impoverished and weakened by disease, might be the descendents of the people who had created the monuments preserved. It was astonishing but true that many of the leaders of the Western Cincinnati did not restrict their sympathies to dead Indians. To living ones they often offered grave and diffident attention. The practical consequences of such a respectful relationship included a due regard for Indian sovereignty beyond a policed frontier, and even proposals for statehood for Indian confederacies within the United States.*

Alexander Hamilton and Aaron Burr shared with Albert Gallatin a fundamental difference from Thomas Jefferson; they accepted the possibility that dark-skinned people freed from slavery might become equal to Whites in all attainments, in science as in the arts. After Jefferson's presidency, Hamilton was already dead, Burr disgraced and exiled, but Gallatin fought on, never acquiescing to the expansion of a slave system based upon racial prejudice and exploitation. The victims would be the Blacks, within the system, and the Indians, against whom it was being expanded.

Gallatin was not the first to recognize that violence against Blacks was occurring upon an internal frontier, with the same motivation and grounded in the same ideology as violence against Indians upon an external frontier. Implicitly, the antislavery views of the Cincinnati in the Northwest Territory were grounded in the same morality as their regard for Indian sovereignty. And their hallowing of the work-products

---

*We come to the details of these proposals for reservations, "asylums", Indian territories and states in a few more pages.

of the Indians, through preservation of the monumental architecture created in the Northwest was part of the same compound of ideas.

What would the West become? That was increasingly the defining question of American history as the West, after 1763, reassumed that centrality in American affairs it had occupied in the third century and, again, in the thirteenth.

The weight of the West was the weight of America's ancient Egypt, nourisher of twenty-two millennia of people, mother of nations, silent determinant of power on the continent. That was why holding it within the United States was so important, and why the Whiskey Rebellion was not, as some modern sophisticates have averred, "almost charmingly benign," nor was it (as another modern commentator said): "duck soup," a mere hayseed embarrassment to the new Republic.[4]

Of course the rebellion, and the possible loss of the West, were known to be important at the time, and among those who knew better—and worse—than to think it charming were the dead and crippled after the battle at Bower Hill in 1794, the prisoners quick-marched ahead of the federal cavalry, and the poor fools executed because they had not the wit to defend themselves against bloodthirsty prosecutors. People died in that rebellion. Though the threat of secession whimpered to a sordid end, it was a real threat, a disaster which did not *quite* occur. Washington believed that he had no choice but to put it down quickly and firmly. The nation was full of disgruntled officers, any one of whom might have made himself general of the insurrection. On the sidelines were hostile powers, among them France, represented by General Georges Collot, who had an interest in just such a separation occurring.

This was Collot's judgment:

> Had the chiefs of the insurrection of 1794 been soldiers, or had they any military knowledge of these mountains, they might, with the troops under their orders—they had more than eight thousand men at their disposal, all excellent light infantry—have blocked up the passages of the Alleganies against the federal army, by seizing these defiles, and stationing their principal force at Bedford . . . perhaps have determined the inhabitants between the Alleganies and the Susquehannah to take an active part in their resistance.[5]

Collot was there to stoke the flames and, if he could, to recover Louisiana for France amid the ensuing conflagration. Washington's firmness disappointed Collot, who had to content himself with observations of Native American architecture.*

---

*We return to him in that role in Chapter Eight.

Albert Gallatin had something to do with that disappointment as well, managing to persuade the insurgents not to provoke the armed confrontation expected by Collot. Washington *was* a man who had ample "military knowledge of these mountains"; his emphatic action made it certain that—for a time—there would be no fissure opened in the United States between East and West.

A BAND OF HEROES

Washington was a general. That was his profession. Planter and president, too, but his training was military and so was his inclination, when it came to the management of civil crisis or colonial organization, history, drama, or comradeship.

A year before his death, in pain and with business difficulties dogging his steps, Washington traveled for the last time away from Mount Vernon. He did not do so to negotiate with his creditors nor even to press his agent, Clement Biddle, to increase his grain sales to Haiti. Instead, he struggled into a coach and bumped along the torturing, rutty, boggy roads all the way to Philadelphia to attend a last meeting with the Society of the Cincinnati.

Washington had a predilection for Romans. His favorite play was Addison's *Cato,* his favorite role, Cincinnatus, the protypical citizen-soldier. Cincinnatus was, to be more precise, a citizen general, a gentleman reduced to doing his own plowing with the aid of but a single slave, but remaining exceedingly proud. He was twice made military dictator of Rome. Twice he was called from the plow to defeat its enemies (leaving the slave to finish the furrow), always insisting, however, that he preferred the barnyard to the drillyard.

Washington's love of glory was as great as his love of land; he managed, however, to discipline the first by remembering always the satisfaction of the second. If not a general, or a president, he might always be a squire. The same modulated and balanced aspirations he offered to those of his officers who might have formed a junta if they had been led by another, such as Alexander Hamilton. When he gave them the name for their postwar organization, the Society of the Cincinnati, he bequeathed to them his own doctrine of self-abnegation. "Back to the plow, gentlemen," he seemed to be saying.

We have already met many of these gentlemen at the city named after them, Cincinnati, Ohio, and upstream at Marietta: Colonel Winthrop Sargent and General "Mad Anthony" Wayne. We will have occasion to record the western adventures of many other officers who served under Washington, among them George and Daniel Morgan, Baron von Steuben, George Rogers Clark, James Wilkinson, and

Aaron Burr. A few had no inducement to relinquish their fertile fields, fat kine, and their battalions of slaves to seek a new life west of the mountains, but many had no slaves nor inherited acres to which to return; some were so poor as to envy Cincinnatus his solitary slave and his plow. At Valley Forge, around their campfires, Washington had spoken to them all, however, in equal eloquence of a world to be won beyond the mountains, a new, purged, open chance.

Won—and then to be organized. The Cincinnatian dream he offered in their encampment was of a hierarchic, deferential, Roman colony—differing from those of the Romans in being without the abomination of slavery. Life with old comrades in such a community still called to George Washington at the end of the 1780s. It called so strongly that his anticlericalism yielded to what might be called a congregational sense of what such a colony might be. He suggested settling Ohio with "particular societies, or religious sectaries with their pastors." Such societies might also be a "means of connecting friends in a small circle." As we shall see in a moment, Washington's conventional deism was given another twist by another Western imperative, the power of Indian religion, but his political preferences remained constant on either side of the mountains.[6]

The West did not respond to Washington's hopes in precisely the form he envisaged, though there were plenty of religious communities formed in the westering process, of which probably the most famous was that of Joseph Smith. Many paid attention to the mounds, though none made ancient architecture so central to their systems of belief as the Mormons. There were also purely secular colonies formed on Cincinnatian lines, some of which were laid down upon previous settlements marked by ruined mounds. We will visit them, but nowhere were Washington's preferences in colonization so closely related to that study of antiquity which he espoused as in Marietta. It was to be a place of refuge, a place to start anew. It was also a place full of memories of old friends, and of places where their friendship had been enjoyed intensely.

Washington's message to the Cincinnati at Marietta saying that he wished he could join them there might seem nothing more than an old man's gesture of solicitude and camaraderie, but as the mouse-shredded evidence has suggested, a place *near* Marietta was already dear to him. Besides, though his presidential responsibilities held him in the East, as Edmond Randolph knew, repulsion as well as attraction might have moved him to Ohio; as we have seen, Washington was thinking of abandoning Virginia. In the generation of the founders, a third of the people born in the tidewater region, slave and free, did exactly that.

Perhaps Washington had something less radical in mind; perhaps he was considering arrangements to sojourn, from time to time, in the "new and rising empire," without completely tearing himself away from Mount Vernon. As if to encourage him, the Cincinnati established their military colony on shores scouted for them by their commander in chief. In 1770 he had reconnoitered the future site of Marietta on the way downriver, and he paused on the way back to disembark for a survey of a proper site for a fortress on the opposite bank of the Muskingum.*[7]

ROMANISM ON THE MUSKINGUM

In 1783, even before news came of the treaty of peace with Great Britain, Colonel Timothy Pickering of Massachusetts (afterward Secretary of State Pickering) wrote of "a new plan in contemplation,—no less than forming a new State westward of the Ohio. Some of the principal officers of the army are heartily engaged in it."[8] In 1788, they were there at Marietta, Washington's townsite, in a turreted stockade. Beetling down upon these heroes were earthworks, believed by them to be fortifications, considerably more ambitious than those they had been able to create out of the frozen ground of Valley Forge or even from the more acquiescent red earth outside Yorktown. All about their new encampment a mysterious antiquity reigned; they did not know it at the time, but the ruins of ancient Marietta were as old as those of Rome.

As they ascended from the riverbank to those ruins, they found it easy to trundle their wagons up a graded ramp, one hundred forty feet wide and seven hundred feet in length, while their apprehensions of Indian attack were alleviated by its high protective embankments. This broad ceremonial ascent they rightly called the "Sacra Via."

Naming it never a trivial act; these classical scholars revered ancient Rome, but theirs was more than passive reverence. They imagined what life was like long ago, picturing people passing along a sacra via to a fortress-village. As the Cincinnati laid out their fields among the earth-bounded enclosures of their ancient predecessors, these old revolutionaries considered how those plazas might have served as liturgical centers. As they constructed their fort, they again drew upon Roman models; it became a turreted, quadrilateral, wooden building, like those from which Varus set forth in A.D. 9 upon his ill-omened invasion of the Teutoburger Wald, though they were luckier. "Varus, give me back my legions!" cried Augustus Caesar. It is quite possible that at the

---

*In a tall folio at Mount Vernon is the longest document written in Washington's own hand, roughly six thousand words, recording all land grants made or requested along the Ohio from 1745 to 1769. As Arthur Miller's salesman might have put it, he knew the territory.

moment his general Varus was ambushed by the Germans, the Adena/ Hopewell were at work upon the cone, the sacra via, and the plazas at Marietta. In the wilds of Ohio, the Cincinnati called their stockade their Campus Martius.

Within the walls of their new Campus Martius, Washington's companions at Valley Forge, generals Samuel Holden Parsons and Rufus Putnam* and Major Winthrop Sargent recorded their impressions of the prehistoric architecture which so overbalanced their relatively modest establishment. The sacra via led immediately into an enclosure about a quarter of a mile square, bounded by earthen walls which were then "6 to 10 feet high, and from 20 to 40 feet thick." It contained two platform mounds, one 120 by 130 feet, the other somewhat smaller. Next to it was another square nearly identical in size to those in Newark and along the Scioto. Beyond the square, surrounded by a circular wall of earth, was a cone, 50 feet high and 760 feet in circumference.[9]

Most of the Marietta earthworks have been destroyed, except for the cone as we have noted earlier. After reverence had dissipated for the antiquities into which the Cincinnati had intruded, after nearly all they had sought to preserve of the past had disappeared, their own graves were kept inviolate by their descendants, and, shielded thereby, the tomb of the ancient ones was spared.

NEW BEGINNINGS

The citizens of Marietta are today proud that the founders of their town were sufficiently respectful of Native American antiquity to lay out its streets to preserve as much as possible of the ruins and, as we have noted, to enact the nation's first historic preservation ordinance.[†] Yet their purpose in coming there was not to preserve the past. They were in Ohio to start something new. As their primary ideologist, Manasseh Cutler, put it, they meant to leave behind them the ugly inheritances of the past; "in order to begin *right,* there will be no *wrong* habits to combat, no inveterate systems to overturn—there is no rubbish to remove, before you can lay the foundation." By rubbish they meant the trash and the bad habits of the undisciplined rabble—of

---

*Putnam was not a parochial Yankee; in 1774–75, he had commenced a settlement in the Spanish possessions along the lower Mississippi, but it had been aborted by the onset of the Revolutionary War. Parsons had been recruited for the Marietta colony by Putnam, who had also served as a general of George Washington's army.

†Ostensibly, Marietta was named for Marie Antoinette, Queen of France, but really for the French comrades-in-arms who died in the common struggle against Britain, "our brave Gallican friends on the first beginnings . . . of our great labor."

their own race. They did *not* mean the evidence of the accomplishments of their Native American predescessors.[10]

The Cincinnati at Marietta shared with Albert Gallatin, Benjamin Franklin, and with Washington a remarkably respectful view of Indians, past and present. They also shared an equally remarkable determination to commence, in the West, colonies which might have Roman names, might apply other Latin terms to roads and fortresses, but would be free of the worst vice of Rome—human slavery. That does not mean that they were democratic by inclination or that they welcomed a multiracial society. It merely means that they were adamant in their opposition to the enslavement of others or to the allocation of what were, in effect, penal conditions on the basis of race. They were not admirable in everything, but they can be conceded that, and the same cannot be said for many of their contemporaries.[*]

Cutler joined Rufus Putnam's Cincinnatian project in 1786, and was the most important shepherd of its passage through the Congress. He raised one million dollars to buy the land in Ohio for which Marietta was intended as the capital. And Cutler saw to it that the leverage of that vast sum would be applied to the nation's Revolutionary debt *only* if running with that land were covenants that slavery would not be permitted upon it. Cutler's money was persuasive in the passage of the antislavery provision in the Northwest Ordinance; it overcame the pressure of Southerners hoping to transplant their plantation system north of the Ohio. That money was even more persuasive than the subtleties of those Virginians who favored the ordinance precisely because it would deny to the Northwest the slaves they believed necessary to produce crops competitive to their own.

The Marietta colony distilled the idealism of a proud, conservative officer-corps. Cincinnatian obduracy in the face of governments "tinctured by democracy" (as St. Clair expressed the matter to Pickering) was coupled among these Yankees-gone-westward with an equally intransigent opposition to slavery. To see what the West might have been like had they triumphed, one can examine the constitution prepared for the Black Republic of Toussaint Louverture[†] by Alexander Hamilton. Hamilton proposed a military government, under a leader supported by a junta, but one carefully balanced among the Blacks,

---

[*]The commentary of Michael Zuckerman at this point may commend itself to many who do not share my enthusiasm for the Cincinnati: "When they spoke of beginning right and eliminating wrong habits, it seems as plausible to suppose they referred to democracy and lower-class vice as to slavery. . . . The Marietta settlers were much more concerned to keep democracy and the unruly multitudes away." (Letter of November 27, 1992).

[†]Later editors have inserted a literalist apostrophe, making his surname into a noun meaning "opening", but this is how he himself spelled it.

Whites, and mulattoes who composed the people of the island after Toussaint freed the slaves and before the invasion of Haiti by Napoleon with the complicity of Thomas Jefferson—see Chapter Seven.[11]

The coupling of tight discipline under Federalist officers to a prohibition of slavery produced in Ohio a series of conflicts with Jeffersonian principles. These interactions were noted in the earlier discussion of the career of Thomas Worthington. The Federalists made Worthington's success easier by appointing Arthur St. Clair as governor of the Northwest Territory. St. Clair's ineptitude as a politician might have been forgiven had he been a competent general. Even his inadequacies in the field, which led to the most embarrassing defeats of American armies until the War of 1812, might have been forgiven had he not been arrogant and stupid. There was much justice in the charge that he had "british & princely ideas," as if he were one of the old colonial governors. Worthington was correct in asserting that "the present arbitrary government [is] better suited for an English or Spanish colony than for citizens of the United States."[12]

St. Clair acted as if he, rather than Washington, were the true heir of Cincinnatus. Despite his admirable qualities, the old Roman was as famous for high-handedness as for high-mindedness, and renowned for his mordant disdain for plebeians. His views squared comfortably with those of the Ohio Cincinnati.

SLAVES IN THE GARDEN

Washington himself was somewhat more inclined toward democracy than Arthur St. Clair; on the other hand, he was considerably less willing than Jefferson to acquiesce in the growth in the West of a greater Virginia—plantations, slavery and all. He is not often described as a Yankee, but when he stated his aspirations for the trans-Appalachian region, he sketched a greater New England, advancing in compact settlements of yeomen farmers and artisans—under strong leaders. Thus might "laws, customs, and civil police . . . extend" across the valley, obliterating the "scattered settlements," in which, he lamented without apparently any embarrassment about his own record, "nothing is thought of by scrambling for land, which more than probably would involve confusion and bloodshed."*[13]

With some justice, the Jeffersonians asserted that the Cincinnati were attempting to establish themselves as border captains—mar-

---

*Washington and Jefferson also differed in balancing the interests of frontiersmen and the Native American residents of the West. As we shall see, Aaron Burr was the first statesman to reveal this difference.

quises, marcher lords, margraves, as such men had been called in Europe.* One only gained membership in the Cincinnati by inheritance, as one does in the Daughters of the American Revolution and the Colonial Dames. Jefferson held that this disqualified them from a role in the West, because his followers had pressed legislation through Congress requiring that all states created in the West should have "republican forms, and shall admit no person to be a citizen who holds any hereditary title."[14]

Winthrop Sargent, Arthur St. Clair, and Rufus Putnam blandly asserted that they were not there to form states, but to govern territories. They opposed early statehood for Ohio or Indiana for their own reasons, despite Pickering's reference to a *new State*. The division of the western territories into *states of the Union* as we now think of them was not yet settled doctrine. There was no process for forming them until 1787, four more years after he wrote. In the meantime several other models were discussed, including tangential "states" ruled by juntas.[†]

Their concept for the governance of territories was that these should remain satrapies of military gentlemen, keeping the hardy but rambunctious pioneers under tight reign. Sargent described the Ohioans under his governance as "very licentious . . . and extremely debouched"; St. Clair thought them "a multitude of indigent and ignorant people . . . ill qualified to form a constitution and government for themselves." The western Jeffersonians, including Gallatin, were coming to be called "Jacobins" by Federalists, or in St. Clair's ungrammatical variant, "San Culottes."[15]

The plan of Rufus Putnam and Timothy Pickering was to discipline this scruffy populace by setting them within a "semimilitary state, settled by officers and men . . . a private was to have 100 acres, an ensign, 150, a colonel, 500, and a major general, 1,100." These officers, like retired Roman legionaries, would be available to defend the realm or defend their states within the realm.[‡16]

The federalists responded to the attacks on St. Clair that the rush to

---

*Some Cincinnati sought to persuade Prince Henry of Prussia or the Duke of York to assume an American throne. Neither the prince nor the duke thought the prospect appetizing, but the Jeffersonians in Congress had to rush to prevent thirty-six Cincinnati from accepting knighthoods in the Polish Order of Divine Providence.

†This may have been what Alexander Hamilton contemplated in 1799 and Aaron Burr endeavored to create in 1805.

‡The revolutionary veterans initiated several systems of this sort, both within the territories of the United States and, as we shall see, in Spanish Louisiana. Nothing quite like these hierarchic colonies had been suggested in America since the seventeenth century, when British governors of New York established military "manors" to stand off the French threat, and the French created "seigneuries" in reply. Neither had its desired effect, since the manor

end rule by a military elite and commence statehood was only a device to open the region to slavery. It was forbidden in the Northwest Territory, but each *state,* hewn thereafter out of the Territory, could, after admission to the Union, make its own decisions in the matter. If Ohio went for slavery, said one farmer, "we shall have gentlemen enough, and their negroes too . . . they would be riding over us with their coaches." Fourth of July resolutions were offered that "freeborn sons . . . [of Ohio] never permit the foul form of slavery to tread on their sacred soil."[17]

Scholars have carefully differentiated an aversion to slavery from a willingness to accept free Blacks in the territories. It is important to note, therefore, that some men, such as Cutler, Worthington, Hamilton, Washington, and Aaron Burr expressed a desire to *integrate* free Blacks into their ideal communities.* Washington and St. John Tucker, among the leaders of Virginia, advocated freeing slaves *and* permitting them to emigrate to the West. In 1816, the Kentucky Abolition Society proposed that Congress set aside "vast tracts of unappropriated lands . . . [as] suitable territory . . . to be laid off as an asylum for all those negroes and mulattoes who have been, or those who may hereafter be, emancipated within the United States.[18] The Kentucky proposal sounds somewhat like a South African homeland, but one need not be too derisive of the intentions of the Abolition Society. There *was* plenty of suitable and pleasant land in the West, though it was in the possession of neither Whites nor Blacks. And none of the other suggestions coupled free land to segregation; there is no evidence that there was aversion to Blacks, free or slave, in the Cincinnattian experiment at Marietta. Washington's proposal to the British investors would have left free Blacks as farmers at Mount Vernon.

Jefferson and Madison, by contrast, never considered either manumission or abolition without at the same time insisting upon the return of Blacks to Africa or shipping them off to Haiti. But neither Washington nor Cutler sought to exclude free Blacks from the American polity. Their chief stated reason for excluding slavery from the Northwest was that it would then be settled by "men of . . . robust constitutions, in-

---

lords and seigneurs quickly sold out to commercial gentlemen such as the Van Rensselaers and Livingstons.

There was, it is true, a more heartening if distant example: amid the detritus of the Roman Empire, in the seventh century, the Merovingian kings of France adapted the *patrocinia* of the Romans to create feudalism.

*The role of Alexander Hamilton, either on his own account or as agent for Washington, in the formation and direction of the Putnam's Ohio Company requires more research into the Company's records. As we will note, Hamilton's hope for an endowment to support his widow and children required the success of the company.

ured to labor, and free from the habits of idleness." That would rule out slave-driving planters along with the slaves who deprived them of healthful exercise.

Pickering was proceeding from a principled and relatively color-blind commitment to a meritocracy in Ohio. He did not suffer from Jefferson's ambiguity in matters of race. He insisted on "the total exclusion of slavery" from Marietta and Ohio in 1779, five years *before* he was joined by Jefferson in what was for the latter a tentative and unconsummated effort to keep it out of all the trans-Appalachian West. Though Jefferson thereafter abandoned the struggle for total exclusion of slavery from the West, Pickering sustained the fight.

Fierce in their loathing of frontier democracy, unrelenting in their abhorrence of slavery, and conscientious custodians of the evidence of ancient Indian achievement, the Ohio Federalists were rewarded by appointments under Washington's successor as president, John Adams. Sargent became first secretary of the Northwest Territory and then, in 1798, governor of Mississippi Territory.

Sargent was unbending and cranky; despite efforts on his behalf by Burr, he was removed from his post in Mississippi as soon as Jefferson came to power in 1801. Sargent had met Jefferson at meetings of the Philosophical Society and discussed with him their common interest in the mound building of the Ohio Valley. His letters in 1800 expressed the hope that their common scholarly interests would be enough for Jefferson to abstain from replacing him in the Mississippi governorship. Idle wishes of that sort were frequently disappointed that year; Jefferson made as clean a sweep of his opponents' political appointments as did Andrew Jackson in 1829.

Sargent's old comrades in Ohio remained in the field, and, in alliance with Worthington, prevented the introduction of slavery into the new state of Ohio in 1802. They lost their first battle in Indiana as the Jeffersonians under William Henry Harrison adopted thinly disguised slavery in its "indenture laws" of 1803 and 1805, but Albert Gallatin prevented Harrison's full triumph in Indiana, and Edward Coles kept Illinois a free state in the campaigns of 1811 and 1819.

THE NEW WORLD GARDEN

For nearly three hundred years, Europeans could imagine America as a New Eden. Until 1800 or so, many conjured, in the West, Prospero's island, a New World garden in the midst of which there bubbled a Fountain of Youth—youth for the nation. The fountain was to be a place of renewal, where the dust of failure might be washed away.

The Cincinnati combined this myth with another, more specific to their condition, "a safe, an honorable asylum . . . [for] the generous, the brave, the oppressed defenders of their country." The New World garden might be domesticated into a rural retreat for heroes. The Great Valley was to be a stage on which to play out, once more, the Cincinnatian drama of military heroes commuting between plow and saddle.[19]

That was its "pull." There was also the "push." They were not a happy lot. Many of them sought to escape a political system for which they had sacrificed much and in which they were losing faith. Though several had large stakes in the East, their wavering hopes induced them to look westward. General Henry Knox, artillerist, patron of the architecture of Charles Bulfinch, and soon to be secretary of war, wrote General Parsons, in 1788, that if Massachusetts failed to ratify the Constitution, and the eastern states degenerated into anarchy, "we must all I believe become inhabitants of Ohio." That was not because Knox had speculated in lands there; his stake was in Maine, then still a part of Massachusetts, where he was owner and promotor of a million acres.[*][20] It was because the western lands of Ohio stood for new beginnings.

Timothy Pickering supported the Marietta venture though he himself owned thirty thousand acres on the Kanawha, seeking to attract the same potential settlers. William Constable stood to lose as much as any of them if his brothers among the Cincinnati were successful in the West, for he had a hundred twenty thousand acres at risk between the Mohawk and the St. Lawrence. Yet Constable, too, wished them well. Some years later, he added that if the civil war they had all feared had broken out, "I meant to go to the Ohio," where there might be for them all a new start, a true "asylum."[21]

In 1788, the year of Constable's endorsement, settlement began on the 311,682 acres west of Marietta and the holdings of the Ohio Company acquired by Colonel John Cleves Symmes as a colony largely for his fellow veterans of New Jersey.[†] When Arthur St. Clair was appointed governor of the Northwest Territory, he did not join the other Cincinnati at Marietta, but set up his capital within the Symmes Tract, where he changed the name of the hamlet of Losantiville to "Cincinnati," and began sending Indian artifacts to Thomas Jefferson.[22] Winthrop Sargent moved with the capital; his archaeological interests continued; when the burgeoning town, fattening on hogs and West

---

[*]Michael Zuckerman offers a less admiring view than mine of the disaffection of the Cincinnati: "The Ohio of the Cincinnati and the Marietta colony is the most crabbed, weedy garden in all of English America; the least buoyant, exuberant, ecstatic, democratic, the most pushed, the least pulled. Compare the promotional literature of South Carolina, of Virginia, of Pennsylvania . . . none of it [is] so sour" (Letter of November 27, 1992).

[†]It was Symmes's estate which endowed William Henry Harrison, who married John Symmes's daughter.

Virginia salt, widened Main Street in 1794, one of its principal mounds was demolished, and burials were exposed (probably Hopewell).[23]

ASYLUMS?

In the eighteenth century, the term "asylum" meant a place of honorable refuge, larger but similar to a medieval sanctuary. Both the Cincinnati and the French refugees who came into the West in the 1790s used that word to describe the colonies they sought to create for themselves and others. For a time, creation of very large refuges, in some cases larger than the present states of the union, was an objective of the Indian policy of President Washington, of the Cincinnati, and of Aaron Burr.

The term "reservation," which they used as a rough synonym for "asylum," had not yet become so wizened as to describe only property thought unfit for occupation by Whites or so small as to become, in effect, a concentration camp. Instead it was thought that there might be some spacious western reservations limited to Whites, and others to Indians, with a few intersections for trade or commingling of cultures.

This all sounded rather familiar, though many recalled that Washington had led the opposition to the "Proclamation Lines" of Bouquet, Dunmore, and their king. The French did not understand any better than the British how intent were the Americans upon their expansion into the Great Valley. The Franco-American romance of the Revolutionary years began to turn sour at the moment the negotiations for peace began in Paris, when the French government showed signs of agreeing with Spain that the western boundary of the United States might just as well be at the Appalachians, with Indian buffer states beyond.

There had even been suggestions in some treaties with the Indians that the Americans would consider what would, in effect, be statehood for those remaining in their ancestral lands. The Treaty of Fort Pitt in 1778 had such a provision for the Delaware nation; the Treaty of Hopewell of 1785 held out such a prospect for the Cherokee; and two years later Alexander McGillivray of the Creeks made such a proposal to James White, superintendent of Indian affairs for the southwestern frontier, who sent it along to Henry Knox, the Secretary of War.*

---

*The story of Indian territories and states remains to be brought up to date by fresh research. The best treatments are those cited in fn. 13 on p. 222 of Dowd, *Spirited Resistance*. They include a summary article by Annie H. Abel, "Proposals for an Indian State, 1778–1878," in the *Annual Report of the American Historical Association*, 1907, pp. 89–104, which cites other secondary sources including *Atlantic Monthly* 93, pp. 809 ff. and *American Historical Review* 10, p. 253.

The similarities of Washington's proposals as president to those of the kings of France, Spain, and Great Britain struck no one as amusing, for the rapacity of the frontiersmen, of whom Washington himself had been one in the 1770s, raged unabated in the 1790s and rendered Washington's program once in power as unenforceable as that of King George.

Unenforceable, that is, unless the frontier were given over to military governors recruited from the Cincinnati, and history was rapidly moving past that possibility. Washington's program for the West had been consistent since 1783, when he expressed the view that "the settlement of the western country and making a peace with the Indians are so analogous" that they required the pacific policy that "our interest dictates . . . [and] an enlightened people ought to adopt." It would be better, he said, to seek a surcease from "disputes both with the savages and among ourselves . . . [than to] aggrandize a few avaricious men to the prejudice of many, and the embarrassment of the government."[24]

Washington's plan called for a clear line dividing the frontiersmen and the Indians (one, it must be admitted, beyond his own holdings). That line should, he said, be garrisoned against "overspeading . . . by a parcel of banditti. Then, it would be felonious for Whites to trespass. Troops would enforce the law; it would be a felony to invade Indian reservations, otherwise those "banditti" would "bid defiance to all authority." Washington took this matter seriously; he coupled it with a proposal to lay out two new states which would be opened to settlement without violating the reservations.[25]

For the remainder of his tenure as president, Washington continued to propose the Cincinnatian program of carefully controlled nuclear settlements, under competent military supervision, and meticulous observance of Indian rights. James Flexner concluded that even as he was equipping Wayne's force in 1793, "Washington believed that the Indians had equal rights with frontiersmen. . . . [However,] communities which had suffered from scalpings could have little sympathy with Washington's holding back the military until [negotiation was tried one more time]. . . . Jefferson espoused the western point of view."[26]

In the West, holding back the army infuriated the still unscalped frontiersmen, and his holding back large tracts of land infuriated the speculators on both sides of the mountains. Not only did Washington propose large Indian reservations on desirable property, he would constrain the colonies in the Northwest Territory with the army guarding their frontiers. He actually deployed additional troops to recover Indian lands already acquired by Whites through fraud or trespass.

This was not Jefferson's policy. According to Flexner, Washington's biographer, the arguments of the Secretary of State "would, by legitimizing even the most notorious land-grabs, hamstring all efforts to achieve peace by negotiation. The government, Jefferson insisted, would be exceeding its constitutional powers if it alienated [recognized Indian claims for] any land that had ever been annexed [however illegally]."[27]

Though Hamilton joined in Washington's position, Jefferson refused to budge, and it is likely that Jefferson had the votes. Seeking consensus, Washington did not press his program. Another opportunity was lost.[28]

Washington's concept of frontier states coupled with large, protected reservations might have worked, but it has been buried under a pile of drawings by Jefferson of neat rectangular appropriations of *all* Indian claims east of the Mississippi.

It is not necessary to see in Washington's Indian policy the considered diffidence in the presence of another culture which one might expect of an anthropologically trained statesman of the 1990s (though one might expect those expectations to be disappointed). Washington was living before the invention of anthropology; it was beyond the ken of his time to consider "civilized" and "savage" races as meriting equal regard. In our final chapters we turn to the question of how terms such as these fit into the religious conceptions of the Europeans and Americans; especially do we attend to the brief moment of openness to the religious convictions even of Indians which made possible for the generation of the Founders the thought that Indians might create monumental architecture for religious purposes. As we do, it may be well to bear in mind an act of President Washington which, so far as I know, has never been repeated by a subsequent occupant of the office. He acknowledged that a reference to his Christian God—and he was a firm believer in such a God—might be offensive to the Cherokee, and that their religious views were as worthy of honor as his own. From a draft of a message to them prepared for his signature, he removed the word "God" and substituted for it, in his own hand, "Great Spirit Above."[29]

CHAPTER SEVEN

THOMAS JEFFERSON
AND THE PERSISTENCE
OF PREJUDICE

O ne day, as he was surveying the western extremities of the Fairfax lands, Peter Jefferson stood on the continental divide and carved his initials into a tree. Beyond him were waters flowing into the Mississippi, behind him those eventuating in the Atlantic. At the top of an Appalachian Ridge there may still be today a great beech bearing the initials "P.J." and marking a point farther toward the Western Waters than his son Thomas ever ventured.

Peter Jefferson intended to explore beyond that tree but was never able to do so. He died when his son Thomas was only fourteen, giving him and his shadowy, barely literate, older brother, Randolph, into the guardianship of another man with western aspirations, Dr. Thomas Walker. Squire "Walker of Walkerton" lived upon seventeen thousand acres acquired through marriage to the widow of Nicholas Meriwether. These holdings, extending along ten miles of the Mattaponi River, were the base for his joint speculations with Peter Jefferson.

In the 1740s, Walker made his way into Kentucky, by way of a pass to which he gave the name Cumberland Gap. Once upon the western side he laid claim through the Greenbrier Land Company to one hundred thousand acres. By the time of his death, Walker's western speculations included eight hundred thousand more.

While Walker was off exploring, Thomas Jefferson was entrusted to the care of James Maury, a fierce Anglican teacher who took up the western theme and turned it into a rhapsody of imperial avarice. The Mississippi Valley, he said, could be "an exhaustless fund of wealth superior to Potosi and all the other South American mines!"[1]

Maury said of himself that he was "forever dwelling with pleasure on . . . whatever bids fair to extend the empire and augment the strength of our mother island [England] . . . and at the same time aggrandizing and enriching this spot of the globe [Virginia]. . . ." Others who dwelt on these possibilities included a series of governors of Canada who refused as late as 1795 to give up hope that the Mississippi Valley, the "second India . . . the granary of America," might be rescued from the Americans.[2]

Maury and Walker died before the full importance of the valley had been learned; only their prodigious student lived long enough to demonstrate that this was a "rising empire" of its own, not to be constrained by its utility to "extend" or "augment" the strength of England, and also an empire with its own past, its own role in the chronicles of humankind.

JEFFERSON AND THE YEOMANRY

The past of the great valley was inscrutable when Jefferson, Gallatin, Washington, and their contemporaries first became conscious that it, in fact, had a past in the same sense that Europe had had one. That rising consciousness was, of course, acquired slowly and was always tinctured by the expectations they brought to learning. Imbedded in their consciousness were school book lessons, and imbedded in their unconscious were prejudices. Those prejudices were not identical, as we have shown to some extent already. We are now to go forward in an adventure of discovery of our own, hewing aside prejudices of our own, hacking our way through school book lessons learned by us about these men, lessons of which we must rid ourselves before we can assess how these learners learned, and what they could not bring themselves to learn.

Let us try to understand Thomas Jefferson, and to follow him as he brought his magnificent intellect to bear upon the lessons of the valley. To begin with, we must get rid of the barriers placed in our way by even the best of historians, and clearly the best of them all to turn his attention to the time we are now considering was Henry Adams. Yet even he could slip, as when he wrote of the future desired by Jefferson and his party for the West as a program grounded in their own past.

Adams would have us believe that Jefferson derived from his mentors, Walker and Maury among them, a desire that the West should be Greater Virginia of "idyllic conservatism . . . perpetuating the simple and isolated lives of their fathers." Which fathers? What simplicity? The imperial Walker of Walkerton, with his eight hundred thousand acres? Jefferson was no "up-country gentleman farmer" nor was he the son of a rough yeoman. No man who takes his ease in the largest library in his hemisphere, surrounded by furniture and paintings from Paris in a mansion worked by battalions of slaves can be mistaken for a proto-Kansan. Jefferson could not be Jefferson with one hundred sixty acres and a mule.[3]

Jefferson was a magnate, son and grandson of magnates. His grandfather Randolph owned hundreds of slaves and twelve thousand acres. His brother-in-law owned three thousand acres. His father was an Addison-reading squire who served his king as magistrate, sheriff (an office of great prestige), militia colonel, and member of the House of Burgesses. A man is no small holder who leaves a son as only half his estate many slaves and two thousand five hundred acres.[4]

Neither Thomas nor his brother Randolph Jefferson grew to manhood as yeomen among yeomen. Thomas quickly distinguished himself from his unremarkable brother, but never broke away from their common heritage, drawing his friends, aides, and his political cronies from among a small circle of Piedmont squires. His neighbors and friends, the Carters, owned ten thousand acres in Albemarle County alone, and another ten thousand in Amherst; the Coles owned another fifteen thousand acres, half of them in a single, contiguous fiefdom just to the south of Jefferson's own. Thousands of acres and hundreds of slaves were possessed by each of his close acquaintances, including the Madisons, Cockes, and Barbours.

Jefferson began as an up-country squire. No one knew more precisely than he what that meant—where the Piedmont gentry fitted into the hierarchy of Virginia society:

> Certain families had risen to splendor . . . some had produced a series of men of talents. . . . In such a state of things, society would settle itself down into several strata . . . aristocrats, half-breeds, pretenders, a solid independent yeomanry, looking askance at those above, yet not venturing to jostle them, and last and lowest, a seculum of human beings called overseers, the most abject, degraded, and unprincipled race.[5]

Henry Adams might be read as suggesting that while Jefferson might be a sophisticate, the other Piedmont squires were "simple," as if Jefferson were in some way peculiar in having the "instincts . . . of a liberal European nobleman." It is true that he "built for himself at Monticello a chateau above contact with man," but so did all of them, when they could. Perhaps it was the site of Monticello, on a sheared-off mountaintop, which distracted Adams, for it is true that Monticello's elevated situation is peculiar, and the plans Jefferson provided to his peers were for houses lying deep within deer parks, insulated by thousands of acres of slave-worked fields.[6]

In such places, of which Jefferson's own Poplar Forest, near Lynchburg, Virginia, is a good example, they lived as much as they could as the English Whig magnates who were their prototypes, within walls,

fences, and hedges composing rings of the cabalistic geometry of disso-
ciation derived from the ideal fortess-cities of the Renaissance. The distinction of Poplar Forest is, as we shall see, that Jefferson combined in
its design the insulating symbolism of the European Renaissance and
potent symbols of separation from Europe drawn from the architecture of the American West and of the American past. Their placement
by Jefferson as part of his scheme for Poplar Forest demonstrates how
successfully he had himself become a synthesis of cosmopolitan gentleman and complete American.

But he was never a yeoman-leader of yeomen. He was a squire-
philosopher-statesman. And there is nothing in his record of action to
indicate that what he had in mind for the West was an open scene for
"solid and independent yeomanry" each working his own broad acres,
neatly marked out in rectangles—prefiguring Kansas as it was in 1920.

The rectangles are, indeed, Jeffersonian. The rest of these proposi-
tions are interlocked fallacies, of no more help in drawing a picture of
Thomas Jefferson's West than taking him literally when he said that
"those who labor in the earth are the chosen people of God if ever he
had a chosen people." If he believed that, it would follow that Negro
slaves would inherit the Western earth, and no one can believe that to
be Jefferson's West.

JEFFERSON, HIERARCHY, AND THE WEST

What would have been Jefferson's West? How would he have shaped
it, and in whose interest? There were moments before the pivotal year,
1784, when he showed some willingness to act apart from the interests
of Virginia speculators in western land and in the breeding of slaves for
sale, of whom Walker was the most conspicuous. But after failure of
the efforts of the New England Federalists to keep slavery out of the
trans-Appalachian region (efforts Jefferson joined in 1784 but did not
initiate) he was never again guilty of a political action offensive to
those Virginia "families risen in grandeur" who had slaves to sell to
new latifundiasts rising in the West.*†

During the last years of the Revolution, Jefferson had served as war-

---

*The Yankees' proposals for the prohibition of slavery north of Ohio in the Northwest
Ordinance of 1787 found little or no resistance in Virginia because some in the Old Dominion believed that there would be little market for slaves. This was consoling, for otherwise
crops produced by non-Virginian operators of slave-driven plantations might compete with
their own and those of their kinsmen in Tennessee and Kentucky.

†Some historians, troubled by Jefferson's steadfast adherence to the interests of Virginia
land speculators and slaveowners, have found solace in his statement to James Madison that
he himself did not own land beyond the Blue Ridge. That was true at the time, but, as noted

time governor of Virginia. With his customary prescience, he grasped the postwar economic objectives of the Virginians "risen in grandeur" by fiercely opposing those who were in competition with them, whether British, Tory, or merely Pennsylvanian. It is noteworthy how much more parochial he was at the time than Washington, who, while hungry for western land, did not attempt to keep others out.

As wartime governor of Virginia, Jefferson made use of George Rogers Clark to lead a Virginian army to cut off the Pennsylvanians from renewing their forty-year-old trading ventures in Ohio, part of which had been wiped out by the French at the end of the 1750s and the rest absorbed by the British, operating out of Detroit. The best face to be put on the matter was put there by an admirer of Jefferson (Anthony Marc Lewis) in 1948, conceding that "an indispensable military advantage was . . . sacrificed, probably for the sake of Virginia's freedom to raise her western sons in her own way.[7]*

If this were Jefferson's objective, he did not admit it to Commander in Chief Washington, who by 1783 was taking a more "continental" view. The two might participate in canal company projects to draw the commerce of the West down the Potomac into Virginia, but Jefferson's version of Virginia's "own way" was diverging from Washington's. They manifested that divergence in their choice of personal companions: Jefferson, as we noted, consistently preferred the Virginia squires and sons of squires with whom he had grown to manhood. Perhaps because Washington's father was not a squire, but a peripatetic ironmaster and entrepreneur, the young men in his entourage, such as Hamilton, Laurens, and Humphreys (see Chapter Five), were not Virginia latafundiasts like those gathered about Jefferson.

Surely no one should charge Washington with democracy, but he did campaign among the yeomanry, regularly, in the eighteenth century manner, dispensing plenty of rum, while Jefferson was always loathe to do so. He was not at ease with simple farmers, indeed he was uneasy with most simple people anywhere. As Henry Adams observed:

---

earlier, Ohio land records and his own correspondence show that his abstemiousness soon diminished, and he became a speculator like his father and his mentor, Dr. Walker.

It would have been better for him had he not, for, like Alexander Hamilton, he made nothing on his Ohio lands. His financial difficulties, late in life, largely arose from the even larger speculations of his kinsman, Wilson Cary Nicholas. Jefferson went into debt aiding Nicholas to acquire over a million acres in the West.

*The contest between Virginia and Pennsylvania was less violent but otherwise similar to the contest between the British and Russians to determine in whose way the Balkans would be organized after the Second World War. It was not a disreputable contest, though the imperiled Kentuckians may have thought themselves as much pawns in the game as the contending partisans of Yugoslavia knew themselves to be in the contest between Churchill and Stalin.

As a leader of democracy he appeared singularly out of place. As reserved as President Washington in the face of popular familiarities, he
never showed himself in crowds . . . nor indeed was he seen at all except
on horseback, or by his friends and visitors in his own house.[8]

It was not that yeomen were unimportant to Jefferson. He could only
achieve power by adding them to his natural constituency among the
gentry, along with the artisans of the cities, the owners of few slaves or
of no slaves at all. Surely some yeomen did think of themselves as
"free" and "independent," and rightly. But even those who were, in
fact, dependent upon the local magnate had reason to retain a sort of
pride, for after the Constitution was ratified each of them was valued,
for electoral purposes at two or three times the value of any northerner.
As the election of 1800 demonstrated, the White southerners, whether
their feet touched the soil or only their stirrups, could make Mr. Jefferson president with fewer votes than those cast for his Yankee opponent, John Adams.* The allegedly democratic "Revolution of 1800,"
as Jefferson called his triumph, was, in fact, the triumph of a sequence
of slick antidemocratic maneuvers bringing to the rolls a shadowy bat-
talion of nonvoting three-fifths persons whose voting power attended
each White.

In 1774, Jefferson's *Summary View of the Rights of British America*
set forth a tableau of freeholders hewing out their destinies by their
own brawn and sweat. His biographers have made much of his pro-
nouncements at this time, as they have of his denunciations of the slave
trade, disregarding the fact that he did all he could to protect the interstate commerce in slaves (Virginia being an exporter of slaves) and
only opposed the international trade introducing competition to
Virginia's "products." We are told in one essay, for example, that Jefferson "attacked absentee masters with all the fire to be expected of
this upcountry gentleman farmer," advocating squatters' rights and re-
sisting Philadelphia-based speculators (such as those with whom Benjamin Franklin was associated) in the interest of a simpler, nobler
West.[9]

This is absurd on all counts: he was no "gentleman farmer" but a
grandee operating thousands of acres with hundreds of slaves, and he
and his friends were themselves avid absentee masters.

Jefferson was also a scientist and philosopher; there is no doubt that
he approached the West with a more encompassing scientific curiosity
than did George Washington, though Washington was a better field

---

*Actual popular vote statistics for the election of 1800 are very hard to come by. They did
not matter very much, because of the peculiarities of the electoral college system, but it is
my impression that of the voters who actually voted, Adams probably secured a majority.

ornithologist and natural historian. Jefferson commenced his inquiry into the heart of the American continent with a record of archaeology already established, grounded in the encyclopedic discipline of his French mentors. He ascended the heights of the Blue Ridge and looked westward toward the distant ridges and valleys his father had explored. Beyond those ridges Washington was even then exploring—as a British squire would explore them, not with the comprehensive, taxonomic procedures of the Jefferson's French friends. Furthermore, Washington looked at the West with only the corner of an eye for its previous occupants, whereas Jefferson had an avid curiosity about Indians, living and dead. Yet, to the fury of speculators and squatters alike, Washington treated Indians as persons having just rights to their own land; Jefferson did not—for him they were not quite persons, and, therefore, almost as unlikely to be be accorded protection of life, liberty, or property as Blacks, free or slave. He learned much about their past, but that did not lead him ever to consider that they had traditions worthy of being sustained into the present. He never deviated from the view that they must either assimilate or be swept aside. Albert Gallatin and George Washington reviewed the evidence and reached other conclusions. But Thomas Jefferson's prejudices in racial matters were more stubborn than those of either of these fellow Virginians.*

Jefferson, Indians, and Blacks

The Virginia Indians known to Thomas Jefferson in his youth were the diminished and demoralized remnants of many mighty nations who had lived about the Chesapeake. Disease and warfare had debilitated them; their social structure and means of supporting themselves had been destroyed, their religious places and burial grounds desecrated.

Indians passed through Charlottesville on their way to negotiate with the British governors at Williamsburg, but their presence was formal and occasional. The "others" who surrounded Jefferson every day were Blacks toward whom little movement can be discerned in his views from his youth to his dying day. As we have noted, Jefferson never brought himself to take the position reached by Albert Gallatin (and, for that matter, by Benjamin Franklin, Alexander Hamilton, and Aaron Burr) that Blacks could be the equals of Whites.

---

*Gallatin became an American citizen in Virginia. It is also true, though we lack the space to prove the point, that Jefferson was less willing than either Benjamin Franklin or Alexander Hamilton to abandon his prejudices against Blacks and Indians, and that Aaron Burr began as a friend to Indians and was a consistent, lifetime abolitionist, taking great political risks for this conviction.

Indians, he came to believe, *might* be. Otherwise he would not have been so pleased with his daughters' marriages to men who claimed Pocahontas as an ancestress. Nor would he have suggested in 1808 that some of the tensions of the frontier might be resolved by marriage between Indians and Whites. "Your blood will mix with ours," he said. This was not a shocking idea; William Byrd II and Robert Beverly had advocated it, and lamented that a "false delicacy" among the first English settlers had prevented more of it. The French made intermarriage state policy, "in order that, having one law and one master, they may form only one people and one blood."[10]

More than any "false delicacy" stood in the path of such a mixture of Blacks and Whites, solemnized by matrimony or not. The thought was abhorrent to Jefferson.* He saw too much evidence of its consequences, all about him, as his wife's half-Black half-sisters and half-brothers grew up unacknowledged and in slavery about his own children at Monticello. Virginians and southerners in general admixed the races, but seldom respectfully. To live in such circumstances can only have been a source of shame for a man of Jefferson's sensibilities.[†]

Like Benjamin Franklin, Jefferson was shocked into a further recognition of the personhood of Indians by the brutality of Whites against them. In 1763, Franklin led Pennsylvania Quakers to protect the "praying Indians" of Pennsylvania from the massacres perpetrated by the "Paxton Boys." Jefferson never had occasion to take up arms in defense of Indians, but in 1774 he was angered by the slaughter of the family of Chief Logan of the Mingo by another set of border ruffians.[‡]

Logan's speech after the defeat of his campaign of retribution so moved Jefferson that he set it down in his notebook. In 1782, when he composed *Notes on Virginia* for a French audience, he recalled Logan's eloquence as proof of the verbal sophistication of a people "without letters." It was a lawyer's trick, but an effective one, for Jefferson knew, though the French did not, that though Logan may very well have made such a speech, he was no untutored savage. His excellent command of English had been acquired during several years' residence in Philadelphia. The point Jefferson was making was valid; the Indians

---

*Gilbert Imlay was one of the very few of Jefferson's contemporaries to advocate an overt, legalized mixture of Blacks and Whites—as distinguished from liaisons of plantation owners and female slaves. See "The Enlightenment of Thomas Jefferson," below.

†Jefferson's father-in-law and his nephews all produced a number of progeny by slave women. There is no dispute about that. What is remarkable is the furor attending the allegation that Jefferson did as well, considering how little comment there has been upon the general moral tone of plantation life at the time.

‡The event itself occurred in the mound country along the upper Ohio, north of Steubenville.

were capable of oratory and, as he was learning, they were capable of monumental architecture as well.[11]

In the *Notes on Virginia,* however, he had not gotten that far:

> I know of no such thing as an Indian monument. . . . Of labor on the large scale, I think there is no remain as respectable as would be a common ditch for the draining of lands; unless indeed it would be the barrows [the small conical mounds of his own area] of which many are to be found all over this country.[12]

He went on to describe his exploration of such a mound on the banks of the Rivanna River, in the neighborhood of Monticello, in pursuit of what he called "natural history," meaning in this context, archaeology. Though admiring, empathetic, and respectful toward exceptional Indians such as Logan, Jefferson wrote of Indian eloquence as he might of the achievements of remarkable children.[13]

Jefferson did not have the good fortune to have an Indian as a friend. As he approached life's pivot-point, at forty, he still treated them as "other"—objects of study, though they might be, he suggested, "formed in mind as well as in body, on the same module with the 'Homo Sapiens Europaeus,'" they occupied an intermediate level in his scheme of science.[14]

In 1779, the College of William and Mary was seeking to accommodate a donor's bequest intended to support teachers among the Indians in reading, writing, and religion. This is the sort of thing the college might do for a remote colony of Europeans. Jefferson, an eminent graduate, suggested instead that a proto-anthropologist be dispatched for the *study* of "Indian law, customs, religions, traditions, and more particularly their languages," reporting to the faculty and filing reports in the library. A little "instruction in the principles of Christianity" might be vouchsafed along the way to accommodate the terms of a bequest, but the inspection team should keep on moving.[15]

We cannot be certain of the reasons for Jefferson's response. He was averse to religious instruction, in general. On that ground alone, he might have favored replacing the instruction of Indians in "the catechism and principles" of Christianity with a neutral study of their existing practices, a more conventional position, at the time, than that of the evangelistic donor to the college. Only Quakers, Moravians, and a very few Puritans and Anglicans held an Indian soul to be equal in value to that of a European. Virginians might be willing to study Indians, but not to take them to church.[16]

In his *Notes,* in 1782, Jefferson responded to French natural historians who had opined that all animals and persons born in the Americas were likely to be smaller and otherwise inferior to those of Europe and

Asia. The comte de Buffon had suggested that Indians were lacking in sexual ardor or intellect (a curious linkage) because of alleged disparities between their organs for such activities and those of Europeans. Jefferson acknowledged that "there are varieties in the race of man distinguished by their powers both of body and mind . . . as I see to be the case in the races of other animals." But he tartly observed that "the bulk and faculties of animals depend on the side of the Atlantic on which their food happens to grow, or which furnishes the elements of which they are compounded." Though insisting that Native Americans were as fully human as native Frenchmen, Jefferson at this stage saw both through French lenses, allowing Indians little more than the status of "noble savages," with the emphasis on the noun, not the adjective. Though Logan might be capable of find language, no Indian could be expected to make fine buildings.[17]

It is astonishing but true that Jefferson's friend, the philosophical Volney, who made his reputation as a travel writer with accurate descriptions of the ancient ruins of the Middle East, was so blinded by his prejudice that Indians were noble savages that he could not admit that the mounds he later saw along the Ohio River were in fact ruins of architecture as well. In his influential *View of the Soil and Climate of the United States of America* Volney told the world that even those at Marietta and Cincinnati "afford no indication of skill in the military or in any other other art."[18]

Enlightenment for Indians, under proper instruction, might be possible. That much Jefferson and the French might allow at this stage, but not art. Then in the 1780s, irony intruded upon history, and brought enlightenment for Jefferson in the matter of Indian architecture—in Paris, of all places.

THE ENLIGHTENMENT
OF THOMAS JEFFERSON

Benjamin Henry Latrobe was not fair to Jefferson when he wrote of his having fished *all* he knew of architecture out of old French books. Jefferson had more practical experience with building than any other president of the United States, and was the only one to earn the honor of being called an architect. But Latrobe was right in implying that Jefferson's classical taste was bookish—and so, after his youthful digs along the Rivanna River in Virginia, was his archaeology. Jefferson made practical use of what he learned from his volumes of architectural history and from what his correspondents told him about American archaeology, but archaeology, like architecture and politics, must be learned by firsthand experience. All these activities produce dirty fingernails. Though one can study architectural history in books, the practice of the profession, like that of politics, is not so tidy and comfortable.

Jefferson made no effort to survey the architecture of the American West. That was not his way; neither did he do field research in the architecture of Italy. He wrote of the Ohio as "the most beautiful river on earth, its current gentle, waters clear, and bosom smooth" quoting the reports of French visitors of a place he had never seen, and though he referred to Palladio's book about the villas of the Veneto as his architectural Bible, he remained nearby for two weeks studying rice production but never made the day's journey to see Palladio's buildings.[19]

However, he had already learned enough from books—and letters and magazines—to abandon his skepticism about Indians being capable of "monuments" larger than "barrows." The evidence leading him to a larger vision of the capabilities of the Native Americans had begun to accumulate in his library even before 1781, when he wrote the *Notes on Virginia,* though it became thoroughly persuasive to him only during and after his years in France, commencing in 1784.

Within the next twenty-five years he became fully informed about the circles, squares, and octagons used by the Adena-Hopewell. Here is a summary of that process:

Jefferson's earliest acquaintance with linked Hopewellian circles and squares probably came from the accounts of Circleville and Hopeton by the Reverend David Jones, in 1774—see Chapter Three. By 1780, Jefferson owned an early edition of Jonathan Carver's *Travels,* first published in 1778, in which Carver wrote of the entrenchment with angles on the upper Mississippi, as if it were an octagon. That would attract Jefferson's notice, for he took intense interest in things octagonal.

In 1789, Jefferson was in France as minister to the Bourbon court, replacing Benjamin Franklin. He received a letter from Ezra Stiles, President of Yale College, written on May 8, 1786, enclosing another letter, this one from Samuel Holden Parsons, together with a drawing of "works of earth in lines of circumvallation found at Muskingham on Ohio, lately taken by General Parsons on the spot." Stiles had pressed Benjamin Franklin for an opinion about the earthworks of Ohio, but Franklin could not bring himself to believe they were of Indian origin. None the less, by the late 1780s many learned people in Paris and in the United States knew they were *there.*[20]

By 1790, Jefferson was already moving some distance toward accepting the possibility that the Indians themselves might be capable of something beyond noble savagery, but he still held to his view that though "the Indians on the waters of the Ohio . . . might indeed make

. . . entrenchments of earth," they were, and always had been, "in the hunter state." In April, 1789, Charles Thomson of Philadelphia gave Jefferson more information about the "antiquities found in the Western country." Responding from Paris, Jefferson recommended "that persons who go thither . . . make very exact descriptions of what they see of that kind, without forming any theories. The moment a person forms a theory, his imagination sees in every object only the tracts which favor that theory. . . . It is too early to form theories on those antiquities."[21]

Jefferson probably read, at this time, the accounts of the Ohio written by other members of the scientific community of Philadelphia. The mathematician and astronomer, David Rittenhouse, and Benjamin S. Barton, a physician and naturalist, published their reports in London in 1787.[*] Throughout the 1790s, hundreds of alert and articulate visitors to the West returned with reports of the scale of the ancient Indian achievements. Another Philadelphian, the naturalist William Bartram, reported his explorations of the mound-building territory of the South in 1791. At least five more published descriptions and maps of the Marietta "works" became available, before 1807.

The issue of the *Transactions of the American Philosophical Society* which in 1793 carried Jonathan Heart's posthumous article on the mounds also carried an article by Jefferson. Even if that were not enough to assure that the Sage of Monticello saw Heart's discussion of the Marietta works, he might well have seen the earlier version published in 1787, in *Columbian Magazine.*

Actually, it is most unlikely he missed the more extended discourse in the *Transactions,* for the journal also carried Gilbert Imlay's obituary of Heart. Imlay was by then the best known critic of Jefferson's racial prejudices. His fame came first, in 1792, with the publication in London, of *The Emigrants,* one of the two earliest novels which may be fairly described as Westerns.[†] Almost coincidentally came *A Topographical Description of the Western Territory of the United States,* a beguiling best-seller in several languages, combining a travel narrative and political treatise. Imlay's florid text about the wonders of the Ohio Valley contained Benjamin Barton's excellent descriptions of its earth-

---

[*]In 1796, Barton engaged the attention of another of Jefferson's correspondents, the English scientist and anticlerical, Joseph Priestley. Priestley, a restless seeker after what he called "primitive Christianity," and anathema to the orthodox, shared friendships with Jefferson and Rittenhouse and exchanged letters about their common enthusiasm for Indian archaeology with Bishop James Madison, cousin of the future president. Madison's treatise on the Ohio earthworks appeared in the *Transactions of the American Philosophical Society* in 1803.

[†]The other was Hugh Brackenridge's *Western Chivalry.*

works, and his political text was a merciless dissection of Jefferson's *Notes on Virginia*, focusing upon his prejudice against Blacks, in general, and specifically against Phillis Wheatley, the poet.*[22]

The Ohio Valley earthworks were presented on a second occasion with company compelling to the political Jefferson. In 1809 a map showing the circle and square at Hopeton was published in a Philadelphia magazine called the *Port Folio*. The *Port Folio* had been a Federalist journal so notorious for its attacks upon his reputation that Jefferson had done all he could to have it suppressed. There can be no doubt that he was watching its pages with furious intensity. (See Appendix A: Thomas Jefferson and Nicholas Biddle.)

In 1805, an account appeared of Ohio geometrics which might (if we could be certain Jefferson saw it) lead us directly to his own architectural planning, specifically for Poplar Forest. The *Journal* of Thaddeus Mason Harris was published in Boston, including a good description of the circle, square, and octagon at Newark. Between that date and 1820, the total of published maps of Marietta reached eight, accompanied by new accounts of the circles, squares, and octagons at Newark and in the Scioto River valleys. English, Swiss, and American travel writers scoured the countryside for romantic mounts.[23]

After reading Sargent's report to the Philosophical Society in 1799, Jefferson began calling the earthen architecture of the West "monuments." That was a change from the *Notes on Virginia*. He now knew that they were not only larger than the Rivanna River tumuli; they were parts of larger complexes. More important still, they were laid out in accordance with the science of geometry, always a subject of intense interest to him. That alone would force a revision in his perception of those who built them.

The American Antiquarian Society was formed in 1812, largely to expatiate upon the western earthworks. Not long thereafter, President James Monroe appointed Caleb Atwater to be postmaster in Circleville. In 1820, Atwater produced the first volume of the Society's *Transactions,* gaining an enthusiastic response from Dewitt Clinton, John Marshall, and Jefferson, and containing an excellent map of the circle and octagon at Newark. Jefferson wrote to the Society that he found it "truly pleasing to hope that, by their exertions, the monuments of the character and condition of the people who preceded us in the occupation of this great country will be rescued from oblivion before they will have entirely disappeared." He told the Antiquarians that he prayed for the success of the society's archaeologists, and

---

*Imlay was a friend of poets. He introduced the literary work of Daniel Boone to Lord Byron, and was, one might say, several times the father-in-law of Percy Bysshe Shelley.

"would gladly take a part in their labors, but nature had limited the term of his services to an earlier day."[*][24]

POPLAR FOREST

From 1805 until 1825, Jefferson was designing and building his retreat at Poplar Forest, south of Lynchburg. As was always the case with him, there was a burst of clarity about form at the outset, then decades of fussing over details and worse fussing over the financial means to complete the program. As late as 1815 he still warned a friend to come "with ears stuffed full of cotton to fortify them against the noise of hammers, saws, planes, etc."; only in 1825 was the ornamentation complete.[25]

Jefferson split his force of two hundred slaves roughly equally between the five thousand acres he owned around Monticello and the four thousand of which Poplar Forest was headquarters. In 1812 he proudly asserted that Poplar Forest would be "the best dwelling house in the state, except that of Monticello; and perhaps preferable to that, as more proportioned to the faculties of a private person."[26]

It was Jefferson's custom to establish himself three times a year at Poplar Forest. At first he camped there himself; he removed his entire family there after he declared it fit for female occupancy in 1815.[†] Poplar Forest was more than Jefferson's distillation of the ideal American gentleman's residence: it was his statement of the proper relationship of such a geometrically ordered villa to an ideal, geometrically ordered, American landscape.[‡]

As he was working out this construct, public interest in the architecture of Ohio was at its most intense, with reports delivered to him in

---

[*]Jefferson's sentiments echoes those of George Washington's letter to the Cincinnati of Marietta, regretting that he could not join them in their archaeology, a letter so widely known and so compelling that St. John de Crevecoeur invented similar sentiments for Benjamin Franklin: "Were it not for my advanced age, I would myself cross the mountains to examine those old military works. . . . What a field for reflection!" (Crevecoeur for Franklin, quoted in Percy G. Adams, *Travellers and Travel Liars*, p. 160).

[†]Jefferson offered Poplar Forest to his grandson, Francis Eppes, in 1822, the year before he went there for the last time. He never saw the house in its final, finished, ornamented form. Two years after Jefferson's death, Eppes sold it in 1828 to a neighbor, whose family retained it for 118 years. There was a fire in 1845, which they repaired and did considerable remodeling to turn a villa into a farmhouse.

[‡]Most of the plans for the University of Virginia came later, but not all were Jefferson's. Generations of scholars have been baffled by attempting to sort out which were exclusively his, which suggested by Benjamin Henry Latrobe, and which by Dr. William Thornton. Poplar Forest was his own.

many a morning's pouch of mail. For a person with a passion for both architecture and archaeology, a demonstration of *one* in the *other* intensified what might have been merely interesting in either. When this intensification was heightened by the presence of pure geometrical forms—especially octagons—Thomas Jefferson paid attention. Jefferson was aware of linked circles and squares in the Renaissance fortress designs of Europe. Probably by 1780 and certainly by 1810, he had learned that these figures were also a part of American architecture. Earthen architecture—on a monumental scale, American in origin, employing his beloved octagons and circles—might be a way to declare the artistic independence of America.*[27]

Many villas in eighteenth-century Britain were composed of a large central structure, with a "hyphen" (a short, low, connecting structure) at each end eventuating in a pavilion. In Virginia and its colonies, Kentucky and Tennessee, this "five part" format was frequently associated with buildings designed or influenced by Jefferson, and is often called "Jeffersonian." But Jefferson's designs for Monticello and especially for Poplar Forest demonstrate that he was also at work upon new patterns and new methods. The most extraordinary of these—the use of earthen mounds rather than pavillions to terminate the hyphens—is "Jeffersonian" as well, unprecedented, and undeniably as American as the bison Jefferson defended from Beffon.

Jefferson's mounds, each about a hundred feet in diameter, were located about a hundred feet from the house at Poplar Forest at the end of the hyphens and rising twelve feet from the level. As if to be certain that no one might think this deployment casual, Jefferson ordered his gardeners to echo the twenty-foot square of the central room of the house by planting "on each mound, four weeping willows on the top in a square twenty feet apart."[28]

Though the house was begun in 1806, and the south parterre in the next year, Jefferson kept adjusting his mounds until 1812. That was the year in which the American Antiquarian Society was founded, with its primary task to inquire further into the architecture of ancient Ohio. The *floor* plan of the central villa is a square within an octagon. The *ground* plan of the estate places that house within a circular planting of trees bordering a circular drive—and, probably, an octagonal fence. The trees and road were broken to permit an extension to the south—a short, straight road running on a line from the main entrance

---

*The process by which Jefferson became informed about specific structures in Ohio is a lengthy and complicated story, which I attempted to tell in the Winter 1992–1993 issue of the *Winterthur Portfolio*. That portion of it which relates to Nicholas Biddle, a Burrite in Jefferson's day and later the arch-Whig, is a plum pudding of political ironies so delicious that I could not bring myself to omit it wholly from this necessarily low-calorie version. It appears in Appendix A.

of the house and connecting the great circle to a garden. We do not know that this garden was square. It was probably fenced with split rails, and split rails do not leave much to archaeology. But gardens of the time were conventionally square: the site is squarish, and so, it is likely, was the garden.

A square or octagon attached to a circle is the configuration of many earthworks in Ohio. What did Jefferson know of them while he was shaping the landscape at Poplar Forest? It is probable, though not certain, that he was acquainted with the reports of Harris, Heart, and Jones. Jefferson *did* acknowledge receipt of letters containing full reports and several maps of the Marietta complex, and it would be very strange if he had not seen the sequence of publications following Benjamin Barton's account of 1787, with an excellent diagram emphasizing the geometry of its earthworks. And he is even more likely to have read Barton's letter as printed in Gilbert Imlay's *Topographical Description* of 1792–93, Imlay's obituary of Heart, and *The Portfolio* in 1809.[29]

Poplar Forest is Jefferson's final exploration of a favorite theme, octagons, but the mounds made it different from all its preliminary exercises. He designed an octagonal house full of suboctagons; one of its tables, probably designed by him, is also an octagon. There was, as well, an octagonal fence within the circular drive. And it is even possible that the underlayment of each mound was an octagon.[30]

THE SOLACE OF GEOMETRY

Size is important, but shape is more so; we ordering animals return, over and over again, to familiar shapes. Thomas Jefferson was a person to whom order and geometry (which is familiar shape) and science were all one, and all of importance. From his first to his last architectural work, he demonstrated a craving for the solace of recognizable physical arrangements, as if he felt a healing in the archetypal power of certain geometric forms, especially the octagon and circle, and from the mathematics associated with them.

He had experimented with geometry in his youth. In middle age, he conducted his grandson's "course in mathematics," and, he said, "resumed that study with great avidity. It was ever my favorite one. We have no theories there, no uncertainties remain on the mind; all is demonstration and satisfaction." What longing there is in that sentence! At the end of his life he sought "satisfaction" in the mathematical geometry at Poplar Forest. Gone were the fragmentations, the disorientations, the "theories."[31]

"Natural history," he had said, using that term in a discussion of archaeology, was his "passion." Architecture was a beloved companion from youth to age. At Poplar Forest, Jefferson brought together work the fruits of archaeology, of geometry, and of architecture, in his last work—his *Falstaff.* "Satisfaction," he had said, "satisfaction" is a good translation of the term Verdi used for his feelings while he composed his last two operas, *Otello* and *Falstaff,* the "old man's toys."

What was Jefferson composing? All he would say was that he passed his time at Poplar Forest "in tranquility and retirement much adapted to my age and indolence." There he could exclude what his granddaughter called "disagreeable intrusions," the "indelicate and improper visits" of the throngs pressing in upon him at Monticello: "the crowd . . . of friends and strangers, of stationary or ever-varying guests, the coming and going, the incessant calls upon his attention, the want of leisure. . . ." Jefferson went on to say that at Poplar Forest, within its rings of octagons and circles, "I slumber without fear, and review in my dreams the visions of antiquity."[32]

What antiquity might this be? Might it not be, in part, an American antiquity? Or was his entire intention to be able to "slumber without fear?" In 1819, in the aftermath of yet another slave revolt, he wrote of the fear of the "firebell in the night." The South was full of fear; the nation was convulsed; many in the North were angry over the admission of Missouri into the Union as a slave state. The Founders' compromise over slavery was no longer tenable. There were fire bells in the night; uprisings were constantly reported. The end of the slave-driving plantocracy of Virginia was drawing ever nearer; from fire bells and from a society desperately riven, Jefferson sought a place of refuge. Keeping the world at a distance, he might in his final years deny the terror at the gates.

Within his gates, Jefferson created the circular walk that provided an ancient protective liturgy, a *circumambulation,* around the space he wished to keep private, his *temenos,* his sacred space. Safe within, he might seek solace in the geometric calculations which had beguiled him all along, especially in the circles. For him as for all of us, circles are incantations to wholeness, quietude, and completion. As Aniela Jaffe, the Jungian scholar, once wrote of "every building, sacred or secular, that has a mandala" ground plan, the estate at Poplar Forest was formed to accommodate "symbols of psychic wholeness, and in this way exercise a specific influence on the human being who enters or lives in the place."[33]

It is a disservice to Thomas Jefferson to avow that he settled into a selfish and oblivious old age. He knew too much to escape the moral tensions which had been brought to his attention by his French friends among the Amis des Noirs (the Friends of the Blacks) and by the eloquence of Logan, though he acquiesced in slavery and in the violent "removal" of Indians. True, he had lost his youthful fervor for the abolition of slavery, but Jefferson was constantly reminded by younger men such as Edward Coles and Thomas Worthington of what he had once said, and of what he had left undone. It is no wonder that he surrounded himself with ring after ring of geometric abstractions, circles, octagons, and squares. He was keeping away demons.

The plan of Poplar Forest is like one of those fortresses of which Leonardo di Vinci drew exquisite plans; though of dubious defensive value, they might exorcise fear by imposing an ideal order.

GALLATIN, JEFFERSON, AND SLAVERY

The Sage of Monticello was not a saint; he was a gentleman-politician-slaveowner avid for politics. His public career could thrive only so long as he did nothing offensive to the gentry he represented, who raised crops for market with slave labor and who also raised slaves for market as a second crop. The gentlemen of the Old Dominion were articulate, rich, charming, and controlled the largest single constituency in American politics. Largely, though not solely because of their influence, slavery permeated every aspect of the nation's life: its Constitution, its economy, its religion, and its psychology.*

Jefferson was at once the beneficiary of slavery and its victim. His sweet and cultivated leisure, his books, wine, and cigars, were purchased by the sweat of his slaves. He knew it. And because he gave constant thought to his place in history, he knew full well that posterity would be aware of it as well. Whatever else he accomplished, his reputation was and is shadowed by his failure to grapple with the shame of slavery.

Though it is wearisomely repeated of him in amelioration of this failure that he was a man of his time and class, others of his time and class did take the political risks and suffered the financial losses required to be consistent foes to slavery. Among them were Benjamin Franklin, George Washington, John Randolph, Alexander Hamilton, Aaron Burr, Edward Coles, and Thomas Worthington. They acted upon their professed beliefs, though it would have been easy for Coles,

---

*This statement may seem to some an old-fashioned point of view. It is; it represents the view common to most histories of the United States written during the last half of the nineteenth century.

It was, however, unacceptable to the mainstream of historians during the Jim Crow period of American historiography, between 1900 and the 1950s. Neither the Beardians, Turnerites, nor most Marxists were much interested in race-based slavery. The perspective of the Dixiecrat historians was even more embarrassing; those of us who took our Jefferson from Claude Bowers cannot read him today without a shudder.

Worthington, Washington, and Randolph to add locale to time and class as excuses; they, like Jefferson, were Virginians. Coles and Worthington freed their slaves during their lifetimes, Randolph set all his hundreds free at his death, and Washington did so at the death of his spouse. Jefferson freed only a handful of his slaves and those few only on his death.

In his public life, Jefferson did attempt on occasion to ameliorate the evil they all acknowledged. The two most widely celebrated of these actions are the condemnation of the slave trade in the Declaration of Independence and the termination of that trade during his presidency. His courage on both occasions has been overpraised.

Let us look closely at the Declaration, reserving the termination of the slave trade for its place in a larger story. In 1776, Jefferson placed in his draft of the Declaration of Independence a forceful indictment of Britain's king for the *international* slave trade, though refraining from any indictment of slavery itself. He did not propose that the Declaration utter a word about the American purchasers of slaves or the merchants engaged in the *domestic* slave trade, of whom Virginians were especially active. Jefferson had his mild say to the international audience, but in any case, his colleagues struck even his modest and measured attack on the slave system from the final version of the Declaration.*

Jefferson *was* a man of his time; he had an acute sense of the winds of change, and as he entered the national and international political arena, in the early 1780s, he must have felt those winds rising about him. Slavery was abolished in Vermont in the 1770s, and in 1781 was held incompatible in Massachusetts with the theorem of the Declaration that all men were created equal. Even in Virginia, the right of slave owners to manumit was formally recognized by law in 1782 and reaffirmed by a two-to-one majority in the House of Delegates in 1785.[†] Slavery was being questioned by all civilized peoples.[‡]

---

*Those who have not read the Declaration sometimes are heard to say that it proclaimed that all men were born "free and equal". It spoke only of equality, and it obviously did not proclaim any intention to extend political equality to the enslaved.

[†]In his autobiography, Jefferson wrote: "In 1769, I became a member of the legislature. . . . I made one effort in that body for the permission of the emancipation of slaves, which was rejected: and indeed, during the regal government, nothing liberal could expect success." (Jefferson, *Autobiography*, p. 5). His biographers have striven without success to confirm that statement. (See Randall, *Jefferson*, 1, p. 58, and Malone, *Jefferson the Virginian*, p. 141.)

Jefferson also wrote that while he was still in the Virginia legislature, in 1778 or early 1779, he and others considered bringing in an amendment to the Virginia slave code, which would provide for "freedom of all born after a certain day, and deportation at a proper age. But it was found that the public mind would not yet bear the proposition. . . . The two

This was the context of his preparation for recording his strongest sentiments against slavery, in his *Notes on Virginia*, written for an audience of French *philosophes*. (Jefferson resisted publication of the *Notes* in America until pirated copies forced his hand.)

Our subject is the discovery of the Great Valley and the prejudices brought into the discovering by Jefferson and his contemporaries. While considerably more could be said of how Jefferson's actions projected those prejudices on the world stage, with regard to the Valley the most important facts to be born in mind are that whatever he might have written for the French, slavery was battened upon the people of the Great Valley during his presidency, from 1801 to 1809, and that he had done little to oppose its expansion into the region since 1784.* Those are severe charges, and to their weight must be added this: he also diminished the benign influence in the West of Gallatin, who was hobbled from his full effectiveness as a friend to freedom by his loyalty to Jefferson. As early as 1792, Gallatin had led a committee of the Pennsylvania legislature to declare that slavery was "obviously contrary to the laws of nature, the dictates of justice . . . and natural

---

races, equally free, cannot live in the same government." He always coupled emancipation and deportation. In his *Notes* he repeted the theme: "When freed, he is to be removed beyond the reach of mixture." (Lib. of Am. *Jefferson*, pp. 44, 270).

Dumas Malone tells us that Jefferson drew a draft of a constitution for Virginia in 1783, "containing a provision for the emancipation of slaves born after 1800," but, once again, nothing came of it. (Malone, *Sage*, p. 317.)

In 1814, Jefferson wrote privately to Edward Coles that he favored gradual emancipation, but would not speak of it openly.

In the aftermath of the Missouri debate of 1819–20, Jefferson supported the proposal by his son-in-law, Thomas Mann Randolph, who was then Governor of Virginia, that a plan close to that offered by Jefferson in 1779–89 be followed, for gradual emancipation and deportation.

Once again, the legislature refused to take up the matter. So, in 1824, Jefferson proposed a plan of his own, his last address to the problem of slavery. He proposed taking all Black children from their parents at the age of five, putting them at forced labor until they became adults, and shipping them off to Haiti, while their parents and grandparents remained in slavery until their deaths. This scheme commended itself to no one, least of all, probably, to those Black families who would be affected.

†It was on its way to abolition nearly everywhere—though it did surge once more in Cuba, Brazil, in the Old South, and because of the influence of southern statesmen in the American West.

*Commencing in Virginia in the middle of the seventeenth century, Europeans and their descendants coupled slavery to race, at first as to Indians and then as to Africans, making it hereditary. In effect, therefore, Europeans acted as if those afflicted by slavery had committed a crime, applying penalties otherwise reserved only for felons of the most vicious sort to people guiltless of any failing except their color. Among these penalties were the loss of personal freedom, the exposure to violence without appeal, and hereditary "attainder," by which the recompense for guilt was required through inheritance from the guiltless.

right." But by 1799 he had lapsed, his compass thrown off course by the power of Jefferson's magnetism, and he failed to speak out publicly against slavery until after Jefferson's retirement from public office in 1809.[34]*

The crucial year is 1784, when, as chairman of a committee of the Congress dealing with the organization of the western territories, Jefferson acceded to a proposal by David Hail of Rhode Island and Timothy Pickering of Massachusetts that would set the statutory limit to the spread of slavery at the Appalachians, beyond which there were still few slaves, and they would be set free after 1800. Though six states voted for Hail's proposal and only three opposed, seven were needed, and it failed. Jefferson cast an "aye" vote and wrote James Madison of his regret at that outcome, but there is no record of any strenuous effort on his part in support of Hail's idea.[35]

Things fell out quite differently in 1787. Jefferson is sometimes credited with the Northwest Ordinance. When many of us learned history, we were told that Jefferson saw to it that the Ordinance prohibited slavery north of the Ohio. Jefferson *was* the final draftsman of the Ordinance, but was *not* the proponent of the limitation of slavery. Once again, that honor must be accorded to the Federalists: Rufus King, Timothy Pickering, Nathan Dane, and Manassah Cutler. The precise language of limitation was introduced by Dane of Massachusetts, and lobbied through the Congress by Cutler.

The Southwest Ordinance came along shortly thereafter, and is somewhat less often celebrated, for it is not a source of pride; it permitted all territories organized south of the Ohio to come in as greater Virginias—with slavery. Operating in tandem thereafter, the two ordinances implicitly encouraged the expansion of slavery into those parts of the trans-Appalachian Southwest which it had not yet polluted,

---

*In 1799, during the maritime war with France, the Federalists passed a law which cut off trade with that country but opened commercial relations with Haiti, which, under the leadership of Toussaint Louverture, had cast off slavery and French rule and was ruled by a multiracial coalition.

Gallatin had the loathsome task of opposing the Federalist legislation, taking Jefferson's side in what has come to be known as his "Black Speech," praising Toussaint but also playing upon fears that his success might lead other Negroes to think of achieving freedom by violent means. The word "black" was a litany; the twists and turns of Gallatin's rhetoric about the word mark the contortions of his own thinking at the time. Even his admiring biographers have been forced to concede that he used language he might have disdained in earlier or later years. After Jefferson's election as president in 1800, the United States broke off the support the Federalists had given Toussaint. In 1800, Jefferson entered into a conspiracy with Napoleon to starve out the Haitian regime. It was unsuccessful, but Toussaint was kidnapped and died in a French prison. (This unhappy story is told at greater length in Kennedy, *Orders from France*).

while crimping the slaveowning style of only a few French residents of Illinois.*

These were acts of the old Confederation. As they were swept into the first set of laws drawn by a Congress operating under the Constitution, they became components of a set of interlocked compromises: the Constitution itself provided to the slaveholders their disproportionate voting power, while the Yankees got the assumption of state debts and protection of their shipping, including those ships engaged in a slave trade constitutionally protected until 1808.

The passes so quickly abandoned in 1784 were open, and slavery rushed into the West. In 1792, Kentucky was admitted to the Union with a slaveowners' constitution, despite the protests of many Kentuckians taking their abolitionist lead from Aaron Burr, but receiving no word of encouragement from Thomas Jefferson. He was silent again as Tennessee followed Kentucky's model in 1796, though Federalists opposed to slavery delayed its entry as long as possible. In 1798, the citizens of Mississippi came to the Congress asking to be organized under the same terms as the Northwest Territory, but with a signal exception. They wanted no part of its prohibition of slavery. George Thacher of Massachusetts attempted to reinsert that inhibition, setting off an explosion of debate, but the power of the South was too great for him. As Georgia and North Carolina conceded their western lands to the nation, they forced a condition that slaves would be permitted to inhabit them. Jefferson, observing and giving counsel throughout these events, never again expressed in public his doubts of 1784.

Jefferson's model republic for the West was fully tested with the organization of Louisiana after his purchase in 1803; it was not to be reserved for free and independent yeomen. Instead, under explicit arrangements with Napoleon, the slaves of Louisiana had shackled upon them the American system of servitude. Under the terms of the Purchase, the slaveowners of Louisiana were assured that they would enjoy all the privileges and immunities of citizens of the United States, which was read by Jefferson to mean that they might keep their slaves.[†]

The debate on this interpretation, in 1805–06, is one of the defining political events of American history.[‡] It set the course of all subsequent

---

*These Frenchmen had received assurances from George Rogers Clark that they might keep their slaves (see Chapter Eight).

[†]Actually, slavery worsened for Blacks in Louisiana; the new American regulations were more burdensome and humiliating than those of the French *Code Noir*.

[‡]That debate was limited in its effects to the area now included in the state of Louisiana, then known as the Orleans Territory. The much greater remainder of the region was then the District of Louisiana.

debates and compromises on the future of the Great Valley, the Missouri Compromise of 1819, the Compromise of 1850, and the Kansas-Nebraska Act. When the next of these, the Missouri Compromise, came before the congress, it elicited from Jefferson an explicit reversal of his policy of 1784.

He had not been so candid during the debate of 1805–6, but his closest supporters revealed what later became his "dispersion theory": slavery was said to become less noxious to the degree that it was spread out. The debate brought into the fray the opponents of the expansion of slavery who had fought beside Jefferson in 1784, had kept the faith, and might have expected his support as president two decades later. They included other southerners who deplored slavery, John Randolph of Roanoke and that marvelous character, Jesse Franklin of North Carolina.

Jefferson failed them, apparently perplexing Gallatin. He wrote to Jefferson a private memorandum responding to the argument that the French citizens of Louisiana must be protected in their slave holdings because Napoleon had received such assurance about privileges and immunities:

> They [the Louisiana French] seem to be but one degree above the French West Indians, than whom a more ignorant and depraved race of civilized men did not exist. Give them slaves and let them *speak* French (for they cannot write it) and they would be satisfied. The first is inadmissible; how far their language should, as they wish, be legally recognized is questionable; but their officers should at least understand them.[36]

Jefferson's reply is not recorded; he remained silent. Gallatin, having attempted conversion throughout, was bound in loyalty and held his peace as well. It is likely that privately he shared the unhappiness of most of the circle of friends he shared with Jefferson in the city of Washington. Among them was the tactless Thomas Paine, back from Europe and still full of common sense; Paine proposed settling the lower valley with Germans, who might serve as antidotes to slave labor. As many a citizen of the "German Coast" of Louisiana can now avow, that was not a foolish idea. It did not, it seems, much commend itself to Jefferson.

Even less was the president inclined to the suggestion of Paine's host in Washington, the poet Joel Barlow, that the Jeffersonians should embrace the proposal of Senator James Hillhouse of Connecticut that the

---

The debate was, in effect, about whether the provisions of the Northwest Ordinance, which had been applied to Ohio, Indiana, and Illinois, should be applied to Orleans Territory in its pure form, or taken with the express exception of the antislavery clause, as applied in the cases of the Southwest Territory and Mississippi.

new territory be organized without slavery, whatever the lawyers might say about the intent of the treaty. Hillhouse was another Federalist, and known to share the opinion of Alexander Hamilton that Louisiana could be taken without paying Napoleon for his doubtful title to it. Why, asked the northern Federalists, should Jefferson profess to feel bound to include the "privilege" of owning slaves within those assured to the Louisianans? Most citizens of the United States lived in areas where that "privilege" was denied them. How could Napoleon enforce such an interpretation? His failed amphibious assault upon Haiti had demonstrated his incapacity to mount naval operations in the Western Hemisphere. What, then, would happen if the United States insisted upon applying the principles of the Northwest Ordinance to Louisiana? Napoleon could not take it back. Besides, he did not own it in the first place. The earlier treaty by which he took it from Spain explicitly required its reversion to the Spaniards if he were to seek to dispose of it as he did.

But the Jeffersonians controlled the Senate; all they would permit was a limitation on *selling* slaves within Louisiana itself. This diminished competition from abroad, but permitted those sold next door, in Mississippi, to be brought across the river and put to work. If slave-owning was a privilege, they argued, then slave-selling was, too.*

---

*The debate in 1804 upon the Hillhouse Amendment (to the Breckenridge Bill of 1803 for the organization of Louisiana) is full of piquant moments:

The renegade Federalist, Lyman Dayton of New Jersey, joined in the advocacy of slavery with the sanctimonious James Jackson of Georgia. Jackson spoke with such self-congratulatory hypocrisy that even Jefferson's slaveowning neighbor, Senator Cocke of Virginia, could stand him no longer. Cocke rose to proclaim that he rejoiced that Jackson had made it clear that he was the one honest man in Georgia.

Dayton attempted to elicit from Aaron Burr assent to his position that slavery was a positive good in Louisiana, and failed. (See Burr *Papers,* p. 867.)

James Wilkinson later attributed to Burr a coded letter written him by Dayton, a deliberate falsification, though it was one of many letters believed by most historians to be part of the Burr "Conspiracy" until it was demonstrated to be false by the editors of the Burr Papers. (See *Papers,* pp. 985–86.)

Standing beside Jackson and Dayton was John Breckenridge of Kentucky, a slaveowner, who said he was "opposed to slavery . . . and am for confining it within as small a compass as possible . . . I hope the time is not far distant when not a slave will exist in this Union. . . . [*But*—the "disperson argument" appears] This will disperse and weaken that race—and free the southern states from a part of its black population, and of its danger. If you do not permit slaves from the United States to go there, you will thereby prohibit men of wealth from the southern States going to settle in that country. . . . Out constitution recognizes slavery—it does more—it expressly protects it."

Jesse Franklin, leading the antislavery forces, took the view that "slavery is in every respect an evil. . . . It will soon, I fear, become a dreadful one—negro insurrections have already been frequent. . . . My wish is to prohibit slaves altogether from that country."

And Thomas Worthington of Ohio, infuriated by the sententious defense of slavery by Jackson, together with Jackson's threat that the people of the West might become so numer-

On the basis of this elastic doctrine, slaves sold by Virginians and Carolinians poured into Louisiana.* South Carolina reopened its slave trade in 1803 to take advantage of the opportunity provided by Jefferson, and commenced a brisk business in Africans for transshipment to Louisiana.

And so the year 1808 approached, with the much-praised abolition of the slave trade. All that Jefferson actually did was to permit the slave trade from *Africa* to expire; he merely supported a bill to do what the Constitution permitted. It cost him nothing; there was virtually no one on the other side; the vote in the House of Representatives was 113 to 5, with two of those *opposed* from the North. By then, "ending the slave trade" was understood by every Virginian slave breeder to mean terminating price competition from Africa; terminating that trade was scarcely an act of political courage deserving a listing among Jefferson's accomplishments. Jefferson did *not* abolish the slave trade. He engaged in that trade—the protected *domestic* slave trade. He rejoiced in the fecundity of his Negro women and sold slaves of his own into a thriving market; they were his most profitable crop. On the other hand, his cousin Randolph of Roanoke watched with horror as people were "raised for the market, like oxen for the shambles." Three hundred thousand Americans were sold in bondage by Virginians to customers in the Mississippi Valley.[37]

Thomas Jefferson was a European colonial, steeped in the cultures which had arisen around the Mediterranean and North seas, who happened to live in Virginia among more people from the continent of Africa than those like himself. Even after many were sold to do the heavy work of the West, they still outnumbered the whites. In 1800

---

ous as to effect "a separation of this Union," responded that "the western States will not separate unless the eastern States by their conduct render it absolutely necessary." (These proceedings appear in Plumer, and in the *American Historical Review* 22, October 1916 to July 1917, pp. 340 ff.)

*In fairness, Jefferson was merely recognizing that every state had *already* banned the importation of slaves despite the constitutional bargain that *Congress* could not terminate the traffic until 1808. They had the right, however, to reopen, which South Carolina did, assisted by slavers from Bristol and other Rhode Island ports.

After the Hillhouse amendments secured only the prohibition of the slave trade from the territory (or rather, of slave trading, as such), though not the continued ownership of slaves, in 1805 the assembly of Louisiana was organized, deploying the Mississippi Territory language, thereby wiping out the Hillhouse amendments.

Simultaneously, when the District of Louisiana was made into a territory, no mention was made of slavery one way or another, an omission of enormous importance for the future.

In 1812, when Lousiana became a state, the name of the remainder of the Louisiana Territory was changed to Missouri Territory, and a feeble effort was made to prohibit slavery in it. (See Fehrenbacher, *Slavery, Law, and Politics,* pp. 47 ff.)

there were probably still, despite the hideous consequences of recurrent plagues, more Indians in the United States than there were people of European descent. As a thoughtful man, Jefferson was forced to reach some conclusions about the nature of people dissimilar in appearance and tradition from himself. He did so. His assessment of Blacks did not alter much throughout his life; Jefferson's prejudices ran deep: nothing could persuade him that Blacks could exhibit "talents" equal to those of the "other colors of men." It was impossible to find, he asserted, a Black "capable of tracing and comprehending the investigations of Euclid."[38]

Later, he went so far as to acknowledge that the mathematician and surveyor, Benjamin Banneker, might have mastered trigonometry, but derided Banneker's letters as "very childish and trivial." Though Phillis Wheatley's verse went into five editions, praised by Washington and described by Voltaire as "polished," Jefferson could not bring himself to call her a poet. When the Abbe Gregoire compiled lists of Blacks showing genius, Jefferson dismissed him as credulous, and sought to find an infusion of white blood to explain any example of Negro genius.[*39]

Jefferson was a good scholar, and his response to the evidence of Indian genius presented by their architecture demonstrates that he was capable of pulling his views up from their roots in prejudice, and replacing them with better stock, when the justification for doing so was irresistable. He lived a little early to have the opportunity to assimilate an equivalent store of information about the ancient architecture of Zimbabwe, Punt, Kush, Meroe, Kumbi Selah, Jebel Uri, of Sheba, and upon the islands off the coast of Tanzania. These ancient cities of Africa only became widely known to Americans and Europeans after his death, and their magnitude was not fully apprehended until the 1960s. Still, there may have been moments in which, as he thought of what he had learned about Indians from their architecture, he might have pondered the possibility that the pyramids of Egypt and the temples of Carthage had been built by the ancestors of his own slaves.[40]

*   *   *

---

*Even his highly developed ironic sense did not lead Jefferson to note the discomfiting fact that he could investigate this hypothesis without leaving home. Intermixture between Whites and Blacks was commonplace enough in Jefferson's Virginia, where little of William Byrd's "false delicacy" stood in the way of the exploitation of Negro women (see also p. 132). Jefferson's father-in-law and his nephews produced a number of progeny by slave women. There is no dispute about that. What is remarkable is the furor attending the allegation that Jefferson did as well, considering how little comment there has been upon the general moral tone of plantation life at the time.

At the end of history, there is biography. At the end of politics, there is, sometimes, friendship. Albert Gallatin and Thomas Jefferson came to life with profoundly differing psychologies, and grew to take, as a consequence, radically different views of the relationship of white Europeans like themselves to people of darker skins. But first and last, they were friends. Like James Madison, Gallatin brought forth from Jefferson a deep affection which belies that public chilliness and impenetrability of which so much has been written.

It is no surprise to read of Jefferson as an old man romping with his grandchildren, or of his reconciliation with John Adams. One expects even impenetrable grandfathers to romp. The Adams-Jefferson friendship was a respectful relation of intellect to intellect. But with Gallatin, feelings went much deeper.

In August 1823, Jefferson was eighty. Gallatin was a mere stripling of sixty-two, but apparently frail. Jefferson wrote him entreating a last visit to Monticello while both were alive:

> Your visit to this place would indeed be a day of jubilee; but your age and distance forbid the hope. Be this as it will, I shall love you forever, and rejoice in your rejoicing, and sympathize with your evils. God bless you and have you ever in his holy keeping![41]

This letter should be required reading for those who believe they understand all there is to understand about Thomas Jefferson.

CHAPTER EIGHT

JEFFERSON'S ARCHAEOLOGISTS: PART ONE

In 1803, Thomas Jefferson, the great geometer, presented his countrymen with a Mississippi Basin completed in bilateral symmetry. Besides a fragment of the eastern bank surrounding the piratic little entrepot of New Orleans, his purchase from Napoleon added the whole western half of the valley, as far as the Rocky Mountains. Jefferson moved the Mississippi River from the edge of the American page to its centerfold.

He set upon that page a cast of characters beyond the contrivances of any novelist—without him not one of them could have played their parts, for good or ill. In this chapter and the next, we will tell their stories, one by one. Jefferson was president; he was busy and therefore required to rely upon these agents to advance his science, stimulating them to learn, persuading the Congress to appropriate for their expeditions, corresponding with them, and encouraging their publication. No president, and no chief of state elsewhere, has ever contributed so much to the store of a nation's information about the record of human habitation on its territory.

JAMES WILKINSON

Among these amateur archaeologists, James Wilkinson, commander of the armies of the United States in the Mississippi Valley, was the most assiduous in pleasing Jefferson, and the most dangerous to his reputation. The most embarrassing events of Jefferson's career arose from his dependence upon Wilkinson, though not in archaeological matters. Jefferson gave Louisiana into Wilkinson's hands, entrusting to this blackguard both his Nile and its pyramids.[1]

To whom may James Wilkinson best be compared? Lucifer? Alkibiades?* No one who met him denied his charm, whether as a dashing and corrupt young officer, a military dictator striding the streets of New Orleans in uniforms of his own design, or even as a seedy pensioner waddling about Mexico City. In his youth he was devastating, in both the figurative and literal sense of that word. He wooed and won a Philadelphia Biddle, and destroyed a succession of careers. Wilkinson may not have been evil; he may not have known what evil is. Some people have such an utter absorption with self that they do not hear the screech of tires or the thump of something beneath the wheels.

An archaeologist of sorts himself, he once happened to take aboard his borrowed riverboat headquarters a boy who became the first American to give a detailed description of the mound city of Cahokia, Henry Brackenridge. Decades later, Brackenridge was still entranced with the Wilkinson he first met on a barge fitted up as sumptuously as Cleopatra's.

> The general's countenance was continually lighted up with smiles, and he seemed *faire le bonheur* of all around him,—it seemed to be his pleasure to make everyone happy. His countenance and manners . . . were such as better fitted him for a court than a republic.[2]

Faire de bonheur! Wilkinson contaminated the happiness of everyone he met; all but a few of his allies and friends ended in disgrace or bankruptcy He accelerated the decline of Alexander Hamilton and led George Washington into his last and worst political error. Aaron Burr was one of scores of otherwise intelligent people deceived by him. Wilkinson had good taste in food, wine, and dupes; the list of those he fooled was a noble one. Thomas Jefferson remained on that list for forty years.

---

*Alkibiades was beloved of Socrates and darling of Athenian democracy in decay, rich, so beautiful that he caused a catching of breath as he passed, a superb athlete—and utterly without moral compunction. "Superficial and opportunist to the last, he owed [his] . . . successes purely to personal magnetism and an almost incredible capacity for deception." (From the entry for Alkibiades in the *Encyclopedia Britannica*, 11th Edition)

In the fifth century B.C., as the Adena people were building their conical burial mounds in Ohio, this paragon of egocentricity created in Athens such a reputation for wit and elegance that his conversations were later reconstructed by Plutarch, Plato, and Xenophon. The populace of Athens loved him, awarding him high office though he asserted with mock modesty that was because his horses won the Olympic Games.

The debouches of Alkibiades, like those of Wilkinson, were as famous as his hypocrisy. Only when his charm was removed from the scene by his departure to command an Athenian force in Sicily could he be tried for impiety and (implicitly) for sedition. He turned to Sparta, and, after Sparta, to stirring up the other enemies of Athens, in Greece and Asia, including Persia. He managed to charm himself back into the command of the Athenian fleet, defeated the Spartans, and returned to his grateful and credulous countrymen. He was finally defeated in battle, however, and died in exile.

Wilkinson was, when young, slim and charming, his face "mild, capacious, and beaming with intelligence . . . manly, and facile . . . he conciliated . . . he captivated." Born in Maryland, he joined Washington's army of revolution, was breveted a brigadier general, conspired against Washington, drunkenly betrayed his fellow conspirators, and charmed his way back into Washington's confidence until he was discharged for embezzlement. Once again, he deployed his mesmerizing guile, was reengaged as clothier general, and again cashiered for dishonesty.[3]

He removed himself to Kentucky in 1784. Three years later, he put an array of produce on a flatboat and set out for New Orleans, where he sold his crop to an eager market and sold himself to the Spanish government through its governor at New Orleans. For an annual fee payable in silver or gold, he became a secret agent of the Spanish Crown. In 1788, he insinuated himself into a group of plotters attempting to return the West to Britain, betrayed them, and followed this with the betrayal of an American military force to the Creek Indians. In 1791, Wilkinson reentered the United States Army; he was thought to have a useful following among the militia of the turbulent West. President George Washington not only gave him this commission, despite the manifest fact that he had long ago ceased to be a gentleman, but was subsequently persuaded by Alexander Hamilton to put Wilkinson in command of the armies of Louisiana Territory. Hamilton had taken the bait which Burr was to take: they both thought they could use Wilkinson.

They were both wrong, though Hamilton died before he found how wrong he had been. Wilkinson recycled plans developed for Hamilton in 1799 to Burr in 1805, a year after Burr killed Hamilton. Even then, Burr was still a hero to many in the West and South, and therefore useful to Wilkinson. At first, it seemed that Burr might merely reestablish himself upon the political base of some two hundred thousand acres purchased in Louisiana, but Wilkinsons urged him to larger ambitions—an invasion of Mexico. When Burr stumbled, Wilkinson turned to Jefferson, who was already apprehensive of Burr, who had been at once his rival and his vice president—the two distrusted each other, and both were right in doing so.

Wilkinson inflamed Jefferson's fears, persuading him that Burr was engaged in treason, creating a smokescreen behind which his own treason might escape notice. Jefferson issued a presidential proclamation charging Burr with conspiracy against the laws of the United States. And the president rewarded Wilkinson by making him military dictator of New Orleans, where he kidnapped potential witnesses for Burr with Jefferson's assent, ruled without *habeas corpus,* threatened to shoot federal judges, sought to extort Mexican gold from bankers, and intimidated citizens.*

The testimony Wilkinson gave against Burr during the trial of Burr's alleged treason was encrusted with perjury so rococo as to be almost admirable in the fertility of its invention: letters written by Wilkinson were attributed to Burr; people were place in locations they never occupied. Chief Justice John Marshall, who had no love for his cousin Jefferson or for Jeffersonian politics, dismissed the charge levied by the president's public proclamation against Burr. Marshall was confirming, thereby, the judgment of four juries in the West.†

After the trial, and Burr's release from the charge of treason, the tide of opinion turned against Wilkinson, so much so that it was he who was next tried for treason, as word crept out about his transactions with Spain. Relying once more upon his gift for persuasive perjury, he won a hung decision in 1811. An array of witnesses implicated him, but he was still a convincing liar. Until the records of the Spanish Foreign Office confirmed the charges against him in detail long after his death, those who had a stake in his veracity chose to believe him. Many others did not. Though he retained command in the West under Jefferson's protection, his tyranny and extortion in New Orleans were not forgotten. At the onset of the War of 1812 both senators from Louisiana urged his recall.

Instead, President Madison's secretary of war, John Armstrong, now fell under Wilkinson's spell; the commander of the West was commissioned a major general and put in command of an army, and produced a series of disasters along the Canadian border.‡

In his old age, Wilkinson remained so charming that when New Orleans became inhospitable, the Mexican authorities took him in. By this time, even *they* might have tired of him. Perhaps they felt he had earned his fees to the degree that he had somewhat confused American

---

*For Wilkinson and extortion, see "The Great Silver Scheme" in Kennedy, *Orders From France.*

†Marshall was the son of a Federalist Kentuckian who had already spiked several real secessionist plots.

‡It is not fair to blame Wilkinson alone for the botched campaign which ensued. His old partner in speculations in Mississippi, Wade Hampton of South Carolina, now also a general, bears part of the onus, though surely not so much of it as Wilkinson attributed to him in demanding Hampton's court martial. Memories of Wilkinson as clothier general, thirty-three years before, were reawakened when he abandoned his raw troops at the onset of winter. They were found in the spring "scandalously and infamously" clad, amid "unrelieved squalor . . . in filthy conditions . . . six to eight months behind in their pay." Wilkinson was once again brought to trial, and once again escaped justice. (Stagg, *Mr. Madison's War,* pp. 387–88.)

policy, and thus delayed expansion of the United States into the Great Valley. Under their rooftree, he composed three volumes of marvelously mendacious memoirs. It was as if, having lived a liar, he thought that he could deceive posterity. He got away with everything but that: the Spanish Archives failed him by not burning, and the record of his repeated treasons and betrayals was there to confound his most resourceful inventions. In the end, he like Alkibiades died in exile, but unlike Alkibiades Wilkinson died in comfort.[4]

* * *

During the 1790s, the Federalists were still in power, and Wilkinson prospered through the patronage of Alexander Hamilton. But Jefferson's star was rising and the commander of the American forces west of the Appalachians was therefore pleased to participate in research attracting the approval of the Sage of Monticello. From 1797 onward, Wilkinson sent him a succession of archaeological reports on what was "marvelous" in the West, and found his way to membership in a select committee of the American Philosophical Society, under Jefferson's chairmanship. Its task was

> to obtain accurate plans, drawings, and descriptions . . . [of the western] ancient fortifications, tumuli, and other Indian works of art, ascertaining the materials composing them, their contents, the purposes for which they were probably designed, etc . . . the length, breadth, and height of the walls . . . carefully measured.[5]

In 1800, Jefferson received from Wilkinson extensive meterological records and artifacts, including "petrifactions," tools, and maps; in 1802, bottles of water from the Arkansas and Mississippi; in 1804, a compendium of maps; in 1805, more artifacts, "to amuse a leisure moment," together with more serious data anticipating the ethnological studies of Albert Gallatin: "an enumeration of some of the Indian Nations southwest of the Missouri River." Wilkinson unctuously claimed as well to have been a provider of other "little services" drawing the "acknowledgments of Washington, Adams, and Jefferson."[6]

Wilkinson's little services included urging his partners in real estate speculations to send along to Mr. Jefferson artifacts turned out of Indian graves by the plow. There is no indication in all Wilkinson's correspondence that he had any interest in antiquity, but Jefferson did, and Jefferson was powerful. As is often the case, much good may be done when even the venal are solicited by the good in power, and some of Wilkinson's closest associates were themselves honorable men who would probably have sought to serve scholarship even if Jefferson had not made it so worthwhile for them to do so. Harry Innes, for example, was Wilkinson's agent in Kentucky, as well as Burr's and Jefferson's.

Innes was the presiding judge in a territory which not only possessed much evidence of antiquity but also such dazzling archaeologists as Constantine Rafinesque-Schmalz.

Innes sent to Jefferson the first piece of his collection of Native American sculpture. It had come together with a description of a "fort" on the south fork of the Elkhorn Creek, near Lexington, Kentucky, in July, 1790. The gift from Innes was nine-and-three-quarter-inch statuette "found by a farmer as he was plowing his corn field" near the Cumberland River, seventy miles south and west of Lexington. Jefferson replied with delight, saying it was "the best piece of workmanship I ever saw from their hands. . . . The artist . . . has very happily hit on the representation of a woman in the first moments of parturition."[7]

Morgan Brown of Tennessee vied with Innes, shipping Indian antiquities to Jefferson from the Cumberland settlements. In 1799, Brown, living in the vicinity in which Innes's figurine had been found, wrote Jefferson that he wished to contribute to the gallery at Monticello two more figures, "of a male and a female . . . found by some laborers digging at a place called Palmyra" in Tennessee. They were later said to be "nearly of the natural size" of the upper half of their bodies; this could be true, for each weighed nearly seventy pounds.[8]

Brown's sculptural contributions were slow to arrive. Jefferson was forced to ask Wilkinson to superintend the transportation of these "two Indian busts from Palmyra." The kneeling figures were of marble found beside the Cumberland near Palmyra, Tennessee. They were carved in workshops nearby in the triangle between the present villages of Castalian Springs, Sellers, and Dixon Creek, thirty miles northeast of Nashville; the figurines sent to Jefferson by Harry Innes and, later, by Morgan Brown were products of that school.[9] Wilkinson had other more pressing matters on his mind, did not read Jefferson's letter closely, and took it to be about "Italian busts from Palmyra in the Old World." (*That* Palmyra lies five days by camel from Damascus, in Syria.) Italian, Syrian, *or* Indian, Wilkinson could not find the busts, offering instead a series of contributions of his own to American archaeology: "productions of nature and art with several original modern manuscripts of some interest"—Indian knives and some maps.[10]

While architecture was the art most beloved by Thomas Jefferson, he had a healthy respect for sculpture and painting. As the gifts from the West accumulated, he created at Monticello the nation's first museum of the American Indian—"a kind of Indian hall." That balconied space just within Monticello, where crowds are today divided into cohorts and given their first extended lecture on the house, is now somewhat austere, with only his mechanical contrivances, pulleys and clocks, and a few sturdy, tourist-proof chairs to give it life, but by the time he had completed his collecting of the marble and granite sculpture of the Tennessee and Cumberland Valleys, and added to it the buffalo hide paintings, bows, arrows, lances, pipes, wampum, clothing, and pottery, brought back by Lewis and Clark, it was a jumble worthy of the Smithsonian in its most ebullient phase.[11]

After Brown's figures finally arrived at Monticello, visitors were aroused to speculate about the antiquity of Tennessee, and "whether they are idols, or only images of distinguished men." Jefferson responded that it was enough for him that they furnished "new and strong proof how far the patience and perseverance of the Indian artist supplied the very limited means of creation he possessed." On the other hand, it does not appear that they were admired by Europeans trained in another tradition; the baron de Montlezun pronounced them to be "by savages—very hideous."[12]

Meanwhile, in the Bluegrass, more sculpture was discovered. No one in the eighteenth century believed any silliness about an empty continent; there were plenty of Indians to fight, there was plenty of ancient Indian architecture to admire, and the nation's foremost advocate of Indian archaeology was constantly exhortating aspiring politicians to follow his example.

ANDREW JACKSON AND JUDGE OVERTON

The Cumberland School of sculpture flourished during the period the Plantagenet kings of England held sway, or attempted to do so—roughly from 1100 to 1475. Central Tennessee yields evidence of many other varieties of human experience: bits of chain mail left behind by Pardo's Spaniards of the 1560s, ruins of a French trading post, built about 1714 by M. Charleville, and around Charleville's post another "old fort" probably constructed by Shawnee, making use of good sightlines from the top of a mound dating from the thirteenth century. Eighteen miles to the southwest, in a loop of the Harpeth River, there remains to this day a great temple-mound complex known as Mound Bottom, bounded as late as 1804 by remnants of a palisade. Mound Bottom contains many truncated pyramids, the largest of which is forty feet high and three hundred feet by two hundred eighty at the base. A raised sacra via, nearly a mile long and seventy feet wide, once led across the floodplain to another site with its own mounds and plaza.*

---

*Mound Bottom can be visited by the public; it belongs to the state of Tennessee, and lies within Montgomery Bell State Park near Dickson. William M. Clark found twenty-nine sites along the Harpeth, in Williamson County alone, with much sculpture of the kind received by Jefferson.

In 1779, five hundred years after this complex was completed, Mound Bottom was surveyed by John Donelson, Andrew Jackson's father-in-law. Donelson was as avid a collector of Indian antiquities as Thomas Jefferson. Jackson learned much from both of them; it is likely that his collection of antiquities came from Donelson, and that the idea of placing them in an Indian Hall at Jackson's house, The Hermitage, came from Monticello, where Jackson had visited Jefferson. One of Jackson's earlier remodelings of his mansion emulated the designs Jefferson was sending to their mutual acquaintances in Kentucky; his final transformation of the house, containing his Indian Hall, was probably directed (by mail order) during his own presidential years by Robert Mills, who had been trained at Monticello.

Jackson's collection of antiquities could not vie with that of Jefferson, but his neighbors received the clear impression that to him, as to Jefferson, things made by Indians were important enough to place where Europeans placed the treasures, or at least the curiosities, they collected. While he was a fierce antagonist to any Indian nation that stood in his way, Jackson was at the same time genuine in his affection for several Indians he knew, and respectful of the past of them all, his individual friends and his collective foes.

Despite the absence of a literary record as to how and when he acquired his collection—Jackson was not a literary man—here is what was reported by Gates P. Thruston in his *The Antiquities of Tennessee* in 1890:

> It may not be generally known that President Andrew Jackson, at his home at the Hermitage, had a most interesting cabinet of relics. It embraced a number of fine stone pipes, ancient medals and coins, old china, and many antiques of great historical and antiquarian interest. They are now the property of the Hermitage Memorial Association. Colonel Andrew Jackson, of the Hermitage, kindly loaned us this pipe and other relics, to be photographed and engraved.[13]

The two pipes illustrated by Thruston as the most interesting of Jackson's collection appear to have come from the same area (and to have been carved at about the same time) as the figurines belonging to Jefferson.

In 1799, Judge Overton, Jackson's partner, built his own house, Traveller's Rest, in the midst of a complex of Mississippian mounds somewhat south of Charleville's post, six miles south of Nashville.* When Overton came to the place, the large eminence on which the house was constructed appeared to be a natural one, but as the founda-

---

*Traveller's Rest is maintained as an historic site—because of the house, not the mound.

tions were dug it became clear that it was full of ancient graves, boxed in stone slabs. After thirty-five skulls were taken from the excavation for the cellar, Overton called the place "Golgotha" (Matthew 27:33).

To Golgotha in 1805 came Rush Nutt, who had come to Jefferson's attention through Nutt's early studies with Benjamin Rush and David Rittenhouse in Philadelphia.* In Tennessee, Nutt was on no presidential commission, but came as a wandering scholar, hacking his way through the cane and poison ivy in search of understanding who the Indians were and they might have been.

Nutt found Overton's new house on a small rise in the midst of an entrenchment spanning twelve acres. Some of Overton's slaves had begun to find the skulls in the basement, others were finding them wherever they attempted to dig postholes for a post-and-rail fence. It appeared to Nutt that "the whole face of the enclosed earth was used as burying places." Recent excavators have found that he was right. Overton had chosen for his plantation the site of a large village densely inhabited between 1000 and 1300; the breezy place he had selected for his house had been its principal burial mound.† [14]

Overton's friend Thomas Brown Craighead, clergyman and antiquarian, chose a more difficult site. His stone house, which he called Glen Echo, avoided an eminence now known as the Hayesborough Mound, so grand that Craighead looped his entrance road about it to form a circle-and-square pattern with a rectilinear formal garden at the back—somewhat like that at Poplar Forest. Within Craighead's garden, we are told, were beds of "old-fashioned maiden bush, micro-

---

*Born in 1784 in tidewater Westmoreland County, Virginia (from which also came George Washington, James Monroe, and Robert E. Lee), Nutt attended the University of Pennsylvania, and, in 1801, began studying medicine with Rush and mathematics with Rittenhouse. As a tribute to the former he shortened his own first name, descended from his Rushford ancestors, to that of his mentor and friend. (Later he named one son Rittenhouse.)

Nutt returned to Virginia to marry. His wife died soon afterward; her death seems to have driven him into the wilderness as a similar shock sent Sam Houston to live among the Cherokee. In 1805, he made an anthropological journey, traveling alone along the bandit-infested Natchez Trace. Nutt's field notes tell of yet another Shiloh group of mounds (in Chickasaw County, Mississippi) about a mile from De Soto's winter camp of 1540–41, and give us our most exact impression of the Old Stone Fort on the Harpeth River, one of four fortified sites in the neighborhood of Franklin, Tennessee.

†Golgotha gained fresh skulls in 1864, when thousands of Union troops died charging up the hill toward Overton's house, which was then serving as the headquarters of the Confederate army led by John Bell Hood.

Overton and Jackson had an eye for places fit for settlement; their taste was that of their Indian predecessors. In 1794, they bought five thousand acres at Chickasaw Bluffs, now known as Memphis. Three hundred years earlier it too had been a large Indian community. (There is a good museum with interesting archaeological displays, including sections of mounds, at Chucalissa Indian Village, on Mitchell Road in Memphis.)

philia, little yellow, hundred leaf and red velvet roses, jonquils, narcissi, and buttercups." One wonders what the mound's builders had grown.* [15]

THE LAND OF SHILOH

Overton and Craighead lived in a bluegrass section of Tennessee, but when we think of fields of that lovely legume, we tend to picture, instead, the bluegrass region of Kentucky, opulent, gentle, and well watered in Adena/Hopewell times, as it was in the nineteenth century. Today, mile after mile of freshly painted white fences set apart bluegrass paddocks owned by sheiks, streetcar magnates, steelmasters, Chicago butchers to the millions, and by those investment bankers who got out in time.

Why was this lovely land so empty when George Rogers Clark and Daniel Boone came into it in the 1770s? Despite its manifest fertility and profusion of game, why was it so lightly settled? The seed of an answer may be contained in the admonitions of the Indians to Boone that his companions would not find Kentucky hospitable, that it was "dark and bloody ground." There were not, in fact, many struggles with the Indians in Kentucky or Tennessee, largely because there were few of them there to fight with. The phrase "dark and bloody" is a rough translation of what the Indians themselves called this sunny garden of the earth. It did not *appear* to be dark, though it contained solemn places shaded by great oaks, elms, maples, and beeches. Most of it was sun-dappled savannah, browsed by elk and buffalo feeding upon luxuriant grasses, with just enough trees to provide pools of shade but not so many as to require much clearing.

If it was felt to be so dark, it must have held dark secrets. Even before the Europeans arrived, their diseases had preceded them, leaving the inhabitants so weakened that they offered little resistance to the Iroquois, pressing in from the northeast, or to the Cherokee who swept through at will from their settlements to the south and east. Or later to Boone.†

As we have observed, it is likely that as many as five million people in the Mississippi Valley were reduced in the Great Dying to a few

---

*This site is now occupied by a K mart store and a parking lot.

†We are cautioned by Henderson, Jobe, and Turnbow in *Indian Occupation* to eschew the "myth that Kentucky was only a hunting ground, never permanently inhabited by the Indians. . . . While this statement is perhaps partially correct for the period after 1760, it generally reflects the poor understanding" of the preceding centuries (p. 192). They list many settlements which were occupied all during this long stretch of time, including several after 1760.

hundred thousand. It is also likely that some areas were especially hard hit. One can imagine that in those places there was no time to bury the dead; corpses were torn apart by animals, and their bones scattered to dry and become dust. Perhaps this is what happened in Kentucky, where there is no concentration of burial sites ("cemeteries," as the earliest Euramericans called them) like those to be found in Tennessee, where coffins made from slabs of stone suggest that the dying left some mourners to tend the dead and give them proper burial.*

Death by disease does not make for drama, even when it leaves behind enigmatic architecture; death by intention, either murder (warfare among individuals) or warfare itself, is celebrated in plaques and monuments all through the border states of the South. There are few markers to remind us of the prehistoric events of the region, though there are hundreds of truncated pyramids still brooding upon its riverbanks—hundreds surviving out of thousands. Though some of the largest have been destroyed, those at Shiloh, on the west bank of the Tennessee just above the Mississippi line, remain, confusing tourists who come there believing that history began with the Civil War.

At Shiloh, in 1862, the military careers of Ulysses S. Grant and William Tecumseh Sherman nearly ended. Their breakfasting forces were surprised on the first of April by a Confederate army of forty thousand men led by Albert Sidney Johnston. The Union forces rallied barely in time, in what Grant later called "the severest battle" fought in the West. Though the slaughter was great, Grant's reputation, and that of Sherman—and the Union—survived.

The carnage occurred in a space sacred to Native Americans. The word "Shiloh"—temple on a high place—came from the little Methodist church on the site, but it could as well have been derived from any of the sixty earthen platforms and seven large, truncated pyramids which lay within an earth-based palisade wall stretching for several miles. Most of these features can still be seen today; the pyramids are especially interesting because of the precise squares of their bases. They appear to date from the eleventh and twelfth centuries, a chronology confirmed by sculpture found in one grave and by other indications that the people of Shiloh were in close communication with those of Cahokia, three hundred miles to the north. But like those at Pinson,

---

*At Lindsley, near Lebanon, Tennessee, sixty miles east of Nashville on a tributary of the Cumberland River, there was an embankment, clearly intended to support a stockade which was probably plastered, with bastions at regular intervals. Within, there were small building platforms, a large platform mound (possibly for an ossuary or charnel house), and a burial mound containing sixty stone coffins arranged around a square, in three tiers. Like the interior of the Spiro Mound, in Oklahoma, built about the same time (between 1000 and 1400) this room was probably lined with tapestries, and contained pottery, copper, stone, and shell ornaments. (See Morgan, "Houses and House-life," p. 107)

they might have been built considerably earlier, in Adena/Hopewell times, as were other platform mounds on the Ames Plantation at Grand Junction, about forty-five miles closer to Memphis, and the Ingomar site just beyond the Mississippi border.

The hidden pocket of fertility around Shiloh must have seemed to the first Europeans who came there from the north to be like Canaan, having come into it out of the "pennyrile" region of Southern Kentucky, more eerie than any Egyptian desert. Cursed by the Indians and full of dread, it is a pockmarked, treeless barren, where rivers disappear into the earth and can be heard coursing underground through caverns covered by brittle, crystalline limestone domes. Horses or cattle sometimes disappear through holes in these domes, and sometimes people who go in search of their animals fail to return. Those travelers who survived the pennyrile route were next forced to work their way through terrible thickets of "cane," a thorny, twisted growth each stem of which might be three inches thick and thirty feet long, as vicious as barbed wire.*

Later settlers generally avoided the pennyrile and approached from the northwest, breasting the current of the Cumberland River as it rushed down to the Ohio. To come directly from the east would have required them to find passes across "very stoney and nobby" mountains, and then to cross eleven fords in twenty-eight miles along the upper tributaries of the river.[16] But when pioneers did reach the Cumberland basin, in 12,000 B.C. or in the 1780s, they found a very Canaan; one chronicler wrote of its black loam "as fine as flour" and fifty feet deep, nourishing cedars four feet thick and "forty feet to the first limb," walnuts eleven feet in diameter, as tall as English elms, set in park land deep in clover—"Clover Bottom" is a common name in Tennessee.†[17]

---

*Cane was the chief adversary to agriculture when the Napoleonic veterans attempted their settlements at Aigleville and Demopolis, in Alabama. See Kennedy, *Orders from France*. It was ultimately extirpated by cutting it in windrows, burning it, and letting hogs grub up its roots, a long and very painful process.

†Like Canaan, the region has been inhabited for at least 12,000 years. The Cumberland-Tennessee valley was a mosaic of ancient habitation. In 1822, Constantine Rafinesque-Schmalz surveyed Trigg County, Kentucky, for archaeology; without going beneath its surface he found twenty-four Indian "monuments" and five village sites.

Seventy years earlier, far up on the headwaters of the Cumberland, Thomas Walker's successors in invasive speculation claimed the entire region by virtue of a "treaty" transacted at Sycamore Shoals in 1775. Richard Henderson exchanged with certain compliant Cherokee chiefs ten thousand pounds in trade goods for most of Kentucky and Tennessee. Sycamore Shoals connotes to archaeologists not an extortionate treaty but what has been lost to dams and to the waters of an impounded river. Gordon Willey and the Bureau of American Ethnology found near Carthage, in land now submerged, twenty-eight village sites, three truncated pyramids, and three caves showing occupation much older than the Adena/Hopewell period.

GEORGE ROGERS CLARK AND OTHER
DISAFFECTED HEROES

The archaeologist-pioneers of Tennessee who investigated the ancient architecture of the Cumberland basin included many veterans of the Revolutionary Armies who might he expected to be fierce patriots. But their settlements were isolated among Indian nations that did not rejoice in their presence. Far beyond help from the tiny remnant of an army left in place by their demobilization, in fear and isolation, they sought protection from whatever military force might be at hand. Every important leader of the transmountain settlements but Andrew Jackson offered his services to one or another of the European powers which might give support for their colonization of this hostile terrain—Spain or France or Britain.

In this they differed from the Cincinnati of Marietta, who, though blimpish at times and crotchety, remained loyal. No longer treated as heroes, the southerners responded by taking extreme positions—taking them literally, at the edge of the known portions of the West—and morally—beyond the limits of what, a few years earlier, they might have thought honorable.

Fealty to the king of Spain was offered by George Morgan, Daniel Boone, James Wilkinson, George Rogers Clark, and Baron von Steuben, all disgruntled former officers of the Continental Army. Boone set the example, early, asking in return the grant of a satrapy within Spanish domains, which he might garrison against the next set of American interlopers.

While voyaging down the Ohio to take up his duties as a judge in Illinois territory, in 1768, Morgan explored the Ohio Valley even before the Revolutionary War. He had investigated the ground around great Portsmouth Mound to determine its salubriousness for a colony, but went elsewhere, possibly because the place was also occupied by the recent debris of a large Indian settlement, called Lower Shawneetown by the English, that had flourished from the 1730s until its abandonment in 1758.*†

---

*Morgan's map of the earthworks was extant until the 1840s but has not yet reappeared. The first extended references to the earthworks were not written until the 1770s, when the traders permitted themselves to cease transacting and give time to make measurements of the evidence of prehistory beneath the brush and trees. (For the history of Shawneetown and its archaeology, see Henderson, Jobe, and Turnbow, *Indian Occupation,* Chapter 5.)

†Baron Friedrich Wilhelm Augustus von Steuben, drillmaster of the Revolutionary army and co-founder with Knox of the Order of Cincinnati, became tired of guiding his old horse "Cincinnatus" about the sinkholes in the bogs around "Cincinnatus Creek," a rivulet flowing disconsolately through starveling acres granted him by the New York legislature. He

After the Revolution, Morgan assembled a following and descended the river all the way to the Spanish dominions west of the Mississippi. Just south of its confluence with the Ohio, he laid out an elaborately planned town to be known as "New Madrid," proposing to become a colonist for Spain. New Madrid gained fame as the epicenter of the famous New Madrid earthquakes of 1810–11, which were felt as far away as Boston, New Orleans, and Washington, D.C.* Those disposed to take earthquakes to be Biblical retribution may be pleased to know that before its demise, Morgan's hamlet had become the Macao or Tangier of the West, where intrigues came together and plots were hatched.†

New Madrid has became a center for archaeology. The site, which commended itself to settlers in 1811, had been attractive, it seems,

---

was not so plausible a land hawker as his neighbor and comrade of old, William Constable, who had more fertile holdings to sell.

After the failure of his effort to induce Prince Henry of Prussia to come to America to straighten things out (the prince prudently declined), Steuben settled for the course taken by Clark and Morgan. Casting about for a more appreciative sovereign than the Congress, he asked the Spanish government for 200,000 acres within its Mississippi Valley domain. In exchange, he offered himself as commander of four battalions he promised to recruit with offers of 230 acres to each soldier. With these troops he proposed to stand off the Americans or the British.

Steuben died before his concept could be tested, but the first outpost of Revolutionary soldiers in the West was Fort Steuben, a bastioned palisade constructed a little over a year earlier than Marietta. Like the Campus Martius, a hundred miles downstream, Fort Steuben was set amid "aboriginal mounds and entrenchments on the fertile alluvial lands." This otherwise handsome village had no historic preservation ordinance, so, at the expense of some important ancient Indian sites, Fort Steuben grew into the present industrial town of Steubenville, Ohio. (Another Steuben legacy, Steuben, Illinois, has been immortalized in the name of a period in archaeology in that region contemporaneous with the Ohio Hopewell. The description of Steubenville is from Thomas Nuttall, Nuttall, *A Journal of Travels,* pp. 32 ff.)

These posthumous honors were of little practical use to the Baron.

* As we will observe, it had the effects of deranging the Hopewellian topography of Newark, Ohio and changing the course of the Mississippi around Poverty Point.

† It was the base for the covert operations of Thomas Power, an Irish adventurer who acted as paymaster to Wilkinson for the Spanish authorities and a depot to which he and Wilkinson shipped murderers whose testimony in American courts might be embarrassing. When a Spanish agent was murdered on his way with three barrels of silver to make remittance to Wilkinson, dispatches to him were found by the murderers sewn into the decedent's coat. Instead of bringing the matter to light by holding the murderer's trial in Kentucky, Wilkinson's partner, Judge Harry Innes, rushed them under an armed guard to Wilkinson. The guard, commanded by Innes's own brother-in-law, barely got to its destination. It was intercepted on orders from Anthony Wayne. By a stroke of luck, however, the local commander was Wilkinson's protégé, Captain Zebulon Pike. Pike sought out an interpreter to question them—in Spanish. They were found sufficiently guiltless to be sent off to the Spanish authorities in New Madrid. The interpreter was Colonel Thomas Power.

more than a thousand years earlier. Those who prefer more localized theories of retribution, of the King Tut variety, may consider Morgan's intrusion upon the tombs of the ancients at New Madrid as the occasion for the tremors.*

George Rogers Clark has been too often portrayed as a rough Fenimore Cooper frontiersman; an otherwise careful historian, Thomas Marshall Green, said of him that his "intuitive knowledge of men more than compensated for his deficiency in the learning of the schools." Clark was, in fact, a Virginia gentleman, reared at Castle Hill, a few miles from Jefferson at Shadwell. He attended Dr. Robertson's Academy in Newtown, which was good enough for President James Madison, Judge Edmund Pendleton, Judge Harry Innes, and the agronomist and philosopher John Taylor of Caroline.[18]

Clark drank too much.[†] And he refused to spell as others spell. But his records of discoveries in Native American architecture are among the earliest and the most entertaining. His research commenced when he was barely twenty, encamped at the base of the Grave Creek Mound. He was found there by a British merchant, James Nourse, who arrived upon the scene with his wife, nine daughters, and "a great array" of trade goods. Nourse and his entourage were bound for Kentucky, and Clark found then irresistible. They found *him* an "intelligent man," obviously a gentleman though acquainted with the management of birchbark canoes and dugouts. Together they voyaged down the Ohio and up the Kentucky to the Bluegrass plain.[19]

---

*Harvard's Stephen Williams has done extensive research in what he has called "a wonderful, large and well preserved mound site," of ten mounds, with eight ranged abound a central plaza, built as early as 900 and occupied until after 1500.

Lilbourn lies on the other side of Interstate fifty-five miles from New Madrid, and about four miles to the southwest. "Beckwith's Fort," lies within the Towosaghy State Archaeological Site, about fifteen miles to the east, on State Route 77. It, too was a palisade with bastions, and was occupied at the same time as Lilbourn.

Near the village of Hickman, in Fulton Country, Kentucky, across the Mississippi from New Madrid, lies a curious earthwork which now appears as a turning fork, but may have been initially formed as a square about 1,000 feet on a side, introduced by a sacra via another thousand feet long lined by embankments 190 feet apart.

†Alcoholism was the endemic infirmity of what has been truly called "an alcoholic republic." When George Washington reviewed the possible commanders for the forces of the United States in the West, in 1792, he pronounced two of the five major generals alcoholic, a third, Anthony Wayne, "whether sober or a little addicted to the bottle I know not." (*The Alcoholic Republic* is the title of an excellent book on the subject by W. J. Rorabaugh. Washington's remarks are from Flexner, *George Washington and the New Nation,* pp. 302–3.)

In 1791, Jefferson urged Harry Innes to attempt to "bring General Clarke [sic] forward. . . . I know the greatness of his mind, and am the more mortified at the cause which obscures it. . . . Could it be surmounted, his lost ground might yet be recovered." (Jefferson to Innes, letter dated March 7, 1791).

One reason for tearing himself away from the Nourse menage was that Clark was under an obligation to George Washington, to Washington's neighbor, George Mason of Gunstan Hall, and to other investors in the Virginia branch of the Ohio Company to survey two hundred thousand acres claimed by the company in Kentucky since the 1740s. He knew the Elkhorn basin thoroughly; it may be that he was the source for a map of the ruins of that area sent Jefferson in 1790.

Clark was a restless sort, for which we may be grateful. He did not long remain in Kentucky but pressed westward. He was the first of the Founding Fathers to provide a glimpse of the ruins of the urban complex at Cahokia, describing them as the "works on the Mississippi near the Caw [hokia] River . . . one of the largest we know of." Monks Mound, he said, could have supported "a real palace." Clark also referred mysteriously to "the little mountain we their [there] saw flung up with a bason [bastion or depression?] on the top was a tower that contained part of the guards."[20] *

Until 1775, the ruins of Cahokia, though very large and numerous, were unknown beyond their immediate vicinity. After being abandoned in the fourteenth century, they lay beyond sight from the Mississippi, the main artery of traffic. Sometime during the early eighteenth century, the rich alluvium of which they had been heaped was occupied by French farmers, who built a mission church on the first terrace of the great mound, but they did not tell the world of their ancient neighbors, nor did the silent Trappists who amplified that simple structure into a monastery.

In the late 1770s, Clark rediscovered those mounds while camped on American Bottom to prepare the Spanish and French citizens of St. Louis and Cahokia to defend themselves against the British and Indians. Clark made his archaeological inquiries in Cahokia as he was basking in the glow of his triumphant winter campaign of 1779, the most famous of the Revolutionary War in the West; pictures of Clark's men slogging through the slush of drowned prairies on the way to Vincennes hung in many schoolrooms in my own youth, and we heard tales of how Clark achieved the capture of Hamilton, commander of that British post, surprising him at breakfast.†

---

*Clark may have alluded to a little knob, now lost, atop the uppermost platform of Monk's Mound.

†He might have returned to Kentucky to relieve refugee-thronged forts besieged by the British and Indians. But Jefferson stretched Clark's loyalty to the Old Dominion to its fullest, dispatching him and his small army northward, *toward* the British base at Detroit, *away from* Kentucky.

In explanation, one of Jefferson's admirers, Anthony Marc Leis, has written that the governor had concluded that "the Old Dominion must play a lone hand at any cost! . . .

Clark was next commissioned by Jefferson, then governor of Virginia, to attempt the kidnapping of Benedict Arnold, the turncoat whose British forces were burning Virginia ports in the early 1780s.*

Clark was himself particular in his patriotism, though he was never so estranged from the general fortunes of the United States as Arnold. In 1775, the Kentuckians had organized themselves as the Transylvania Colony and solemnly notified the Congress that they would stand aside from any revolution against the king. In the course of the next winter, some of them changed their minds, but Virginia failed to welcome them with arms and equipment. Clark threatened that he would organize them into an independent state if his native state did not do better. It was in that context that we should read his famous statement that "a country that is not worth defending is not worth claiming." It was not a patriotic utterance; it was a statement equivalent to "put up or shut up!" Clark's loyalties never ran primarily to the United States. Transylvania came first and then Virginia, and Virginia only when it was ready to defend Transylvania.

There *is* a Yugoslavian quality about the politics of Kentucky and Tennessee, even leaving aside the British, Spanish, French, and Indians.

[Therefore he] risked very briefly the very security of Kentucky." (Lewis, *Jefferson and Virginia's Pioneers*, pp. 573 and 577.)

In their correspondence, Jefferson and Clark reminded each other of conversations giving reasons too sensitive to be entrusted to the mails. Still writing of Virginia as their "country," they were, it is likely, referring to the contest between Virginia speculators and Pennsylvania speculators for control of the West. Clark was instructed to proceed with "your expedition up the Wabash" rather than to cooperate with the commanders appointed by Washington as leader of the armies of the Continental Congress. These commanders, Edward Hand, Daniel Brodhead, and George Morgan, were disqualified as allies by Jefferson because, we are informed by Lewis, they were also "investors in land schemes with the Pennsylvania interests." Jefferson despised those interests. (Lewis, Ibid.)

Clark was induced to remove himself from his position covering the defenses of Kentucky, and sent forth with a force of Virginians only, to worry the British at Detroit. He was also to cut off any movement westward of the forces of Pennsylvania. Jefferson wrote privately to Clark that his assignment would "have an important bearing ultimately in establishing our [Virginia's] northwestern boundary." Then he wrote blandly to Washington declining any "joint expedition" on the grounds that "these two officers [Clark and hand's successor, Colonel Daniel Brodhead] cannot act together." He did not trouble to inform Washington that he had told Clark to decline to do so. (Ibid., p. 579)

Jefferson was right about Brodhead; no patriotic scruples were standing in his way, either. He wrote to President [that was his title] Reed of Pennsylvania: "Should our State determine to extend its settlements over the Allegheny River I should be happy to have an early hint of it because it would be in my power to serve several of my friends." (James, *Clark*, p. 236)

Four hundred men, probably partisans of Virginia, signed a petition for the removal of Brodhead on the grounds that he was "actuated by motives, selfish and interested and his views are totally confined to land, manors and millseats." (Ibid.)

*Arnold got away to become an unsuccessful trader in the West Indies.

The North Carolinians led the Transylvanian independence movement, to which Clark lent his support. The tidewater Virginians, the Washingtons, Masons, Carters, and Lees, organized the Ohio Company, in competition with the Piedmonters, including Walker and Peter Jefferson, whose vehicles were the Loyal and Greenbrier Companies. Then, of course, there were the Pennsylvanian interests; there is no way to be certain what their policies might have been toward slavery, but it is a fair guess that they would have been more like those of Gallatin than those of Jefferson and Clark. When Clark arrived among the French in St. Louis, Cahokia, Kaskaskia, and Vincennes, he found there a considerable number of Blacks, held in bondage. As we noted earlier, one of his first acts was to reassure their owners that they had nothing to fear from Virginia.

Even after the passage of the Northwest Ordinance, seven years later, the governor of Indiana Territory confirmed to the French that they might hold on to those slaves. Under pressure from the Yankees of Marietta, Governor St. Clair, a Pennsylvanian, declared that Blacks born in the Northwest Territory thereafter would be free.*

As soon as peace was concluded with the British, in 1783, Jefferson attempted to induce Clark to undertake a mission in the interest of an even more extended Virginia. He was asked to return to Cahokia and then to set forth up the Missouri Valley on a private version of the exploration his brother William undertook at Jefferson's behest a decade later. Clark declined; he was otherwise engaged. He was setting himself free even from Virginia, operating as a frontier brigand and raiding Spanish traders' boats on the Wabash from his base at Vincennes. The Constitution had not yet brought forth an executive; a

---

*Among slaveowners in the Southwest, there flourished a theory that, having failed to hold back the flood of southern emigration, the Yankees would be just as happy for Spanish intransigence or Spanish gold to take the West *out* of the Union. Otherwise the growing power of a conjoint West and South would overbalance the East (or North—both terms were used).

This is what James Monroe meant when he asserted that the Yankees were seeking a "means of throwing the western people and territory without the government of the United States and keeping the weight of population and government here," meaning east of the mountains.

John Jay was known to have said "the western country will one day give us trouble," a view which some thought explained his quiet support of Burr's western ambitions in the 1790s and, perhaps, later.

Among the reasons most northern Federalists had supported the Northwest Ordinance was that it would bind into the Union a region likely to grow in Yankeeness, producing more slave-free states, each with two Senate votes. It is not improbable that some narrow-minded partisans among the northerners might also have been willing to attempt to tilt the balance of the Senate in their direction by lopping off the possibility of new southwestern states and votes being added to the South.

feverish and inept Congress was unable to govern, to pay its debts, to defend its frontiers or protect its shipping. The British were in smug occupancy of forts well within American territory, some of them on land Clark had himself conquered for Virginia and had relinquished to a federal government which failed to keep them. When in dismay he wrote the Spanish authorities to offer his services to them, and, by implication, offered to abandon his piracy, he complained "that no property or person is safe under a . . . meak and unfirm" America government, he was not far from the truth.[21]

FRENCH PLOTS AND ARCHAEOLOGY

At this time a more distant friend of Jefferson's, the philosopher Brissot de Warville, was briefly enjoying power in France. Brissot caused to be published a euphoric report on a visit to the United States including a paean to the Mississippi Valley with the undisguised suggestion that Spain was unworthy of such an endowment. Brissot sent Edmond-Charles Genet to the United States to see what could be done to stir up French-inclining separatism in the West. Initially, the plan had been that Genet would help Louis XVI to escape the guillotine and would thereafter smuggle him to America, where he might be safe. Brissot and Genet planned thereby to spare their country the blood of a martyred monarch and the disaffection of their American counterparts, such as Washington and Alexander Hamilton, who were revolutionary but not radical.

The plot to spirit away the king failed. He went to the guillotine on January 21, 1793. Though the Brissotins were losing power to the more radical Jacobins and to people still more radical than they, Genet came to the United States anyway, with sedition, rather than the salvation of a king, as his agenda. At Charleston, South Carolina, this rash, vainglorious young man was placed ashore in gold epaulets, flowered cravat and satins, carrying with him a commission as Major General in the Armies of the French Republic for George Rogers Clark. Clark had turned from Spain to France; his friends in Paris had asked him if he would be willing to lead an army of frontiersmen to secure New Orleans by force and set up an independent western state under French protection.

After a triumphal progress amid choruses of the brand-new anthem *La Marseillaise*, Genet finally arrived in the capital. Intoxicated with adulation, he disclosed his plans to Jefferson, still secretary of state in the administration of George Washington. Jefferson might have been expected to heed Washington's clear admonition that his cabinet officers should not encourage invasions of the territories of nations with which the United States was at peace. But Jefferson had his own plans for the West, plans more compatible with those of Genet than those of Washington. He arranged with Genet that their mutual friend, the botanist Andre Michaux, would be their emissary to the people of the Mississippi Valley. Among those to whom Michaux would carry messages was Clark; to him the scientist-seditionist bore his commission in the French colonial army. Michaux could do research along the way—any constitutional qualms felt by the secretary of state seem to have been overwhelmed by the prospect of advancements in science.*

To the botanist and to the frontier general was added another soldier, who combined the roles of scholar and spy, and, as was often the case with Jefferson's maneuvers, archaeology was the beneficiary. The Genet-Michaux-Clark venture brought to the scene the first engineer to make clear maps of the Indian architecture of the central Mississippi valley, General Georges Collot. Collot was assigned by Genet to determine how separatism under French auspices might lead to a successful joint invasion of the Spanish holdings in Mexico. In the process, he was to make a detailed survey of the Ohio and Mississippi valleys. Though sedition was his business, he did permit himself to be distracted by archaeology, perhaps because his focus was rendered imprecise by a severe case of Genet's disease. This is a contagion *still* to be encountered among French diplomats. Its symptoms manifest themselves in the following propensities:

1. to denigrate living foreigners
2. to romanticize long-extinct occupants of the territory of those foreigners
3. to rhapsodize upon such territory as fit—only—for Frenchmen

In Collot's view, contemporary Americans were scruffy and discourteous; their military engineering was contemptible and their failure to defer to French officers and gentlemen was incomprehensible. To his credit, he had a good eye for Native American antiquities; at the time, only George Rogers Clark and the Marietta Cincinnati could rival him in that.

As Collot progressed from Pittsburgh down the Ohio to Kentucky, he began to record in his diary notations of what the Indians had ac-

---

*At the time, Alexander Hamilton was calling for a break with regicidal France; Jefferson wrote to Monroe that Hamilton was so antithetical to France that he was willing to present "our breach to every kick which Great Britain may chose to give it." But Genet had some kicks for Jefferson, too. (quoted in Schachner, *Aaron Burr*, p. 318)

complished. While engaging in a little sedition in the neighborhood of Frankfort and Lexington, he took time to admire an "irregular hexagon," thereby commencing the systematic survey of the archaeological and political potentials of the Elkhorn Valley.[22]

Collot's hexagon was probably the "fort" on the south fork of the Elkhorn described by Harry Innes to Thomas Jefferson in July, 1790, as Innes submitted the first of the works of sculpture Jefferson collected from Kentucky and Tennessee.* Collot described "the parapets behind the ditch, . . . the entrance . . . covered by two small turrets on a little eminence, . . . a kind of a small horn work, and a redoubt." At this stage of his travels, Collot was still unwilling to give credit where it due: he was in "no doubt that the work was constructed by Europeans, and even by persons well versed in fortification." Collot gives the location as "between Lexington and Frankfort, nine miles distant from this last town, and on a small river called the Elk River." The Elk is now the Elkhorn.[23]

When Collot came to Cincinnati, Anthony Wayne made every effort to prevent his reconnaissance of American military installations, but he managed to explore

> . . . an Indian building, having the form of a rotunda. Here the Indians held their councils, made their sacrifices, and celebrated their feasts. If we may judge from the size of the trees which have grown up since its construction, this senate-house must be very ancient. . . . Had it not been for the persecutions with which we were menaced by General Wayne, . . . we should have taken a plan of this building, but it was prudent to . . . depart as speedily as possible.[24]

This must be one of very few instances in which a spy expressed regret to his superiors that counterespionage had forced him to desist from archaeology. Nor could Collot resist making observations of natural history. After leaving Locust Creek, he saw

> . . . a multitude of wild turkeys, and in such numbers that the trees were literally rendered grey. . . . This bird, in America, is of singular size and beauty. . . . The feathers of the body are of a fine ashen grey, and those of the neck and under the wings of a copper color. When exposed to the sun . . . the plumage is as bright as gold. . . . Towards four o'clock in the afternoon, we perceived on the horizon a kind of white riband of great length, which was a flock of pelicans. . . . These birds travel always in flocks; when they reach any great river, they range themselves all in one line, their heads turned against the steam, and thus suffer themselves to

---

*This was the structure also reported by John Filson in 1784 (see Chapter Three, "Forts Ancient.")

be carried down: they swallow all the fish that come their way, and deposit them in the great bag."[25]

Callot did not always forget his task. If separatism did take place, "a fort placed at Red Bank would be extremely useful to stop whatever ascends the Ohio. . . . The head of the Wabash . . . forms militarily speaking, a fine position . . . the first which ought to be fortified if the North Western States ever make a schism." And he reported to Paris the lamentable condition of George Rogers Clark. "Often found lying in a state of stupor in the streets," Clark could hardly be expected to lead a separatist party.[26]

If someone better could be found, Collot envisaged "battalions composed of the vigorous woodsmen and robust farmers of the Western states," led, one assumes, by impeccably uniformed French officers against "Anglo-federal legions, clerks, shopkeepers, and wholesale dealers, notaries, and lawyers, English agents and factors."[27]

His prejudices ran deep: though Collot did include on his maps "Indian ancient tombs," such as those southwest of French Cahokia, he never could credit the Indians with architecture of any distinction, dismissing such an idea as "fictitious." All the Indians had done, he insisted, was to create

> Mounds of different heights, which have served as fortresses. . . . These mounds are scattered in all directions. . . . They have built no cities nor constructed any public works. . . . They overrun . . . [the country] only in the character of hunters.[28]

Genet's disease was rampant at the time, infuriating even to the Francophile Jefferson. As the tenor of his *Notes on Virginia* makes clear, he was induced to believe the better of the Indians in part because the French lumped all Americans, red and white, together, as inferior to Europeans. In defending the Indians from their doubts, he was, in effect defending himself.

But always Jefferson preferred a French alliance to any other, and, at the outset, failed to restrain the follies of Genet, Collot, and Clark. To the delight of his comrades, Clark briefly diminished his intake of alcohol; an invasion of Spanish Louisiana once more offered hope of booty, glory, and some embarrassment to American leaders insufficiently grateful to aging heroes. Virginia had refused to honor Clark's request for the reimbursement of his personal expenses during the Revolution:

> I have given the United States half the territory they possess, and for them to suffer me to remain in poverty, in consequence of it, will not redound much to their honor hereafter.[29]

In a letter which might have been written by von Steuben or George Morgan, Clark assured his French sponsors:

> I can raise an abundance of men in this western country . . . who have repeatedly fought, [and] obtained laurels. . . . I can by my name alone . . . raise 1500 brave men. . . . I can take the whole of Louisiana for France. If France will be hearty and secret in this business—my success borders on certainty.[30]

But Anthony Wayne swept down upon Clark's recruiters and disbursed them, while President George Washington was provoked by Genet's outfitting the brigantine *Little Democrat* in Philadelphia to lead a fleet to attack New Orleans from the sea. In the face of a direct order from Washington not to do so, Genet assaulted British shipping and brought his prizes into Delaware Bay. Washington convened his cabinet and Genet was ordered to be recalled to France on September 15, 1793. George Rogers Clark was deprived of his last campaign.

LEWIS AND CLARK

Thomas Jefferson's imperial ambition might have played itself out in 1793, with a scientific filibuster led by George Rogers Clark and Andre Michaux at the expense of Spain. Because of the intervention of Wayne and Washington, he had to wait for a decade to send forth Clark's younger brother, William, and Meriwether Lewis on his next scientific assault upon "the Dons."

The boldness, one might say the effrontery, of Lewis, Clark, and Jefferson is often underrated in our schoolbooks. When the two explorer-provocateurs set forth down the Ohio toward St. Louis, there had not yet been a Louisiana Purchase. That negotiation was completed as they were underway, but even then the government of Spain took the view that the boundary of the purchase lay considerably to the north of the line imagined by Jefferson, mapped by Gallatin, and to be explored by Lewis and Clark. The Spanish position was thereafter that Mr. Jefferson's explorers trespassed upon Spanish territory every time they walked the mud flats and hunted deer and antelope through the willows on the south bank of the Missouri. Accordingly, the Spanish authorities sent an Indian detachment dry-gulch the Americans. The detachment and expedition passed each other by. Things might have been unpleasant for Lewis and Clark if the Spanish-sponsored Indians had caught them, but in the vastness of the plains one tributary is difficult to distinguish from another. Rivers hide in folds in gently swelling prairie; only straggling cottonwoods mark their courses.*

Jefferson had other expeditions underway, and by the end of 1806, four detachments of troops and scientists were probing and Spanish defenses. Each professed the scientific and archaeological purposes assigned to Lewis and Clark. Geopolitically, however, their function was to extend the sway of a nation Jefferson had found as an uneasy alliance and which he made into an imperial power.

On their way westward, Lewis and Clark were to collect natural history, to report on Indians and their "monuments." On January 9, 1804, after a snowy night and in a "hard wind," Clark found himself amid the northern group of mounds on American Bottom not far from those his brother had explored at Cahokia. He had gone after some prairie chickens and ducks for dinner, but after breaking through the ice of a partly frozen slough he "discovered an Indian fortification . . . 9 mounds forming a circle." There was still archaeological evidence aplenty to be found on the surface: "great quantities of earthen ware and flints—about ½ [a mile north] . . . is a grave on an eminence. I returned before sunset, and found that my feet, which were wet, had frozen to my shoes. . . . The wind from the W, across the sand islands . . . raised such a dust that I could not see in that direction. It had been an exceeding cold day."[31]

In the papers of Lewis and Clark there are many references to Indian villages, active or abandoned, but after the passage quoted above they did not describe "monuments" comparable to those at Cahokia. Along the flood plains of the upper Missouri they did come across walls of sand and earth, which they thought might be early fortifications, but which tiresome subsequent investigators have reduced to natural sandbars and silt deposits.

The explorers were, however, able to investigate many individual burial mounds. Clark reached a point just within the borders of the present state of Nebraska on July 12, 1804, and went out to seek game while his "much fatigued" men took a day off. After ascending "a high artificial knoll," he had an "extensive and pleasing prospect" across a plain of "15 or 20,000 acres of high bottom land covered with grass about 4 ½ feet high." Upon this blooming prairie Clark saw many

---

*The Missouri Valley cottonwood is not a stately tree like an English oak or a German linden or the white pine of Maine. It is a disheveled, battered old poke of a tree—no giant of the forest, just a survivor of the plains, but a provider of welcome shade in summer. Plains people are fond of cottonwoods.

Despite frequent assertions to the contrary, Lewis and Clark were not the first explorers to cross the continent from the Atlantic to the Pacific. Sir Alexander MacKenzie, having found his way to the Arctic, preceded them to the Pacific Northwest in 1793.

"mounds or ancient graves which is to me a strong evidence of this country having been thickly settled.[32]

On August 25th, Clark and Lewis together reconnoitered a "mountain of evil spirits" on White Stone Creek (the present Vermillion River), which he also called a "mound" and said to be about seventy feet high. Earlier, the expedition passed, but did not come close enough to observe, two hilltop "forts" lying some distance back from the Missouri, which have subsequently become known as the Utz Site and Old Fort.* [33]

What would Lewis and Clark have told President Jefferson of these "hillforts" had they come upon them while chasing a deer or a covey of wild turkeys? Would they have brought to this ancient architecture expectations learned from books about Iron Age Britain, and looked about for stone circles and "pi" shaped megaliths? Like their contemporaries who explored the earth and stone enclosures along the Scioto, the Paint, the Elkhorn, the Miamis, and the central Mississippi, they would have been likely to see them as defensive; that preconception held until the 1990s.

Now, however, a fresh interpretation is possible; a combination of pottery analysis and carbon dating has forced reconsideration of both the timing and use of the Ohio Valley sites (see Chapter Eleven). If they were commenced as ceremonial spaces, then used defensively, and finally returned to liturgical use, as now seems likely, and if all this occurred during the Adena/Hopewell period rather than in the later transition period once denominated as "Fort Ancient," then it would be well to reexamine the traditional dating for Utz and Old Fort as well. The conventional wisdom has been that these are evidence of the Mississippian Emergence (the title of an excellent book on the subject). If that were true, Lewis and Clark were only pushing backward in time a few centuries from Cahokia to Old Fort, as they ascended the Missouri, and these enclosures were created as pockets of repose at the same time Western Europeans were summoning one of their own miracles of political coherance, giving philosophy that nurture which is the blossoming of tranquility. Utz might have been underway as Charlemagne was crowned Holy Roman Emperor in the year 800, advised by Alcuin, the sage.

The traditional chronology would give us more poetry than that of revision, for near Old Fort the American explorers sought out a sage of their own, paying a call on Daniel Boone. Boone had come there to his final residence; he was not at home when they called, though his householders supplied them with some corn and butter.[34, 35] I think it likely that they had hoped the old man himself could provide them with in-

---

*These "forts" are both in Saline County.

formation about ancient architecture. They had come close, but had found disappointingly little.

As we have observed in the case of Georges Collot, explorers are apt to find what they expect, and, if sufficiently patronizing about the people among whom they are exploring, they are more prone to indifference than to surprise at what they do not expect. Lewis and Clark expected more Indian mounds along the Missouri than they did, in fact, encounter. Their sponsor had, by that time, heard much of what had been discovered in Ohio, and had urged them to find the like. They themselves had made their base at Cahokia, in the region of the Mississippi Valley holding its most spectacular earthen architecture. What they did discover was its significant absence: when the ancient Indians moved up the Missouri River and came into regions of light rainfall, where the cultivation of corn was no longer predictable enough to nourish large populations without irrigation, they did not make big buildings. In the desert Southwest, irrigation was the sister of architecture, or, perhaps one might say, a branch of architecture. But it was not so in the Mississippi Valley, probably because there was plenty of well-watered land to support a concentration of both population and architecture.·

So Lewis and Clark were disappointed.

HENRY BRACKENRIDGE

As the eighteenth century came to its end, a literature of the West itself began to emerge. The first westerner to write comprehensively about the West was Henry Brackenridge, son of Hugh Henry Brackenridge, who was himself the first novelist to have a book published west of the Appalachians.* The elder Brackenridge had been a versifier, country lawyer, partner to Albert Gallatin, and, briefly, both courtier and

---

*The third volume of *Modern Chivalry* was that book. Gilbert Imlay's *The Emigrants* is its only challenger for the distinction of being the first "western." Both were published in 1793; both were, explicitly, works of fiction about the West. Plenty of fiction had been published in Europe about America before that, but none of it admitted itself to be such.

Parts of Jonathan Carver's *Travels,* for example, clearly qualify as fiction, as do several of the Spanish and French chronicles. If one turns to nonfiction, or largely nonfiction, one must give pride of place to Imlay's *Topographical Description* of 1792.

The exact day within the following year when Imlay's *Emigrants* came from the printer cannot be established, but since both his works were published in England, the distinction of Brackenridge's novel, also published in 1793, is its combination of American writer, subject, and publisher.

The third volume of *Modern Chivalry*—and there were many volumes from 1793 through 1815—came off a shiny new press in Pittsburgh. (Pittsburgh is a *western* city, with sewage flowing to the Mississippi, as Philadelphia is an eastern, bestowing its effluents upon

masque-maker to George Washington.* The mother of Henry
Brackenridge died in 1788, when he was eighteen months old, and he
was given into the charge of the wife "of a respectable cobbler, my
father's tenant, in an adjacent log-cabin where the Bank of Pittsburgh
now stands, and where I fared as well as might be expected: that is, I
was half-starved, half clad, and well scorched and meazled in the hot
ashes and embers."

The rest of his life turned out better than might be expected from
such a beginning. He was even reconciled, at the end, to the curmud-
geonly novelist, having established himself as a literary craftsman of
sufficient eloquence to describe Indian antiquity, the best to address
himself to the task until Mark Twain took forth his pen to describe
Troyville in flood.

We owe to Brackenridge the most extensive archaeological reports
of the first two decades of the nineteenth century, some portions of
which follow, told mostly in his own words. He began his acquaintance with them on the way down the Ohio to learn French in Ste. Genevieve. He was left for a time among the mounds of Cincinnati to en-
large his command of military English among the soldiers of Anthony
Wayne. They were encamped at what was then called Hopson's
Choice, just north of Losantiville which was later merged into Arthur
St. Clair's Cincinnati. Brackenridge then moved west another step,
picking up Spanish at George Morgan's New Madrid, where his
growth was fueled by "coarse black bread, a kind of catfish soup, hot
with pepper, and seasoned with garlic . . . almost the only food they
gave me."[†]

When at last he reached Ste. Genevieve, there was an improvement
in the gastronomy, for "with the poorest French peasant, cookery is an
art well understood." In the course of the next two, idyllic years, young
Brackenridge learned cooking and two more languages. He and the

---

the Atlantic). This occurred after the first two had tamely emerged from an eastern publisher.

Hugh Brackenridge had previously founded the city's first book store, first newspaper,
and the Pittsburgh Academy.

*The general and the poet did meet as Washington was taking the waters at Warm Springs,
Virginia, readying himself for his final journey to the Ohio Valley. For the occasion,
Brackenridge brought forth "a masque . . . in the style of Ben Jonson or Milton. . . . The
characters included the Genius of the Springs, the Potomac, the Delaware, and the Ohio."
We are not told whether there was a subplot about Portages or Canals among the principal
players. (See Brooks, *Washington Irving*, fn. on p. 286).

[†]I am indebted to George Knepper for straightening out the crinkles in the history of Cincinnati.

local French children played with the offspring of the remnant nation of Kickapoo, settled near Ste. Genevieve peacefully growing corn, where their ancestors (or perhaps another group displaced by those ancestors) had been practicing maize agriculture for a thousand years. Inadvertently, the elder Brackenridge had provided his son with the defining experience of his youth, a knowledge of Indians as individuals, qualifying for admission into the human family. (His father's view, stated in 1782, was that they were "the animals vulgarly called Indians.")[36]

Next, he was introduced to Thomas Power, soldier of fortune and secret agent masquerading as archaeologist, and to the general to whom Power brought Spanish bribes, James Wilkinson. Power was with Brackenridge during an epiphany of the fecundity of the valley:

> It was now the middle of summer; the air was delightfully mild and clear, while nature was clad in her most luxuriant robes. . . . We gathered the wild pea-vine and made ourselves soft beds under the shade of the trees, which stretched their giant vine-clad arms over the stream. Flocks of screaming parakeets frequently lighted over our head, and the humming bird, attracted by the neighboring honeysuckles, came whizzing and flitting around us, and then flashed away again.
>
> Mr. Power had a handkerchief full of dollars, which he permitted me to take out and jingle on the rock. . . .
>
> [A day or so later] I witnessed a phenomenon which I have never observed since. . . . The day was excessively hot and calm; on a sudden, the river appeared to be alive with fish of all kinds, jumping out of their element, darting in every direction, and actually lashing the water into a foam. They appeared all around our boat, and in their frantic capers, sometimes dashed themselves against it, and almost ran aground. A number were shot with rifles. . . . [37]

This frenzy of fishes was followed by another experience then commonplace though now difficult even to imagine; as he passed along the Ohio near Louisville,

> in a part of the river where the vision extended at least ten miles . . . the whole heavens to the edge of the horizon were covered and concealed by a flight of wild pigeons, and remained so for upwards of two hours. . . . During the whole of the day immense flocks continued to pass. According to my computation the principal flock was at least . . . ten miles in width, by one hundred and twenty in length.[38]

In 1993, fishing is improving in the Ohio, but the Carolina parakeet and the carrier pigeon have been hunted to extinction.

At the age of ten, Brackenridge completed his training in French at Gallipolis, and was returning toward Pittsburgh, when he was overtaken by the imperial barge of Wilkinson.

> when . . . I was transferred on board . . . as a playmate . . . for his son Biddle, a boy of my own age. . . . The boat . . . was fitted up in a style of . . . magnificence. . . . It was propelled . . . by twenty-five or thirty men, sometimes by pole . . . and often by oar.
>
> There was also a band of musicians, and the whole had the appearance of a mere party of pleasure. My senses were overpowered—it seemed an Elysium! The splendor of the furniture—the elegance of the dresses—and then the luxuries of the table. . . . Every repast was a royal banquet.[39]

Wilkinson's banquets were, in point of fact, royal—paid out of royal funds, brought to the commander of the American army of the West from the king of Spain by Colonel Power. Presiding over these festivities was the queen of the Ohio, the General's lady:

> a most estimable person, of the mildest and softest manners. . . . She saw us catching minnows with pin hooks—made us desist, and then explained in the sweetest manner, the cruelty of taking away life, wantonly, from the humblest thing in the creation.[40]

Wilkinson's only loyalty seems to have been to this consort, who saw him through all his courts-martial and cashierings, his treasons and betrayals.

Brackenridge was a man of deeper loyalties, chief among which was archaeology, which came to him by carom shot in two bounces. His delight in *Tom Jones* led his father to emphasize the virtues of another Jones, the Jones of *Jones on Bailments,* a work known to their sorrow by law students even so late as 1993. In compensation for inscribing the entire second Jones in perfect penmanship, he was permitted, for recreation, to read *Potter's Antiquities.*

His curiosity thus aroused, Henry Brackenridge looked about the neighborhood of his father's residence "in that delightful spot on Grant's Hill, where the ancient Indian mound . . . overlooks . . . the clear and beautiful Allegheny, the loveliest stream that ever glistened in the moon, gliding over its polished pebbles, being the Ohio, La Belle Riviere, under a different name . . . still the boundary of civilization."[41]

Even on that boundary, Brackenridge was set to dancing lessons as far as the hornpipe, while fencing was gained through the instruction of a M. de Lisle. He learned to entertain at parties, on a high wire; on one occasion he replaced a traveling acrobat who came late to an engagement.*

In 1810, Brackenridge embarked on a keel boat from Pittsburgh, back to Ste. Genevieve, where he planned to commence a new legal career in the West.† A year later, he had the good fortune to encounter William Clark, who had become an Indian agent in St. Louis, and had accumulated the most magnificent collection of Indian antiquities outside the walls of Monticello.

Clark confirmed his enthusiasm for archaeological research. Soon Brackenridge began publishing "sketches" of the antiquities of the Mississippi Basin.‡ He might have become a fixture of the literary and legal scene in St. Louis, as his father had been in Pittsburgh, but he was not done wandering. His "destiny called [him] to Lower Louisiana" and at the end of 1811, he left St. Louis for Natchez, Baton Rouge, and New Orleans. Energetic and diligent, his erudition must have been impressive, for the good people of Louisiana quickly engaged him to write a new code of laws required to bring the French legal system into conformity with the English system of the rest of the United States. The Brackenridge Code has been employed in Louisiana ever since. By the end of 1813 he was a judge—like his father.

His first published book, *Views of Louisiana; Together with a Journal of a Voyage up the Missouri River, in 1811,* was full of rollicking tales of adventure, some of which Washington Irving retold, with Brackenridge as hero, in his *Astoria* in 1836. Brackenridge was becoming a celebrity.

*   *   *

Brackenridge does not tell us when first he began to bring analogies from the old world archaeology of *Potter's Antiquities* to bear upon

---

*In 1799, the senior Brackenridge was made a judge of the Pennsylvania Supreme Court, and a highly partisan judge he was, having lampooned the Federalist Cincinnati in the famous tavern scene in *Modern Chivalry*. Its Quixotian hero, Captain Farrago, had gone into an inn and there met a man wearing the eagle of the Order. According to Brackenridge, Farrago's Sancho expressed the thought that it meant that the wearer liked to dine on roast goose. To demonstrate that the Cincinnati had something more solemn in mind, the eagle bearer delivered a Fourth of July oration no funnier than many, but less coherent than most. Farrago, told that some Cincinnati were "honorary," did not understand. "Nature," he said, "makes no honorary animals." On scarcely sober reflection, he suggested that the "real animals" distinguish themselves according to their contributions to the Revolution by wearing eagles of silver, brass, tin, or pot metal. (Brackenridge, *Modern Chivalry*, pp. 69–75)

†Ste. Genevieve had a population of about 4,600; St. Louis was only a little larger, 5,667.

‡Stephen Williams has informed me that this term was in common parlance in the nineteenth century to describe the Missouri, Ohio, and Mississippi watersheds. (Private communication, December 1992.)

the Indian mounds in the American West. It may have been while he was still reading Potter, on Grant's Hill, or it may have been when he first read the Reverend Dr. Thaddeus Harris's poetic descriptions of the antiquities of Grave Creek and Marietta (see Chapters Five and Seven). Brackenridge had no shortage of role models; he had read Jefferson's account of his own archaeological investigations, and he knew thoroughly Bishop Madison's *Supposed Fortifications of the Western Country.**

These authorities were in his mental inventory, he tells us, as he surveyed the hundreds of mounds to be found on the shores of the Mississippi, south of Ste. Genevieve, where he had first been acquainted with Indians as companions. That childhood experience had disposed him to accept Indians as fully capable of either friendship or art, even before his reading of the classics of literature and archaeology permitted him to deduce that human settlement would be drawn to salubrious circumstances in either the Old Old World or the New Old World.

In his *Views on Louisiana,* Brackenridge made the connection between the bounteousness of the Mississippi and Ohio valleys and its capacity to support the large populations required to produce advanced architecture.

> All these vestiges invariably occupy the most eligible situations for towns or settlements; and on the Ohio and Mississippi, they are the most numerous and considerable. There is not a rising town or a farm of an eligible situation, in whose vicinity some of them may not be found.
>
> I have heard a surveyor of the public lands observe, that where ever any of these remains were met with, he was sure to find an extensive body of fertile land. An immense population has once been supported in this country.

Brackenridge classified these vestiges by shape, beginning with the conical barrows.

> [Barrows] such as [those] described by Mr. Jefferson [are] . . . extremely numerous in every part of the western country. The traces of a village may always be found near them, and they have been used exclusively, as places of interment, at least of deposit for the dead. The height is usually eight or ten feet above the surrounding ground, the shape manifesting little or no design.

---

*It is possible that he read those antislavery writings of Madison which led Edward Coles and, probably, Thomas Worthington, to free their own slaves. Perhaps it was Madison who emboldened him, before he was eleven, to free the runaway he found hiding in the haystack in Pittsburgh. As we shall see, his subsequent responses to slavery were not so energetic.

Watson Brake, near Monroe, Louisiana — the oldest circular monumental building yet discovered in North America. It was probably begun at least 5000 years ago. *(Credit: Smithsonian Institution)*

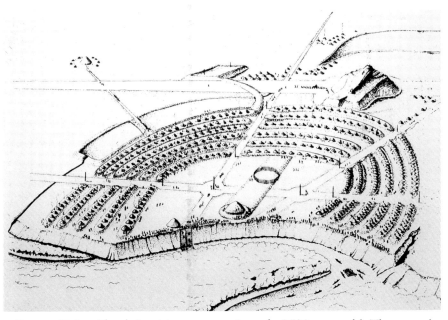

Poverty Point, Floyd, Louisiana, approximately 3000 years old. The central mound, top right, may have been an effigy of a falcon. It consists of a platform at the top, reached by another, lower platform, 13 feet above the surrounding plain.

Owl sculpted from jasper by the people of Poverty Point, circa 1500–1000 B.C. *(Credit: Smithsonian Institution)*

The cone at Grave Creek, Ohio, along the Ohio river, is the largest remaining burial building of a people we call the Adena. It was constructed around the time of Christ. Here it is shown in a drawing from one of the most important nineteenth-century reports of ancient architecture: E.G. Squier and E.H. Davis's *Ancient Monuments of the Mississippi Valley* (1847).

The Hopewell people were near contemporaries and perhaps competitors to the Adena, though their culture lasted several centuries longer. They constructed precisely geometrical octagons, squares, and circles. The Fairgrounds Circle at Newark, Ohio, is a quarter of a mile across and three stories high. This diagram shows how the New Mexico Indian buildings at Pueblo Bonito (A.D. 920–1025) and Pueblo Del Arroyo (A.D. 1065–1110), drawn to the same scale, could fit inside the Newark Circle. *(Credit: William N. Morgan)*

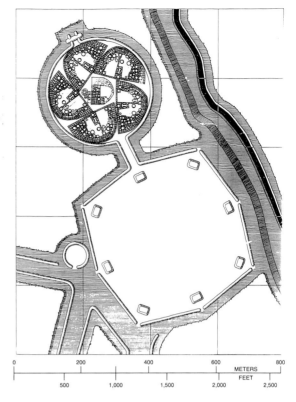

Hopewell beaver effigy pipe. *(Credit: Gilcrease Museum)*

Monk's Mound at Cahokia, Illinois, built between A.D. 800 and 1300. The great pyramid at Cahokia is greater in extent than that at Gizeh, in Egypt. Cahokia's structures, with those in the immediate surroundings, comprised North America's largest metropolis from the tenth through the fourteenth centuries. Similar but smaller urban centers appeared along the Missouri, the lower Mississippi, the Cumberland, and Tennessee rivers, among others. *(Credit: Painting by Lloyd K. Townsend)*

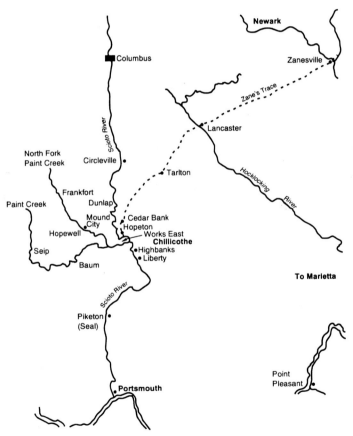

Sites in central Ohio associated with the Great Hopewell Road which ran from the mound complex at Newark to mounds in the neighborhood of Chilicothe. The modern city of Columbus is shown on the Scioto River north of these ancient communities. It too had mounds, but probably not in the geometric configurations to be found south in the other sites.

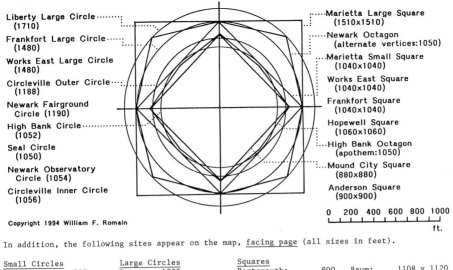

Liberty Large Circle (1710)	Marietta Large Square (1510x1510)
Frankfort Large Circle (1480)	Newark Octagon (alternate vertices:1050)
Works East Large Circle (1480)	Marietta Small Square (1040x1040)
Circleville Outer Circle (1188)	Works East Square (1040x1040)
Newark Fairground Circle (1190)	Frankfort Square (1040x1040)
High Bank Circle (1052)	Hopewell Square (1060x1060)
Seal Circle (1050)	High Bank Octagon (apothem:1050)
Newark Observatory Circle (1054)	Mound City Square (880x880)
Circleville Inner Circle (1056)	Anderson Square (900x900)

0 200 400 600 800 1000
ft.

In addition, the following sites appear on the map, facing page (all sizes in feet).

Small Circles		Large Circles		Squares			
Works East:	760	Baum:	1320	Portsmouth:	800	Baum:	1108 x 1120
Frankfort:	720	Seip:	1632	Dunlap:	800	Liberty:	1108 x 1108
Seip:	750			Hopeton:	960		
Baum:	760			Newark:	960		
Hopeton:	960			Seal:	854 x 852		
				Circleville:	841 x 841		
				Seip:	1108 x 1120		

Comparison of sizes of Ohio sites. *(Credit: William F. Romain)*

The Serpent Mound in southern Ohio, a quarter-mile-long effigy of a serpent holding a circle in its mouth, built about 1066. It may possibly refer to the same comet that was woven into the Bayeux tapestry celebrating William of Normandy's invasion of England in that year. *(Credit: Dache M. Reeves Collection, National Anthropological Archives)*

Albert Gallatin, leader of Jefferson's Democratic Republicans, Senator from Pennsylvania, Secretary of the Treasury, and Minister to France and then England. He studied the Indians comprehensively, wrote several books about them and learned many of their languages. Gallatin helped sponsor the first major study of the mounds, *Ancient Monuments of the Mississippi Valley* by Ephraim George Squier and Edwin H. Davis. *(Credit: National Portrait Gallery)*

George Rogers Clark, older brother of William Clark, the partner of Meriwether Lewis. Veteran of the Revolutionary War, reared a Virginia gentleman but plagued by alcoholism, Clark was the first of the Founders to discover the great complex at Cahokia, of which he reported that Monk's Mound could have supported "a real palace." *(Credit: National Portrait Gallery)*

James Wilkinson, who at various points betrayed Washington, spied for Spain, betrayed Aaron Burr, and survived a trial for treason by dint of a hung jury. Nonetheless, his archaeological reports to Jefferson earned him membership in the American Philosophical Society, and he gathered many artifacts, including kneeling figures from the ancient cultures of Tennessee. *(Credit: National Portrait Gallery)*

Henry Brackenridge, the first westerner to write comprehensively about the American West, and the finest literary craftsman to describe Indian antiquity in his day. He wrote of the mounds that "all of these vestiges invariably occupy the most eligible situations for towns or settlements. . . . An immense population has once been supported in this country." *(Credit: National Portrait Gallery)*

Thomas Worthington, governor, senator, student of mounds, and friend of Albert Gallatin.

Diagram of Jefferson's estate at Poplar Forest, Virginia. Begun in 1806 and by 1812 designed to include mounds 100 feet in diameter and 12 feet high, 100 feet from the house and on the same axis, with four weeping willows marking a 20-foot square on each mound, echoing the 20-foot-square central room of the house. The floor plan of the central villa is a square within an octagon; the ground plan places the house within a circle of trees, in turn within a circular drive. It is likely that these circles were attached to a square garden to the south. The parallels with the Adena-Hopewell Ohio mound shapes are striking; Jefferson knew in detail the configuration of the Marietta complex and perhaps of others. In 1819 he wrote that at Poplar Forest, "I slumber without fear, and review in my dreams the vision of antiquity." *(Credit: Sketch by Timothy Deal; concept of estate plan by C. Allan Brown)*

Brackenridge contrasted these simple tumuli to the platform "mounds or pyramids" such as those within the squares at Marietta, and those to be seen in their multitudes around St. Louis and Cahokia. These, he said, "belong to a period different from the others, and are easily distinguished from the barrows, by their size and the design which they manifest."

His taxonomy of ancient architecture is still useful, and he has much else to teach us. Because it is wearisome to read great blocks of single-spaced type, representative sections of Brackenridge's descriptive prose are placed in an appendix, entitled Mr. Brackenridge Speaks for Himself, with comfortable spaces between the lines, while we proceed with his own story.

* * *

On July 25, 1813, Henry Brackenridge gave Thomas Jefferson an extended account of his researches into ancient American architecture. His sketches had been printed in a St. Louis newspaper and then in Niles's *Weekly Register* in Baltimore, so all Brackenridge was required to do was to accompany reprints with a map to make them more easily understood.[42] On the strength of these researches he was bold enough to follow up with the suggestion that as he passed "through Virginia this coming autumn or the spring following . . . [he might] pay my respects in person at Monticello."[43]

Brackenridge wrote later in his *Recollections of Persons and Places in the West* that he was not quite sure enough of his right to ask the Sage to read his manuscript until he found in what he called "Mr. Jefferson's Memoirs" that presumably about 1798, "some information had been communicated, by my father, of the business [Thomas] Power was engaged in."[44]

Jefferson left no "memoirs" covering the 1790s, and no correspondence about Power appears in any other of his voluminous papers. There does not seem to be any mention of Power in all those papers, though, as we have seen, there are several other exchanges, including an appalling recommendation by the elder Brackenridge that Washington give greater authority to the man Power was bribing into sedition, James Wilkinson.

Perhaps at some point Brackenridge, senior, did reverse himself and warn Jefferson about both paymaster and payee. If so, that document was not kept in those papers. Brackenridge may have been right; in any case, Jefferson went to unusual courtesies in acknowledging the archaeological discoveries made by the son of his informant at Cahokia. He responded in a personal letter, dated September 20, 1813, acknowledging that he had read with pleasure the "account . . . of the ancient fortifications in the Western country" and acknowledging that he had "never before had an idea that they were so numerous."[45]

Jefferson went on to say that he had forwarded the accounts of Brackenridge to the American Philosophical Society. Then he composed a more formal response dated March 16, 1814, apparently intended as a testimonial to help Brackenridge toward publication. The fine aroma of presidential authentication rises from his endorsement of "this valuable contribution towards the knowledge of a Great Country." As the result of such reports, he declared, the rising empire of the West was "destined to become the most interesting portion of the western world."[46]

Brackenridge knew how to ingratiate himself with a Francophile sage: he invoked the authority of Jefferson's friend Volney, and the prepotency of the French view of the abundance and antiquity of America's ancient Egypt:[47]

> Throughout what is denominated by Volney . . . there exist traces of a population far beyond what this extensive and fertile portion of the continent is supposed to have possessed, greater, perhaps, than could be supported by the present white inhabitants, even with the careful agriculture practiced by the most populous states of Europe. . . . There are certainly may districts on the Ohio and Mississippi equally favorable to a numerous population. When I contemplated the beauty and fertility of those spots, I could scarcely believe it possible, that they should never have supported a numerous population.[48]

The land was rich, the climate kindly, and the evidence clear that "at the junction of all the considerable rivers, in the most eligible positions for towns, and in the most extensive bodies of fertile land" there would be an attraction which permitted, nay, required, "a population as numerous as that which once animated the borders of the Nile."[49]

It did not require a leap of the imagination for Brackenridge to envisage what had happened to that population. He and his contemporaries were well acquainted with plague and other sorrows. A great epidemic would naturally come to the minds of people who themselves lost to disease nearly half their children in infancy, and to whom death came so early that most never reached what we blithely call "middle age." As he walked about the desolate landscape around Cahokia, Brackenridge was, therefore, inevitably led to intuit the events we have called the Great Dying, an "astonishing diminution in numbers [that might have struck the Indians] immediately before we became acquainted with them."

"Nearly opposite St. Louis . . . on the banks of the Cahokia," Brackenridge followed a shambling, uncertain, and boggy stream as it traversed a plain of deep brown soil, nearly fifty miles in extent. In 1810, this vastness, hummocked with huge earthen platforms, lay almost completely empty of human life. He reported two complexes containing "not less than on hundred mounds."

> One of the mounds falls little short of the Egyptian pyramid Mycerius. When I examined it in 1811, I was astonished that this stupendous monument of antiquity should have been unnoticed by any traveller. . . . The mounds at St. Louis, at New Madrid, and at the commencement of Black River, are all larger than those of Marietta.[50]

The astonishment of Brackenridge was justified. But it is even more amazing that after the Cahokia complex was registered in its magnitude by Brackenridge, many Americans were still so trapped in a European point of view that they responded with a yawn. As Brackenridge observed in 1813:

> Who will pretend to speak with certainty as to the antiquity of America—of the races of men who have flourished and disappeared—of the thousand revolutions, which, like other parts of the globe, it has undergone? The philosophers of Europe, with a narrowness and selfishness of mind, have endeavored to depreciate every thing which relates to it. They have called it the *New World,* as though its formation was posterior to the rest of the habitable globe.[51]

The fault, of course, was not with the eighteenth century philosophers of Europe, against whom Jefferson had contended in his *Notes*. It lay with nineteenth century Americans—and with some Americans still—whose diffidence about the value of their past, and about their distinct character as a people, underlies an apparent truculence about whatever wealth or power they may achieve in a precarious present.

*   *   *

As he wandered from city to city, Brackenridge found himself for a time in Baltimore, where he produced an "Ode to Jackson's Victory" and a second short-order history, his *History of the Late War, Between the United States and Great Britain,* composed and printed in less than two months' time. His next book, *Voyage to South America,* in two neat octavo volumes and receiving good reviews, came after a stint in Latin America. Meanwhile he set about rebuilding a legal practice in Baltimore based upon service in the Maryland legislature. Once again, Jefferson came to his aid, reviewing the *Voyage* with approval. It was a great success, being published again in London and in a Spanish edition. Brackenridge was established as the most popular writer on Latin America in the English-speaking world; not until 1840 was he replaced by Prescott.

Literary celebrity is nice, but it seldom pays the bills. In 1820 Brackenridge started another round of searches for fortune commensurate with fame, setting off for St. Louis and another go at the law. On this occasion his trajectory *was* right; once again, however, it was through a carom shot, for his next career was not in the West. It happened that the Paladin of Missouri, Thomas Hart Benton, was in Washington to lobby for the admission of Missouri into the Union. He had read in Brackenridge's *Views* an eloquent statement of the geographical determinism which later became known as *Manifest Destiny*. Benton delighted in the prospect that America was fated to occupy the great valley and then to thrust westward to the Pacific, where trade with the Orient would flourish and a new culture emerge along what we call "the Pacific rim." Commerce with China and Japan would flow into Benton's St. Louis by way of the Columbia and Missouri rivers— despite small obstacles such as the Rocky Mountains, the Indians, and the Pacific Ocean. "The first idea of it," said Benton to Brackenridge, "was from your book on Louisiana." Would Brackenridge please set to work, immediately, so that all these wonders might unfold? Benton was ready to subsidize pamphlets and articles "agreeable to our friends" supporting the admission of Missouri to the Union.[52]

What was "agreeable" to Benton would surely be agreeable as well to General Jackson.

Jackson had already carried out his private invasion of the Spanish territory of Florida, and had demonstrated that the territory could not be held by Spain; it was thereupon ceded—or, rather, conceded—to the United States in 1821. Like any border baron of the British Middle Ages, Jackson had won by the sword his appointment as governor of a territory.

By coincidence, as General and Mrs. Jackson were descending the Mississippi from St. Louis toward Baton Rouge, Brackenridge was in transit to the same destination. The Jacksons' steamboat was disabled. They transferred to that bearing Brackenridge. The old Brackenridge charm sparkled once more. Brackenridge became Governor Jackson's civilian secretary and translator.

In Florida he went to work once again as "Judge Brackenridge" (Jackson's term for him) to rework an alien legal system into rough compatibility with that of the United States.* In March, Old Hickory came in like the lion he was. In October, he went out rather more tamely, "disappointed," as his wife put it. The Spanish elite still dominated the scene, encouraged by the solicitousness of other American appointees. These were agents of John Quincy Adams and James Monroe, who subverted Jackson's authority to prevent the broadening of his political base. Finally Jackson put his Spanish predecessor "in the

---

*His partner in this work was that magnificent character Richard K. Call, who in 1861 became the Sam Houston of Florida, an anti-secessionist Governor of a seceding state.

calaboose" and told Monroe he was going home to The Hermitage. Brackenridge was serving as Jackson's ghostwriter, and crafted his farewell address as governor.[53]

Jackson's retirement left Brackenridge in a vacuum. He had no Florida constituency of his own. Jackson was pretending he had no further ambitions: "Do they think that I am such a damned fool as to think myself fit for the Presidency of the United States? No, sir, I know what I am fit for; I can command a body of men in a rough way; but I am not fit to be President."[54]

While Jackson was playing Cincinnatus and consolidating his base in Tennessee, Brackenridge was moving incautiously into the vacuum left in Florida, behaving as if Jackson were still governor. He became a member of the legislative council of the territory and, on July 17, 1822, was appointed U.S. district judge for West Florida, Monroe's choice having declined the post. It appeared that he had entered on the uplands the outlines of which he had been so long reconnoitering. He even got married: "Now that the flower of my youth has faded away . . . I . . . hope for the enjoyment of those pleasures which have their seat and center in the heart . . . [otherwise] existence itself will seem but a cold, and dank, and dreary way." On March 22, 1827, the forty-one-year-old judge married Caroline Marie, whom he had known since her birth in Pittsburgh thirty-one years earlier.[55]

On his return to Florida, ahead of his bride, he began a rigorous exercise course, walking four or five miles a day, and told her proudly he was losing weight. He also found time to prepare his own counterpart to Jefferson's *Notes on Virginia,* a long article for the *North American Review* which might have been called *Notes on Florida.* The voice was the same as that of the young man who had recognized the necessary conditions for a great city in the fertile American Bottom and evidence of an ancient civilization in the mounds of Cahokia. Around Tallahassee, Brackenridge saw larger trees and deeper soil than elsewhere in Florida, together with "the appearances of a dense population, which seems at one time to have covered this country."[56]

Brackenridge did not pursue his researches into the archaeology of Florida, nor did he sustain his ties to Jackson, though he was counseled to do so by his old Louisiana friend Edward Livingston. In 1831–32, when Jackson was president, the administration and the judicial system were purged of the followers of John C. Calhoun. As the presidential knife extended to prune away even those judges who were politically ambiguous, Brackenridge was among them.

The cold steel came as a shock. Brackenridge thought he had a pledge from the president to renew his term, given at a family dinner at the White House. He responded with a violent political attack on Jackson. Jackson returned the favor, calling Brackenridge "an ingrate of baseness."[57]

Four years later, Jackson retired, bestowing the presidency upon Martin Van Buren. Brackenridge supported William Henry Harrison, another writer on Native American antiquities. Jackson's coattails were still strong enough to pull Van Buren into the White House, but in 1840 Harrison ran again and won. Brackenridge rode behind him into the House of Representatives. Though aging, a stately equanimity was still beyond his range of deportment, and the Congress required more composure than he could summon. It bored him. Restless once again, he returned to Pittsburgh and resumed his legal practice.

As a boy, Henry Brackenridge had played upon that Indian mound, built eighteen hundred years earlier, in a neighborhood called Grant's Hill. As he grew older, he had steadily expanded his neighborhood; the narrative he eventually sent to Jefferson began:

> I often visited the mound and other remains of Indian antiquity in the neighborhood of Pittsburgh. . . . Since the year 1810 . . . I have visited almost everything of this kind, worthy of note on the Ohio and Mississippi.[58]

Pittsburgh had lost the mound, however. In the 1830s, a level *temenos* (sacred precinct) was required for a new Grecian courthouse. The mound was obliterated, though as Brackenridge, now a venerable former judge, entered the *temenos* to file his pleadings, he traversed space the Indians had made sacred long before.

On two thousand acres acquired by Mrs. Brackenridge eighteen miles up the Allegheny, the middle-aged couple built a comfortable house and founded a town they called "Tarentum". He had become a sage, not so much out of wisdom as out of geriatric tenacity, and as the property of Mrs. Brackenridge burgeoned in value after the panic of 1837, he became wise in the wallet as well: the wallet is for many the seat of wisdom.

In 1848, Squier and Davis acknowledged the pioneering inquiries into the architecture of Cahokia made by Brackenridge four decades earlier. So did George Glidden, the Egyptologist, who moved into "a shantee" across the Allegheny from Brackenridge and commenced to "talk *archaeology* to our full content."[59]

Brackenridge was already returning to the subject, extending his scope to New Mexico. In 1850, he found in the city of Washington an archive of materials assembled by Peter Force on the antiquities of the upper Rio Grande Valley, and produced a pamphlet on the subject that caught the attention of Alexander von Humboldt—the renowned explorer was still extant—and of Brantz Mayer, a lawyer, antiquarian

and ethnologist, to whom Brackenridge made a wholly sensible suggestion: that the chimerical city of Quivira, sought by Coronado in 1540–
41, was Cahokia. The "large river" described to the Spaniards by the
Indian they called "The Turk," with its sailing canoes, was the Mississippi. When Coronado reached the neighborhood of Lindsborg, Kansas, just south of the complex of mounds at Salina, he had gone three-
fifths of his way to Quivira-Cahokia.

History was beginning to coil in upon itself, as it does for old men.
Brackenridge edited his father's papers and brought out a new edition
of *Modern Chivalry*. He wrote Louis Philippe, now King of France,
that he recalled "as if it were yesterday" the king and his two brothers
as refugees in the Brackenridge house in Pittsburgh fifty years before.[60]

By 1860, Brackenridge was even richer, having reaped the benefits
of the industrialization of the Allegheny valley. In East Tarentum
(which has become the little city of Brackenridge), there had been created the largest chemical complex west of the Appalachians. And, as
old men are wont to do, he became conservative. In 1864, Brackenridge campaigned for George B. McClellan against Abraham Lincoln,
revealing, it is sorrowful to record, an unbecoming wordiness and bit-
terness. His speeches were full of invective against the "demon of abolition": *Uncle Tom's Cabin* was a "slanderous novel." In his youth he
had rescued a slave, but now he now would support only the slowest
and most gradual of compensated abolition.[61]

He had always had a propensity for swimming against whatever tide
was running at the time. And he was appalled at "the mutual hatred
. . . [and the] bloody, destructive civil war." The 1864 campaign was
his last major public effort; he died on January 18, 1871. His tombstone in Prospect Cemetery describes Henry Brackenridge as traveler,
author, jurist—and man of honor. That he was, though, as he grew
older, honor ceased to be coupled to a vigorous historical imagination.
He forgot what he had learned about people who did not look or live
like Anglo-Saxons. He could not abandon his prejudices against people
of color. He was a Jeffersonian, not a Gallatinian.

CHAPTER NINE

JEFFERSON'S ARCHAEOLOGISTS: PART TWO

The French knew from the beginning that Natchez was a healthier place to build a city than New Orleans, where malaria was recurrent. Only if one kept high above the river was there was some hope of a breeze and relief from the plague-bearing mosquitoes, and Natchez had a bluff, upon which, in 1716, was placed the most important outpost of the empire of the Bourbons in the Mississippi Valley. Fort Rosalie, at Natchez, was complete two years before the French attempted to do anything in the swamp at New Orleans, which for fifty more years remained a few hovels amid dwarf palmettos and willow thickets from which at nightfall slithered cotton-mouth adders, and its streets were as dangerous from alligators as from cutpurse thugs.*

"The hill" at Natchez is the first high land to which one comes ascending the Mississippi, a compost heap of brown loess (a fine, calcareous earth) a hundred feet deep and two hundred miles in extent, some of the richest soil in the world. This elevation stands four hundred miles from the mouth of a river which from the air appears to be a blue dragon, or a great boa, devouring, now and again, the ruins of another Indian city, an old French town, a cornfield, or a plantation complex—columns, garconnieres, pigeonaires, "quarters" and all. Seen on the map, the river suggests something less formidable, something from an anatomical chart—a lower intestine grinding and dissolving those substances the continent needs for nourishment, and carrying what it does not require to deposit in the sea.

These digestive processes have been proceeding for tens of thousands of years. Rivers and rain and wind have done their work at their own pace. Mud flats have been produced, extending for hundreds of

---

*Natchez below the hill served a different clientele; it was a den of prostitutes, gamblers, drunks, and desperados.

miles. Gaining fresh deposits, they rise high enough to stand above the river, except when the river chooses to flood. On these mud banks, enormous beech trees and cottonwoods thrive; almost anything grows there after the trees are removed. By 1820, these fertile flatlands were planted in indigo and sugar and cotton, replacing earlier crops which had been cultivated for at least two thousand years.

For a thousand of those years, the valley of the Mississippi had supported monumental architecture in complexes of platform mounds set about plazas, until in the central valley around Cahokia, that unaccountable decline in activity occurred around 1350, and the Empty Quarter opened. As it widened southward, pressing displaced people ahead of it there seem to have been frenzies of building and warfare, as successive nations were threatened and sought to protect themselves. At Natchez, this outbreak of desperate energy and mound building continued a late as 1500, perhaps until 1540, producing at Emerald (ten miles north of Natchez on the Natchez trace) the shaping of a loess hillock into a great mound, about 235 feet by 771 bearing on its upper surface two smaller, but still very considerable structures, one for a temple and the other for the palace of a chieftain.*

About forty years after work ceased on Emerald Mound, De Soto's expedition burnt and pillaged its way through this countryside, then heavily populated. The Spaniards exhausted themselves in assaults against walled towns, contending against the ancestors of the Natchez Nation who came against them in armies of thousands and navies of hundreds of war canoes. After the ravagers departed, there was a pause in visible politics as the diseases they deposited in the region did their work, and the French appeared. After a series of mutual slaughters, the French endeavored to exterminate the remaining Natchez in 1719. As often happened during the expansion of Europe into other continents, the natives were massacred first and then romanticized.†

The romance of the nearly exterminated was achieved by Chateaubriand in his novel *Les Natchez,†* while amid the ruins of ancient Natchez, "Natchez above the hill" was becoming an elegant village of

---

*Neighboring the Emerald site is another group, with a plaza, apparently built a little earlier, at Anna.

†A chronicle written in 1808 by the English traveler Fortescue Coming said, with a little inaccuracy as to date, that: "In 1731 the Indians, disgusted with the tyranny and cruelty of the French colonists, massacred most of them, for which . . . the French took ample vengeance, almost extirpated the whole Natchez race."

A descendent of the Natchez has recently reminded me that the word "almost" is important: reports of the extirpation of his people were premature. A few escaped two massacres and deportation to Haiti, and retreated to Alabama to live for a time on the Coosa river and create descendants such as my informant. (Coming on Natchez, *Travels*, pp. 125–26. My informant spoke privately.)

verandas and gardens. The little city on the loess was almost genteel by 1789, when Andrew Jackson began trading there; great landowners had begun to congregate in Natchez, administering through resident overseers their hundreds of thousands of acres in the bayou lands to the north and south of the city.*

Nineteenth century Natchez was the base for a prosperous band of scientist-planter-entrepreneurs with close financial and intellectual links to Philadelphia—New Orleans was rising, but Philadelphia had arisen. The Natchez Junto, as they were called, could afford to keep up their links with the eastern metropolis; in fact, they could not afford not to do so. Their capital requirements were huge, and Philadelphia, not New Orleans, was the banking center of America. Money was of interest to all of them; to some, the subjects of this chapter, Philadelphia was important for another reason: it was the capital of their intellectual and scientific life, headquarters of American science, collating and assessing the evidence of American antiquity. Natchez commanded the field forces deployed upon the grand arena for research sold by Napoleon to Jefferson.

The chief guides to the western half of the Mississippi Valley below that portion explored by Lewis and Clark were the scientist, astronomer, explorer, archaeologist, physiocrat, physician, and planter, William Dunbar, and a pirate-architect named Barthelemy Lafon.

We will find Lafon in Barataria, amid his swag and his specimens, having executed an exquisite map of Dunbar's citadel, Natchez, and of the archaeological wonders of the Ouachita River valley.

WILLIAM DUNBAR AND THE NATCHEZ

When one considers the variety of persons congregating along the Mississippi at the time of the Louisiana Purchase who had no love for his government, it is no wonder that Thomas Jefferson took frequently to his bed with blinding, black-and-red headaches.

In the West there were unhappy politicians such as Aaron Burr, agents of foreign governments such as James Wilkinson, George Rogers Clark, Harry Innes, and John Sevier, suborned judges and intriguing generals, aggrieved Cincinnati convinced Jefferson was a Jacobin, adherents to Spain, France, and Britain, Irish and Scottish ref-

---

*The first traders and small planters who established themselves at Natchez between 1729 and 1800 reproduced on the escarpment above the Mississippi the architecture of the Caribbean lowlands, balconies and piazzas, some raised on posts. The streets were thronged with Americans, French and Spanish creoles, mulattoes, free Blacks, and slaves.

This was the Natchez of 1806, where Aaron Burr gathered his forces for his final assault on New Orleans.

ugees constitutionally averse to authority of any kind, pirates on the coast and brigands on the land, and an array of nations who had occupied the land long before any of these Europeans came upon the scene.

Yet also present were beneficiaries of the finest education Europe could offer, which, at the time, could be found in Scotland, and who shared with Jefferson a firm adherence both to the United States and to scientific research. At their head was William Dunbar.*

Dunbar came from Elgin, the Scotland of ruined cathedrals, bishops' palaces, and royal residences, of Prince Charlie, and of a museum of fossils collected by the Elgin Society. Though it was hoary with age and resonant with memories, Elgin had not always been tranquil. As the youngest son of Sir Archibald Dunbar, William grew up to tales of "The Wolf of Badenoch" and his "wyld, wykked Helandmen," of the Bloody Vespers when the Dunbar and Innes clans fought it out in the cathedral itself. Bonnie Prince Charlie himself had spent eleven days with the Dunbars at Thunterton House just before the disaster at Culloden, and three years before William's birth.†

William inherited the estate on the death of his father and brothers, but chose to set his course to the south and west. He studied the classics in Glasgow, and mathematics and astronomy in London. In 1771, he was at Fort Pitt, trading with the Indians, and two years later at Baton Rouge, where he became a Spanish subject. Things did not go well for a while: we are told by the *Dictionary of American Biography* that "some of his most valuable slaves were lost to him in an insurrection." It might have been called a "Revolutionary War" if the slaves had been white—and won.

By 1792, however, Dunbar had recovered and established himself at The Forest. In 1798 he welcomed there the new governor of Mississippi Territory, Winthrop Sargent. Despite Dunbar's hospitality, and a fresh set of Indian antiquities to compare to Marietta and Cincinnati, Sargent did not think much of Natchez: he wrote James Wilkinson, that fastidious soul, that "the perverseness of some of the people, the inebriety of the Indians and Negroes on Sundays" made Natchez "a most abominable place."[1]

But Dunbar was able to appeal to both Sargent's love of antiquity and his speculative instincts by including him in the glorious possibili-

---

*In some local histories he is still called "Sir" William Dunbar. He was, in fact, the son of a baron's second wife and had a baronial half-brother.

Dunbar made a joke of the matter at one stage, asserting that it was his republican principles which required him, when ordering a carriage, to settle for a mere monogram rather than a coat of arms on the door.

†Sad to report, I have found no reference by either Judge Dunbar of Mississippi or Judge Innes of Kentucky to family lore about these earlier associations.

ties of a hamlet he called Clarksville, named for his friend Daniel
Clark, then the most powerful trader in New Orleans and a partner of
Wilkinson's. Clarksville was barely within the United States, at the
edge of Spanish Louisiana, on "an handsome plain ornamented by
seven elegant indian mounts." Dunbar predicted that it would become
"a great commercial town." Wilkinson agreed: sensing opportunity
during the previous fall, he had begun building at Loftus Heights, two
miles away, a stockade he called Fort Adams.[2]

How could Sargent resist? The Clarksville complex was more elaborate and architecturally sophisticated than that at Marietta. And to
the north of Natchez Sargent and Dunbar were made conscious of the
presence of antiquity every time they rode past Emerald and Anna on
their way to the seat of government, at Washington, Mississippi. Of
course, Natchez itself was then dominated by the presence of another
complex, occupied until the French eliminated the Natchez threat to
their settlement.

The scientific community of Natchez included Dr. David Ker, late of
Trinity College, Dublin, who had gone on to study medicine at Edinburgh, and a cadre of scientist-doctors who had been trained along
Scottish lines in Philadelphia. These included Ker's son-in-law, Rush
Nutt, whom we met earlier at Golgotha, and his grandson Dr. Haller
Nutt, as well as Dr. Stephen Duncan and Dr. Frederick Stanton (Stanton may also have been trained at Trinity and Edinburgh). I suppose
we should add James Wilkinson—Dr. James Wilkinson, for he, too,
had been trained in medicine.[3]

Dunbar had served the Spanish Crown as surveyor general of the
Natchez district, working along the southwestern border of the United
States in parallel with Andrew Ellicott, the American representative
charged with establishing the extent of West Florida, and beguiling
Ellicott with his inquiries into astronomy. Dunbar built a sophisticated
astronomical laboratory, and conducted the first meteorological observations made in the Mississippi Valley since the great days of Indian
astronomy three centuries earlier. Duncan could have been introduced
to Jefferson either by Ellicott or by Daniel Clark; there is much correspondence among the four on scientific and political subjects. Dunbar
became a member of the American Philosophical Society at Jefferson's
recommendation.

Nutt and Dunbar made their greatest contributions to an understanding of Native American architecture in 1804–5, during the early
days of Burr's "conspiracy." They joined Sargent in the exploration of
this very ancient land, which, as Nutt put it, bore evidence that it had
once been "in a greater state of cultivation than when we found it . . .
& [it] possessed the art of architecture."[4]

THE OUACHITA EXPEDITION

In the winter of 1804–5, while William Clark was at Cahokia, William Dunbar led a Jeffersonian expedition up the Ouachita River. Its charter was the same as that of Lewis and Clark, except that the provocation of Spain was somewhat less blatant because the Ouachita flowed entirely within territory conceded by the bureaucracy in Madrid to have been purchased by the United States.

The Ouachita (always spelled by these partners as it is pronounced and sometimes spelled when applied to wildlife areas, "Washita") rises in the Ouachita Mountains and above Hot Springs, Arkansas. After leaving the hills it wanders indolently southward, in parallel to the Mississippi, passing fifteen or twenty miles to the west of Natchez. It is not emphatic about its intentions, looping about, gathering in the equally unhurried Tensas, Red, and Catahoula, to become for a few miles the Black River (though brown would be more like it), and ultimately contributing accumulations of water and silt to the Mississippi below Angola, Louisiana.

Dunbar's deputy for the Washita expedition was Dr. George Hunter, another Scot, but one sprung from the artisan class of Edinburgh rather than of Dunbar's gentry. Hunter had ascended through indenture and apprenticeship to become an "Eminent Druggist." He came to America in 1774, served in the Revolutionary Army as an apothecary, escalated through a succession of chemical factories until he was forty-nine and earned Jefferson's estimate that he had "probably no equal in the united States . . . in the practical branch of that science." However practical, he was not a gentleman in Dunbar's terms, and, possibly because he was also a Scot, Dunbar's terms were particularly severe. Writing to Jefferson, Dunbar dryly noted that Hunter displayed "a very warm temper" and that he was guilty of applying his "practical" knowledge of chemistry "to the object of making money." They all did *that* of course, but it seems Hunter did so with ungentlemanly candor.[5]

The first set of ruins passed by Dunbar and Hunter was a mound complex twenty miles to the west of Natchez, lying under the present town of Jonesville, Louisiana. It was once known as Troyville, and its ancient architecture attracted the attention of people from a greater world including Mark Twain. The wounds are gone; the discouraged little town has lost all distinction, and all claim to the attention of tourists, because in the 1950s the Louisiana Highway Department completely obliterated all significant evidence of antiquity to obtain fill for a highway.[6]

The hamlet which had grown in the shadow of these ruins was

known to Dunbar and Hunter as the trading post of "Monsieur Cadet, who has built his house on an Indian mound" keeping a ferry "which even now is very lucrative" under the shadow of a "stupendous turret, situate on the back part . . . tapering as you ascend, the whole surmounted by a great cone with the top cut off. This tower of earth on measurement proved to be about 80 feet perpendicular . . . [and a platform mound] 100 feet broad & 300 feet long at the top." The eighty-foot earthen tower was the highest mound in the United States but for Monks Mound at Cahokia. (Sauls Mound at Pinson, Tennessee, is close behind, at seventy-two feet).* †

Dunbar and Hunter pressed northwestward from M. Cadet's stupendous pile through a maze of bayous and deep alluvial soil formed by the many early meandering of the Mississippi and its tributaries, and now occupied by the Upper Washita National Wildlife Refuge. They were penetrating the most profound mysteries of American ancient architecture. They passed a few hundred yards below that modest elevation which supports the five-thousand-year-old earthworks at Watson Brake, past the bayou which leads into the Ouachita River from Frenchman's Bend, and not far from the great earthen rings at Poverty Point. All these ancient works eluded them because they were not directly upon the river bank and were so eroded and covered with brush. Only the middle of the twentieth century did they become easily accessible to pulp-cutters and cotton farmers. The Ouachita expedition pressed up the river until it came into the foothills of the Ouachitas, and, uneventfully turned back to Natchez.

THE RED RIVER EXPEDITION

The second Dunbar expedition did not have so tranquil a history. After Hunter, nursing his warm temper, went back to his commercial ventures in Philadelphia, Dunbar looked about for another leader to complete the reconnoitering of the Spanish borderlands. Dunbar and Jef-

---

*They went on to say: "If one may judge from the immense labor required to erect those Indian monuments located here, this place must once have been very populous. There is an entrenchment or embankment running from the Catahoula to the Black river, enclosing about 200 acres of rich land, at present [the embankment] is about 10 feet high & fifty broad. This surrounds four large mounds of earth, at a distance of a bow shot from each other. . . . Cadet owns about two or three thousand acres of rich bottom land here, which is never overflowed except in very high freshet." (Hunter, *Western Journals*, pp. 5 ff.)

†If this had been De Soto's Anilco, this would have been the "stupendous turret" which was an island when his forces came upon it while the river was in flood. Often during the nineteenth century, townspeople took refuge upon it; in the 1870s Twain was there to describe such a flood and such a use.

ferson both knew from the maps Baron von Humboldt had shared with them (with Gallatin, and with Aaron Burr), that the Red River swings westward into territory claimed both by Spain and by the still-potent survivors of the Caddo Confederacy. The task of mobilizing enough force for archaeology, natural history, and whatever else might be useful upon the Red occupied Dunbar's energies for months after he returned from the Ouachita, and in April, 1806, an expedition to explore the Red was ready. By that time, Dunbar's health was failing, and Burr was in Natchez as well, with his own ideas for the Ouachita in particular and the borderlands in general.

Dunbar, with growing apprehension, acknowledged that he must hand to others the field responsibility for the Red River expedition. He considered that old mound-seeker, William Bartram, whose book of *Travels* of 1791 had informed the Philadelphia and Natchez intellectuals about the platform mounds of Ohio and the American South. But Bartram was in his late sixties, and seldom emerged from his botanical lair in Philadelphia.

Benjamin Smith Barton was next consulted. Barton, like Bartram, was known both as a scholar of Ohio Valley antiquities and as a naturalist. His *New Views of the Origins of the Tribes and Nations of America* had been published in 1797. Barton declined, but recommended the twenty-five-year-old Peter Custis, yet another scientific Virginian and "a good botanist," Jefferson told Dunbar.*[7] Though Custis turned out to be competent enough, Jefferson and Dunbar lost the opportunity of the epoch by refusing the application of an even more colorful mound-seeker, Constantine Samuel Rafinesque-Schmalz. Rafinesque was barely twenty-one, but he had already made a name for himself as a researcher into Kentucky ornithology and Native American antiquities. Born in Constantinople, of French and German parentage, trained in Italy, he described himself correctly as

botanist, naturalist, geologist, historian, poet, phiosopher, philologist, economist, philanthropist, . . . traveller, merchant, manufacturer, col-

---

*Peter was an eastern shore Custis, like the first husband of Martha Washington, but he had done his college thesis in Jefferson's Albemarle County.

His kinfolk included Washington himself, George Washington Parke Custis of both Arlingtons (one now in the National Cemetery and the other on the eastern shore), and Dr. David Stuart, the whistleblower on the intrigues of the Jeffersonians of Kentucky. Though they were at the core of the Federalist party, it does not seem that Peter was political at any time in his life. Certainly he left the politics of their expedition to Freeman.

I owe Professor Donald Jackson thanks for sorting out the Custises. Peter was a descendant of Thomas, whose brother John became father of Daniel, who left Martha Dandridge a very rich widow at twenty-six. She became Martha Washington. See Donald Jackson, *Letters*, p. 239

lector, improver, professor . . . surveyor, draftsman, architect, engineer, palmist, author, editor, bookseller, librarian, secretary . . . and I hardly know myself what I may become as yet.[8]

Rafinesque was all of these, and a good philologist to boot; his speculations about the translation of Mayan glyphs were achieved by sheer brainpower, and anticipated what has only been achieved in the 1980s by making full use of computer technology. But though he had mapped the antiquities of Kentucky, he seemed too exotic for Dunbar and his offer was refused.[9]

The method used to select Thomas Freeman as the other leader of the expedition put Dunbar and Hunter once more into the hands of James Wilkinson, who had his own agenda for the expedition. Freeman was a recently reformed alcoholic,* born in Ireland and trained as a surveyor. He came into Wilkinson's entourage as early as 1797 or 1798 when his employment as a surveyor around Natchez with Andrew Ellicott erupted in a noisy falling out.†

Wilkinson acquired Freeman as a dependent, and was therefore especially useful to both Wilkinson and Jefferson. This may explain why "a careful scan of the correspondence between Jefferson and various influential persons . . . in the period before Freeman's selection failed

---

*As noted in our discussion of George Rogers Clark, alcohol was a national addiction during these decades. (There is further discussion of this point in Kennedy, *Greek Revival America*.) Recruiting requirements for scientific expeditions such as those of Freeman and Dunbar often included specific stipulations for *sober* officers and *sober* men.

Wilkinson used alcohol as one of his methods of beguilement. Humphrey Marshall said of him that he knew that the way to a man's heart was down his gullet. He was on occasion charged with drinking too much, but he was also famous for limiting himself and his guests to very fine French wine. It is likely that he understood alcoholics—and reformed alcoholics. With his instinct for the vulnerable, he was in authority over Freeman's life when that able man managed to break his habit. The best evidence that this happened during the two years in which Freeman worked for Wilkinson at Fort Adams is that he was notoriously alcoholic theretofore, and thereafter for the rest of his career, and in his obituary, Freeman was commended for his sobriety.

†Ellicott charged Freeman with drunkenness and a propensity for Shakespearian performances while on company time, "impropriety [and] . . . inflammatory conversation." Freeman responded by asserting that Ellicott was living in a ménage à trois with a washerwoman and his own son. "I was even pressed by the old sinner Ellicott, to take part of his bed with his washerwoman and himself for the night."

Others reported that Freeman was "frequently drunk and . . . absent without leave" and that Falstaff was a favored role.

(Opinions on Freeman and on Ellicott from Jacobs, *Tarnished Warrior* p. 180 and Flores, *Jefferson and Southwest Exploration*, p. 315. Wilkinson gives an extended version of Freeman's testimony in his memoirs, apparently savoring it.)

to turn up any clues explaining why Jefferson thought of Freeman in the summer of 1805."*[10]

During that summer, Aaron Burr's "Conspiracy" was being formed. It defeated itself at the end of 1806 and early in 1807, as a mere sideshow to our tale of science. Wilkinson, Burr, and Jefferson were joined in this gallimauferous undertaking, and joined as well in two sets of simultaneous endeavors in the same arena. These were a series of provocative probes of the borders of the Spanish Empire which were also scientific expeditions into the territory along the western edges of the Louisiana Purchase which was claimed by both Wilkinson's Spanish employers and his American employers. As an agent of Spain, Wilkinson manipulated both governments, seeking to find advantage in their reciprocal misunderstandings. Though he did his best to provoke confrontation between them, it appears that he had no strategy beyond a general expectation that in turmoil there might be opportunity. In all this, as in science, Freeman was a useful tool.

On the other side of the disputed territory, the Spanish commissioner of boundaries reported to the Spanish governor of Texas that he had learned (probably from Wilkinson) of Jefferson's specific plans for

---

*It is true that Freeman, like the much more eminent Ellicott, had worked upon the survey of Washington, but it was probably more important to Jefferson and Wilkinson that he have good reason to be discreet.

By rescuing and recruiting Freeman, Wilkinson earned the distaste of Ellicott, who later joined the ranks of those seeking means of bringing Wilkinson down. Freeman went into the general's own household at Clarksville, and was employed by Wilkinson for the next two years as an engineer in the construction of Fort Adams.

As Freeman's loyalty was purchased, Ellicott was placing himself naively in the deepest peril. He escaped with his life, though not, thanks to Wilkinson and Freeman, with his reputation.

In 1798, Ellicott made the mistake of telling Wilkinson that one of Freeman's colleagues, John McClary, was "under hostile influence" and that he had seen "a letter in the handwriting of M. Power [then a merchant in New Orleans] in which your name is mentioned in a manner which astonishes me. . . . I am confident it is false."

When Freeman arrived to take up his duties for Wilkinson he handed over "a certificate of [from] old Bare Bones" [Ellicott]. Wilkinson gloated that the "certificate" dealt with "my Spanish Commission" and that it was, in effect "a letter of vindication." (Wilkinson quoted in Jacobs, *Tarnished Warrior*, pp. 180–81).

By 1811, Daniel Clark and Colonel Power had had enough of Wilkinson. (Clark had been his business partner, with Governor Miro as silent partner, in the 1780s, and knew him as well as Power, who had been his paymaster for Spain).

They charged Wilkinson with crimes leading to his indictment for treason. Ellicott became an important corroborating witness against Wilkinson—thereby, in implication, *for* Burr and *against* Jefferson, Wilkinson's sponsor. Freeman's "letter of vindication," purchased by a two-year commission, was then less important than the destruction of Ellicott's credibility. Freeman's salacious story did the trick, just enough to spring Wilkinson once again.

explorations of the Red, Arkansas, and Saint Francis rivers, and recommended that it was easy and important to "divert and even to destroy these expeditions."[11]

If Wilkinson had read Jefferson's comment to Governor Clairborne
of Louisiana that "any violence . . . offered the party by subjects of
Spain . . . will have serious consequences" he would have had ample
reason to rejoice. Clearly such an altercation was anticipated; Freeman
had been instructed by Jefferson to turn back only if "a superior force
. . . be arrayed against your further progress and inflexibility determined to resist it."

As the clouds rolled in, William Dunbar, full of foreboding and increasing apprehensions of the motives of Wilkinson—and, by implication, those of Jefferson as well—assembled the expeditionary force to
be led into the disputed territory by Freeman and Custis. He had been
drawn into Jefferson's web by love of science and loyalty to his
adopted country—or rather, to the country which by its expansion had
adopted him. The president had assured him in 1803 that "nothing but
the failure of every peaceable mode of redress, nothing but dire necessity should force us from the path of peace . . . in all possible means to
re-establish our rights" to navigate past New Orleans. Surely a war
with Spain or France would be painful, for "the Mississippi would be
blockaded . . . by a superior naval power, and all our Western States
be deprived of their commerce unless they would surrender themselves
to the blockading power."[12]

But now, two years later, that same president was involving Dunbar
in a succession of scientific expeditions conceived by Jefferson himself
and articulated by Wilkinson which were also planned encounters with
Spain. Colleagues of Dunbar in Natchez warned him about this and
about Wilkinson. Their apprehensions were confirmed by Ellicot and
his own partner, Daniel Clark.* Suspicion gathered into doubt, and
doubt crystalized into dismay as Freeman and Custis set out in April,
1806, from Wilkinson's little capital, Wilkinsonbourg, Mississippi
Territory, a hamlet of saloons and sutleries about the stockade of Fort
Adams.

The party included Dr. Custis, Freeman, two other officers, two
noncommissioned officers, seventeen privates, and a black slave.
Meanwhile, Captain Edward Turner and one hundred fifty troopers
from Fort Clairborne had assaulted the old Spanish capital of Texas,

---

*The *Louisiana Gazette*, which kept an eye on all these plans, concluded in 1811 that "these
secret expeditions, secret orders and secret plans" arose from "that same philosophic mind
[that] has long wished to emancipate the people of *Old and New Mexico*" [its emphasis].
(Quoted in Flores, *Southwest Exploration*, p. 312.)

Las Adaes, sending Jose Maria Gonzales and his eighteen defenders into retreat to the Sabine River. Secretary of War Henry Dearborn gave his western commanders a prod toward provocation by sending them *The Articles of War.* On the other side of the lines, Governor Antonio Corderoy Bustamente called for more troops and resolved "to attack and destroy every Anglo-American party." Aaron Burr wrote his son-in-law that "all reflecting men consider a war with Spain to be inevitable," and Freeman and Custis prepared themselves for that eventuality.[13]

Theirs was a larger party than the garrison of Gonzales at Las Adaes; it could handle all but a determined Spanish response. It was also quite capable of ornithology, natural history, anthropology, and a little archaeology.

Jefferson's written instructions to Freeman and Custis were essentially the same as those to Lewis and Clark. They were to explore, to probe, report on flora and fauna, and "to learn the names and numbers of the nations through which your route lies . . . the extent and limits of their possessions their relations with other tribes and nations their language, traditions, monuments. . . ."*[14]

GUNSHOTS IN EDEN

After the Red River leaves Louisiana and enters Arkansas, it makes a sharp bend to the west to take up its responsibilities as the border between the states of Oklahoma and Texas. Along the Great Bend, Hunter and Freeman found themselves in the heartland of Caddonia, a region whose stem is the river the Indians called "the Mother Red."

The Caddo were a confederation of nations who survived as mound builders well after Europeans came among them, and survived as a people after the Natchez had been destroyed by the French. They spoke a tongue with Iroquoian associations, and were in active dialogue with Spiroan mound builders who created an entrepreneurial culture, trading between the buffalo-hunting tribes of the plains and the urban, corn-growing Cahokians. The Spiroans left an astonishing hoard of sculpture, textiles, and ornaments in burial mounds at their largest center, Spiro, in Oklahoma, and may have spoken a Tunican

---

*The abrupt changes in Jefferson's behavior during the Burr affair are not easy to explain. The best explanation of his oscillations is that, at the last minute, in 1806, he recoiled from the thought that Burr might be useful to him in his imperial adventures against Spain, and turned his entire network of agents and colleagues to dissociating himself from Burr's plans. There can be little doubt that he knew those plans in detail, and implied his approval of them. (This thesis is developed in Kennedy, *Orders from France.*)

tongue.* Both the Caddo and Spiroans created magnificent truncated pyramids of earth set about ceremonial plazas, and along the northern borders of their realm the fury of Caddoan resistance forced De Soto back toward the Mississippi in 1542. The survivors of his force straggled through the fringes of Caddonia after De Soto's death, marching southward toward the Texas coast.

Close to the places where these tests of strength and resolve had occurred two and a half centuries earlier, Hunter and Freeman were themselves forced to turn back in 1806. They had passed the holy Medicine Mount of the Caddo, a two-mile-long, two-hundred foot-high calcareous ridge with such sharp sides that it might be called a "butte" if found in New Mexico. A few miles to the south, there still exists the largest of the surviving Caddo mounds, five hundred ninety-two feet long, one hundred fifty-seven feet wide, and thirty-three feet high. This has been called by recent archaeologists "Battle Place"; with two platforms, it was probably the central ceremonial structure of the principality the Spaniards called "Naguatex" when they came upon its ruins in July, 1542. Today, the Medicine Mount is prosaically known as Boyds Hill, six miles northwest of Lewisville, Lafayette County, Arkansas.

A little farther along, Hunter and Freeman were met by three runners, sent by a chief who may well have been a descendant of the cacique of Naguatex who had confronted Moscoso, the successor to De Soto as leader of the Spanish invasion. The Caddo informed these new intruders that a thousand Spanish troops had passed through their village to intercept the Americans. Two days later gunshots were heard upriver, either warning shots or a Spanish hunting party. Sentinels and outriders increased, and, coming around a turn in the river, they saw a Spanish camp high on what is now called "Spanish Bluff."[†]

On July 29, 1806, according to Freeman:

> The party continued to advance, until the usual time of dining, when the boats stopped, and the men were directed to make their fires, and prepare for dinner as soon as possible. The Spanish guard was distinctly seen from hence, about half a mile further up. A party of horse was observed to gallop up to the next bend of the river, through the Cotton Wood bushes, and return with the same speed to the sentinel. They were observed at short intervals passing from the sentinel to the camp.

---

*For the Tunica's language, see Schambach, *Some New Interpretations*, pp. 187. In the late 1980s, state governments and the Archaeological Conservancy managed to rescue several of the Caddo mound complexes.

[†]A mile southwest of the point where Texas Highway 8 crosses the Red just north of New Boston, Texas.

About half an hour after the party landed, a large detachment of Horse, with four officers in front, advanced in a full gallop from the Spanish camp, along the beach towards us. As soon as they reached the water, and were about crossing to the side on which the Americans were, the men were ordered to ascend the bank and range themselves along it in the cane brake and bushes, and be ready to fire at the same time with the sentinels below, and to keep up their fire in the most effectual manner possible.

The men being thus concealed from sight, with rests for their pieces, in a position inaccessible to horse, could, with perfect safety to themselves, have given the enemy a severe reception. A non-commissioned officer and six privates were pushed along the bank so far as to be in the rear of the Spaniards, when their attack should be made. The Spanish column passed on at full speed through the water, and came on towards the party. The sentinels placed about 100 yards in advance of the barges, hailed them according to orders and bid them halt. They continued to advance with the apparent determination to charge. The sentinels a second time bid them halt, cocked their pieces, and were in the act of presenting to fire, when the Spanish Squadron halted, and displayed on the beach, at about 150 yards from the sentinels. The officers slowly advanced, and were met about 50 yards in front of the sentinels by Capt. Sparks, who was soon joined by myself, when a parley of nearly three-quarters of an hour ensued. . . .

In this conference, the Spanish Commanding Officer stated that his orders were not to suffer any body of armed troops to march through the territory of the Spanish Government; to stop the exploring party by force, and to fire on them if they persisted in ascending the river before the limits of the territory were defined. . . .

The great superiority of the Spanish force, and the difficulty the party had already experienced in ascending the river, from the shallowness of the water rendering a further progress impracticable. I replied that I should remain in my present position that day, and would return the day following.

On the Captain of the Spanish troops saying to his interpreter something respecting sending a detachment of foot below the American party; I became apprehensive they wanted to place sentinels round my party and perhaps surround us; I therefor directed Lt. Duforest to inform him, that none of the Americans should cross the river until the next day; and that if a Spanish guard was placed near us they should be fired upon. The intention was politely disavowed; he only wanted permission for an officer and a party to pass the sentinels and fetch up the Spanish detachment from below, lest any accident should happen from their not knowing the result of the conference which had taken place.

This request was acceded to; the party passed the sentinels, and soon returned with the troops that had been posted below.

Fortunately, the party were not stopped before we had made almost the greatest progress that the state of the water would admit of; we were then nearly 200 miles from the Panis nation, where only the necessary supply of pack horses could be obtained for the prosecution of our route, and we had not with us a sufficiency of Indian goods for their purchase. The practicability of exploring this river completely, was established, and sufficient information collected, to enable the party to execute it in future, more advantageously, than it could have been done at this time, and against any opposition the Spaniards can make.[15]

This time the remnants of the Caddoan confederacy merely looked on, as De Soto's Spanish successors faced down the American advance guard.

AFTER THE CONFRONTATION

In 1811, the *Louisiana Gazette* noted that "although a foreigner," Freeman continued "a favorite of government," suggesting that the explanation of this puzzle might be the fact that "cabinet secrets relating to the expedition were entirely confided to Mr. Freeman. . . . [Knowledge of] those secret expeditions, secret orders, and secret plans wonderfully enhance talents, respectability and worth." Freeman's report of the altercation with the Spaniards was intercepted, almost certainly on Wilkinson's orders, by one of his subordinates, Colonel Cushing, and the public denied information about it. Dunbar was infuriated by this further evidence that he had been duped as to the provocative purpose of the expedition; he protested it to Dearborn.[16]

Despite the suppression of evidence, the account of the expedition still included some damning information. According to Dan Flores, the only modern historian to ferret out the process by which Wilkinson and Jefferson dealt with their embarrassments, that information was excised next: When Jefferson transmitted the expedition's reports to one of his scientific advisers, Nicholas King,

> apparently he included instructions for King to delete from the accounts several references implying that the expedition was attempting to win the Indians and was preparing for a military showdown with the Spaniards. While King was thus engaged, Jefferson had occasion to deliver his annual message to Congress. He mentioned both his Louisiana [Purchase] explorations, lingering on the achievements of Lewis and Clark, and reducing those of Freeman and Custis to a bare notation that they had examined the Red River "nearly as far as the French settlements had extended . . . with zeal and prudence" but their work had "not been so successful as that of Lewis and Clark"[17]

From Wilkinson's point of view, their work had not been a success at all. He had been deprived of an altercation from which he might emerge as a hero, or, alternatively, emerge richer in fees for having avoided heroism. A bloodless confrontation between an expedition (within his responsibility though led by others) and his Spanish paymasters did not quite serve his purpose. Therefore he raised the stakes, providing the Spaniards with detailed instruction on how they might confront and destroy, if they desired, the American force under his own command.

Taking a trumpet to his lips, he proclaimed "the Spanish are coming!"

Wilkinson sent dispatches to Jefferson and Clairborne warning of a nonexistent threat to Natchitoches (in American Louisiana)—whereas, in fact, he had sent his own troops to seize Las Adaes, the Spanish capital of Texas and to reconnoiter Nacogdoches (in Spanish Texas). Furthermore, as Wilkinson well knew, Zebulon Pike might shortly be found in the willow thickets along the Rio Grande above Santa Fe. The aggression was the other way round. Nonetheless, the stage management prevailed, and, on cue, Anglo-American and French-Creole indignation erupted against "the Dons." Governor Clayborne called out the militia, and Wilkinson, hero once more, appeared magnificently uniformed at the head of a force of fifteen hundred men at Natchitoches. The long-awaited altercation was at hand.

History did not accommodate Wilkinson's ambitions. The "bloodthirsty" Spaniards had, it seemed, lost their edge since de Soto cut off the hands of his Indian captives to teach them submission. Pursuant to orders from the governor of Texas to avoid a defeat by a superior force, the Spanish force on the Sabine, two months and only a little more than a hundred miles across Caddonia from the point at which Freeman and Custis had bowed to the inevitable, retreated to the south bank of the river. There would be no war, unless Thomas Jefferson ordained it.

He did not; instead, he ordered Wilkinson to cease his provocations. *This* change of course was occasioned by events in Paris and London. Napoleon, persuaded by Tallyrand, suddenly announced that France would to to war alongside Spain if the Americans provoked a confrontation on the Louisiana-Texas border, and Charles James Fox died. Fox had been prime minister during the escalation of Jefferson's campaign—Fox and Jefferson saw many things alike. With his death went the prospect of a British alliance against Spain.

Wilkinson had already become a dove, for his own reasons. The Spanish, in a sudden burst of energy, produced a thousand men on the frontier. There would be no easy victory, no silver mines on the cheap. Now all smiles and charm, Wilkinson negotiated what has been called the "Neutral Ground Agreement" with the Spanish force opposite him.

So ended Thomas Jefferson's set of explorations of the lower tribu-

taries of the Mississippi River. There was a sputtering, inglorious ending: at the request of Secretary of War Dearborn, speaking for Jefferson, William Dunbar had equipped and recruited a fresh effort to explore the Arkansas River basin, in which forty or more mound complexes
awaited discovery. There would be a long wait, for Dunbar's proposed
Arkansas expedition, no longer useful to either Wilkinson or Jefferson,
was mysteriously aborted, so mysteriously that Dunbar was never informed of its cancellation by either Dearborn or Jefferson.

Perhaps his view of events had been made too clear a little earlier, in
his one recorded letter to Wilkinson. In May, 1807, while continuing
dutifully to comply with what he believed to be Jefferson's wishes (but
increasingly dubious of the purity of the government's scientific interests), Dunbar wrote Wilkinson to urge that the Arkansas expedition
into the Spanish borderlands be given full military protection. American soldiers or scientists should no longer be put at risks they could not
counter. This was not Wilkinson's new line: Spain was no threat, he
was saying; he had been covering his tracks by making a great stir that
the enemy had been Burr, not Spain, and Burr had been apprehended.
Dunbar seems to have been among the Westerners who scented the
commanding general's Spanish connections, for he could not resist
adding to his letter a note of irony. He and others in the Natchez circle
were on to the game:

> I have a perfect knowledge of those fine sensibilities, by which the honor
> of a soldier is impelled to brave every shadow of danger, but there are
> moments, when . . . the ultimate good of our country ought to be the
> object perpetually in view.[18]

Betrayed and humiliated, the old man thereupon ceased all correspondence with Wilkinson and Jefferson.[19]

CUSTIS

As Freeman maneuvered amid the Spanish forces in August, 1806,
Peter Custis was dodging enemy patrols in order to complete a different sort of reconnaissance, recording observations of interest to Jefferson, including an account of the Caddoan creation myth.* Aside from
that, Custis was only of marginal use to archeology, for though he re-

---

*The search for Madoc was underway. Creation myths were much in vogue, in major part
because similarities of ancient Welsh myths to those of the Indians were given as evidence
of the truth of the Welsh tale of American colonization by their Prince Madoc. Jefferson
took these stories with sufficient seriousness to ask Lewis and Clark to seek for Welsh
descendents where they had been reported, on the upper Missouri. (See also Chapter Ten.)

ferred in passing to natural features which might have been mounds, he was primarily a botanist and in a hurry. His chief attention, when he was not looking out the corner of his eye for Spanish snipers, was upon the fascinations of a botanical frontier. Caddonia contained both hardwood lowlands and prairie; it lies at the point at which the heavily forested Ozark Highlands straggle downward into the plains which commence another but now imperceptible ascent. Amid increasing altitude and decreasing rainfall, the Staked Plains of Texas and New Mexico prepare the way for the sudden escarpments of the southern Rockies, the terrain into which Pike penetrated on his way to Santa Fe.

As the Red and Sabine rivers traverse the prairie, the climate is benign, the soil deep and black, the rainfall ample. Custis had found his way into the very Eden of the Jeffersonian dream, "in point of beauty and salubrity and fertility there is not its equal in America, nay the world." The ancient ones had again chosen well. Custis noted that their descendants (descendants they probably were, for historians have concluded that this region did not experience the violent dislocations of Indian nations characteristic of the Ohio Valley and the Northeast) had improved the high-grass and well-watered prairie by regularly burning off the shoots of brush. Thus they sustained a convenient balance between open range land, into which herds of buffalo and deer might be driven, and the woodland gardens on which they grew the corn which, with beans and squash, produced an opulent and balanced diet. Well-fed and well-organized, they were able to devote considerable energy to architecture.*[20]

Already, however, this paradisic ecosystem was under silent siege. Custis noted that European bindweed was beginning to spread across the meadowlands; in the Indian settlements European microbes had already done their deadly work. Other immigrants from Europe were more benign: bulbous buttercups, hollyhocks, and comfrey competed with indigenous black-eyed Susans, the jimsonweed used by the Caddo as a hallucinogen and the horehound used to soothe sore throats. There were loblolly pines as tall as 170 feet, and even larger were bald cypress, some 1,200 years old. Some of the Indian monuments on the terraces above them were, of course, four times older.†

---

*Earlier French visitors had described the terrain as rapturously as Custis. In 1687, Joutel wrote of "lovely plains and meadows, bordered with fine groves of beautiful trees, where the grass was so high, that it hindered our horses." Le Sieur de la Tonti noted that the Caddo's "fields are beautiful" and in 1719 la Harpe described a neighboring set of villages as being situated upon "a prairie most beautiful and most fertile" bordering a lake or bayou "two leagues long covered with ducks, swans and bustards." (Quoted in Flores, *Southwest Exploration*, p. 195, fn.)

†Only five years later, Freeman complained to Albert Gallatin that illegal cutting of cypress was making the landscape of the region both poorer and uglier.

It is scarcely possible to imagine this landscape as Freeman and Custis saw it, for Arkansas has had less luck in saving its old growth than states settled earlier by Europeans. Large stands of mature cypress are still to be found along the Wabash in Illinois and Indiana; they are scarce in Louisiana and Arkansas because their lowlands were drained when, in the antebellum period, the heartland of Caddonia from Shreveport to Texarkana became the consummate province of King Cotton.

The archaeologists or Arkansas, Mississippi, and Louisiana have bravely endeavored to save what little remains of the evidence of the ancient peoples who had lived so opulently in this fertile province. At Toltec, near Little Rock, and at Poverty Point, just beyond the state border in Louisiana, there are brave state parks, and across the Mississippi, at Winterville, there is another. Closer to Natchez, Emerald Mound, untended, unexplained but astounding and protected, gives a hint of the architecture of the princely states through which De Soto and Moscoso passed, still magnificent, still thriving even after the Great Dying. The peculiar cross-purposes which deranged Jefferson's expeditions into the Louisiana Purchase, and his misjudgment in selecting as their commander the despicable Wilkinson, denied to him and to us the full satisfaction of his scientific intent: much remained just beyond their vision, much was scrutinized in haste.

Alexander the Great encouraged his commanders to give heed to the ancient wonders among which they passed in Asia and Africa, a lesson emulated when Napoleon, two thousand years later, took his own stand beneath the pyramids, and Thomas Jefferson sought as well to combine imperial conquest and inquiry into antiquity. Taunted by his hated rival, Aaron Burr, traduced by his unworthy agent, James Wilkinson, buffeted by abrupt geopolitical shifts of the ground upon which he trod, as Britain, France, and Spain circled his operations in hostile and inconstant formations, Jefferson still managed to add immeasurably to his countryman's knowledge while doubling his country's size.

We may regret that Wilkinson was able to distract Jefferson from his scientific intentions by playing upon his fear that Burr might lead a slave revolt—and Wilkinson did so, in concert with Jefferson's Postmaster General, Gideon Granger. We may regret as well that the expansionary ambitions of the slaveowning constituency which was crucial to Jefferson's political power led him for thirty years to take great risks in support of the expansion of the plantation system at the expense of the territories of Spain—and he did so, from 1790 to 1820. Perhaps our greatest scholar-president might have given greater attention to the sheer growth of scholarship if these matters had not contended for his attention.

Yet no one else in his time, except Albert Gallatin, contributed so much to our knowledge of American antiquity. That there might have been more is a complaint to be made of the perfect. He was not perfect. He was merely the best. And under his huge aegis there flourished a multitude of lesser inquirers, including a pirate-archaeologist he may have met in the great city of Washington, while that pirate was the houseguest of the president's architect.

THE PIRATE-ARCHITECT AND THE LOST CITY OF BALBANSHA

Every climber through the branches of history has moments when some unexpected and delicious fruit appears on a branch which seemed barren. So it was one evening when, amid the correspondence of William Dunbar, I come upon a letter written to him by Barthelemy Lafon. That letter provides a glimpse of the state of knowledge about Native American architecture in the lower Mississippi Valley in 1806 from the point of view of a pirate.

We will come to the content of that letter, probably the most important written by any of the Jeffersonian archaeologists. But here we owe some introduction to Lafon for those who were not acquainted with him as he appeared in my *Orders from France,* welcoming Benjamin Henry Latrobe to New Orleans,* and providing him instruction about how architecture must be conducted in a corrupt city. Though large portions of his biography are lost in the sea mist of Louisiana's shores, much is known. Though we do not have his portrait, we do have a description of him as a small, bandy-legged figure observing the unloading of swag from boats on Barataria Bay, southwest of New Orleans. His refitting station was the depot of a consortium of pirates headed by the brothers Pierre and Jean Lafitte. Sometime around 1800, Lafon joined them as architect, partner, and as a sort of arbitrator of the competing claims of freebooters.[21]

However, it was not the geographic reach of Lafon's imagination that is most amazing, but his ability to range temporally and among

---

*Latrobe had fallen on hard times after his triumphs under the patronage of President Thomas Jefferson. In retirement, after 1808, Jefferson was able only to provide enthusiastic references, eliciting in return ideas for the design of the University of Virginia. The university did not deign to pay architectural fees, and Latrobe, though nearly bankrupt, did not feel that he could accept any even if offered, there could not be much of this sort of charity work. Younger competitors such as Robert Mills and William Strickland were able to solicit the rising generation of patrons, such as Andrew Jackson (for Mills) and Nicholas Biddle (for Strickland).

Latrobe had grown irritable and erratic, but in New Orleans, with Lafon as his guide, his disposition and his prospects improved. New Orleans was, however, still plague-ridden. Latrobe died there of yellow fever in 1819.

cultures. He was constantly on the alert for evidence of American antiquity, though it was not only this which led him into his relationship
with William Dunbar. Lafon was a surveyor, cartographer, military
and hydraulic engineer as well as an architect, and schooled in chemistry and astronomy.

He was a native of the vineyards shadowed by the curtain walls of
Carcassone, in southwest France. He learned enough metallurgy in
that decaying but picturesque old town to be welcomed as an ironmaster in New Orleans after emigrating about 1790, when he was still
under twenty-one.

Many houses in the French Quarter are attributed to Lafon; among
those which can be said with decent proof to be his is one at 638 Royal
Street which has for long been known locally as "the first skyscraper,"
though that claim seems a trifle excessive. He certainly designed the
city's beef market and the drainage projects which somewhat improved
the mouth-puckering salinity of the town's wells.

Alderman Lafon became an important politician, and by 1811 a personage. His reputation in politics, engineering, and architecture preceded him to Washington, where he was recommended to several eminent people by Edward Livingston, a lawyer and former mayor of New
York, who had found New Orleans more to his taste and whose clients
included many pirates. Among the recommendees was Latrobe, then
busy designing the Capitol and remodeling the White House. Lafon
was endearing; in 1811–12, the Latrobes took him in as their houseguest and he remained with them for several months.

Both Latrobes expressed amusement at Lagon's pursuit of hiero-
glyphics, though they might have been a little less amused at his skill in
a related field: breaking the Spanish code. As a linguist who spoke and
wrote Hebrew, Spanish, French, Latin, English, and enough of the Indian dialects to permit him to pass comfortably through the wildest of
the bayous, Lafon found uses for decoding as he plied his other profession, piracy in Spanish waters.

Lafon was also the most competent city planner to work in the Mississippi Valley until Daniel Burnham appeared at the end of the nineteenth century. He provided the speculative community of Donaldsonville the plan to which it adheres today, and gave both shape and street
names to the Garden Districts, upper and lower. His most ambitious
venture was a civic complex for which he provided a series of place
names which still appear on the map of New Orleans, though, lamentably, the buildings designed for it by Lafon do not.* He recommended

---

*It would be impolite to contrast the elegance and flair of his designs with the offerings of
the post Second World War generation of architects who finally were given the opportunity
to fulfill Lafon's program.

a school to be called a prytaneum, to offer a classical curriculum—Prytinee Street remains. Tivoli Circle commemorates his proposal for an amusement park, and Colossée Street a colosseum. There was to have been a magnificent public baths, with an arcade of great Ionic columns derived from Lafon's copy of Vignola's *Orders*. While no signed plans survive, I believe that Lafon made use of Vignola for another grand commission, a house for Dunbar called The Forest, which was erected after both the architect and the client had died by Dunbar's widow, just south of Natchez.

Other surviving maps and pamphlets by Lafon suggest he laid out other cities in Louisiana and Arkansas, such as Vidalia, opposite Natchez, while extending his imagination as far as the Yellowstone. His pamphlet on Yellowstone was the earliest to give it the standing which later led to its becoming the nation's first national park.

The profession of ironmaster was used as a cover for Lafon as it was for Jean Lafitte, the most famous pirate of the Gulf. Lafon designed and built Lafitte's Red House, the finest structure on Galveston Island and the headquarters for their depredations of Spanish shipping. It was also a sort of courthouse, where Lafon settled disputes among the other pirates, and organized a consortium of the brothers Lafitte and other venturers which had more power in the Gulf than the fleet of any nation after the departure of Sir Francis Drake in the sixteenth century and before the British reappeared in force Louisiana during the War of 1812.

That war was a major disruption of the pirates' operations—and not only of their piracy: they had to desist from archaeology as well. Lafon had gone directly from his genteel residence in the Washington with the Latrobes to unloading silver taken from a Spanish Vessel, and, because he was not a simple fellow, to measuring the thousand-year-old mounds between Barataria and the Mississippi. The eruption of imperial conflict along the coast caused Lafon, the Lafittes, and the other Baratarians to take a sabbatical from both swag and research and to gather in New Orleans patriotically to resist the British invasion of 1814.

* * *

Now, as to that letter: dated August 19, 1805, it established Lafon's claim to eminence in the chronicles of archaeology. Dunbar and Lafon probably met each other along the boundary line between Spanish Louisiana and American Mississippi, as Dunbar was also becoming acquainted with Thomas Freeman and Andrew Ellicott, before the Louisiana Purchase. Dunbar served as surveyor general of the Natchez District, while Lafon was serving Spain as its principal surveyor in New Orleans. He crossed the border to Natchez often enough, however, to produce a map of the city, which includes a portion of a speculative town to be called Vidalia, drawn along the lines of Donaldsonville and the Lower Garden District. Dunbar had interests in Vidalia. Perhaps he, like William Donaldson, made use of the most eminent planner available in the Mississippi Valley.

Dunbar's report to Jefferson had lamentably little to say about this remarkable man of dubious reputation; had he related to the president more about the architectural interests shared by all three, we might know more about Lafon. All Dunbar would say was that Lafon was "the author of the map of Louisiana and the View of New Orleans though I do not think that he himself is much of an astronomer."[22]

Why so tepid a recommendation? A gentleman-planter might be excused from waxing too warm in praise of the scientific attainments of a well-known pirate. Only later did Lafon become the houseguest of the President's friend Latrobe. In justice to Lafon, however, we must note that Dunbar knew better—Lafon's achievements as an astronomer were second in importance only to his own. There was no one living west of the Appalachians who could contest the eminence of either of these two.

No speculation is required to place the letter from Lafon to Dunbar in the history of American archaeology: it contains the first proposal for a systematic effort to discover and map the monuments of the ancient Americans. Jefferson and Gallatin had urged the Antiquarian and Philosophical societies to do the research, but only Lafon was so bold as to suggest an atlas of American antiquity. It would have been an archaeological predecessor to the National Geological Survey of John Wesley Powell or the National Biological Survey now (1994) underway.

This proposal by a distinguished architect and cartographer, a good idea then and a good idea now, was backed by potent apparatus; between them, Dunbar and Lafon possessed the best scientific equipment for astronomy and surveying in the West. James Wilkinson depended upon that equipment, and upon other research produced by both Dunbar and Lafon, to enhance his reputation with Jefferson—it was their work he sent along with such unction to the President.

Yet it was not merely for their precise observations that they deserve our respect. They were men of wide ambition for learning, restless with the received wisdom of their time, especially when that wisdom failed to give proper credit to the architecture of the Native Americans. That is why the letter from Lafon to Dunbar on that subject is a document of such immense importance in the history of American archaeology.

It is greatly to be desired for the advancement of the sciences that there should be a scientific paper here in which observations and discoveries in the country would be recorded. For example would it not be not only curious for the reader, but useful for the perfect knowledge of the epoch at which great nations inhabited these vast countries that there should be established an ancient map of America, that is to say a map on which would be represented all the ancient monuments, their positions and their extent. . . .

And would [it] not be possible to infer from such a work the place from which they came and the gradations of the power of each of these nations?

You have doubtless seen the monuments of Catahoula. The pyramid is remarkable for its height and indicates to me that the peoples who used to inhabit that country were more numerous and more powerful than those who inhabited the lower part of the Mississippi River.

One league from Pointe a la Hache one finds some of these monuments scattered throughout the entire interior of North America. They are at a distance of 130 fathoms from the Mississippi. The first is a parallelogram 20 fathoms long, 10 fathoms wide, 9 feet high with a slope of two fathoms; the second is a truncated cone 36 fathoms in circumference at the base, 6 fathoms in diameter at the summit and 12 feet height; the third is a rectangular triangle, with a perpendicular of 15 fathoms, a base of 12 fathoms, a hypotenuse of 20 fathoms, 2 feet in height at the base and the hypotenuse slopes gradually.

These monuments, as you see, are less extensive than those of Catahoula and nevertheless present the same circumstances with the exception of the pyramid.

Those monuments indicate to us unquestionably that they were the headquarters for assembling. I infer this opinion from what the Lepage Duprat says in his history.

"On our arrival in this country," says he, "the river was called Mississippi as far as New Orleans, but the lower part was called Balbansha. This word means city." Does not this name come from these monuments which really were the city?

When Lepage, who did not understand the language well, heard Balbansha pronounced to express the place where the city was and [sic] he probably took the part for the whole.[23]

Since Lafon knew that Dunbar was acquainted with "the monuments of Catahoula," the subject must, at the very least, have been discussed between them. It is not impossible that Lafon accompanied Dunbar on his Ouachita expedition; he had made the best map of the region, and was also the most renowned military engineer in the Mississippi Valley. "Catahoula" was a name for a complex of mounds where the Ouashita joins the Black River that was "larger than those of Marietta." They are now given the names Greenhouse and Marksville, the latter for the Louisiana town which has all but obliterated them.*[24]

---

*What is left is maintained in the Marksville State Commemorative Area, including the small museum at 700 Allen Street housing a map of the Mississippi's peregrinations. It is interesting to note the presence of platform mounds at Marksville, which gives further credence to the possibility disclosed in recent archaeology by N'omi Greber that similar

Most of the mounds at Marksville/Catahoula can be dated to
Roman or Adena/Hopewell times, roughly halfway in the six thousand
year history of monumental architecture in the Delta. At Marksville
and other associated sites, there are no circular, square, or octagonal
Hopewellian earthworks, but, instead, platform mounds coupled with
conical burial mounds, like those at Pinson and Marietta. But part of
the Marksville complex may go as far back as the Poverty Point period;
there have been objects found there which do come from around 1200
B.C., and the configuration of its surrounding embankment is intriguing. As noted earlier (p. 13), it is about 600 meters or 1,970 feet, as
is the innermost ring at Poverty Point, constructed about 1200 B.C.
There are other 600-meter D-shaped figures in the region, lying at river
bends, as if doubling the configurations of the streams themselves.
Several are to be found in the state of Mississippi just west of Yazoo
City, about fifty miles east of Poverty Point. They are called Spanish
Fort and Leist. A third is at Jaketown, another thirty miles to the
northeast.

All these sites have produced archaeological evidence, in the form of
points and baked clay, potato-shaped, "Poverty Point objects", indicating that they were occupied at the same time as Poverty Point. Fixing occupancy to construction of earthen architecture is difficult, but
such coincidences are suggestive.*†

*   *   *

The mounds of the Catahoula are, indeed, impressive enough, but
Lafon saved his climax for an ancient, hidden city below New Orleans
near Pointe a la Hache, the outermost and most mysterious of these
complexes. It was, he said, large enough to be called Balbansha, "really
a city."[25]

I have searched for Balbansha. In 1994, the visitor to these marshes
who borrows a boat and an archaeologist, and explores afoot when the
tide is low, will find occasional hummocks bearing trees hoary with
Spanish moss, under the roots of which are layer upon layer of history.

---

mounds at Marietta may be of the same date. Maybe archaeologists will come to speak of
Marietta as "Marksville" in style.

†Three miles north of the Marksville plaza, and also on the route of Dunbar's expedition,
lies another complex, on an island in an old river channel. It is called Greenhouse, and it,
too, has a plaza surrounded by truncated pyramids. It is smaller than the assemblage at
Marksville/Catahoula, but more survives of it. Unlike the mounds at Catahoula, Greenhouse does not appear on any surviving map by Lafon.

Along the highway there are oil refineries and bedraggled fishing villages; architectural distinction is rare; a mission-style, modern church of St. Thomas at Point a la Hache bravely carries on, having replaced a tabby building constructed in 1820. Having re-edited some WPA Guides, I used the 1941 Guide to Louisiana, which reported that there was then "beside the road by a lone oak, overhung with moss" and a house standing "on top of an Indian mound."[26]

Fishing shacks fill most of the open spaces. The mound is gone, and so is the moat, reported in the Guide, for another structure which would have been the base from which Lafon explored the region, as it was for "Lepage" (Antoine Simon Le Page du Pratz, 1718–1758) before him and for Georges Collot, who also explored these marshes. Fort Iberville was the first European military post to be constructed in Louisiana, created by le sieur d'Iberville in 1700 to head off a recurrence of the English threat to the Delta. His troops had just turned back—courteously but firmly, a British flotilla claiming to be lost in these French waters.

Iberville's post occupied one of the outermost points at which there was much dry land. That lone oak then had companions: "oaks, ash, elms, plaines, poplars." The WPA Guide goes on to describe "the ridge upon which the old fort was built . . . [as] plainly visible, and the lines of the moat may easily be traced." This is no longer true, as a crew of frustrated archaeologists reported in the 1980s after searching for Iberville's work, though they did find the ruins of Andrew Jackson's entrenchments of 1814, also arrayed against the British. In 1994 there was no difficulty in getting one's bearings because a later fort has been added to the flat, grassy landscape: a peculiar little brick fort created in the 1840s and used by the Confederates in 1860, with a moat and a neo-classical doorway.[27]

Lafon mapped Iberville's moat, but his contemporary and campatriot Collot, who also provided a chart of the area, did not. Neither gave posterity a map showing Balbansha. There is a tantalizing reference to a plaza bounded by mounds five or six miles southwest of Pointe a la Hache in the summary of researches in the year 1927 submitted to the Smithsonian Institution by Henry B. Collins. It appears to square with the description Lafon quotes from Le Page du Pratz, and implies that he himself has found accurate. I have made a diligent search of the Smithsonian archives for any field notes about this phase of his work by Collins, who ranged freely from the Arctic to Central Americas, but have found none.[28]

As the burden of earth brought to the delta by the great river weighs down the land beneath the marshes, the water level has appeared to rise steadily. It is probably twenty or thirty feet below what it was when Balbansha was constructed, and at least ten below that seen by Lepage, Collot, and Lafon. Even Collins saw more of the plazas bounded by mounds than can we; some of what he described as dry are now underwater. Though there are mounds roughly where he said they might be, there is nothing as grand as the complex described by him, by Lafon or Le Page. No Balbansha so far.

Lafon knew every inch of these bayous and marshes; when he was not measuring the possible lineaments of Balbansha with his surveyor's instruments, he was busy in the neighborhood on other business. According to the Spanish archives, his provisioning point for Lafitte's fleet was about ten miles away, and Barataria Pass was not far to the West. He and his partners were thorough; when they took the brig *Nueva Delores* and her twenty thousand pesos of silver, they even made off with her mainmast. His maps of the very end of the Mississippi have been lost, but the Historic New Orleans Collection has portions of his lost atlas and his elegant depiction of Galveston Bay can be found in the archives of the City of Mexico.*

Lafon was remarkable in many ways. From his variegated professions he was able to endow handsomely his two children, who were born to a black woman, and to set a standard of civic responsibility. At the time of his death in 1820, he left an immense estate, worth perhaps eight million in 1993 dollars. There were several claimants; relatives appeared from France who contended that he could not possibly have intended to leave so vast a sum to mulatto offspring. Their contention, which might have prevailed a few decades later, was dismissed. Lafon's respectful relationship to his wife and to the American Indians extended after his death, as his son and namesake, "Thomy" Lafon, became the most important nineteenth century philanthropist in New Orleans.[29]

Lafon did not have the gift for publicity that made Jean Lafitte a folk hero, proud to distribute to his acquaintances Lord Byron's admiring description of him as a corsair. But Lafon was a considerably more important figure. Like Gallatin, Washington, Jefferson, and Henry Brackenridge, he contributed mightily to our store of knowledge of the life of the ancients in the Mississippi Valley. But like them all, he had so much else to do. A pity. Lafon might have been our best guide to the lost cities of the Delta.

We are reduced to piecing out. We have better scientific instruments to do the piecing than Lafon possessed, but that is scarcely consolation; he needed them less than we do. The next two chapters are attempts to construct portions of a story of which Barthelemy Lafon possessed

---

*Details of all this appear in my *Orders from France*, together with an account of Lafon's sponsorship of Latrobe in New Orleans.

many clues subsequently lost. What a companion this bandy-legged, beguiling polymath would have been as we enter, now, a Baratarian delta of our own, into which so much has flowed, a confusion of possibilities, channels and false channels, bayous and meanders—the world of might have beens.

CHAPTER TEN

EVANGELISM AND AMNESIA: EXPLAINING AWAY THE MOUNDS

M onticello.
White ball on green table.
White dome above green lawn.
White-domed villa on flattened mountaintop given an Italian name.
Your villa, Mr. Jefferson: is it Venetian?

Or is it English, cousin to the domical villas of London grandees, villas to be pronounced Chizzik and Merrywood though spelled Chiswick and Merewood? How did you and Mr. Adams do with this little test of sophistication as you made the colonial's obligatory tour of British country houses, learning how such things should be done, and how pronounced?

If put to the test, you could, of course, note that the English had themselves, not long before, made such grand tours to acquire sophistication from the Venetians.

And note as well that, in truth, the Venetians had not been wholly self-assured; the architect of the most famous of their domical villas, Andrea Palladio, had assumed the name of a Roman architect* as he assumed the domical style of Roman architecture.

* * *

In the 1770s, Thomas Jefferson, country squire, caused his slaves to cart away in wheelbarrows the top of a mountain he had inherited, and began to build thereon the house preceding the one we see today. That first house, called Monticello after its platform, had no dome. The domical presence of the Emperor Hadrian only became obvious in Virginia in 1790, after Jefferson rejected that first plan and began the present building.

Well versed in classical culture, Jefferson knew that Hadrian dis-

---

*The Venetian's name had been Andrea di Pietro.

218

pensed his imperial wisdom from a throne directly under the aperture in the domed ceiling of the Pantheon; at high noon the sun and the emperor would be in entire agreement as to the location of the center of the universe.

Jefferson *did* make use of Hadrian's dome, as reinterpreted by Palladio and the English neo-Palladians. He *did* create a great central drawing room, where *he* dispensed wisdom directly beneath the center of the dome. But as a good republican he interposed a ceiling between his seat and the domed space above. That gave the drawing room becoming modesty. The dome room thus left over, having made its statement to the cognoscenti, remained so inaccessible as to be to this day off-limits to those touring Monticello.

As we have observed, Jefferson was a man quite capable of holding contraries in his mind at once. Magnate and democratic leader, slaveowner, slave seller, and political representative of an expansionary slaveocracy, he advocated the rights of man and hymned the virtues of free and independent yeomen. At Monticello he demonstrated the post-Renaissance European way of dealing with landscape at its most controlling, domineering, and mountaintop-shearing, and at Poplar Forest he showed how to pay homage to the American earth, the American land, and its ancient, pre-European people.

Inside Monticello, Jefferson's Americanness is revealed the moment one enters the galleried reception hall. In 1994, for the first time since his death, that hall is once again the testament to his pride in his continent, once again the proclamation that he was no longer a colonial European. The fruits of long exertion by the present staff are on display; they have reassembled Jefferson's "Indian Hall," the nation's first museum of the American Indian.

Beside one door lie those Kentucky mastodon bones which, together with the hide of a moose, he believed might rebut French aspersions upon the sheer size of American animals, and, by implication, of Americans as well. There, in the center, is the Mandan hide-painting which came to him from Lewis and Clark, depicting an attack on a Missouri valley village. Under his busts of philosophers—Voltaire, Turgot, and the philosophical Franklin who preceded him to Paris—are two of the stone heads and one of the half-figures presented to him by the pioneers of Tennessee. Scattered about are the jumble of animal heads, hides, weapons, and wampum which his countrymen came to expect of natural history museums until, by the 1990s, it became obvious that Indians and animals are not quite in the same category of being.

The hall equals the height of the grand salon beyond, lined with its paintings and statuary. The dome room above the salon is merely implied, for anyone who has walked about the house before entering knows it is there. One can feel all the glory of eighteenth century En-

gland in this salon hung with baroque pictures, Rubensian and Carpac-
cian. It is no more domestic than Sir John Vanbrugh's grandeurs at
Castle Howard or Blenheim; no yeoman in the world ever lived amid
such splendor.

The Sage of Monticello carried over for this part of the house the
floor plan of his first Monticello, which he doubled and replaced with
the present mansion after his return from France. He carried over, also,
the notion that it would have two stories, but substituted for a simple,
gable-roofed, second-floor library the dome—constructed in the manner of the most breathtaking room he had ever seen, the grain market
in Paris.*

Having been introduced to America by the Indian Hall, the visitor
would enter the salon for introduction to the Sage, a finished cosmopolitan gentleman, fully American yet fully civilized, who knew how to
pronounce Chiswick and Mereworth, and also knew how to pronounce Cherokee and Mandan.† There in the Indian Hall were laid out
the shipments he had received from James Wilkinson, Harry Innes, and
Morgan Brown—busts and heads from the Castillian Springs School of
Sculpture. Throughout his life, everyone seeking Jefferson's favor ca-
tered to his ardor for collecting such things. For him and for others of
his time, that enthusiasm was uncontaminated by any requirement that
the artists be of the collector's religion. Their works of art might be
beautiful or merely interesting, attractive aesthetically but, primarily,
objects of science.

Jefferson was a child of the Enlightenment, living in a cool, brief,
suspended, scientific moment between epochs of excitement. Before
Enlightenment, he often wrote, there had been "superstition" and
"priestcraft." And as his life was coming to an end, he feared that these
ancient foes were arising once more in a cacophony of "sects" and religious enthusiasts. Instead of "priestcraft" there was evangelism,
which, to Jefferson, was just as bad.

Daniel Boorstin wrote not long ago of "the lost world of Thomas
Jefferson"—which we may find *too* cool for our taste, *too* detached in
its political morality, *too* willing to see other humans as specimens. But
it had the virtues as well as the deficiencies of detachment; it was free
to accept and consider and draw conclusions without making every
tale a parable and every object a pretext for a sermon.

That suspended moment did not last long; it had commenced with a

---

*I have offered in detail in *Orders from France* the hypothesis that he intended this dome as
a shrine to his epiphanic moment in the grain market with Maria Cosway, a lady with
whom he fell in love.

†Chicago had not yet been invented. No President before James K. Polk knew how to pronounce *it*.

precarious victory over the forces Jefferson called the "combination of the altar and the throne." Though Jefferson, Franklin, Gallatin, and John Adams professed to be Christian, they deplored the "disfiguring" of the ideas of Jesus by his "schismatizing followers . . . perverting the simple doctrines he taught . . . frittering them into subtleties, and obscuring them with jargon, until they have caused good men to reject the whole in disgust and to view Jesus himself as an imposter." Jefferson's tombstone, for which he selected the accomplishments for which he wished to be remembered, did not include his presidency or the Louisiana Purchase. Instead, it placed his sponsorship of that Virginia Statute of Religious Freedom, by which altar and throne were severed within that commonwealth, beside his authorship of the Declaration of Independence and his founding of the University of Virginia.[1]

As his life was drawing to a close, and sectarianism proliferated, the religious temperature rose again. He wrote his friend Dr. Thomas Cooper that "in Richmond . . . there is much fanaticism, but chiefly among the women. They have their night meetings and praying parties . . . attended by their priests and . . . pour forth the effusions of their love to Jesus in terms as amatory and carnal as their modesty would permit to a mere earthly lover."[2]

Though Jefferson eschewed effusions of any sort, he and his contemporaries had shown a strange sort of passion of their own in their detachment, in their scrupulously diffident treatment of the religious objects and architecture of Native Americans. They prized their science, untroubled by evidence of achievement on the part of non-Christians. This enthusiasm probably arose from their being themselves assaulted by those who derogated those achievements. They were often called "heathen" by the same people who rejected art on the ground that *it* was heathen. John Adams wrote Jefferson that he would hold to his "love of God and his creation . . . [his] delight, joy, triumph, exultation in my own existence" whatever might be said of him by the priests and the sectarians.[3]

> Howl, snarl, bite, ye Calvinistic, ye Athanasian divines, if you will; ye will say I am no Christian; I say ye are no Christians, and there the account is balanced.[4]

Adams, like Jefferson, deplored the recrudescence of sectarian "fanaticism":

> We have now, it seems, a national Bible Society, to propagate King James's Bible. . . . Would it not be better to apply those pious subscriptions to purify Christendom from the corruptions of Christianity than to propagate those corruptions in Europe, Asia, Africa and America?[5]

To Adams, evangelical Christianity was merely another of those "en-thusiasms, crusades . . . [and] epidemical and endemical distempers, to which mankind is liable." The proliferation of sects so distempered *him* as to draw forth this injunction to his old friend Jefferson: "abol-ish pantheism . . . in every shape, if you can, and unfrock every priest who teaches it, if you can."[6]

By 1819, the cool blossoms of the American enlightenment were crisp at the edges, browning, and disappearing into the molten lava of sectarian evangelism. Though Adams might deplore "pantheism" and Jefferson a resumption of "fanaticism" and "superstition," evangelism swept up John Jay, John Randolph, Noah Webster, and Elias Boudinot. Even Benjamin Rush, the archdeist, came to the view that "only the gospel of Jesus Christ will effect the mighty work of making nations happy."[7]

Amid these events, Thomas Jefferson died insolvent, and of necessity the collection of Indian artifacts at Monticello was dispersed. His In-dian sculpture and paintings passed out of the laboratory lighting of his Indian Hall into an atmosphere flickering with invidious rectitude and sectarian passion in which they acquired the menacing glow of heathen objects. Others were merely jettisoned into the trash bins of a society obsessed with the moment and amnesiac about the history of the continent, as objects thought to be curious but insignificant. Fi-nally, and only lately, have some of the objects he collected reemerged to reconstitute his Indian Hall.

The vicissitudes of that collection between Jefferson's death on July 4, 1826 and its partial reinstallation in Monticello in the 1990s mark the stages of a larger story, in which much the sequence can be ob-served: the loss of the newly rediscovered, amnesia and, finally, aston-ished and embarrassed recovery of a few fragments. What was true in the history of Jefferson's "heathen" works of art was also true of the architecture from which they originated. By the time of his death, the world of Thomas Jefferson was lost, replaced by a fervid and unreflec-tive period in which the determining qualities by which antiquities were judged were their place within a sectarian and ethnic scheme. There ensued a long interval of indifference, followed by another of distraction with what was current and fashionable in Europe. Finally, there has been some partial recapture of the scientific spirit of Jefferson and his contemporaries, accompanied now by that deeper sympathy which often arises only in the presence of irrecoverable loss.

If one wishes to observe in microcosm how nineteenth and twentieth century Americans of European descent viewed Native Americans and their artistic capacities, including their prowess in architecture, there is no better way of doing so than to follow the fortunes of Thomas Jefferson's Indian collection. As it was being sold, the old view of Indians as mere savages, against which Jefferson had contended, once again prevailed. His countrymen unlearned what Jefferson had learned over his lifetime about Indian antiquity, as they pursued policies toward contemporary Indians which, it is sad to admit, he himself had permitted to supplant those of George Washington and the Cincinnati. Hastily and unrepentently, Jeffersonians and Jacksonians thrust the Indians aside by means which might lie easier on the conscience if those displaced were thought to have neither history, art nor religion worthy of the respect of the displacers. They collected cases full of Indian artifacts; but the spirit of collection became increasingly dissociated from a regard for the people whose work was collected.

We have lost the two extraordinary busts Jefferson received from Morgan Brown because the next generation gave them a more sinister description than "hideous."* From 1830 onward they were deemed dangerous—"pagan." No longer might one view with detachment "idols" made by "savages." As a consequence, Indian figurative art was consigned to the shadows, where it might no longer offend. The busts which so delighted Jefferson were last sighted in 1831, when Dr. J. T. Barclay presented a "collection of heathen images" found at Monticello to "Dr. Plummer, of the Presbyterian Board of Missions," and then "removed to the rooms of the American Board of Commissioners for Foreign Missions in Boston." They were not thought important by the commissioners, who sent them to the Andover-Newton Seminary, which in turn, it appears, has lost track of them.[8]

So much for "heathen" busts. The votive heads (perhaps all the plows of the pioneers had left of larger figures like the Morgan Brown busts) suffered even greater indignities. Two "carved stone heads, which he believed to be of primitive origin," probably from the same Tennessee workshop as the figurines, had come into Jefferson's collection about the time he acquired his buffalo-hide paintings from Lewis and Clark.[†] He displayed them proudly, but after his death the two heads went in auction to Captain Stockton, a neighbor, who "mounted them on his gateposts."[9]

In 1861, after the Stockton heads were found again, one was donated to the collections of the Smithsonian Institution and the other to the Valentine Museum in Richmond. The Smithsonian had not yet entered its better years as a collector of Indian art; its Secretary, Spencer

---

*That was the aesthetic judgment, acceptable, one supposes, as such, though not our own; a *philosophe* might go so far. Though deemed less than beautiful, they were at least being regarded with care, deserving of scientific interest.

†As noted elsewhere, there may be a misdating in Jefferson's catalogue, and these may be the same two heads sent earlier, in the 1790s. But, on balance, I think not, and that there were four.

F. Baird and its Assistant Secretary, Alexander Wetmore, turned to certain unnamed "archaeologists," who concluded that Jefferson had been duped. These heads, said these alleged experts, were "likely to have been carved by Negro servants to serve as ornaments for gateposts."[10]

Dismissed so lightly, the heads joined the "heathen" idols—obscene at worst, insignificant at best, so insignificant that the Smithsonian's experts did not bother to reexamine the letter accompanying them to the two museum collections. It had specifically stated that though they *had* been used on gateposts by Stockton, that indignity was suffered after Stockton acquired them from the Jefferson estate, and long after Jefferson's grandson, Colonel T. J. Randolph saw at least one of them as it "sat on a stand in the Hall at Monticello."[11]

THE EARLIER HISTORY OF OBSCURANTISM IN AMERICA

Thus did ignorance, grounded in prejudice and devoted to obscuring truth, do its heinous work. And not for the first time. Earlier zealots were guilty of wholesale obliteration of the evidence; in the 1530s, the first archbishop of Mexico, Juan de Zumarraga, systematically destroyed whatever Aztec art, architecture, and literature fell into his hands, to reduce the competition offered by the testaments of the Indians to the New and Old Testaments of the Christians. Roman Catholic evangelism swept across Mexico, seeking to eliminate all traces of that competition. This first Old Testament Age in the Americas commenced with the landing of twelve Franciscan apostles in Mexico, hard on the heels of Cortez; it continued with the arrival of the Pilgrim Fathers at Plymouth a hundred years later, and only expired in Jefferson's youth.

While it prevailed, sixteenth and seventeenth century Europeans found in the Old Testament texts to justify their own ferocious civil wars. Accompanied by hymns, princes and peasants burnt and pillaged, murdered and mutilated in Europe. When they came to the Americas they treated the Indians no worse than they treated each other; their sectarian cruelties were extended to new victims. In New England as in New Spain, dissenters and heathen were treated with equal savagery. Flames were flames, as searing when administered by the Inquisition as by the General Court.

Always, however, there were dissenters; there *had* been a New Testament. Bartolomé das Casas took to the Hapsburg court itself the cause of justice and of respect for Indians, and in the English colonies there were Anne Hutchison, Roger Williams, the Moravians and Quakers. It remained generally true, however, that from 1492 onward for nearly three centuries, violent and vicious people made use of ancient Hebrew texts to justify their worst behavior toward the people who obtruded upon their imperial ambitions.*

There was no comfort for the Indians in the assertion of the pilgrims under John Winthrop that "the God of Israel is among us. . . . We shall be as a city upon a hill." Their God of Israel had seen fit to bring only a furious favor. Once it had been shown to the ancient Jews; now it was vouchsafed to the Puritan invaders of what they sought to mold into a New England, redeemed of the sins of the Old. There was little of the New Testament in this, and not much more of the compassionate side of Judaism, only cold fury, grim wrath and convenient rectitude. When it pleased the invaders to expand their beachheads into the lands of the Pequots, they buckled on the armor of "David's war." It was, they said, conducted with "light from the word of God," in this case the word of an Old Testament, offering the justification in New World forests of Old World desert killings. Thus might the conscience be salved in the carrying forth of whatever English ambitions might require. As he watched the flames consume the men, women, and children in a Pequot fort in May, 1637, John Underhill exclaimed that the Lord was "burning them up in the fire of His wrath . . . it was the Lord's doings, and it is marvelous in our eyes!" Yet through it all Roger Williams persisted in his truth; killing Indians was spilling "innocent blood."[12]

LOST TRIBES

Williams found support from some strange allies, who took their position not only out of compassion but also from an unorthodox reading of the Old Testament, drawing from ancient Hebrew accounts reasons to treat the Indians not as subhumans but instead as persons deserving *special* regard: they were Jews, descendants of the Lost Tribes of Israel. It was a little unclear how these Hebrews might have reached America, but the *theory* they had done so reached New England from New Spain, via Holland and the heterodox Puritans of England. In the six-

---

*This book is not large enough to include the responses of the French, Dutch, Swedes, Portuguese, or Spaniards to the evidence of ancient America, though the French and Spaniards had ample opportunity to do so even within the geographic confines we have set for ourselves, the Mississippi Valley. Some effort in that direction was made in an earlier draft, but was abandoned in the interest of portability.

teenth century, a Dominican friar, Diego Duran, probably of Jewish descent, had asserted that the Indians, too, were Jews. The Sevillian intellectuals from whom he sprang were being exiled and persecuted; he found some solace in stories of Lost Tribes escaping tribulation. Duran's idea was picked up by another Dominican, Gregorio Garcia, who published a survey of the *Origin of the Indians of the New World* in the year of the founding of Jamestown by the English (1607). For good measure, Garcia added the possibilities that the Indians might have originated in Carthage, Atlantis, or East Asia.[13]

The Jesuits were less capacious in their imaginings. Their Jose de Acosta derided the Lost Tribes theory as fanciful: he took, instead, the modern view that the Indians had come in a series of invasions by a land bridge from Asia. Seekers after lost tribes were not to be deterred, however. In the middle of the seventeenth century, a Portuguese Jew, Antonio de Montezinos, wrote that while exploring the interior of Ecuador, he had come upon some Indians who professed regret at ill treatment they had meted out to "a holy people." Had they not driven them into the woods, where they were "now hidden," these people might now be recruited to redeem the Indians from Spanish rule. Montezinos did not then think the hidden people to be Jews, but after he was jailed by the Inquisition, he had a sudden revelation while praying for strength to resist his captors: an inner voice told him: "Those people were Hebrews!"[14]

Upon his release, reported Montezinos, he returned to the jungle, once again found his guides, and was led by them to three men and a woman who greeted him with the words "Sherma, Yisrael, Adonai Elohenu Adonai Ehod"—"Hear, O Israel, the Lord our God, the Lord is One". They told him they were of the tribe of Reuben, that the tribe of Joseph was close at hand, and that "the God of these children of Israel is the true God, and everything inscribed on their tablets is true. At the end of days, they will be lords over all the earth." Having promised to bring twelve bearded men back to the jungle to write down what these lost tribes might recall, for they had forgotten the art of writing, Montezinos once more departed Ecuador.[15]

He made his way to the Sephardic community in Amsterdam, where he persuaded the venerable Rabbi Manasseh ben Israel of the truth of his story. While the twelve bearded scribes were unavailable, the rabbi had his own printing press, and commenced propagating the account of the lost Reubenites and Josephites. An English clergyman in Holland, John Drury, brought the good news to another, Thomas Thorowgood, in England, who wrote it down in a book entitled *Jews in America, or, Probabilities that those Indians Are Judaical*. From Thorowgood the new gospel about the Old Testament was brought to the Reverend John Eliot, of Roxbury, in Massachusetts, who was inspirited by it to redouble his effort to convert the Algonquians.

Eliot produced his own book, a translation of the Bible into the Algonquian language, the better to sustain his missionary endeavors—he and Roger Williams were of that branch of the Puritans still cleaving to the view that Indians were people, and worthy of salvation. In this he was an inconvenience to the more orthodox view that they were of a lesser order, to be swept away by the cleansing power of the English. The humanity of Indians was as uncertain to Cotton Mather as the humanity of Blacks was to Jefferson. Mather pounced upon Eliot's "lost Israelites among the Indians," and upon other "learned men" and poured his derision upon their "thorowgood reasons" for taking seriously Manasseh ben Israel.[16]

Manasseh ben Israel had not been idle. His *Hope of Israel* was published in Latin and Spanish, espousing much the same idea as de Acosta, but with a twist: Jewish Indians had come with other emigrants from Asia via the "strait of Anian" after the Assyrian conquest of Israel had dispersed the lost tribes. To Montezinos's story he added another from the Andes: tall, white-bearded patriarchs who regarded the use of canoes with the same disdain with which a Doge might respond to the suggestion he propel a gondola.[17]

The *Hope of Israel* had considerable influence among those Englishmen who were disposed toward conversion rather than extinction of Indians. Not only were Williamsite Puritans persuaded to justify a respect for Indians on the ground that they might be the people of the Old Testament; so, too, were Quaker settlers of Pennsylvania and New Jersey, and Quaker merchants who had learned the blessings of accommodation with their Sephardic colleagues everywhere. William Penn reported that the Indians of Pennsylvania resembled the Jews of London.

By the 1820s, there was among reformist Protestants a settled body of opinion holding that Indians should be handled more gingerly than mere imperial convenience might dictate. This delicacy was grounded in the opinion that they were not, so to speak, Indians at all. While others were calling for extermination of bloodthirsty savages, the reformers asked some consideration at least for impoverished descendants of Lost Tribes, who might be as capable of redemption as New Testament Jews. This strain of Puritanism bore fruit again in 1823, when Ethan Smith published his *View of the Hebrews; or the Lost Tribes of Israel in America*. This Smith was no kin to Joseph Smith, the founder of the Church of Christ of the Latter Day Saints, but his book offers passages of battles and tribal annihilation which presage *The Book of Mormon*.

Conventional evangelism had swept into the nineteenth century with very little interest in converting Indians—*that* had been left to Catholics, Moravians, and Quakers. Few of the sects that effloresced in the 1820s and 1830s gave much heed to the possibility that Indians might have religious insights worth the attention of more orthodox Protestants or Catholics. It followed that Native American religious art was relegated to the trash heap, and even scientific interest in "savage" architecture abated among the orthodox, as it had among a shrinking number of deists and Unitarians.

This was not the case with those who held to the Lost Tribes hypothesis. If the Indians had emerged from the pages of the Old Testament they might be worth saving, and so might their art. It is true to this day that the Mormon church, the largest denomination to accept the Lost Tribes view of Indian origins, has been consistently interested in evangelistic—that is, respectful—relations with Native Americans. This is not to say that the followers of Joseph Smith have been conspicuously attentive to Native American religious precepts. They have, however, not been as willing as other Americans to treat Indians as beings sufficiently *less* than human as to be justifiably exterminated. The Mormons have sought to gather converts among Indians. They have also paid rapt attention to Native American architecture.

JOSEPH SMITH, NEPHITES, AND JEREDITES

Mormonism was a rejection of the deism and scientism of the Founding Fathers. The contemporaries of Joseph Smith, Mormons and non-Mormons alike, were rediscovering the Old Testament. Rediscovered and restored to currency, the ancient texts were provided with supplements, of which the Book of Mormon is the most famous. It was by far the most successful fusion of personal revelation, archaeology, and proselytizing by literature in the history of Christendom. But it did not stand alone, nor was it unprecedented.

The revelations of Joseph Smith came as the culmination of a sequence which began with Duran, Garcia, and Montezinos, and continued through the labors of Thorowgood and Eliot. Smith was born in Vermont in 1805, and grew to manhood south of Rochester, New York, in yet another village named Palmyra, set all about by ancient Indian mounds, while in western New York, preachers were bringing swaying, singing crowds to raptures with sermons cadenced in the rhythms of the Old Testament from which they brought passages indistinguishable from their own inspired texts. The very air throbbed with Hebraic verses, as the metronome of daily life was set to a beat established by daily prayers and prayer meetings convened as often as chores allowed. This testamentary atmosphere flowed across a landscape the principal features of which were ancient mounds, while a folk religion crept through those mounds bearing European traditions of magic stones for discovering riches, and Hebraic tales of tablets bearing wisdom and divine injunction.

Smith was a seer, equipped with a prodigious memory. He had been a conjurer and dowser, in trouble with the law for responding to the craving of his neighbors for new discoveries by offering them holy stones for treasure hunting.* He was the child of passionately religious parents, deeply read in the scriptures, living in a region in which so many fiery sects were thriving that it became known as the "burnt over district." The air was thick with revelations and incantations, as the Old Testament was quarried for truth. It was an unsettling time, in which the whole of America seemed swept from its moorings and on the move, west, north, south. Continuities were desperately sought. Some might be found in ancient religion, especially in the Old Testament, the chronicle of a people which never lost its identity despite disruptions and disasters, a story especially consoling to Americans of the nineteenth century. (Its more universal consolations are to be derived, I think, from another emphasis).

Another continuum was to be found upon the land itself; intimations of antiquity emanated from mounds set conspicuously and mysteriously upon the landscape of Ohio and western New York.

Mormonism answered a longing for continuity, as it was organized to provide community. In the process, it offered a synthesis of ancient American history and ancient Hebrew theology. The Old Testament was made the explanation for the mysteries of archaeology; the Mormons became the legitimate heirs both of the Mound Builders and the testamentary Hebrews. The tablets of Joseph Smith proclaimed them to be kin.

In 1827, his neighbors began to bruit the story that Smith had discovered treasure which somehow revealed the truth about the builders of the mounds. He had told some of them that he had been visited by the angel Moroni, who, with his father Mormon, had been the only survivors of a lost tribe of Israelites, the Nephites. They had buried, in the hill of Cumorah in western New York, golden tablets or plates, telling the story of architects of earth who had come in three migrations from Asia, by boat. The first of those to arrive had been the

---

*Fawn Brodie commenced her career as a psychohistorian with a biography of Smith which led to her expulsion from the Mormon church; only afterward did she turn her attention to Thomas Jefferson and in the process become the rediscoverer of the story of Jefferson's putative relative to Sally Hemings. (See Brodie, *Jefferson*.) Her Smith is more necromancer than seer, just as her Jefferson was more troubled and passionate romantic than seer. I do not find either portrait wholly compelling.

Jaredites, in 2000 B.C., who prospered for a time but fell into evil, famine, and civil war, culminating in the first battle of Cumorah. There was a survivor, however, the historian Ether who buried his own golden chronicle tablets under the hill later used by Mormon and Moroni.

Fourteen centuries later, the followers of the prophet Lehi escaped the destruction of Jerusalem by the Babylonians, and they, too, came to America, where the Tragedy of the Jaredites was repeated. Once again there was dissension; even the mound-building descendants of the good son of Lehi, Nephi, lost their virtue and were overwhelmed by the depraved Lamanites, who vanquished them in a second battle at Hill Cumorah. The Nephites had rediscovered the lost tablets of Ether; and when their own time had come, they knew where to place their own golden chronicles. This second interment was accomplished by Mormon and Moroni, whose tablets were those discovered by Smith.

As the year 1827 unfolded, Smith dictated the Book of Mormon, including a history of the mound-building Indians in the rhythms of the Old Testament. Twenty-seven thousand words out of a total of 275,000 in his book were only slightly altered from the King James version of the Bible. Smith sat on one side of a curtain, reading, he said, from Mormon and Moroni's tablets, making use of "seer stones" while his wife took down his words.*

Smith became the founder of the only world religion to be based in American archaeology. Because the American Indians have never sought to evangelize Europeans or Africans, Mormonism is also the only world religion to place American Indian experience at the center of its creed.

Smith was lynched in an Illinois jail in 1844. After his death, his inspired successor, Brigham Young, brought to a new Zionism of the West the impassioned religious life of the mound-haunted landscape of western New York. Mormonism sprang from the mounds; according to Smith and Young, the lost tribes of Israel had led to the Americas, and thus explained those mounds. According to Duran and Ben Israel, the lost tribes had found refuge in the New World, and it is probably not coincidental that they were rediscovered in the sixteenth century as Jews were being expelled from Spain and harassed throughout Europe. A newer, nobler Israel might someday emerge from their tribulations, and some might say it *did*, in Brigham Young's Zion. Mound building

---

*Smith had, it is true, been convicted in local court as an "imposter" for alleging that he could find buried money using such stones. But before skeptics draw too quickly the conclusion that he was an imposter in his religious discoveries, it is well to remember that religious revelation does not readily visit those who do not seek it, and have no metaphors for discoveries beyond the range of conventional technology.

had become a religious matter, associated with Mormonism. Lost tablets and lost races took center stage, and science retreated into the shadows.

ENTER THE WELSH

There are passages in the Book of Mormon which assert that the Lamanites were cursed with the characteristic skin color of the Indians, that copper or reddish hue which some (though by no means all) of them seemed to acquire upon exposure to the sun, while Europeans became charred or pink. This may not seem a generous explanation of pigmentation, but it was more so than a theory simultaneously current that the mounds were built by pink people who had arrived during the Middle Ages from Wales. This possibility commended itself to many of that coloring, including Thomas Jefferson. It did not require so much of a leap of faith as the Lost Tribes hypothesis, for instead of treating Indians in general as carrying the genes of a chosen people, and thus capable of doing grand things, it merely suggested a brief intrusion into the affairs of the continent on the part of a few mound-building Welshmen whose descendants might be found in isolation on the upper Missouri. The rest of the Indians could still be regarded as savages, noble or otherwise.

Jefferson was a Celt—those who knew both him and Alexander Hamilton remarked on the similarity of their coloring, their reddish hair and ruddy cheeks. Those who were also acquainted with the Mandan of the upper Missouri noted similar coloring among them, fair skins, hair frequently brown and sometimes red, turning grey, and blue eyes. In the last decades of the eighteenth century a concatenation of wishful ethnic pride, imperial propaganda, and inexplicable coloring among Indians persuaded many people that the Mandan were the descendants of Welsh builders of mounds. Even the French, who had no reason to desire Welsh primacy among Europeans in America, had noted the differences between Mandans and other Indians. Among the first to do so were the two sons of a baronial fur trader, le sieur de la Verendrye. The elder son, le Chevalier, and the younger, merely Francois, reached the Mandan villages on the upper Missouri in 1738. The courtly two noted that the Mandan women did not look Indian, and pronounced their features "fairly good looking, especially the light colored ones; many of them have blonde or fair hair." They added that the Mandan fortifications were "not characteristic of the Indians."[18]

In 1794, the Mandans were visited again by a fervent advocate of a Welsh enclave in North Dakota: John Evans. A decade before Lewis and Clark, Evans went up the Missouri while it was still embraced by the Spanish Empire. Though disappointed that the Mandan did not look as Welsh as he had hoped, he still insisted that their language contained Welsh words. Perhaps it did. How would we know? Evans had as much reason to expect Welshmen on the Missouri, making "fortifications" beyond what seemed at the time to be the skill of mere Indians, as Joseph Smith had to find Israelites buried beneath the mounds of western New York.

Why might Evans expect lost tribes of Wales? Not from Welsh sorrows, but from Welsh pride. Jefferson does not seem to have taken seriously the attribution to lost tribes of Israel of the mounds of the Middle West. He was not a devotee of the Old Testament. He was, instead, a child of the Renaissance, turning more readily to Elizabethan myths generated from the psychic needs of people like himself. The Elizabethans had sought to fuse science, classical humanism and fierce ethnic pride carried by Welshmen and Englishmen into an unstable brew swirling about the Anglo-Welsh court of Queen Elizabeth, the Welsh princess whose grandfather had wrested the crown from an English prince. America for them was the next kingdom to be gained, by wresting that kingdom from Spain.

The valuable portions of the Spanish realm in the New World had been acquired through the exertions of Cortez, who invaded Mexico in 1519. There had been reports of Aztec behavior on that occasion which might, with a little ingenuity, be turned to Anglo-Welsh account. Might there be truth in the tale that when Cortez arrived he was greeted by Montezuma speaking Welsh? And was not one reason given for the success of Cortex that Montezuma did not at first resist him, but, instead, welcomed his arrival in fulfilling an expectation of a return of bearded white men from the sea? If he greeted Cortez in Welsh he must have been expecting Cortez, as a white man, to speak Welsh in return.

The fundament of this theory was that the language instructors to the Aztecs had come four centuries earlier as the companions of Prince Madoc of Wales, who set forth in 1170 with ten ships to explore the western seas and never returned. It was in the British imperial interest that in the twelfth century the Welsh had preceded Cortez to the New World, thereby establishing a claim to it for Elizabeth Tudor, Queen of England, prior to that proclaimed by Cortez for the kings of Spain. This was a better idea than that Montezuma was speaking Hebrew.

Elizabeth's chief of intelligence, Sir Francis Walsingham, welcomed the first written assertion of Elizabeth's priority, prepared for him in 1583 by Sir George Peckham. Peckham's account of the "verie words of Mutuzuma, set down in the Spanish chronicles . . . doo all sufficientlie argue the undoubted title of her Majestie" derived from "Prince Madocke."[19]

A year later, in 1584, David Powell published his *History of Cambria* (Wales), placing in print the speculations of the man who had already provisioned Peckham: John Dee. Dee had much in common with Joseph Smith. He, too, was often called a sorcerer—"a caller of devils"—though both were more famous for their "angelic conversations." Dee was the more cosmopolitan, for Smith was a poor farm boy, and Dee was able to study in Prague and Louvain, where he became a mathematician and geographer, learning as well those alchemical skills which came to justify his appellation as "Arch Conjurer of England." As scientific adviser, Dee served such Elizabethan enterprises as the Muscovy Company and the Company of Cathay, and anticipated Jefferson's explorations by advising the British to seek their own Northwest Passage to the Pacific.[20]

Dee had begun in 1578 to acquaint the British court with the ancient tale that Prince Madoc of Wales had been the first European discoverer and colonizer of America. Dee's original manuscript pleadings for "Royal Titles" was lost, but a printed version appeared in 1580. Lost manuscripts are important to the story of the Elizabethan rediscovery—or deployment—of the Madoc legend. Richard Hakluyt, professor of geography at Oxford, following Dee, asserted that they were basing their assertions upon a lost manuscript by Humphrey Llywyd, which, in turn was based upon another lost manuscript by Caradog of Llancarvan.

As these bardic conveniences were appearing, Walsingham produced an English seaman, David Ingram, who was prepared to testify that he had been marooned on the Gulf Coast in 1568. Ingram, according to Walsingham as reported in Hakluyt, came among elephants, flamingoes, penguins, and Indians using Welsh words to describe these animals.

Another involuntary explorer-linguist soon appeared, Morgan Jones, who said he had been captured by Doeg Indians in South Carolina in 1660 who spared his life because they and he shared a language—Welsh. By now the public had become accustomed to such tales, and by 1770, Welsh dilettanti assembled in London were making anthologies of accounts of Welsh-speaking white Indians. Conveniently, a Britisher turned Indian, William Augustus Bowles, claiming to be chief among the Muskogee in the mound country of Alabama, was willing to inform eager audiences that there were white, Welsh-speaking Indians just over the western horizon—the Padoucahs. Jonathan Carver, that packrat among mythographers, reported in 1784 that there were such people, "whiter than the neighboring tribes, who cultivate the ground, and . . . in some measure the arts," living on the Missouri. So, at last, we come to the Mandans, by way of Wales, Mexico, the Gulf Coast, South Carolina, Alabama, and the ephemeral Padoucahs.[21]

Jefferson owned a copy of Carver's *Travels,* and by 1803 was fully acquainted with the presumptive outreach of his forbears. Morgan Jones had given the world Welshmen sailing with Prince Madoc to America and starting to build mounds; Morgan Edwards, chronicler of the American Baptists, reported that by the 1780s there were scores of reports of their descendants, from such diverse sources as Daniel Boone and Simon Girty. In Tennessee, John Sevier paused to search out evidence of Madoc even while campaigning against the Cherokee. Having invoked Welshmen to explain the presence of the ceremonial center he called "Old Stone Fort," on the Hiwassee River, during a lull in the fighting he asked Oconostota, a Cherokee war leader, to confirm the possibility that these earthworks, strengthened with stone, had been built by a white race which preceded the Cherokee. Oconostota obliged, embellishing the tale with great imagination.

If this were not enough, John Filson, or Daniel Boone (it is not certain which) recounted that

> Captain Abraham Chaplain . . . a gentleman whose veracity may be entirely depended on, assured the author, that in the late war [1775–1781, while at Kaskaskia with George Rogers Clark] . . . some Indians came there, and, speaking in the Welsh dialect, were perfectly understood and conversed with two Welshmen in his company.[22]

It is perilous to the successful pursuit of truth to dismiss any testimony, however unlikely it may seem. Jefferson did not, and as part of that sober inquiry which led him to send Lewis and Clark after Verendrye and Evans up the Missouri, he asked them to find Welsh-speaking white Indians. Two of their men reported they had done so.

As Lewis and Clark pressed toward the Rockies, in England the poet Robert Southey produced his interminable and profitable epic *Madoc.* Many Americans of Welsh decent still assert that the Mound Builders were a separate role and Welsh. As late as the 1980s, a historic plaque placed on the shores of Mobile Bay by the Daughters of the American Revolution proclaimed that upon that proud place the Welsh prince had set foot. The plaque was only recently retired to a warehouse.

Why Welshmen? Because, in the first instance, it was desirable to establish a Tudor claim antecedent to that of Cortez, and the Tudors were Welsh. Later this dynastic imperative was replaced by the need of Europeans to define away Indians from the ranks of those worthy of respectful treatment by denying to them fully human status. If, as Jefferson had once asserted, but later recanted, Indians *were* incapable of monumental architecture, then Welsh builders of mounds producing only a few mixed-blood descendants who would conveniently die off from a plague of smallpox, were a considerable convenience. It is not likely that Jefferson was hoping that Lewis and Clark would corroborate the Madocian hypothesis; Evans was not probing the northernmost extensions of the Spanish Empire to denigrate Native Americans but to replace the claims of Spain to that empire with those of the Anglo-Saxon-Brittonic peoples, and Jefferson, of course, did not have an Elizabethan reason for seeking out Mandans or Welsh speakers. His best source of information before the departure of Lewis and Clark, Winthrop Sargent, was not persuaded that the builders of the Ohio Valley mounds were Welsh, and for Jefferson a search only justified itself if it was in the interest of science. He was, characteristically, just looking.[23]

It must be recalled that Jefferson had his own imperial vision. He sent Lewis and Clark to establish the claim of the United States to the Missouri Valley, to the shores of the Pacific Ocean, and a route to Cathay. For such routes Ferdinand and Isabella dispatched Columbus and Cortez; for them, as well, Elizabeth of England and Wales, as red-headed as Jefferson, made use of the myth of Madoc to animate her own imperial campaign and its search for a Northwest Passage—a water route to Cathay.

* * *

Between Europe and Asia there were, in fact a peoples lost to history, the peoples of America who built earthen architecture. Jefferson's growing wonder at the accomplishments of the early inhabitants of the Ohio and Mississippi valleys quickened his interest in what "monuments" Lewis and Clark might discover on the imperial way westward. Perhaps another instinct, ethnic in origin, enlivened his scientific curiosity about what truth there might be imbedded in the map he sent them, the product of John Evans, "whose original object I believe had been to go in search of the Welsh Indians said to be up the Missouri."[24]

European diseases accompanied these imperial adventures and this scientific probing. As a result, the Mandans nearly became a truly lost tribe. We shall never know whether or not they ever built mounds, or when they first developed their peculiar coloring, or even if some of them might have been descended from Welsh explorers of the twelfth century. The Mandans were virtually gone by 1840; nearly exterminated by European smallpox. Since there are no pure-blood Mandan (whatever that might mean) left, geneticists have been discouraged from pursuing their biological history with twentieth century devices. Jefferson made use of everything available to him for the purpose, however, drawing upon the accounts of the Verendryes to inform Lewis and Clark what they might expect on the upper Missouri. Though by 1840 the scientific tone established by Jefferson and Gallatin still persisted, it was being flooded out by racial apologetics. Indian accomplishments were erased by allocating all that was interesting in

their work to someone—almost anyone—else. What had begun in the
1570s as a device of Tudor propaganda became, by the 1840s, a device
of American racial apologetics.

AN APOLOGETIC POTPOURRI

The first generation of American statesmen-archaeologists did not require exotic peoples to explain the monumental architecture they
found in the Mississippi watershed. As we have seen, Jefferson, Gallatin, and Washington simply assumed that the people they found in the
valley had been preceded by other Indians who had known more effulgent circumstances—"a more populous people" but not a different
one. The Biblical scholars, however, began early to seek American
demonstrations of the texts which they had become accustomed to
quarrying for sermons. Ezra Stiles of Yale substituted, for the Lost
Tribes of Jews, Canaanites driven from Palestine by Israelites.

Stiles offered his Biblical exegetics to Benjamin Franklin, who replied from Paris that he thought De Soto a more likely leader of the
Mound Builders than any Canaanite. Franklin knew better; accounts
of De Soto's expedition were by then widely current and made it quite
clear that the Indians with which De Soto's party contested were still
building and using mounds. None the less, many such mounds came to
be called "Spanish Forts," especially in Tennessee and Mississippi,
where, indeed, Spanish forts might be expected. Some still dot the Mississippi and Tennessee landscape, though they were constructed a
thousand years and more before there was a Spain. Many were there
before there was either a Rome or a Carthage.

Benjamin Barton, like most of us, learned as he went along, but at
the outset he brought his own distorting lenses on his travels down the
Ohio. Though his prejudices were relatively harmless in the reading
room of the American Philosophical Society, they did not help science
in the open air. Barton had been reading the Icelandic sagas, and thus
was able to anticipate what emerged from nineteenth century Scandi-
navian pride. He offered Danish Vikings as the forefathers of the
Mound builders, who had, he suggested, gone on to Mexico to become
Toltecs. De Witt Clinton, father of the Erie Canal and mayor of New
York, concurred with Barton in 1811, having reviewed the evidence of
New York mound building a decade before Joseph Smith adumbrated
the Mormon hypothesis.

Toltecs alone would do, but giving them an infusion of Viking blood
made them almost Normans, who, as everyone knew were first cousins
to the Anglo-Saxons—1066 and all that. Besides, Toltec Vikings assimilated into mound-building apologetics the otherwise indigestible Aztec

tale of a Toltec king named Quetzalcoatl who was bearded and fair-skinned. (Quetzalcoatl the Viking must not be confused with Montezuma the Welsh Bard or Hebrew poet.)

Bishop James Madison did not join Barton in requiring Danish blood for his Mound Builders; neither did Thaddeus Harris nor Caleb Atwater. For Harris, and for many others later, something exotic to the Ohio valley was a pleasant thought, but that something need not be non-Indian. Mexicans would do—Harris accepted the Toltec idea uncomplicated by Viking-Normans.

Toltecs and Aztecs, though resident in the central valley of Mexico, and therefore distant, were better known to the literary world of Boston than the Indians of the American central valley. To Prescott, Stephens, and Catherwood as litterateurs, rather than as archaeologists, we owe such place names as the Aztec ruins of New Mexico, the Toltec site in Arkansas, Montezuma's Castle and Montezuma's Well in Arizona, and Aztalan Mounds in Wisconsin. While the geography is a little off, there is no racial prejudice in these attributions.

The general view in the 1820s was that of Atwater, William Henry Harrison, Albert Gallatin, and Henry Brackenridge. Though they placed their Mound Builders at some distance from "any tribe of North American Indians known in modern times" they did not require for them blood infusions from Europe.[25] Though Atwater might suggest Hindu influence on Indian art, that was because Hindus and Indians both came from Asia. Gallatin made it clear that he did not feel the builders of mounds had learned anything from the Toltecs; rather, he wrote, it was the other way round.

And so it may have been. As we have learned more about archaeology we have become more timorous in our suppositions, and are now ready to admit that we do not know. Still agnosticism does not sell books; confusion does. The hot pseudoscientific best-seller of the 1830s was Josiah Priest's *Antiquities and Discoveries in the West* which added Polynesians, Greeks, Romans, and Chinese to the list of alternative mound builders—anyone would do but Indians. Early nineteenth century novelists such as Sarah J. Hale and Cornelius Matthews, and the poet, William Cullen Bryant (in *The Prairies*, in 1832), and mid-century writers such as Daniel Pierce Thompson offered touching tales of mound-building heroes and heroines of indeterminate race.

Fiction, then as now, tended to accommodate public preference. The Indians were always an annoyance. After the Sioux and Cheyenne refused to accept the invasions of the West, and in 1862 commenced their nearly thirty-year struggle to retain their lands, Indian fighting became the White Man's Burden. The weight of that burden was lightened by denying any redeeming virtues—such as architectural skill—to the enemy.

SCIENCE AFTER JEFFERSON

Literature was one thing, science another. From 1790 until the 1870s, American science remained fairly consistent in supporting the opinion of the founders that the mounds were built by Indians. The father of American physical anthropology, Samuel G. Morton, supported this view after studying skeletons from the mounds and from more recent Indian graves. The Smithsonian Institution has agreed ever since 1848, when it published the reports of Squier and Davis. The Smithsonian's John Wesley Powell, chiefly known as the one-armed hero who made the first expedition through the Grand Canyon, also advanced the cause of respectful scientific inquiry into the ancient history of the Indians. He wished to diminish ignorance, for, as he said, "the blunders we have made and the wrongs we have inflicted upon the Indians . . . have been cruel and inexcusable, except on the ground of our ignorance."[26]

In 1873, J. W. Foster, president of the Chicago Academy of Sciences, contested the Smithsonian's position. The Indian, said Foster, "has been signalized by treachery and cruelty. He repels all efforts to raise him from his degraded position. . . . He has never been known voluntarily to engage in an enterprize requiring methodical labor. . . . To suppose that such a race threw up . . . symmetrical mounds . . . is . . . preposterous."[27]

The fight was on. When Powell appointed Cyrus Thomas to be head of the Smithsonian's Bureau of Ethnology in 1881, Thomas was, he admitted later, "a pronounced believer in . . . a race of Mound Builders distinct from the American Indians." Thomas came to the opposite view, though in 1889, he was still struggling to "reconcile" the precision of the immense geometrics of Newark "with the theory that the works were built by Indians." Upon the truth or falsehood of that theory, "all other problems must turn." If they were, "then there would be no more blind groping . . . and . . . the thousand and one wild theories and romances would be permanently disposed of."[28]

And so they were, in 1894, when Thomas published the 730-page *Twelfth Annual Report of the Bureau of Ethnology*, which laid to rest his doubts, and those of all serious students of the subject thereafter. More than that; with the zest of a convert, he went after the unconverted. They were, he wrote, guilty of "garbling and perversion . . . blind zeal . . . serious errors even when they were not imposed upon by frauds and forgeries.[29]

Frederick Jackson Turner was a more endearing writer than Thomas. His thesis that the frontier had a paramount influence upon the formation of the American character was published in 1890, at the same time as Thomas's *Twelfth Annual Report* of the Bureau of Ethnology, as a commentary on the *Report of the Bureau of the Census*. The frontier thesis and the work of the Census Bureau have received far more attention than the work of the Bureau of Ethnography. One of the purposes of this book is to seek to set a better balance of approbation.

In the 1890s, the Americans of the dominant culture were entering their imperial era with many of the self-doubts of adolescents; they became intensely interested in themselves just as they commenced imposing themselves upon others. It may be too severe to call the age of McKinley and Theodore Roosevelt the age of American Bullying, but it was certainly not a time in which Americans wished to give much attention to the achievements of peoples over which they overlaid their anxious imperium.

In the time of "bully wars" and White Fleets, of Big Sticks and Making the World Safe for a particular version of democracy, it was unlikely that there would be an avid audience for the quiet assertion of Cyrus Thomas that the Americans of European stock leading charges up hills in Cuba and the Philippines had paid too little attention to the artificial hills built by other races in Ohio. Especially when those races were still present.

Albert Gallatin had pointed out the relationship of racial apologetics and imperialism in the 1840s. Cyrus Thomas was writing into the teeth of a resumption of the same apologetics in the 1890s.

THE FATE OF THE ANCIENT ARCHITECTURE

Meanwhile, thousands of mounds were falling to road builders, canal builders, and railroad builders, to developers and farmers, to floods arising from the conversion of gentle rivers into sluiceways, and valleys into recreational lakes. America's ancient past was being obliterated at a pace which, by 1948, had reduced by *ninety percent* the earthen architecture available to Squier and Davis a century earlier—about the same rate of loss as the Great Dying, four centuries earlier, among the people who had built them. Most of the *Twelfth Annual Report* was an obituary.[30]

As late as 1820, enough remained of the Circleville earthworks surveyed fifty years earlier by the Reverend Jones (see Chapter Three) to permit Postmaster Caleb Atwater to describe

two forts [we are back to forts], one being an exact circle, the other an exact square. The former is surrounded by two walls, with a deep ditch between them. The latter is encompassed by one wall, without any ditch. . . . The walls of the circular fort *were* [emphasis supplied] at least 20 feet in height, measuring from the bottom of the ditch. . . .

What surprised me, on measuring these forts was the exact manner in which they had laid down their circle and square; so that after every effort, by the most careful survey, to detect some error in their measurement, we found that it was impossible, and that the measurement was much more correct, than it would have been, in all probability, had the present inhabitants undertaken to construct such a work.[31]

Already the wonderment has taken an elegiac tone. Atwater's past tense tells us that the citizens of Circleville, like those of Marietta, had already lost much of their understanding of the value of the remarkable and distinguishing along with their reverence for the mysterious past. "Development" and "progress" were sweeping Ohio.

In Marietta, the Historic Preservation Ordinance of the Cincinnati did not prove firm enough to save the central square; the sides of the embankments along the Sacra Via were leveled; the conical mound remained, insulated by Revolutionary heroes' graves from the rapacity of real estate development. There had been two sacred ways leading from the cropland on the floodplain to the ceremonial plaza. The smaller is entirely obliterated; the larger, that traveled by the Cincinnati, has been stripped of its flanking embankments, but its dimensions are retained by two pleasant strips of asphalt separated by a strip of grass. The square to which the way led is still there, a city park, containing two flattened pyramids. The town library surmounts one, and the other remains a grassy relic.

The Newark square inconvenienced a railroad, and was obliterated. That at Circleville stood in the way of the construction of the Ohio Canal—it went to progress as well, sacrificed at about the same time as the square in Marietta and that at Newark. The first generation of Europeans at Circleville still retained in its culture enough of Thomas Jefferson's Renaissance to organize its streets as a spider web, with a central, octagonal space where a mound (probably a mortuary) had been in Hopewell times. As time went on, the good citizens of Circleville obliterated the mound, but they did adopt Jeffersonian principles and built their octagonal courthouse where it had been. Each of the sides of that courthouse faced the entry of a radial street coming in from the circle, with blocks, in blunt pie-shapes, between them.

*   *   *

The clay walls of Circleville's interior circle were mined for brickmaking, and then both circles and the ditch (or "moat") were flattened, but not before the citizens' difficulty of plowing them away had given shape to the town, and thus imparted something to stand between it and mediocrity. By 1840, however, avarice had already begun to take its toll. An English traveler, James S. Buckingham, wrote:

> So little veneration . . . have the Americans for ancient remains . . . that . . . Circleville is soon likely to lose all traces of its original peculiarities. . . . Though the octagonal building still remains, the circular streets are fast giving way, to make room for straight ones, and the central edifice itself is already destined to be removed, to give place to stores and dwellings; so that in half a century, or less, there will be no vestige left of that peculiarity which gave the place its name. . . .[32]

The reasons for its demise as a place of individuality were the usual ones. The city council found lots in peculiar shapes inconvenient to developers. On March 2, 1838, urban renewal came to Circleville with a chartered Circleville Squaring Company. Buckingham was right, as John Reps has shown in a recent commentary containing a series of somber drawings of the loss of all individuality and antiquity by this Ohio valley, Circleville looks like every place else, today.[33]

Serpent Mound does not. It lies close to the Ohio River, near the hamlet of Peebles, not far from Marietta. It remains a quarter mile of coiled power, holding a world-circle in its mouth, and located in the center of a compass-unsettling anticline which probably marks the arrival of a meteor long before the Indians composed their effigy. At the end of the nineteenth century, it was saved from destruction by another Yankee Putnam, Frederic Ward Putnam, director of the Peabody Museum in Cambridge. After investigating the mound, Putnam told Bostonians that if it were obliterated by development that event would be more disgraceful than tearing down the Bunker Hill Monument. His pleas raised the money to save it.[34]

The rescue of the Serpent Mound and the issuance of Cyrus Thomas's report on the Mound Builders marked the highwater mark of intelligent and responsible preservation of the architecture of ancient America. As these words are being written in the winter of 1994, a developer is threatening to desecrate the lowlands which supported the life of the people who created the serpent effigy on a promontory above them. Five other unexcavated sites lie exposed to the flood waters that the developer proposes to impound behind a dam, so that speedboats may zoom above what were the sacred grounds of Indians who created a monument without equal in the world.

The people of Peebles are much divided about how they should respond to a proposed development surrounding Serpent Mound. It all sounds glamorous, and theirs is a county much in need of employment. On the other hand, they retain a fierce local pride in their ancient monument, and some of them point to the fate of Circleville, a hundred miles or so distant in central Ohio, as a cautionary instance.

It is probable that the hilltop hearing Serpent Mound was a sacred site for many years before the writhing testament to the other creatures of the earth was created. It is also probable that a template of gravel was precisely gauged to establish where the coils of the serpent should be placed so that they would be illuminated by the sun at recurring points during the course of the year. This would provide for one sort of re-harmonization of human creation with the larger world; the Serpent Mound was, I think, an offering of propitiation, in which the sun over-head, and the creatures of the underworld—of which snakes are the most obvious—were simultaneously beseeched to accept humankind as their fellows.[35]

When humans deliberately seek out places in which they feel mystery and the ordinary rules of physics do not obtain, and leave there offerings to sun and to the underworld, they may well be seeking to recapture a harmony they feel themselves to have lost with the earth. Perhaps by a large sacrifice of labor, and by the application of their most demanding science, they may restore themselves to the good graces of a world they have violated and to which they fell estranged.

The search for harmony is not a new phenomenon in Ohio. Propitiatory sacrifice was not invented in the Middle East. Perhaps, as we move forward toward an attempt to restore our own harmonious relationship to our mound-building predecessors, we may find, in the Old or New Testaments texts, analogies to the physical testaments they have left to us. Analogies do not explain things away. Instead, they may be openings to understanding, declaring that we are all baffled by the enigmas of the universe, and that it is possible that the American Indians, we, and ancient peoples of the Old World, including the Jews, may have sought similar ways of seeking harmony with mysterious systems we cannot understand and cannot control.

In this spirit, let us return to the mounds, and risk some guesses about why and how they were built.

CHAPTER ELEVEN

WHY WERE THE MOUNDS BUILT?

We have come to the end of our tale of exploration and explanation. Our predecessors have done their best for and their worst to what was found in Great Valley. Now we are on our own.

Abraham Lincoln told us what we should do, and why. Thomas Jefferson had put the watershed of the Mississippi River in the center of the American story, but it was left to Lincoln to bring together all that Jefferson had learned about its magnificent past and to make of that a guide to shape its future. In his Second Address to the Congress, Lincoln spoke of the land which had nurtured him, looking backward to its antiquity and forward to the prodigies that might be brought forth from it:

> It is the great body of the republic. The other parts are but marginal borders to it. . . . In the production of provisions, grains, grasses, and all which proceed from them, this great interior region is naturally one of the most important in the world. . . . We shall be overwhelmed by the magnitude of the prospect presented . . . [by] this Egypt of the West.[1]

Elsewhere, Lincoln provided the necessary admonitions; we are, he often said, heirs to a great estate, and as heirs we have obligations. I was reminded of Lincoln's words during a conversation in my office at the National Park Service with David Brower, that fierce conservationist, at the end of January 1994. Brower suggested that we will do better by the Valley if we reformulate and extend Abraham Lincoln's sense of trusteeship: Lincoln looked backward. Brower looks forward and tells us that we do not own the land, we merely borrow it from our children.

Brower's sense of continuous trusteeship encourages us to pay attention to the lessons imparted by the experience of those who had this task before it came to us. While we are borrowing, we may borrow from them, as well. They may have understood some things of which

243

we are only indistinctly aware, and they may have suffered from a lack of recognition of other things which are clear to us in hindsight.

The Founding Fathers sought with all the means at their command to discern what might be learned about those who had been in the Great Valley before them. Though their scientific instruments were not so finicking as ours, they learned enough to gain a great truth: the people who had earlier lived along those streams exerted themselves mightily to live harmoniously with the earth and the sky, but from time to time those people either failed to remind themselves of that endeavor, and became prodigal, or were so unfortunate as to attempt it and fail. In either case, they suffered, and their descendents suffered; it was many years before each recovery occurred, and each fresh start. And this has happened several times.

These oscillations of civilization were baffling to the Founders and baffling also to those who still accept an eighteenth century view of progress. It is hard to accept the uncomfortable fact that humankind has failed before in its relationship to the environment in the Mississippi Valley, despite its best efforts to do better. People have lived here before, have grown crops and raised families, have made sculpture and painting, woven cloth and built cities. But, because their relationship to the land became disharmonious, their civilizations declined, their descendents were impoverished, and their works of art became shards. Their cities crumbled and eroded until they are only to be discerned as ruins barely distinguishable from the natural contours of the land itself.

The cyclical history of the Great Valley before the advent of the Europeans does not corroborate sentimentality about Indians living lightly on the land. Gush of this kind is patronizing; it implies that the Indians were capable only of an architecture of teepees and of an economy of pursuing animals and gathering seeds. It denies that they broke sod and raised crops and laid up pyramids and ringed their cities with walls of stone and wood. Some Indians lived heavily upon the land. Some changed its contours. Some lived so densely together and for so long that the land could no longer support them, though they did their best to propitiate its requirements. Thereafter their descendents could survive only if they scattered and took to living more lightly. The land itself required recovery.

The interval between the cessation of work at Poverty Point and the commencement of construction among the Adena/Hopewell was nearly a thousand years. Only in a few places in the lower Mississippi Delta and along the Gulf Coast do people seem to have been able to remain together in large enough aggregations to continue to create large works of architecture. There was a second flowering, as the

Adena/Hopewell achievement produced prodigies of art and architecture, but there was a second frost, a second period of exhaustion, though a mere three or four hundred years in length, that intervened between their great exertions and the Mississippian emergence. There was such an emergence, however, and mighty cities arose, but once again, after the great days at Cahokia, even before the Europeans brought their diseases, the Vacant Quarter opened. And as people were drawing together once more, around 1500, they were smitten by the Great Dying.

Three hundred years later, the first generation of citizens of the United States to cross the Appalachians saw before them in the Ohio Valley evidence that multitudes had been there before and were no longer present, multitudes capable of building cities and of large-scale agriculture.*

That evidence supports, I believe, the hypothesis offered in this chapter, a hypothesis grounded in scepticism about any theory of progress which assumes a regular ascent from "primitive" people building mounds to ourselves. It *is* only a hypothesis (*an* hypothesis for English readers); I am not a psychoanalyst, archaeologist, nor an anthropolo-

---

*The Founding Fathers had no better way to place that evidence in a time-scheme than to measure the sizes of the trees standing upon the mounds, and, if inclined toward greater precision, to count the number of rings between the lighter and darker concentric circles discerned in cutting across a tree trunk.

Carbon dating and dendrochronology are very recent devices. Even if Jefferson and Gallatin had possessed knowledge of the rates of decomposition of carbon 14 and the conveniences ensuing from flotation of seeds, even if they had used satellite photography and microscopes, they would still have been unable to place their research in the context of long spans of time. They thought and wrote before the study of geology expanded the impression of time within which human history has taken its very late place, and before Darwinism superimposed upon geological duration a comprehension of the immense span of time within which vegetation and animal life, including human life, have assumed their current forms.

Until the last half of the nineteenth century, there was little solid science to replace the means by which Bishop Usher concluded that the earth had been created, with all its creatures upon it, in 4004 B.C. The bishop used the best information at his disposal, and linked the life spans of the patriarchs of Israel set forth in the Bible. These linked biographies accumulated six thousand years, reaching a period when, we now know, the glazed ceramic cubes were placed in the mounds at Watson Brake. In Jefferson's time, most educated people no longer thought the world to be only so young as that; but they had no way of knowing how old it actually was.

Not only were Jefferson and Gallatin less fortunate then we in the possession of certain scientific instruments, not only did they lack what has been derived from modern geology and the theory of evolution, they were forming their ideas within the field of force of the eighteenth century theory of progress. It is not the same thing as that of evolution; the latter is sufficiently capacious to include all significant developments except miracles in the growth and change of our species among others. the former was not.

gist. While people who are expert in these fields have offered much kindly criticism and correction of these pages, the reader should be aware that they were written by an amateur. None the less, a century and a half is sufficient time to justify pressing beyond simple observation of the monumental architecture of the valley to attempt a theory as to why it was built.

Though Thomas Jefferson was at first chary of the attempt, George Washington, did, after all, urge Richard Butler to get on with it: amateur archaeology is, as Washington put it, "very valuable and may lead to some useful discoveries. Those works which are found upon the Ohio . . . show traces of the country's having been once inhabited by a race of people more ingenious, at least, if not more civilized than those who at present dwell there. . . . Any clue . . . which can lead to a knowledge of these must be gratefully received."[2]

And, later, Jefferson *did* urge that the American Antiquarian Society exert itself so that "the monuments of the character and condition of the people who preceded us in the occupation of this great country will be rescued from oblivion before they will have entirely disappeared."[3]

They have not quite all disappeared. The clues are still there toward an answer to the great questions: Why did the American Indians build their earthen architecture?

AMONG NOT IN

Ancient American architecture—geometrics of earth in Ohio, platforms of stone in Mexico, of earth in Missouri, or of adobe in Arizona—does not separate humans from nature by enclosing them within walls, roof, and floor. It directs them up ramps and down, beside and over pyramids and cones, and between embankments or walls of stone—but almost never sends them within. It is only a little too simple to say that American monumental architecture is an exterior art. In Mexico, Yucatan, Illinois, Tennessee, Georgia, Mississippi, or Alabama, people were conducted by architecture itself across flattened spaces bounded by masses. The programming was to move around, through, and upon. One almost never entered a doorway. Doorways were unimportant.*

European monumental architecture, following the great achievements of the dome-making Romans, increasingly focused its genius

---

*Perhaps that is why neither the Mexicans nor the Ohioans troubled to develop any more complex masonry arch than that composed of corbels—overlapping horizontal stones—or balancing upright but inwardly slanting slabs. They used both of these, but only, one suspects, out of convenience, not out of pride in their ingenuity.

upon interior effects.* Following the lead of the Hellenistic architects of the Middle East, the Romans reveled in theatrical effects only possible in controlled spaces. Their largest buildings provided a concave experience. People moved into large spaces, worked, lived, and ate in enclosures, and vast assemblages could be held in the Baths of Caracalla and the Pantheon.

This was not true in America. From Tierra del Fuego to the Arctic, one moved amidst architecture, not within it. When we think of Chillicothe as the Delphi of American antiquity, which many of us have come to do, the further thought arises that its climate is not much more severe that that of Thrace, and that before the Romans made interior space so important, many of the sacred places of the Greeks were in the open air. The word they used for outdoor areas reserved for liturgy—*temenos*—serves as well for spaces bounded by the earthen octagons, squares, and circles at Newark and Chillicothe.

The Fairgrounds Circle is the largest figure in the Newark complex. It has no direct counterpart in Greece, though once again an analogy helps to identify the origin of the feeling of sacred mystery one feels within that circle. It, too is a *temenos,* the more intense because it seals out the world with a nearly complete circular wall of earth, rather than merely implying the sacred as does the rectilinear *temenos* about the Parthenon in Athens. Though they were certainly not a reticent people, it is virtually impossible to reconstruct the feelings of the Greeks within that temple, as they approached the enormous, brilliantly colored statue of the goddess Athena, as much a patriotic as a religious figure. It is considerably easier to imagine how the Hopewell felt within the Fairgrounds Circle, for it was a sacred space centered upon a a charnel house—a building in which bodies were prepared for burial or cremation.

I do not know how the Hopewell regarded these activities, but it

---

*The Romans and Byzantines exhausted the possibilities of sublime interior space experienced all at once. Sir John Vanbrugh, Louis Sullivan, and Frank Lloyd Wright were trickier, keeping down the height of their corridors to provide for an explosion of space in their great chambers, emphasizing an entry *into* constructed space. But theirs, too, was an architecture "about" enclosure.

European architecture uses the ears as well as the eyes to emphasize that it is "about" interiors. One of the supreme ways to experience such architecture is to hear the impact and echo of one's footfalls as space expands and contracts, as when one walks through a space like Bernini's St. Peter's, in Rome.

This is the auditory equivalent of being dazzled by tricks with light—interior light from unexpected places. The Spanish and Mexican *transpirante,* like the Berninian footfall, is not to be sought among the Hopewell, nor are the tricks with little mirrors so beloved of Sir John Soane and Benjamin Henry Latrobe.

The masters of the Gothic also worked in the art of interior light, but whereas Soane and Latrobe dazzled to delight, the Gothicists dazzled to instruct.

seems to me that in the perspective of the hundreds of thousands of years in which our species has been very much as it is, they were modern people, essentially like us. Therefore we need not be excessively chary about imagining ourselves into their spaces, and developing from that imaginary experience some explanations for why those spaces were created. Then we can integrate supplementary evidence into those explanations to see how things fit. The first element of my hypothesis is, accordingly, that the Fairgrounds Circle was a *temenos* in which the Hopewell worked reverently to provide a proper transition of the living spirit from one realm of being to another and a dignified union of the dead body and the earth.

Even today, when the traffic of rush hour is gone, we can feel the presence there of the ancient dead and of those who were dedicated to this place of spiritual passage and of physical reconciliation. The entry to the circle is still, at nightfall, as numinous as it was for Squier and Davis in 1848:

> Here, covered with gigantic trees of a primitive forest, the work truly presents a grand and impressive appearance; and upon entering the ancient avenue for the first time, the visitor does not fail to experience a sensation of awe such as he might feel in passing the portals of an Egyptian Temple.[4]

That sensation of awe is contained in a circle, and thereby focused as a beam of light is focused by a prism. As I suggested at the very outset of this work, similar feelings are aroused and strongly felt, if one attends to them, in tens of thousands of sacred rings of earth and of stones across the American continent. The Ohio Hopewell constructed some of the largest of these, sustaining a much older tradition. The circle at Watson's Brake was already four thousand years old when that on the Newark Fairgrounds was commenced.

CIRCLES OF WATER AND OF EARTH

In many cultures around the world, circle-making has been used to separate profane from sacred space. Carl Jung had something to say about this, in London, in 1935:

> The . . . archetypal idea . . . of the magic circle . . . drawn around something that has to be prevented from escaping or protected against hostile influences . . . is an archaic idea you can still find in folklore. For instance, if a man digs for treasure, he draws the magic circle round the field to keep the devil out. . . . [A] circle within a square . . . is called in

Sanskrit a mandala. The word means a circle, particularly a magic circle. . . . The symbol of the mandala has exactly this meaning of a holy place, a *temenos*, to protect the center.[5]

Many Indians of recent times have held the view that circles of water were especially effective as barriers against ghosts and other spirits. Robert Hall, an anthropologist, has recorded water and circle observances by the Omaha, Iroquois, Ojibwa, Blackfoot, Micmac, Potawatamie, and Cherokee (none, it happens, in Ohio). Hall's findings may explain why even older Indian circular barriers were often created by placing ditches on the inside of *circular* earthworks.[6]

Europeans who came upon such constructions marveled that anyone would put a moat on the inside of a parapet (which they persistently took to be a fort). If defenders had no moat between them and their attacker, but, instead, one at their backs, of what use was it? And how would a military explanation square with the fact that the Hopewell created their squares and octagons, in the same complexes as their circles, by building embankments out of earth that was removed from deep ditches *outside* these figures, where a proper moat should be? Clearly, the military hypothesis was foolish. As early as the 1870s, an inquirer into the Newark mounds, Samuel Park, saw that:

> Nearly all of the circumvalations . . . are constructed with a moat, or ditch inside of the wall, and many of them are very small, ranging from one to two hundred feet in diameter, and of easy approach at any, and all points on the outside. Now to call such works military fortifications, is not only absurd, but supremely ridiculous.[7]

It is *not* absurd, however, to cling to the word "moat" even though the placement inside, rather than outside, the embanked earth clearly confirms Parks's conclusion. For the term "moat" suggests a ring of water to keep something in or something out—and so do these circular ditches, even when they are dry. Ohioans who built mortuary sanctuaries apparently shared that association, for they often deployed stream-suggesting cobbles in lieu of ditches. Stephen Peet quoted the old settler Isaac Smucker as describing a cobbled or "paved circle eight feet wide" around "a group of burial mounds near the old fort" in Newark. This was probably the circle found when the Central Ohio Railroad smashed its right-of-way directly through the center of the Newark earthworks. A group of local antiquaries managed to stand off the road crews long enough to excavate one mound. It was found to contain postholes and layers of cobblestones, sand, ash, charcoal, sheets of mica, blue clay, and a few unburned bones, and "a cobble-stone way about eight feet wide. . . . This oblong circle of stone must have been one hundred years in . . . diameter."[8]

When the clay embankments forming the circle at Circleville were torn down, a symbolic "moat" was discovered inside it, as well, composed of "cobble-like stones, varying in size from 8 to 15 cm. in diameter . . . 10 to 15 cm. deep, and about 1.4 m. wide."[9]

William Romain has collated many reports of the use of puddled clay to cover the central mounds within these circles. These central mounds often (perhaps always) covered either burials or charnel houses; puddled clay is a mixture of water and the kind of earth found in streambeds; once again, water is a medium symbolically insulating the physical remains of the dead from the mundane world.*

If water and earth may be considered as indistinct from each other, as clay is neither one nor the other, and as stream-bed cobbles may be substituted for streams, then we may see these Hopewell circles as water or as earth. Circles, though. Why circles? And why in association with water? Perhaps because when something emerges from a pond, such as a duck returning to the surface or a fish jumping, or even a frog reemerging, it creates on that surface a small wave receding in a widening circle.

Romain has noted that Hall had earlier suggested that water-borne soils such as puddled clay might indicated that the Hopewell may have participated in the Earth-Diver myth. That powerful idea situates the creation of the world with a hero sending a succession of animals into the primordial waters (Jung would surely say into the racial unconscious) to find some earth from the bottom. All fail until the last, which succeeds in returning, exhausted, to the surface with a bit of that earth in its bill or claws, and from that bit the earth expands upon the surface to form our round world.

(Jung might read this myth as depicting a means by which reality might return to an insufficiently grounded psyche by a deliberate though difficult return to the collective unconscious and a reemergence into consciousness with something derived from the depths. That would not diminish its value as a parable of other truths.)

In the 1950s, anthropologists collated instances in which this account of creation has been found among the traditions of historic and contemporary Indians—such amazingly diverse people as the Cherokee, Delaware, Hopi, Navajo, Omaha, Yakima, Seneca, Kansa, Shaw-

---

*Romain lists burial mounds and/or charnel houses at Seip, Liberty, and Circleville as well as within the Fairgrounds Circle at Newark, and puddled clay at Seip and Liberty as well as on the Hopewell site, at the Mount Vernon Mound in Posey County, Indiana, and at Mound City, Ohio. (This information is to be found in Romain's paper, "Hopewell Geomatric Enclosures," which he shared with me early in 1994, before its publication.)

nee, and Acoma. Reviewing that work, Romain suggests that it is "probably the most widely distributed of all North American Indian myths".[10]

The Earth-Diver provides a unifying element among two concepts already implicit in a circle surrounding a charnel house: the transition of spirit from one realm to another and the reconciliation of the body to the earth. The emergence of earth balances the return of the body to earth. Creation is the balance to death; the recurrence of life is completed by the recurrence of death.

It was important to guard these mysteries with interior "moats" and layers of puddled clay. If one were seeking to keep the spirits of the departed from wandering before they were properly propitiated, or to keep evil spirits from the outside from contaminating a holy place, there would be no better way to do so than by erecting a circle of earth to cut off all visual association of the worlds inside and outside, and then by placing within it a circle of water (or a circle of cobbles made round by a stream). Creation and completion are recalled in the same *temenos*.

One could not be permitted to enter such a place capriciously: there was only through a single entry to the Fairgrounds Circle, for example, and that single entry was in reality the only means of access to three nested circles. The first has been lost; it was a low structure outside the presently preserved circle, which was then only two-thirds of its present height (the upper third was added in reconstruction, about the time the outer circle was destroyed). Finally there was the interior "ditch."* At Circleville, there were also three concentric circles, but the "moat" was *between* the two embankments. There, again, there was only one place of entry, another solemn gateway which, one may guess, was guarded by incantations and possibly by wooden sculpture long ago crumbled to dust. The surviving wooden sculptures surrounding and protecting the platform burials within the circular pond beside the circular "moat" at Fort Center, Florida, also probably served as sentinels.[11]

When the mortuary mound within the Fairgrounds Circle was finally excavated professionally, the charnel house beneath it was found to have been a wooden structure, with wings, at the core of which was "an altar built of stone, upon which were found ashes, charcoal and calcined bones."[12]

---

*It was reported as filled with water until the water table and drainage altered by the New Madrid earthquake in 1812. The ditch was "often seen . . . partially and sometimes wholly, filled with water all around the circle." The earthquake raised that terrain relative to the prairie nearby, which became a pond, often washing close to the circle's outer bank. The interior "moat" has emptied out and the means destroyed by which it had been supplied with water." By 1881, it had "not held water of late years to any great extent." (See Smucker, "Mound Builders," p. 265).

We will return to the Fairgrounds charnel house and its circles shortly—as economists. We have other stops to make, and other elements to be added to our working hypothesis. They come from beyond the Ohio and Mississippi valleys. Over four thousand years, circular forms dominated American architecture. That statement contains other implicit assertions about the Indians who chose to deploy their energies in monumental circularity, assertions gleaned from what can be learned about other ancient and modern people who did so. Most of them lived and live in self-sufficient farming communities engaged in the early stages of the development of agriculture, animal domestication, spinning, and pottery making, without much density of settlement—some anthropologists suggest without much hierarchy either. The people gathered together for the construction of liturgical architecture, but apparently not for war, judging from the scarcity of broken and perforated skeletons in their detritus. Perhaps their numbers may not yet have exceeded the resources relatively conveniently at hand. They apparently felt no need to bludgeon each other either for sustainance or for empire.

If we wish to romanticize this state (and many of use are disposed to do so) we might think of these circles as suggesting societies in a Rousseauian state of relatively peaceful relations among people in general, and (a truly romantic thought) of equipoise between the genders.

Societies of this type have survived into the modern age; their leadership tends toward the matrilineal (though not always to an arrangement so severe as matriarchy); in many places (not all) women are likely to share both the work and the leadership with men. Red ocher (hematite—iron oxide) has traditionally been used in association with their circles of earth, painted upon the bodies buried in mounds and upon bones exposed to the air and cleaned, and laid in "lenses" or horizontal layers of red-tinted sand or clay at intervals in the mounds. Here is another clue to their being produced by a culture in which females were important: red is the color of blood, or life, and of menses. Menses are important events in any culture, for pregnancy, or which menses are the precondition, is essential. As Thomas Jefferson observed, the female body is frequently depicted in the sculpture of the Indians as pregnant or nursing a child.

Hematite is not easy to find in the bayou country of Louisiana and Mississippi; it had to be moved considerable distances. In neolithic burials in Europe it appears in association with female figurines, the well-known pregnant "Venuses." In Louisiana, as in Sardinia, such lenses appear in the most ancient earthworks.

Mimi Lobell, a psychiatrist and anthropologist, lists the "Adena-Hopewell cultures of North America" among those to be described as circle-related, along with the Jomon culture in Japan, the Yang Shao in

China, the Indus Valley culture in India, the pre-Sumerian Ubaid forms of Mesopotamia, the predynastic Gerzian period in Egypt, Minoan Greece, the Pre- Indo-European megalith builders in Europe, and, in America, the Mogollon, Anasazi, Hopi, Zuni and Pueblo, early Tehuacan and Tlatilco, and Chilca.[13] *

Though it must be conceded that in some other cultures the circle seems to have a male gender valence or to be androgenous, let us assume for the sake of argument that its associations were female for the Adena, and that it remained so in Hopewell times, when circular ditches and cobbled pavements still occurred together with red ocher and female figurines.

The creation of huge squares and octagons beside great circles may have accompanied purposeful changes in materials. The Hopewell may have made a distinction between earth taken from pits, or deep earth, unexposed to the sun until it is used to make circles, and earth scraped from the surface, or sun earth, deployed upon squares and octagons.

Deep earth may have been an element of a female complex and sun earth of a male one. The female body holds a seed until it is ready to become a child. And the earth holds seeds until they, too, are ready to enter the world of light, welcoming the cooperation between earth and sky which is photosynthesis. That polysyllable is a testament to the power of science to incorporate a very ancient understanding of the importance of the sun to growth which commences beyond its reach, deep in the earth.[14]

Coming to light, out of the earth, is somewhat like coming to light out of water. It is entirely possible that people who deliberately confused what was earth and what was water might have done so to reinforce this point, and to make a symbolic statement in monumental circles that the Earth-Diver had been succeeded in the sequence of creation by the seed planter, the first agriculturalist. Many of us believe that we are called upon to participate in the creation of the world, a feeling especially appropriate for farmers.

And so we come to agriculture—through what the Cincinnati at Marietta called a sacra via.

SACRED WAYS AND AGRICULTURE

The sacred ways we have seen from Tennessee to central Ohio did not commence on the river bank, but, instead, a little ashore, on the fertile

---

*The distinction between the rounding Adena and rounding-and-squaring Hopewell may be matched by an equal distinction between the ambiguous forms of the earliest Anasazi and the more precise rounding and squaring to be found in their Chacoan stage and thereafter.

floodplain, replenished with silt each spring, where the primary crops of Hopewell farmers were grown. From these garden plots the graded and protected ways led to ceremonial spaces on upper terraces, where earthworks were formed to register the regularity of the growing seasons. The sacred ways achieved more than a convenience for motion from river to upland. They clarified a liturgical association.

Sacred ways leading *to* ceremonial architecture *from* bottom lands recognized the interlocking importance of each of these locations. And the temples were composed of the fecund earth.

Thus the ancients offered grateful acknowledgement back to the earth and sky for all thy had gained by tearing up the landscape. Does "tearing up" seem excessive? Would "reconstructing" have a more glozing sound? Not if one wishes to describe the process of an agriculture using crude stone plows, violating surfaces which had previously gone about there diurnal business without presumptuous human interference.[15]

Agriculture alters things. It kills some plants and encourages the growth of others. It collects seeds and puts them in pots or baskets, to be reinserted in the earth after it has been reshaped by tearing. Plowing is tearing. It must precede furrow planting—which is also a radical construction of a surface. Farmers disrupt the continuities of nature. What a discovery! The earth, we learn, may produce food year after year once that earth has been purposefully disturbed. Certain seeds may bring forth food from that earth when planted at the right times.

Having dared to discover agriculture, the deliberate disturbance of earth and of the natural course of vegetable life, the Indians produced an architecture of both obeisance and propitiation, in form as well as in its material. Earth and time together. Architecture and agriculture.

When did the Ohioans first feel confident that however deep the winter, spring would return? When did they gain confidence that the stars and moon and sun would observe their appointed courses? At some forgotten moment, astounded and joyous, they learned that it was safe to celebrate the recurrence of spring, the great event of all religions. If there is a regularity, there might possibly also be justice in the universe. In spring, we give thanks for the past harvests, and, in wonder at such a miracle of continuity, are enjoined to plant again. With so much that disappoints us, so many shocks, so many disasters, springtime affirms again that it was not foolish to have saved the seeds. Some promises are fulfilled.

Though only if we risk disturbing things.

Even today, the food crops domesticated by the Ohioans who created this great geometric architecture are likely to be found in "disturbed earth" along the edges of roads and railroad cuts, near the bottom lands where these plants grew in their wild state. They appear as well where Adena/Hopewell agriculture intervened, where their plows ripped the soil, and, at harvest time, where they took seeds removed from the natural order and hidden in pots, richly decorated with vegetable patterns.

Though there were, as we have noted, earthen circles and conical mounds in the lower Mississippi Valley two thousand years before the rise of the Adena/Hopewell system, there seems little doubt that the first conical burial mounds and sacred circles to be built in the Ohio Valley came together with Adena "houses"—or gathering places—that were also circular. These large circular mortuary mounds, apparantly created by a rapidly increasing population, were probably shared by a number of families, gathered in septs and engaged in common domestication of plants.

Domestication permits aggregations of people in larger communities that in turn may be deployed upon larger architecture. At first, the circular buildings of the Adena (which may have been ceremonial, like the kivas of the Southwest and the council houses of the Southeast) were converted by the labor of the people into burial places, sometimes with the bodies placed in wooden cabins or crypts. These interment structures, surrounded by earthen walls or by paired posts and screens or brush and saplings, have been called "mortuary camps." Some were repeatedly covered with earth and reused. Several stories of buried crypts rose to become mounds, near but apart from the circular ceremonial spaces still in use, themselves growing larger, with earthen walls taking the place of the sapling screens as they came to serve larger family groupings or clans. Ultimately, mortuary mounds become very large indeed, as we saw at Portsmouth and Marietta, where their conical circularity was reinforced by more surrounding circles.[16]

Early agriculture depended upon the sun, as does all agriculture, but unlike much corn culture it remained a floodplain miracle. Thus it was that in the Adena/Hopewell world, before maize production, farmers built sacred ways from these food-production areas to their ceremonial centers. Early accounts and maps show that these ways existed at Hopeton, Marietta, Portsmouth, Dunlap, and Newark. There was probably a sacred way leading from each crop-growing area to each set of circles, squares, or octagons.*

At Marietta, George Washington's grizzled veterans knew at once that their sacra via was not constructed for protection against intru-

---

*This was one of the sacred ways of which the Reverend David Jones wrote that they connected geometric earthworks "built [on a terrace] near a river or run of water . . . and [whose] walls run in a circular form . . . [as they] appear to come together at the bank of the river, leaving . . . only a covered way to go to the water."

The Hopeton sacred way can still be discerned from the air, though each year it has been plowed, and only a last minute action by the Congress in 1992 saved it from a gravel pit.

sion. They were schooled in ceremony, and could recognize a provision for dignified ascent through three zones: the water, the fruiting, cultivated plain, and the terrace were they, and the Hopewell before them, placed their architecture. These broad, graded passages, between embankments sometimes twenty feet high, could not have been built just to get up the bluff. To get *what* up a bluff? Wagons? There were no wagons. Canoes? Canoes are not useful on land. The Cincinnati, with their formality, their parade-ground discipline, and their classical learning, understood that they were built to get from farm to temple with decorum.*

THE RECTILINEAR REVOLUTION

The temple was conical before it was square. After the earth-observing Adena came, I think, the sky-observing Hopewell, who wrought a rectilinear revolution.

That radical shift in architecture accompanied a transition from the circle and cone building of the past to an architecture attuned as much to the sky as to the earth. On a more mundane level, it also was contemporaneous with a more intensive cultivation of fatty and starchy seeds, perhaps made more predictable by close observation of seasons and thus to the passages of the moon. Those seeds were cooked in the sort of thin-walled ceramic containers which do not travel well, the pottery of the Hopewell, as distinguished from the somewhat coarser ware of the Adena. I offer the additional thought, then, that the rectilinear revolution occurred as the Hopewell became more proficient at

---

*One might say of these sacred ways that they were constructed to provide a ceremonial passage through which might be conveyed to holy places the exotic and precious good one finds in Hopewell burials, and one might support this view with the patent truth that many of the minerals worked by Indian artisans—copper, flint, meteoric iron, lead, silver, and obsidian among them—are very heavy. They were almost certainly transported by water. It is certainly true that until the Europeans brought wheeled vehicles together with horses and oxen to draw them, it was more difficult to conduct trade in heavy materials by land rather than along rivers. Though there are many indications of widespread walkways throughout the Ohio Valley, it was amply provided with navigable rivers and with trees large and solid enough to be made into serviceable dugouts.

Yet it is also obvious that the agriculture of the floodplains was a necessity, and a regular, constant part of Hopewell life, while the arrival of exotic minerals was so infrequent and unpredictable an event that it is unlikely to have been the sole cause of the creation of ceremonial ways.

Perhaps the reconciliation of these two ideas lies in the likelihood that some minerals were shaped elsewhere into objects which themselves reinforced the religion of agriculture and the sacred earth. Then they might appropriately be brought to the temple-forms up the sacred ways, perhaps accompanied by their own liturgies of welcome and regard.

astronomy, engineering, and intensified agriculture, becoming as they did so more sedentary. They remained longer in one place.

Furthermore, as the Hopewell geometricians added to all the pre-ceeding circles their conjoined squares and rectangles, their action marked a transition in social organization. The Adena had been held together by a cult of the dead. The Hopewell still accorded the dead great honor, and their greater prosperity permitted that respect to be effulgently expressed. But, as I read their architectural record, it seems to me to indicate that they created a new liturgy, one of growth coupled to what might well be called lunar engineering.

The earth looks to the sky.

Their rectilinear revolution marked a sharp increase in the sophistication both of that sort of engineering and of agriculture, as Hopewellian observation of the sky permitted a new boldness in trusting the seasons. In fact, as some readers will surely have muttered by now, the agricultural revolution did not come "at some forgotten *moment*." It seems to have come in bursts, widely separated in time. The sequence, beginning long before the Hopewell, seems to be roughly as follows:

After 2000 B.C. people east of the Great Plains began to save seeds gathered from floodplains in one season to plant in the next. It would not be a staggering surprise to find that evidence of their early experiments in domestication is to be found at the Poverty Point group of sites in the lower Mississippi Valley, especially where D-shaped earthworks cup the bends of bayous and slow-moving rivers. In the floodplains below such places crops did, in fact, grow, and we might still grow them in the fecundity renewed by fresh silt each spring.

A Smithsonian scientist, Bruce Smith, has defined the domestication of plants as "intentional and sustained planting, . . . deliberate storage of seed stock and intentional planting of seeds in prepared seed beds . . . leading to the intense seedling competition and strong selection for plants that will sprout quickly . . . and grow quickly . . . thereby shading out their neighbors and contributing more to the fall harvest seed stock for next year's planting."[17]

Smith's "Floodplain Weed Theory" has been attacked by some feminist anthropologists for giving inadequate credit to "sustained scrutiny and selection of desired attributes" presumably more likely to be the contribution of women than men. This "Gender-Credit Critique" does not seem to me to be incompatible with my own hypothesis that the circular earthworks spreading throughout the region with domestication were predominantly associated with feminine principles, including a predominantly feminine association with the earth as the nurturer of seeds.[18]

The most significant finding of Smith's work, to which apparently not only the Gender-Credit theorists but an overwhelming majority of ethnobotanists and archeobotantists seem to agree, is that there were "clear and dramatic increases in the representation of seeds of domesticated and cultivated plants at about 250B.C. to A.D. 1 . . . [and] a broad geographical pattern of increasing dependence on food production."[19]

Thus, early in the Adena/Hopewell period, and close to the beginning of the Hopewell emergence, a new society, committed to agriculture, formed in the Ohio and Mississippi valleys. A process of agriculturization had taken several thousand years to reach this point, at which it could truly be said of its practitioners that they were farmers. And, as Smith has informed us, the Hopewell *were* farmers.

> They cleared forests; prepared fields; planted, cultivated, harvested, and stored at least seven different species of high yield, high nutritional profile seed crops. Before the introduction of maize, and more than seven centuries in advance of the transition to maize-centered field agriculture, farming economies and an agrarian way of life had been established in the eastern United States.[20]

Specifically, they garnered and stored seeds of squash (*Cucurbita*), marshelder (*Iva annua*), goosefoot (*Chenopodium berlandieri*) and sunflower (*Helianthus annuus*), erect knotweed (*Polygonum erectum*), maygrass (*Phalaris caroliniana*) and little barley (*Hordeum pusillum*). These plants still make good food. Smith has shown me how to strip the seeds between thumb and forefinger; they can be cooked over a slow fire into a kind of hominy.

Smith and his ethnobotanicl colleagues can read remnants of seeds in fecal remains as Roman priests read the entrails of owls. Though their insights are only retrospective and might not earn them a place among conjurers, their retrospective contribution is sufficient to earn our thanks here, for they have instructed historians to overcome the sway of the maize cult. Until the ethnobotanists had done their work, there were still those who found it difficult to understand how people who paid little attention to corn as a crop managed to achieve prodigious architecture. To these maize cultists may be assigned responsibility for the canard that until the Indians took to corn, they could only have been hunter-gatherers like Stone Age Britons.

Though dumbfounded by the immense dimensions of the Hopewell geometrics, Americans of the nineteenth century were unable to credit much sophistication in agriculture to their builders. By classification as "hunter-gatherers" they remained equivalent to the neolithic people of Europe. And thus, by European analogy, their geometric architecture, including the parallel lines of their sacred ways, could be reduced to conveniences of a "water cult." To the deprecatory effect of the maize cult was added the weight of another means of diminishing the sophistication of the Ohio architect-astronomers. "Water cult" was intoned with the same inflection as the terms "heathen" and "primitive." Unlike *those* people, *we,* it was implied, do not have "cults"; *we* have religion.

Thus is a mystery reduced to a puzzle. An unfathomed religion, shriveled into a "cult," is deprived of its awful power. The early architecture of Ohio was and is so vast in its extent, so refractory to our intelligence and to our imagination, that it has been quite natural for our predecessors to give small names to large things.*

FISH AND BIRDS

If we must speak of cults, a fishing cult is a more likely explanation of large graded ways from streams to ceremonial centers than a water cult. But it, too, falls far short of what is needed to justify the immense labor required to create those geometric constructions linked by sacred ways to a floodplain. It is true that the streams of the Scioto basin, like the waters of the Sea of Galilee, are important sources of protein. Fishermen's trails still are formed along those streams every summer. But the most striking effigies associated with the Hopewell, as with their ideological cousins in Florida to whom we will allude more fully in a moment, are birds, not fish. When we recall what George Washington and Henry Brackenridge told us about sky-darkening flocks, we can only imagine the aviary of the Ohio Valley when its people were armed only with throwing spears, before the advent of bows and arrows. Birds and animals were in ample supply, and consumed in great numbers. Fishing was probably only another provider of protein.†

---

*Students of the American Gothic Revival have observed that during the 1840s, Americans relapsed into loyalties not of *place* but of *race*. They did not begin where they *were*, in America, among *its* antiquities. Instead, they ran the film of history backward, retreating in time and place to Olde England. They became retroactive Europeans.

Similarly, in 1902, the Reverend Stephen D. Peet, Ph.D., sought to understand the sacred ways of Ohio by recalling British theories about "ways" leading to Avebury, Stanton Drew, and Mount Murray. (The water cult is discussed in Peet, *The Mound Builders.*)

In fact, Americans know as much (and as little) about the religious ideas of ancient Americans as Britons do of ancient Britons—speculation may be harmless, but only when it does not get in the way of inquiry—as Thomas Jefferson pointed out in his discussion of the Marietta works.

†Stephen Williams has a great fondness for shrimp and crawfish as sources of protein. While my pacific nature has led me everywhere else to eschew repeating commentary from one

Fish were important in Ohio, especially shellfish, which were good to eat and also produced shells and pearls from which beautiful objects might be made. But exotic marine animals seem to have been especially important in their rituals. Ohio-produced chert blades have been found at Fort Center and in the Florida Panhandle, and, in Ohio, six species of marine shells, barracuda jaws, ocean turtle shells, shark and alligator teeth, some of which would only have been available from Atlantic coastal waters along the Florida peninsula.[21]

Economists have called all this evidence of "trade." Some are willing to add to that evidence indicia of a transfer of ideas from one locality to another, such as the equivalence in size of the Fairgrounds and Circleville circles with that of the circle cut into the earth at "Fort Center" near Lakeport, Florida, and the half-circle in Pinson, Tennessee. This is an advance in the right direction; let us go all the way. Due appreciation of the sophistication of Hopewellian art and architecture requires that we abandon the use of shriveling terms like "cult" and "trade," and progress through the half-world of ideas (such as equivalent circles and other geometric abstractions) toward the realm of myth. Myth can be sophisticated beyond the reach of science, and so I think it was in its power to link the concepts of life, death, birds, and the transmutation of elements in alchemy and in geomancy.

The term "geomancy" has traditionally been used narrowly by students of the use of divination to mean casting earth from the hand upon the ground, or by connecting dots made, ostensibly, at random. It describes just as well the casting of large amounts of earth upon the ground, and leaving it there in the form of monumental architecture, also for incantory reasons.* We will return to that through shortly, and to alchemy as well.

Let us first observe the persistence of bird symbolism in Florida and Ohio in Hopewell times, and of bird myths among peoples once called "primitive" around the globe as well as among those to whom that

---

scholar upon the work of another, I cannot resist passing along his marginal note placed upon this part of my manuscript:

I'm not a corn freak; but I still doubt that my old friend Bruce is really right. I think there's something else besides those . . . little seeds, not CORN, but a nice protein like freshwater shrimp! Hard to discover [their shells don't last— RK], I'll admit, but easier for me to believe than hominy of seeds! (October, 1993.)

*Any good Jungian would recognize the similarity of geomancy to throwing the *I Ching*, and know how archetypes would operate upon ostensibly random dots.

It is good to welcome another contribution to this discourse by William Romain, who brought into contemporary discussion a refreshed use of the word "geomancer," deploying it for the first time, so far as I know, to describe the creation of monumental architecture of earth. (See Romain's unpublished manuscript of January, 1994).

ascription may only be given by those very ignorant of spiritual subtlety.*

Consider, please, the mortuary platform at Fort Center, held aloft on wooden posts, and surrounded by wooden effigies of animals: several varieties of wildcats, an otter or two, perhaps, but the predominant figures are of birds: eagles, falcons, and marine birds of many kinds.

In Ohio, the sculpture was smaller and it was buried with the body in the earth (interment is not desirable in Florida, where the water table is just a few feet below the surface). Midwestern beaver, chipmunks, ducks, and other animals abundant in a woodland setting accompanied the departed—or, one might better say, the transitional. But, once again, birds predominate: owls, ducks, crows, and falcons especially, and those eerie "popeyed" birdstones which are found across the region lying just to the north of the Ohio Hopewell heartland. Birds appear in full three dimensional sculpture, in combinations as ornament on ceramics and upon copper breastplates.

These sculptured birds are most frequently found in association with passage from life to death, and, perhaps, the passage into life as well. These birds of passage faced those engaged in the ritual smoking of "effigy pipes." They looked into the eyes of the smoker, who inhaled

---

*Religion and diplomacy are always closely allied, but inquiry into prehistoric "terms of exchange" should not be polluted by importing into it the narrower meaning of "terms of trade" as that term is used by Adam Smith, Malcolm Forbes, or Milton Friedman. Nothing in the behavior of Americans before the Europeans arrived suggests that they thought of exchange as requiring a balance of giving and getting. In the earliest "trade" in the Chesapeake region and in New England, much misunderstanding arose between the English and the Indians because for the Indians the winner was the one who gave away the most. Even today, where old customs survive among the descendants of the first Americans, there are contests of munificence. Chiefs have been as proud of their capacity to give rich presents as medieval barons were proud of providing rich dowries.

All this talk of exchange should not conjure up images of fairgrounds in medieval Europe—places of trade for profit—emporia. Judging from what we have learned of the exchange practices among historic Indians when Europeans first came among them, we may deduce that objects given from one set of hands into another in the Fairgrounds Circle were offerings of objects carried great distances, and offered in the hope of receiving gifts in return.

Many thoughtful people even today classify gifts roughly in this order:

The richest of gifts is salvation.

The second greatest gift (ranking considerably behind salvation, as martyrs demonstrate) is survival. The survival of a whole people season after season is the work of priests who do what is necessary to propitiate the guardian of the cycles of growth.

Then, at a considerable distance behind salvation and survival, is the mild churchy delight in ceremony.

Next, and unlikely to have occurred at all within the sacred *temenos* of the Fairgrounds Circle, though with a host of celebrants since the Romantic Movement of the nineteenth century, there is aesthetic pleasure.

Only after all these do we settle for "presents." Objects of exchange. Trade goods.

the smoke through his or her mouth by way of a tube cut into the mouthpiece at the base. What was burned? We do not know. Tobacco is a relatively recent arrival in Ohio, but evidence of it has been found in Hopewell burials—strong tobacco, much stronger than the lighter varieties encouraged by the Europeans, so strong as to be a mild hallucinogen.

A religion that brings a believer to a heightened receptivity to the unconscious, and places that person in a rapt relationship to birds and to water animals, such as frogs and beaver, is a religion that might also create an architecture of animal forms. And so it did: "effigy mounds," shaped like the opossum measured by Romain at Granville, Ohio, the famous Serpent Mound in Peebles, Ohio, and vultures and eagles in Iowa and Wisconsin.

Effigies are very old in America, and not only in sculpture. The great structure upon which centered the nested circle forms at Poverty Point was, many think, in the form of a falcon. The Motley Mound, a mile or so to the north, had a similar configuration, and the falcon interpretation is reinforced by the etched falcons on Poverty Point amulets along with those potbellied owls.

What do we know about the meaning of birds in religious life?

Let us begin in the Middle East and Europe, where the dove is the symbol of the Holy Spirit. It delivers messages from one realm of being, "heaven" in common parlance, and another, the world of everyday life. Sometimes it brings the good news of the arrival of a new human into the world, which is, of course, an event marking the intrusion of the spirit into the flesh. In Greece, this event was symbolized by the visit of an amorous dove from the Gods; there is less explicit sexuality in Christian imagery, where the dove mediates and calls humans to attend to the fact that there is another world. Pindar wrote of "the passionate bird" by which the Gods made themselves known to humans. The dove is a Greek lover and a Christian ambassador.

Farther back in human history, the Egyptians included the mediatory and intercessory role of birds in their own version of the concept of the primordial world as an ocean. Birds, especially water birds, were as important to the Egyptians as to the Hopewell and to the people of Fort Center. Like those Indians holding to the Earth-Diver myth, like the peoples of Russia, Finland, Estonia, like the Polynesians and Indonesians, the Egyptians had a creation myth beginning with a visit to the primordial ocean by a bird which laid an egg on its surface from which the world developed.*

---

*Among the sophisticated Orphic cults, creation occurred when black-winged Night produced an egg out of which golden-winged Eros was born, and "the two halves of the shell became Heaven and Earth." (*An Encyclopedia of Archetypal Symbolism*, p., 84).

Many ceramic vessals used for ritual purposes in Native American, Cycladic, Minoan, and Helladic art take the forms of water birds. Some also represent the bird as carrying a large egg in its body.

Whatever else birds may be, they mediate between the earth and sky, as alchemy operated at the intersection of the tangible and the intangible. Its foremost modern student, Edward Edinger, described its operations in this way:

> The transformation of a solid into a gas, representing the process of gaining objectivity, detachment, breadth of vision, and freedom, is symbolized by the bird that flies high in the sky. . . . The opposite procedure . . . is . . . taking whatever is in a gaslike state and transforming it into solid matter. A back-and-forth movement between these two processes, the fluctuation between spiritualization and incarnation, is set in motion. Both processes are evident in the myths, as they are fundamental in human experience. . . . Ascending birds represent . . . translation from the temporal to the eternal, so descending birds represent contents from the archetypal world that are incarnating by breaking into the personal ego realm.[22]

There is a good deal to chew upon in that paragraph, including the possibility that for the Hopewell as for the alchemists birds had a mediating role between the living and the dead, between the spirit of life and the shroud of flesh. Mortuary practice among the Hopewell and probably among the Fort Center people induced flesh to fall from the bones of the dead, either by exposure on platforms or by actual charnel activity, before the bones were interred. Within the northern earth and beneath the waters in Florida, the alchemists' *circulatio* completed itself, as described in the ancient *Emerald Tablet of Hermes:*

> It ascends from the earth to the heavens, and descends again to the earth, and receives the power of the above and below. Thus you will have the glory of the whole world.[23]

Those who came into the Hopewellian sacred spaces had been prepared for them, it is likely, by smoking from effigy pipes carrying effigies of birds. Some had passed through the confined space of the Great Hopewell road, accompanied by flutes and drums and incantations for fifty miles, pausing for preliminary propitiation in the *herradura*. Judging from the formation of the gateways to the largest enclosures, they would arrive at a ceremonial center where entry was permitted *only* after being escorted around a final obstruction, a platform mound high enough to obstruct too easy a view of the space beyond. Then, and only then, might they be ushered into the main space to make a presentation.

It is probable that most people who came there were local, that is to say that they came from the Ohio watershed or from Illinois. A few, however, might have accompanied to this destination the articles presented, all the way from their origin. Were there not among them grizzly-bear hunters or obsidian collectors from Wyoming, fishermen from Florida, or nugget-collecting entrepreneurs from the copper region of upper Michigan?*

Even today, even we, our sight and hearing made indiscriminate by too much trash and thrash and din, our symbolic sense deadened by incessant profanation, even *we* may feel the power of the Ohioans' holy places. These immense husks from which the faith has gone may be only the carapaces of a departed mystery, yet we may still feel the life which was there, the same tremor we experience in places closer to our own tradition, at Pecos or Tumacacori or within the gutted shell of the abbey church of Cluny.

TEMPLES AND FORTS

The Hopewellian rectilinear revolution was a great event in American architectural history, recapitulated in parody, and therefore trivialized, by the squaring of Circleville. In the first four centuries of our era, circles were squared and then quartered, sometimes through the intermediation of octagons.

The squaring began to occur about A.D. 150; I do not know of any rectangular embankments created before that date, though there may be some. Thereafter, squares and rectangles began to appear frequently in the plan (the "footprint") of mounds, as seen from above or on maps. Rectilinearization became obvious, as well, on the ground. Mounds had been rounded like haystacks, or like natural hills.† The Adena had made them pointed as cones. Now they were platforms, sliced across the sky in severely horizontal, linear embankments, or even more arbitrarily truncated as flat-topped pyramids.

The precise relationship between the Adena conebuilders and the Hopewellian geometers is an enigma, but to me it is arresting to observe how often the latter built their monuments close to those of the former, integrating their predecessors' work into the grand schemes of

---

*I have been urged by one friendly archaeologist to avoid any suggestion that evidence has been found that a specific hunter or collector from any of these places went to Ohio, 1,500 years ago. Contrariwise, another, equally friendly, urges that we not be overemphatic that a "trader" from Ohio did *not* go to the sources. Because they are both friendly, we cite neither.

†Architects oddly call this unelevated view "the elevation" of a building.

their own devising. This was true at Chillicothe, where the Hopewell structures at Dunlap and Ginther were placed on the same north-south axis as the Adena Mound. Adena conical mounds were also brought into Hopewell schemes at Marietta and Portsmouth, by rectangles and lengthy parallels.

Was this deference, or triumphal gloating? I prefer to think it the former, and that we will find one day evidence of simultaneous ceremonial use of Adena and Hopewell earthworks.

My preference for reconciliation no doubt works its way into the following speculations about the import of the chronological discoveries of the first three years of the 1990s. For nearly fifty years, archaeologists have held to a time-scheme placing the Adena first, the Hopewell next, and a third people called "Fort Ancient" next, roughly from the sixth to the tenth centuries, following a decline of the Hopewell and preceding the rising to a Mississippian climax. Fort Ancient is a large hilltop enclosure twenty miles or so southwest of the Paint Creek enclosures of the Hopewell.

Some reference was made to this chronology in my discussion of the Utz and Old Fort sites along the route of Lewis and Clark and of the "forts" of Kentucky and Tennessee. We come now to a fuller statement of the reasons stated then for revising the traditional dating of these places by pushing them back in time by five hundred years or more. The archaeology of the early 1990s has forced such a revision for their Ohio equivalents, including Fort Ancient itself, and thereby has suggested a new scenario for their creation in the first place.

It now seems probable that at least the Ohio buildings were not such latecomers, but were, instead, created during the Adena/Hopewell period. This would be true of the eponymous Fort Ancient, of all the other structures along the Miami River that were its contemporaries, such as Miami Fort, Fosters, and the Pollock Works, and also of Fort Hill and Spruce Hill, which look down upon the geometric earth works of Pain Creek and Chillicothe.[24]

The story of their construction seems to be this: they were started about the time of Christ, serving only ceremonial purposes. They were at first separated from the other hilltops on the ridges on which they were placed *only* by a wall of earth and stone, with an opening. Though the sides were not defended, nor was the wall itself fortified, these walls were not casually built. The intention, laboriously executed, was to set them aside from mundane life. Limestone slabs were laid on the *interior* slope at Miami Fort; the walls at Fort Hill and Spruce Hill were of quarried sandstone; at another site called Foster's "fieldnotes and photographs suggest that at least at some points there was a double core of stone within the wall;" stone was used at Fort Ancient for exterior facing, interior buttressing and for the spine of the earthen wall; at Pollock stone pavements led through the gateway and stone was used to face the entry embankments.[25]

Later, palisades of logs were placed on top of these walls, and the hilltops were surrounded in vulnerable places, even along bluff lines, with more walls and palisades. These were composed of vertical timbers, set in holes in the ground and chinked upright with stones. The lower portions of these stockades, past shoulder height, were plastered with mud over a "framework of branches interwoven across the vertical posts."[26]

Robert Riordan, who discovered much of this evidence in recent years, suggests that the first "simple wall" was placed athwart the access to the sacred space as a "formal enclosing of the plateau . . . setting it off as special, sacred, perhaps tabu. It did not establish a fortified position." Within this *temenos,* "a great deal of food preparation and consumption went on . . . , and the construction of linear and circular stone pavements and stone mounds there may suggest ritual activity."[27]

They suggest to me Hopewell, sky-watching ritual activity. The distinction between Adena and Hopewell practices may someday fade away utterly, but enough vitality remains in it to suggest a scenario based upon Riordan's findings. He goes this far: "the hilltop enclosures were places where activities were conducted that were complimentary to, but different from, those conducted at the geometric riverine enclosures" of the Hopewell.[28]

The alteration of these ritual enclosures into fortified positions occurred "late in the second century A.D. . . . [when those who had gathered there] suddenly felt the need to build a 4 m-high stockade. . . . They went to a great deal of trouble to fell, haul, trim and erect the timbers . . . to cut and collect much more wood to weave horizontally through the uprights, to haul thousands of kilograms of rock up from the creek to chink posts and to face the stockade, and to plaster at least 2 meters of its height with mud."[29]

Then something stranger still occurred. The stockades were toppled, to lie in place, burnt, and thereafter a new wall of earth was ceremoniously placed across them.

> Destruction of the stockade and construction of the embankment had to be concerted acts because the burned timbers lie essentially undisturbed beneath the wall. This action was surely taken by the people who used the enclosure, and not the work of a raiding party. It stretches the imagination to think of raiders who would burn a stockade during an attack and then also stop to cover it with almost a meter of earth![30]

Burning of structures was a part of the Adena/Hopewell tradition. Their charnel houses and ceremonial structures were liturgically burnt before they were mounded over, sometimes in succession as multiple-layered mounds were built. It is my guess that the destruction of these fortified ritual places, which occurred at roughly the time when all major Adena construction came to an end, was a respectful closure of a period in American Indian history.

The sequence of events might have been this: the traditional Adena continued to build their conical mounds and to bury their dead in the old way, with the old ceremonies, while the Hopewell astronomer-priests conducted their research on the hilltops and began construction of their geometric architecture on the plains below. That architecture was a commemoration of their conclusions, showing their increasing sway among the populace. Then, at some time in the second century, the priests of the old believers resisted, perhaps violently, and sent the Hopewellians back to the hills. This eruption may not have been very violent; these were not violent people; the only archaeological record of mass burials or of fractured skeletons is at Fort Ancient itself, where "human remains were found haphazardly buried in a mass within an enclosure near a 'gateway.'"[31]

Whatever the urgency may have been, the Hopewell astronomer-priests thought it prudent to fortify their hilltop enclosures where they had, all along, been conducting their observations of the moon and sun. When the Adena elders died out and their surviving followers dispersed, the Hopewell waited until a fitting time had passed, restored the hilltop sanctuaries to their form before the time of anxiety, and gave ceremonial interment to the evidence of its passage.

The presence of burials of the Adena type along the East Coast, probably dating later than the hilltop events just recounted, has suggested to some archaeologiests the work of Adena refugees: "our best evidence for Adena in the East come from the shores of Chesapeake Bay in Maryland and on the Delmarva Peninsula of Delaware." Perhaps they went over the Appalachians through the passes explored by George Washington from the opposite direction a millenium and a half later. Others may have escaped southward along their traditional trade route to Florida as far as northern Alabama, "to found the Copena culture."[32]

GEOMANCY, POLITICS, THOMAS JEFFERSON AND LOUIS SULLIVAN

We will follow them southward in a moment, but first let us reconsider William Romain's idea of Hopewell geomancers in the context of these speculations about the politics of the second century. With a zealousness that would, I think, have delighted Jefferson, Romain has worked out many interlocking relationships among the octagons, circles, and squares of the Hopewell period. He has discovered that the great square which so astounded the Cincinnati at Marietta could precisely contain four of the smaller circles, equal in size to each other, to be found along Paint Creek, and, also, four of the smaller squares to be found, also equal in size to each other, in the same complexes along Pain Creek. Might there not have been a political story in this quartering and circling on the plain, perhaps arising from the turmoil on the heights? The master square at Marietta might have been created first, and the square and circular ceremonial centers afterward, to denote their status as colonies. Or the Paint Creek figures might have already constituted a group of clan-marked towns, and the Mariettans might have denoted a triumphant sway over these clans by enclosing the dimensions of the Paint Creek squares and circles, seven hundred and fifty feet across, in their own one thousand five hundred foot square.

It is not required of these deliberate earth forms that they recover for us the lost politics of the Adena and Hopewell. We may already have asked too much of them. If a Hopewell person were present he or she would already have told us that this line of questioning implies a kind of geomantic imperialism better to be expected of Aztecs or Incas or Romans than of the Ohio Valley people. What justification is there to suggest that the Hopewell sought dominance over their neighbors, using architecture as propaganda? So let us leave this line of inquiry and return to the forms of the architecture itself.

That return was made easier for me as I took the final version of this chapter for editing to the coast of the Gulf of Mexico in February 1994. One day we made a pilgrimage to Ocean Springs, Mississippi, to visit three cottages amid great live oaks and magnolias, set back from a sandy beach, designed and built in the 1890s by Louis Sullivan. Sullivan was a great man, called "the master" by Frank Lloyd Wright. Like Thomas Jefferson and the Hopewell, Sullivan was much interested in octagons as mediating forms between circles and squares.

Anyone with any interest in the workings of genius would find equally engrossing the sketches in which Jefferson and Sullivan worked on this problem, though the latter was trained in nineteenth century ornamental practice and the former was not. As a result, when Sullivan developed the theme in the early 1920s, under the guise of *A Grammar of Ornament*, he integrated natural, leafy forms within the requirements of geometry, using grids of hexagons and octagons as trellises for efflorescence, as if branches had been pruned early in the spring, bent to accommodate the human intellect, and then left to flower. Jefferson's cadenzas were simpler and unbotanical, constrained within the justifications of T square and compass.

Both Sullivan and Jefferson, however, showed in their work the impact of exercises in the same forms by the Hopewell. We have observed the integration by Jefferson of information about those forms sent him by the explorers of the Ohio Valley. Sullivan came to the same terrain in 1915, and learned quite by accident about earthforms of circles, squares, and octagons. He was commissioned to design and direct the construction of a small bank (now an ice cream store) in Newark, Ohio, a little more than a mile from the Fairground Circle. It is said in the town that Sullivan made it his habit in the early evening to walk out Main Street from his construction site, and into that circle. Even in its derelict and desecrated condition, it was still capable of inducing that state of mind reported by Squier and Davis in the 1840s.

Sullivan brooded upon this experience, and upon the other geometric earthworks he visited in the neighborhood, and the results appeared in his cadenzas in *The Grammar of Ornament*, to which he affixed this caption:

> These simple forms of ancient discovery and use were given esoteric meaning and occult powers by the men of that day, in an effort to control, by means of formulas and secret ritual, the destiny of Man amidst the powers of NATURE.[33]

A propensity for these forms was already present in Sullivan's psyche, as it was for Jefferson. A quarter century before he was presented with evidence that he had been preceded in his interest by the Ohio Indians, Sullivan had let his octagonal fancies play on the seashore at Ocean Springs, while his great brick-slab skyscrapers were underway in Chicago and St. Louis. The cottages rotate about octagons as rapturously as Jefferson's buildings of brick and earth at Poplar Forest. Sullivan's own cottage is a shingled octagon, with the two interior rooms and the porch fitted into its cabalistic requirements with an ingenuity as great as that required by the identically shaped but larger container created by Jefferson. The larger cottage at Ocean Springs, built for a client, next door, culminates in an octagonal dining room, around which the rest of the house splays, as if the eight-sided room were the fixed crystalline form and the rest merely a gaggle of appurtenances.*

---

*It is a pleasure to note that while the Sullivan cottage has acquired a wing at the back, and has been treated to some refacing to its fireplaces, its essentials are as he left them, and the family that acquired it in 1993 know what they have and will care for it properly. Fortunate people with an interest in American genius can stay in a bed-and-breakfast cottage behind this small masterpiece. The Villa Capra Rotunda and the Parthenon do not provide such conveniences. Neither, so far, do the people of Owatonna, Minnesota, who possess America's Parthenon, the Merchant's Bank, also by Sullivan.

A day or so before we had come to Ocean Springs, we were nearby, at Fort Walton, Florida, visiting a small museum built to explain the presence of one remaining platform mound of a complex the rest of which has been flattened, asphalted, and desecrated by the disposable architecture of fast-food chains and a cacaphony of highways. Within the museum is a fine small exhibit devoted to the work of the people whose mounds these were, who lived and built in the area from Hopewell times until the middle of the eighteenth century, and had been engaged in exchange of materials—and, one assumes, ideas—with the Hopewell. The chief prizes of the museum are a few examples of the idiosyncratic pottery vessels of this area, flat ceramics shaped like platters, obviously intended for ritual use, and hexagonal in shape.*

So far as I know, these hexagonal ceramics do not occur elsewhere; they seem to be an expression of a peculiar need on the part of people living along the shores of the Gulf of Mexico who had been in regular communication with the octagon builders of Ohio. It is unfortunate that Jefferson never knew of the Fort Walton people, for it is likely that the Indian Hall of Monticello would have been filled with their hexagons. While he was assembling his collection, there must have been many more of these eerie artifacts lying beneath the Florida earth. Only in the 1960s and 1970s did the imperatives of a hasty and hamburger-consuming public eliminate the possibilities of finding them.

Like the Fort Walton people, like Sullivan and Jefferson, the Hopewell may have felt the powers of octagons or hexagons, which are not quite circles and not quite squares. These figures are thus capable of geomantic reconciliation, when made of earth either into architecture or into ceramics. There is a large difference in the persuasive potency of these two uses of earth. Hexagonal platters, being smaller, are more subtle than octagons a quarter of a mile across. But, on the other hand, the vast Newark and Scioto octagons are much more difficult to apprehend than is a ceramic vessal that may be held in one's hands. So the early Americans who built these enormous arrangements of earth saw

---

*In Florida, the contemporaries of the Hopewell are associated with what is there called the Deptford period, with some overlappage into the Weeden Island period. The Fort Walton truncated pyramid may have been commenced as early as 400 or 500 by either of these cultures, and was probably occupied continuously until it was abandoned in the eighteenth century by a group called locally the Fort Walton people, contemporary with the Cahokians of the Mississippian efflorescence, who had lived there from 1300 onward.

The hexagonal platter to which I refer has been dated later than the Hopewell period, but Yulee W. Lazarus, who completed most of the significant archaeology in the area, informed me that she had seen another hexagonal vessel in Vernon, Florida, which bore the characteristic ornament of the Weeden Island people, and was therefore quite close in date to the Hopewellians of Ohio. She saw it in the home of a collector in Vernon, Florida, some years ago; it, too, had the hexagonal shape of the later Fort Walton ceramics. Ms. Lazarus and I discussed the matter by telephone on February 18, 1994.

to it that the people they wished to influence were choreographed through octagonal arrangements of earth only after proper introduction, chemically and architecturally. By such means, emotion can be focused in the service of ideas.*

THE ARCHITECTURE OF THE SKY

Let us follow Louis Sullivan's lead another step toward participating in those ideas about "man amidst the powers of nature." Why were those "formulas and secret ritual" used by the shamanic engineers of Ohio? I believe they meant to link earth and sky, agriculture and astronomy, in a celebration of life. Like the Pythagoreans, these geomancers of an American brotherhood (and sisterhood?) persuaded their fellow Hopewellians over several centuries to build these and many other interlocked celebrations of a new knowledge. Their revolution in thought was made tangible in architecture glorifying growth and order, and, through the sacred ways, connecting production with celebration. The discovery of order was part of their discovery of how to produce food regularly by attending to the recurring cycles of the sun and moon.

The seasons of agriculture are regular and synchronous with the equally regular motions of the moon and sun. Knowing this, farmers have always paid reverent attention to the imperatives of the sky, for the regularity of the heavens steadies and assures an anxious farmer. Perhaps one of the reasons for a farmer's anxiety is that he knows how bold is his action in ripping up the earth. I offered earlier the suggestion that this tearing was propitiated in Hopewell architecture, in the

---

*If this seems strange to us, we need only recall the professed intentions of the Pythagorean brotherhood that created Chartres and other Gothic cathedrals. They, too, used space to move people, with the intention that while being moved they would feel and think, and, like the visitors to Hopewell earthworks, inhale scented smoke. Incense is to Christians what tobacco was to Americans.

To space, the Gothicists added light, having available in their ministrations painted glass. The Hopewell did not have manufactured glass, though they may have worked at obsidian, a natural glass, so intently because they, too, understood the association of light and feeling. A closer analogue to Hopewellian geomancy through the deployment of large solid masses of earth and stone is that of the ancient Egyptians. We know something of what they intended because we know something of their writing. There is no reason to deny the possibility of similar intentions on the part of the Hopewell geomancers.

There was at one stage of this manuscript a detour into Neoplatonic theory, but it has been abandoned in the interest of frugality. The theorists I had in mind are those of the second quarter of the twelfth century, especially Thierry of Chartres, though Otto von Simson suggests we could have started with Johannes Scotus Erigena, or even Abelard—see von Simson, *The Gothic Cathedral*, pp. 25 ff.

sacred earth principle. Now we may have come upon a second mode of propitiation, by offering the justification of the skies for what was done to the earth.

Here is a second paradox to set beside the first. Not only may a violation of the earth be justified by offering earth back to earth, but now we see that a participation in the ordering of the universe may be recorded in an apparently divisive and exclusionary architecture. This is the architecture of rectangles and squares, moderated only by octagons—all requiring distinctions and exclusion. They divide the world into categories, an abrupt though not necessarily a prideful act. It may be, at the outset at least, a respectful or even worshipful recognition of natural patterns—"forms," "ideals," or archetypes—which may guide the behavior of heavenly or human bodies or both.

This may all seem a little abstract. It may be rendered somewhat more accessible (practical, some might say) by walking a line on the ground drawn between the Observatory Mound at Newark impaled by the edge of the Observatory Circle and the southwestern edge of the Fairgrounds Circle. This line is obvious every 18.61 years to anyone standing upon the Observatory Mound, for it extends to the moon as it is seen to set just at that edge of the Fairgrounds Circle. It would be at the southernmost point its setting had ever reached, and would ever reach. A person on the Observatory Mound watching the sky would have noted its presence there precisely 18.61 years earlier, and 18.61 years before that. If these people reported their 18.61-year observations to each other often enough, someone at the end of a few centuries might utter a delighted yelp of recognition. Here was a pattern, matching the preceding marvel that seeds planted would sprout later in the spring.

During the same sidereal month (comprised of twenty-seven and one-third days), our observatory watcher or his friends might have seen the moon achieve its extreme *northernmost* rising, at a point on the horizon to be noted *either* by looking through the parallel earthworks connecting the Observatory Circle to the octagon and directly across the axis of the octagon to its farthermost side, *or* by making the trip to the Fairgrounds Circle and stepping precisely to the midpoint of its entrance and gazing along the axis of the avenue leading toward the Newark square.[34]

Good modern astronomers would expect the Hopewellians to add two more points on the eastern horizon, where the moon records the limits of its narrowest monthly band of risings. During its 18.61-year cycle, the lunar broom sweeps across the sky from this narrow band out to a broad swath to reach the extreme points we have seen. Then it slowly constricts again to the two risings of severest constraint. A crabbed celestial housekeeping thus becomes steadily more ambitious until it seems to stand abashed at its affrontery and begins to retreat to a period in which a lick and a promise will do. Then the increase of ambition sets in once more.

All these eastern four points, with the lines required to reach them, were neatly marked on the earth by the Newark earthworks. Furthermore, as any attentive reader will have anticipated, four other lines, reaching toward four other points, were marked as well. The moon sets in the west as it rises in the east; on the western horizon there are four points matching the eastern four. Lines can be drawn to them as well. These eight lines can be found in the octagon at Newark.[35]

Engineers have discerned in recent years what was known to the engineers of Hopewell times: that there are grids of straight lines upon which their earthen figures are laid, lines invisible but real, leading to the horizon, to be discerned by repeated and patient observation of the heavens, and then traced upon the ground. When that is done, if one desires to be in harmony with the passages of the moon, one might do what the Hopewell did: place earthworks upon those invisible templates.

There is order in the universe. Answering to the cycles of the moon, tides rise and fall, on the Great Lakes as well as on the high seas. Women's bodies answer to that cycle, and so do those of men, though less perceptibly. Farmers today, as in Hopewell times, notice such things. Monthly cycles are convenient punctuations for their planting and reaping. Monthly cycles stipulate the times for breeding. Though the moon does not aid in photosynthesis, it determines the monthly cycles of agriculture as the sun determines both the daily and the annual.

Modern city people may think of the moon as merely picturesque, reduced to a convenience for rhyming songwriters. But country people know better. Even when council fires brought citizens to turn to each other rather than to the moon for guidance, nothing humans could suggest could countermand what could be observed from Observatory Mound. In ancient America, the distant, uninsistent moon was never out of sight and mind for very long.

Having discerned the regularity of the moon's passages, having built architecture to bring themselves into harmony with those passages, the Hopewell connected that architecture across vast stretches of terrain. The Great Hopewell Road did this for the average, literal minded, unenlightened pilgrim, while the more subtle connections were intellectual. The main axis of the *Newark* circle and octagon lies exactly along the same compass bearing as the two parallel embankments leading from the Scioto to the *Hopeton* works fifty miles away. These *Hopeton* lines, which some Hopewell geometer must have drawn on the earth for others to fill out with architecture, are set precisely at right angles to the axis of the compound figure at *Highbanks,* which lies on the

Scioto about a mile from Hopeton. Adept archeoastronomers of our own day have demonstrated that the reach of these systems extended throughout the Hopewell sphere in Ohio and Kentucky.*

Science quails at the possibility that all these monuments coincided so exactly by accident. It is surpassingly likely that they came from astronomical observations over many decades, centering about A.D. 200, that were communicated perhaps through the pilgrimage process suggested by the architecture itself.

Judging from their architecture, the Hopewell were capable not only of the astronomy necessary to observe and record, but also of the engineering to memorialize their conclusions.

We, with our consummate technological prowess, had to await the arrival of the digital computer to comprehend what they observed and what they did, and to correlate the two. They worked in four dimensions. They knew how far *across* their buildings should be, how far *up* and *down*. They also knew how *deep,* how to make a plane into an object, having dealt with its extent and what we call its elevation. And then, to confound us, they made all this consonant with *duration*—with an 18.61 year cycle. To size and place they added time.

Primitive?

Consider once again their achievement, not merely in one complex of figures but in connecting several sets. Every 18.6 years, an informed observed looking toward the Hopeton works from the Scioto between its parallel embankments would see the moon rise at its northernmost pausepoint at the same moment that rise would be noted by another observer looking toward the square from the entrance of the Fairgrounds Circle, along its embankments, by a third observer upon the Observatory Mound looking along the axis of the Newark golf course circle and octagon, and a fourth at Highbanks who turned exactly 90 degrees from the axis of its complex.

Not every schoolchild in Newark or Chillicothe today would know

---

*In 1976, David Brose pointed out that looking along the alignment of these Hopeton northeasterly inclining walls was, in A.D. 200, "within 2 minutes of the 18.6 year lunar cycle's northernmost rise" or pause-point (see Brose p. 64).

This corresponds to the orientation of the main axis of the Newark octagon and circle complex found by Hively and Horn, at Newark. (See Hively and Horn.)

William Romain has amplified the work of these earlier observers to bring into the system lunar alignments at Piketon, Circleville, "Opossum" (the effigy at Granville), Cedar Bank, Dunlap, Seip, Portsmouth, Shriver, Milford, and Frankfort. He has found *both* lunar and solar alignments at Mound City, Hopewell, Turner, Marietta, "Junction Group," Bull, Highbanks, and Works East. As his hypotheses are checked, it would be interesting to see if the solar and lunar sites are not found to have been built *later* than those with purely lunar alignments, *or* that the solar orientations may as readily be explained purely in lunar terms. Romain also offers evidence that the Hopewell also aligned their mortuary establishments to lunar alignments. (See his titles listed by subject in bibliography.)

how to make the calculations necessary to make such observations. But the arithmetic was sufficiently well understood by the Hopewell to induce the loading of hundreds of thousands of baskets full of earth and the placement of that earth in carefully determined, geomantic positions. Some of this work was being done when shepherds, tending their sheep in Palestine, saw a great star, and followed it to Bethlehem. In Ohio, by the time Jesus was born, farmers were thoroughly accustomed to watching the heavens for signs.[36]

Before we descend to the sociology and economy of all this, let us give a final paragraph to the symbolism of birds. Among the Egyptians, and perhaps among the Hopewell, birds are moon symbols. We are solemnly assured by the *Encyclopedia of Archetypal Symbolism* that the gait of the ibis suggested "the movement of the moon to some classical authors. Plutarch has written that the alternating black and white feathers of the male ibis are reminiscent of the dark and light phases of the moon." However that may be, the Egyptian God Thoth was perceived in the form of an ibis.

> Like him, the bird is connected with the moon . . . [and] in addition to being the moon god, was the god of wisdom who maintained the cosmic order. . . . The law that governs the regularity of the heavens is understood to be the nourishing matrix of both the sun's power and the goodness of life [agriculture] that depends thereon.[37]

So after, all, a bird, flying between earth and heaven, also presides over a synthesis of myths. It is an intermediary between life and death and also a creator of life, for it participates in the work of the moon to govern the consistent motions of the sun and thus to nourish agriculture. Of course water birds might merely be important to the people of Fort Center and to the Hopewell because their flights northward in the spring signaled the resumption of plowing and presaged planting. But I think there was more to it than that. Now, on to the economy of the mounds.

THE PROTO-JEFFERSONIANS

Though many people in the circle-building stage of human history lived in small household units, spread widely throughout river valleys, very few outside the Indus Valley matched the architectural achievements of the Adena. Fewer still built anything comparable to the geometric wonders of the Hopewell. We have offered some thoughts about why these Ohioans moved millions of baskets of earth in accordance with meticulous plans, sustaining that effort over extended peri-

ods, and why, though apparently loosely organized, they buried some
of their number amid sheets of pearly and mica, with copper face
masks, surrounded by beautiful works of sculpture.

Works of architecture, great in size, precision, and complexity, were
planned and built, and the clear implication is that this occurred under
the direction of a priesthood of astronomer-engineer-architects. That
conclusion does not, however, imply as well that there was a hereditary
hierarchy. People may gather to support priests in building a church,
but that does not mean that they will submit a political theocracy.*
Perhaps the geomancers selected to lead the creation of architecture did
only that, and were chosen from a larger number from time to time, as
the monks at Cluny, Premontre, and under the rule of St. Benedict select their abbots, and as most Buddhist monks select their lamas to lead
for a time and then return to the ranks, having only earned burial amid
rich celebration of their achievements.

Public architecture according to complex plans is not often achieved
by societies in which the residential pattern is scattered and there are
few distinctions of caste. But let our Jeffersonian preferences lead us
for a moment to consider how pleasant it would have been for Jefferson had he an opportunity to become acquainted with the data un-
earthed in the 1970s and 1980s about the social structure of the
Adena/Hopewell. Bruce Smith tells us that:

> Ohio . . . populations were distributed across the landscape in small set-
> tlements. . . . [They inhabited] agricultural communities consisting of
> individual single family farmsteads scattered along river valley seg-
> ments.[38]

They were capable, it appears, of mighty exertions in a common
purpose, and of architecture having that quality of pertinacity which
Jefferson so passionately desired for his young republic.

Here were no dull, drilled, and doltish peasantry, laboring under the
lash. Instead, we may imagine them as America's first free and independent yeomen, living on their own modest farms, striding the forest

---

*Some might see in this a transition from a female- oriented society to a male-dominant one.
I am not ready to move so rapidly, preferring to defer that transition until a time when
elaborate burials were only of men. I cannot secure from archaeologists assurances that
rectilinearizing was coincident either with the arrival of a new physiological type ("Hopewell" people different from "Adena" people) or with the elimination of females from ceremonial interment.

It would be handy if one could turn to squares for men and circles for women, but it does
not seem to work. It certainly does not in the Southwest, where the use of circular kivas
(sometimes described as "womb chambers" by women writers) in many places seem to have
been permitted only to men.

and prairie after game, neither drawn to bright city lights nor abasing themselves to a primogenitrous, entailed local gentry.

DECLINE AND FALL?

Two interlocked quandaries are presented to us by the behavior of our second and third century predecessors in the Valley. They exchanged goods and services in ways that are inexplicable according to capitalist or Marxist rules, and they lived dispersed while assembling to create large, planned projects over long periods of time.

These quandaries are deepened by the combination, in their architecture, of qualities which in Europe might be in conflict, as representing an age of reason and an age of faith. Their cerebral, geometric, one might say "classical" or renaissance engineering appeared to be motivated by desire to bring their buildings into harmony with nature—with the passages of the sun and moon. Their architectural *forms* implied a search for order in continuous and predictable patterns. Each structure's *orientation*—its placement vis-à-vis the earth and sky—might seem to arise from a deferential spirit, were it not itself grounded in science. Strict shapes and sizes were arranged in accordance with celestial lines. The eighteen-and-a-half-year lunar cycle, the twenty-eight-day monthly cycle, the cycles of the sun and seasons, all observed over many decades, were discerned to have patterns, too—patterns affirmed by the architecture.

Now—why did they *stop* building these works? Some writers, following Joseph Smith, still seek military explanations. Violence is the favorite solvent for the lumps of history.* Was there a Fall of the Hopewell Geometers? Did Lamanite "barbarians" come upon the scene? Archaeologists have looked, so far in vain, for evidence of environmental disaster, for epidemic, or for many mass burials of shattered skeletons which might show military outcomes. But there are few signs of mass destruction, no great battles nor pogroms. It may not be necessary to find such severe shocks as these. Even a mild dislocation might be enough to crack open a fragile system of largely voluntary associations. A row of poor harvests, or early winters, or wet falls might cause people to lose faith. There might have been marginal but malignant environmental change, a drying period, for example, which could have made the growing of crops more difficult along the Scioto.

---

*There is the belief, ineradicable it seems, that there was, at a certain date, an event called the Fall of Rome, with Vandals or Huns or Ostrogoths raping and pillaging and the Baths of Caracalla collapsing in an avalanche of classical masonry before our eyes. But the end of Rome was a slow, inconstant, erratic decline full of false hopes and partial disasters.

People living on more marginal terrain might have been driven to attempt sporadic raids upon the food stores from the floodplain farms by which the geometers had supplemented the diet of the people.

If somehow these proud yet deferential geometers disappointed their people, we can imagine a bleak scene of despair and affliction, in which diseases become more virulent among those whose nutrition had already suffered. And possibly there was an incursion of exotic microbes.*

Thirty years ago, some archaeologists, remembering Aryan invasions and Teutonic *Volkswanderungen* or influenced by Mormon theology, suggested that the Hopewell were a separate race from the Adena, and that their invasion from the west was recompensed by a later retributory invasion of Algonquians, driving a great wedge into the Ohio Valley from the north or east. Thus they explained the division of the Iroquoians in the Hopewellian neighborhood in New York from the Iroquoian-speaking Cherokee, living in the Appalachians. Those of us with Cherokee blood in our families find this theory delightful; it would give us Hopewell relatives. The Iroquois, too, might be gratified, but, sad to admit, no archaeological evidence has appeared in its support.

Such great movements of peoples may not, in fact, have been necessary to bring down, or wind down, the Hopewell. It may have been enough that faith was shaken, authority brought into disrepute, and great collective exertions requiring both faith and subordination were abandoned. The dispirited may simply have gone their own way as the society decomposed. People seem to have coarsened in their habits, reducing their expectations to accommodate greater likelihoods of disappointment—as did contemporary communities from Paris to the Adriatic, and across North Africa.

The center did not hold, but on the periphery, especially in Illinois where geometric complexes had never been attempted, life seems to have gone on without dramatic changes—as it went on in many portions of the Roman Empire long after the "Fall" solemnized in the roast-beef prose of Edward Gibbon. Or, as we savor fine English counterparts, we might turn to Mallory, but we need not imagine an Amer-

---

*Though the skeletal remains do not show evidence of plague, disease may have reduced the population enough as to eliminate the possibility of common work, always a difficult task to organize even in fervent and effulgent times.

From whence might disease come? Possibly from a mutation of Western Hemisphere microbes into greater virulence, afflicting only the architectural work force. Diseases certainly arrived along with the Scandinavians in the eleventh century, and may have wiped out some of the scattered bands of hunters and fishers they encountered, but, probably because the victims *were* so scattered, those Viking epidemics did not spread very widely.

ican Camelot. In King Arthur's time, after the Roman legions withdrew from Britain, across the Atlantic in the Mississippi Valley people
went on living, making pottery and making love, hunting and farming.
But the geometers had laid down their instruments. Construction of
complexes of octagons, circles, and squares ceased. In the Southwest
geometric forms—rectangular plazas and ball courts, D-shaped blocks
of rectangular rooms, and circular kivas—were still constructed. And
on the Gulf Coast platform mounds were still laid up by people now
isolated from their midwestern partners.

Then, after the ninth century, in the Mississippi Valley, there occurred the second stage in the rectilinear revolution, in which there was
an intensified corn culture creating rectilinear plazas and platforms;
people fought and hunted with bows and arrows; I think there was also
a more assertive masculine principal amid these corn-based, rectilinear,
plaza-and-pyramid cultures. By the time the first European historians
came among them, they were almost entirely chiefdoms. Though, as
we have seen, platform mounds, as discrete units, were built by the
Hopewell and their contemporaries in Tennessee, Florida, and the
Delta, these mounds stood either alone or within other figures. Only
after four centuries had passed were truncated pyramids deployed in
the Ohio or Mississippi valleys to bound rectilinear plazas, and then in
connection with an entirely different kind of society, now with the discernable hierarchy of platforms we have observed at Cahokia. These
rectangles bounded by rectangles (that is how rectilinear platform
mounds around a rectilinear plaza appear in plan) announced the completion of the rectilinear revolution.

Thereafter, people remained much longer in the same place, raising
corn, aggregating to build platform-and-plaza complexes such as
Cahokia, St. Louis, and Moundville—sedentary and almost urban.
Diets became imbalanced, though more predictable. Teeth deterio-
rated. Disease resistance declined. Blowguns and *atlatls* were still used,
but bows replaced breath and the muscles of the forearm as propulsion
for missiles. Arrows were more frequently used than darts and spears
to kill.*

The completion of the rectilinear revolution came at the end of a
sequence of events, a sequence, not a "progression" as that concept
might have occurred to Gallatin and Jefferson. At this point, before
venturing further, an Executive Summary of that long continuity may
be useful. It began about 4000 B.C. with the first generalized circles. It
was as if the concept "circle" were present, but not precisely articulated in solid material. Examples of this phase are at Watson Brake,

---

*I was shown how to use a blowgun by a patriarch of the Alabama-Coushatta as late as
1991. He said that when he was young his people were too poor to afford guns.

Sapelo and other shell rings, and most Adena rings. Incomplete, implied circles appeared as early as 1200 B.C., in the D-shapes of the Delta and the precise but incomplete circularesque configurations such as Poverty Point (two linked sets of elypses).*

The Rectilinear Revolution occurred about A.D. 200. Afterward came post-rectilinear circles, precise in the case of the Hopewell. These figures in Ohio do not seem to have stood alone, but always in association with rectilinear forms. It was otherwise in Florida. (The destruction of so much of the evidence makes such generalizations risky, however necessary they may be.) Then came the post-rectilinear implied circles of the Paint Creek group and possibly at Cincinnati, perhaps left incomplete because, once the point was made, it was no longer necessary to finish things off.†

---

*These words were in the line-editing stage when my wife and I took a long weekend off from the exigencies of the National Park Service to explore the mound country of the west coast of Florida, to confirm some earlier reading. Some of the fruits of that reading appear in my discussion of the midwestern links to the Deptford and Fort Walton people. But surely there must be more to the said about the associations of the Poverty Point half-rings and hinge-mound to the nests of ridges associated with large mounds in Charlotte County, Florida. At the John Quiet site on Turtle Bay, there are five concentric half- circles and hinge-mounds, together with an entry "canal," cutting through the rings into the central plaza as the "bisector ridge causeway" discovered by John Gibson cuts through the southwestern sector at Poverty Point. Not far from the John Quiet site is Big Mound Key, east of Gasparilla Sound. Its major mound is conspicuous and was viciously attacked by looters in 1980 before it was protected within a wildlife area. But enough remains of that structure together with its own set of parallel ridges to remind us that roseate spoonbill bones, presumably from this part of Florida, have been found at Poverty Point.

It is also worth noting that Gibson's causeway points directly at a small pond outside the Poverty Point rings, with thoroughly Floridian theatricality. There are eight examples of this device at Big Mound City, east of Lake Okeechobee (not the same place as Big Mound Key). Three are at Big Tonys, and one so marvelous at Mount Royal, on the St. John's River, that is was ecstatically reported by William Bartam in 1771. (See William Morgan, *Prehistoric Architecture*, pp. 124–135, and Bartram, *Travels*, pp. 101–102)

Furthermore, the strange "fishhook" causeway leading to the platform mound at the Jackson site in the Poverty Point complex and described by Clarence B. Moore in 1913 is eerily like that Moore described in 1895 at Shields, near Jacksonville. (See Moore, "Sand Mounds" and "Aboriginal Sites," and Gibson, "Earth Sitting," p. 225).

†On the Great Miami River, six to ten miles south of Dayton, Ohio, about as far to the northwest of the Scioto works as Newark lies to the northeast, are two immense configurations, larger in extent though less precise in configuration than anything in the Scioto or the Licking-Muskingum watersheds. The first centers upon a conical mound, now somewhat reduced, but originally about 70 feet high and 900 feet in circumference (now in the Miamisburg Mound State Memorial). It is similar to those at Grave Creek, Marietta, and Portsmouth, and may have antedated the geometric works. Near it, and on the same side of the river, were a square 1,150 feet on a side, and a circle with a diameter of about 2,000 feet.

After a pause in monumental construction, the Mississippian Emergence occurred after about 800, the year of the crowning of Charlemagne.

PLAZAS, PYRAMIDS AND THE SUN

The moon has a periodicity we mark in months. The sun has another, almost exactly twelve times as long, which we mark in years. When the Indians began to build monumental architecture with solar orientations, therefore, an annual emphasis replaced the earlier monthly one. This was the case in North America as well as in Mexico and Mayaland, where monumental stone architecture was aligned to observations of the rising and setting of the sun at changes in the seasons. All these sun-societies, from Montreal and Wisconsin to Panama, were based upon growing corn.*

Corn, sun symbolism, and solar alignments emerged together after about 800. Some solar alignments in architecture were achieved earlier, during the maturing of the Hopewell system, but they were few before its decline. Indian cultures recrystallized in the corn-growing, hierarchic, more densely compacted "Mississippian" period, with its northern metropolis at St. Louis–Cahokia. It is important to note, however, that there was no such renaissance of monumental building in the Adena/Hopewell heartland of Ohio and Kentucky. The people of the area do not seem to have returned to their previous vigor and prosperity; the skeletal evidence indicates that after 1250 they suffered such a decline in health that their average stature declined by two inches. The sun and corn did not do so well for them as had the moon and starchy seeds.[39]

The broadest study of solar orientations among the earthworks of the lower and central Mississippi Valley is by Clay Sherrod and Martha Ann Rolingson, whose focus is on the Toltec complex in Arkansas.[40] Having reviewed the positioning of hundreds of mounds, in scores of complexes from the confluence of the Ohio and the Mississippi to the Gulf of Mexico, they conclude that "there is no clear evidence in this sample for solar alignment of mounds prior to the Coles Creek period, A.D. 700." Though they did not cover Ohio, Indiana,

---

*The sun rises in the east, as the moon does, and its rising point at the midwinter solstice is about halfway between the extreme northern rising point of the moon (its ultimate rising point in its broadest sweep of the heavens) and its least ambitious sweep of the northern horizon, that is to say, its rising point farthest north during its most constricted monthly cycle. The sun's rise at equinox (the date at which day and night are equal in duration) lies at the centerpoint of all these lunar and solar observations on the easterly horizon. South of the equinoxes lie the minimal southrise, the midsummer solstice, and the maximal sunrise.

and Kentucky, the likelihood is that the same statement could be accurately made across most, if not all, the terrain we have explored. Judging from the predominance of lunar orientations in the architecture of the Hopewell, the moon held sway as long as they held sway.[41]

Then came many more flat-topped pyramids, ranged around, and defining, rectilinear (or, one might say, flat-sided) plazas. Most of these seem to have been laid out to accommodate solar observations. Or, perhaps, it would be better to say that at Moundville, or Cahokia, or Toltec, among the corn-growing, sedentary, corner-inscribing, rectilinearizing Indians after 1000, flat-topped pyramids were placed as they were according to the dictates of the sun.[42]

In Europe, by this time, hierarchical chiefdoms had stratified into caste systems dominated at first by priestly aristocracies and then by men at arms. Patterns of descent became predominantly patriarchal, and shamanic bards gathered all-male secret societies to tell epic tales of deeds of raiding and bloodshed. One man's private property became distinguished from another's by seals and proprietary burial, and the wives of Big Men accompanied them into death. Religious life in Europe became a pantheonic assimilation of many traditions in the service of conquest or the acquisition of fealty, "centered on the Lord of the Four Quarters (Zeus, Indra, Thor, Brahma, Jehovah, Quetzalcoatl, etc.) a mythic projection of the centralized authority of the chieftain in society."[43]

These arrangements are of interest to students of American societies because they may provide borrowing privileges; there do not seem to have been histories written north of the Rio Grande, so European analogies may be instructive. They are also of interest because, with the exception of a warrior princess encountered by de Soto in Georgia, the leadership patterns found by the first European explorers in America seem to have much in common with those becoming obsolete upon their own continent by 1492. Sunworshipping, mound-building, platform-mound-and-plaza societies were found throughout the Mississippi Valley and the Southeast. They may have been degenerate descendants of the Mississippians, for it seems likely that their social structure was not much changed over the preceding centuries. The great days of the Great Man of Cahokia and the Great days of Charles V of Spain were only a few centuries apart.

SOME FINAL THOUGHTS

The European chroniclers have come upon the scene. Let us go back over some of the ground we have covered in anticipation of their arrival, and draw some conclusions.

The ground which interests me that most is that bounded by circles, the innumerable earthen and stone circles built by the Indians from California to Maine over many thousand years. Some of these Indian circles in Utah, Arizona, New Mexico, and Idaho are to be found close to circles of poplars planted by Mormons around their houses. In Kentucky and Ohio, people standing within ancient earthen circles a century and a half ago might have heard the sound of Shakers in their meeting houses nearby, singing and dancing their circle dances.

In *American Churches,* a decade ago, I attempted to trace the history of the circles deployed in the European tradition as devices to hold together a community of believers. The utility of circular spaces arises from the feelings induced in people by such spaces, feelings arising from archetypes accessible to all humans. There was no need to limit that inquiry to round European churches: the use of circles to bound sacred space is not, of course, specifically European or specifically churchly. Circular archetypes are apparently active in the Native American psyche also. As the Sioux wise man, Black Elk, put it: "You have noticed that everything an Indian does is in a circle, and that is because the Power of the World always works in circles, and everything tries to be round."[44]

But, as we have seen, other archetypes are also available to Indians; it is not quite true that among them *everything* tries to be round. The Hopewell tried to harmonize circles and squares, fitting squares within circles, circles within squares, and, like Thomas Jefferson, experimenting with conciliatory octagons. The Fort Walton folk did as much with hexagons as even the cornering Mississippians revered the circular sun.* Europeans brought something new, the heedless linear arrogance of machines driven by explosion. Uprooted, having abandoned their own places, their heedlessness was provided in the nineteenth century with a wider destructive range by the developments of the technology of internal combustion, the operating principle of which is destruction. Then came nuclear fission.

Technology is morally neutral. It is available to any use we desire. We have desired that it should defile holy places, and break open sacred circles.

Bulldozers in Ohio rip through ancient earthen rings in their quest for gravel . . .

---

*I am not sure how important or how illustrative it may be, but I did observe on a recent visit to Cahokia that an early circular enclosure near Monks Mound was replaced by a series of rectilinear enclosures.

Stephen Williams, who does not share my enthusiasm for the notion that Mississippians were cornerers, notes with quiet irony that they had round pots. (Marginalia of September 1993).

Truckloads of pot-hunters gouge parallel tire tracks of desecration across the circles of the desert West . . .

A cold wind strikes the spine.

AN ANIMIST MANIFESTO

Let us try to do better. Though we share with truck-born pot-hunters a motorized mode of transportation, we do not need to share their point of view. Let us get out of the car, change our shoes, and take the time for a walker's preparation to the architecture of our predecessors. It is not well to rush. Their buildings were not created in haste. Nor do they yield to assault. They respond only to a slow and respectful approach. As these buildings make their appearance upon a walker's horizon, their immense scale fills out gradually. As we approach, they may seem impenetrable until a deferred opening appears, like that found by Squier, Davis, and Louis Sullivan at the entrance to the Fairgrounds Circle.

When we trust our feet again, and walk patiently about the Hopewell earthworks in the early morning and at dusk, the magic returns. The early architecture of the Americas is quiet. Great earthworks shut out high frequency sound. They contain places for attending to the stately rhythms of the heavens—statelier than the thumping of boom boxes and the amplified discontents of the age of noise.

They are quiet in another way. But for their regularity, the Ohio geometrics might be taken as natural features. Early Americans did not make "statements" clamoring for attention. They strove instead to attend. Their world and ours is full of wonders lying beyond the blare we have interposed between ourselves and its uninsistent glories. When our predecessors had heard from the moon and the sun and the stars, they strove to use their highest mathematics and engineering to accommodate what they heard.

Let us jettison terms such as "Observatory Mound." The places from which these builders sought to obtain instruction from the skies were not observatories; the Hopewell were not, I think, observing. On the evidence of their architecture, we may conclude that they were, instead, awaiting instruction.

Yet, as I write in this way of them, I do not intend that ethnic diffidence creep into these pages. Native Americans are not alone in having a tradition of respectful attention to the natural order of things. We of largely European descent have such a tradition as well, a tradition that has much in common with those of the medieval Americans. We too have felt a close commonality with the other animals and objects of creation, and we too have reminded ourselves of these commonalities in prayers and architectural forms of communion such as circles and circle dances. We too have invoked the harmonizing forces in the cosmos. We too have practiced geomancy, that search for architecture harmonious to the laws of the cosmos which people as disparate as Louis Sullivan, Le Corbusier, Frank Lloyd Wright, and Mies van der Rohe have sought in our own time.

Long ago, in the middle ages of Europe, earlier builders attended to those laws. Some, who called themselves Pythagorians, preferred to search for the mathematics of cosmic order. Others, at the northwestern extremities of the old world of European Christians, sought more poetic devices. Even before the bardic Norse came into the family, the Irish were accustomed to invoke the aid of forces in the universe other than any Great Chieftain in the sky. Here is a stanza from a traditional prayer called "The Shield of St. Patrick":

> For my shield this day I call:
> Heaven's might,
> Sun's brightness,
> Moon's whiteness,
> Fire's glory,
> Lightning's swiftness,
> Wind's wildness,
> Ocean's depth,
> Earth's solidity,
> Rock's immobility.[45]

The closeness of Irish geography to the Western Hemisphere is a sign. It leads us to look for a corresponding proximity in the religious life of the island to that in the Americas across the Atlantic. At the time the Hopewell were building their sacred geometry in Ohio, Roman religion had not yet penetrated Ireland. Whoever composed that prayer, it had probably been in use for centuries before Saint Patrick or Bishop Palladius, or someone, brought Christianity to the Irish.* So strong

---

*It must be admitted that the hymn called "the Shield of St. Patrick" has been traced only so far as the eighth century. That is not far enough to give meticulous medievalists serenity in attributing it with certainly to the saint himself, who died no later than A.D. 495. But there is no reason to deny it to him on that ground alone. He made no claim upon future royalties. So free of anxiety for reputation was the man, that he left us in a quandary as to whether or not his name was, in fact, Patrick.

There are those of us who prefer to think Patrick to have been the same man as the Bishop Palladius. The records of the missions on the northern frontier of Christendom are spotty and vague; there is a good chance that what we think we know of Patrick is interposed upon and interpenetrated with the saga of Palladius, his precursor in the attempt to evangelize Ireland. Having brought the religion of Christian Rome to the island, Palladius disappeared from the record as Patrick emerged.

Our preference arises from the perhaps puckish desire to call Ireland "Palladian" long

was the hold of the old religion that the first Fathers made in Ireland an ameliorative conversion of the same sort which the Franciscans effected in New Mexico a thousand years later, after the Pueblo Revolt of 1680. Perhaps Patrick saw to it that the old religion became comfortable with the new.

As a result, animism—a participative and respectful view of humankind's relationship to the rest of creation—was never expunged. Patrician Christianity is, therefore, the closest of European Catholic expressions to the religious life articulated in the architecture of the North Americans of his time, especially that of the Hopewell people.*

The Shield of St. Patrick has troubled some theologians of narrow views. Since they have chosen to apply the term "animism" to it as well as to certain Native American prayers, they encourage the rest of us to consider the two together, in a fusion of modern, that is to say Christian, theology, and that of an older point of view. The redoubled energy of two great traditions may help us penetrate more deeply into the meaning of the sculpture and architecture of the American Midwest than was possible for nineteenth century people who dismissed that work as "heathen."

Behind the rise of science for the few, there fell a shadow—impatience and inattention on the part of the many. Science implied objectivity, requiring abrupt distinctions between humans and the rest of God's creation. Raucous and full of pride, many Europeans and Americans abandoned the redeeming animism which until then had refreshed the European religious tradition.

None the less, "heathen" or "animists" have continued to offer supplication to created nature. A decent respect for animism is a precondition, I believe, to any understanding of the ancient architects of America. The tradition of St. Patrick is copious in wisdom old before Christianity, wise in its respect for the earth and the other animals resident with us upon it, and reaching back to an earth-conscious culture on both sides of the North Atlantic. The earliest Americans and Europeans shared in that older wisdom, as their circles and red-ochred burials tell us.

Patrician wisdom is still healing in Ireland, the last island of Europe, the last abutment before the great Atlantic leap. It may, in time, even restore a forest to that ravaged land, as it might repair the sad eroded slopes of Sicily, once shadowed by great pines before it became bounteous with grain. Some day that sort of wisdom may give comfort to

---

before England might justly claim that description through the exertions of Inigo Jones and Lord Burlington.

*St. Francis of Assisi, with whom Patrick had much in common, was a contemporary of the Cahokians.

the desolated slopes of Greece, where only tortured olives and hungry goats survive amid columned ruins evoking the memory of groves.

On our side of the Atlantic we are slowly learning to attend to what the Patrician synthesis teaches us about judgment—judgment in the biblical sense—upon the consequences of profligacy. We are all too slowly beginning to attend to the significance of the successive forced abandonments chronicled in this tale, the Vacant Quarters and inexplicable declines, the cycles of opulence and decay, of celebration and neglect.

The archaeology of the Great Valley presents lessons so poignant, so undeniable, that they require no emphasis. The Hopewell were in advance of us in many ways: they understood the importance of sustaining a respectful relationship with the cosmos. But for them, as for the Poverty Point people, as for the Mississippians, matters went awry, something we are beginning to understand with our advanced means of measuring the effects of failure. Though the Hopewell, like the people of Poverty Point and the Cahokians, made consistent efforts to stay in harmony with the earth, even they did not succeed.

There has been no tidy sequence of ever-ascending cultures upon this continent, nothing resembling "progress." Instead, the evidence of prehistory presents recurrent cycles of endeavor, exhaustion, and failure. Habitation has become uninhabitable, and the people who lived there have moved away.

Now there is nowhere else.

If people as sensitive to their circumstances and careful in their husbandry as these our predecessors failed to strike a balance between population and resources, what may we expect?

The moral is plain. Let us join St. Patrick in a prayer that it becomes a lesson learned in time.

THOMAS JEFFERSON AND NICHOLAS BIDDLE

Even before Nicholas Biddle converted the *Port Folio* from a Federalist scandal sheet into a journal of literature and archaeology, he had already contributed to the Jeffersonian history of the West. He rendered coherent the scattered and episodic accounts by Lewis and Clark of their scientific and provocatory expedition from the Mississippi River to the Pacific Ocean.

In the light of its subsequent celebrity, it is strange how underreported was their expedition of 1805–6. So indifferent were their countrymen that their journals languished uncollated and unkempt until Biddle edited them in 1810 and had them published in 1814.

Biddle came to them in 1809, by way of Thomas Freeman, still enjoying a privileged status, and now employed as a surveyor for Albert Gallatin along the Natchez Trace. One day, Freeman was told that Meriwether Lewis had been found dead, probably from suicide, in a tavern nearby. Freeman brought Lewis's personal effects to Virginia, including a journal which William Clark thereupon entrusted to Biddle. Clark was already eager to bring some order to the million words of journals reposing at his home in the valley of Virginia. With Lewis's now at hand as well, he succeeded in persuading Biddle to undertake the ghostwriting, cutting, ordering, and publication of the consolidated notebooks, while he returned to the West.

Biddle had much else to do; he was a rising lawyer and politician; though he had a livelier first-hand knowledge of antiquity than all but a handful of Americans, his experience with the exotic had been limited to Greece and Italy. None the less, he set aside much of the next year to edit the Lewis and Clark papers, reducing the word count by half with the assistance of Paul Allen, who was working with him to rehabilitate the *Port Folio*. Western archaeology had found the right editors.

In August 1813, Jefferson wrote Biddle and thanked him "for the trouble you have taken" despite Biddle's Burrite connections, and despite Biddle's association with the *Port Folio*.* The edited journals reached the public a year later.[1] As we have observed, they had in common an enthusiasm for Indian archaeology. As Jefferson was gaining information about forms taken by the geometric earthworks around Chillicothe and Newark, Ohio, a map was published in the *Port Folio,* in 1809, showing the circle and square at Hopeton.[2]

The magazine had been an arch-Federalist journal edited by Joseph Dennie. Despite Jefferson's professed devotion to civil liberties and freedom of the press, the president had long wanted printers such as Dennie quieted. They "ravin on the agonies of their victims, as wolves on the blood of the lamb. . . . Nothing can now be believed which is seen in a newspaper," he said, and in his Second Inaugural Address, in 1805, he deplored the "licentiousness" of the press, inviting acting against it.

In that year, Jefferson raised no objection when his partisans filed suit in a Pennsylvania court to put Dennie out of business with a charge of seditious libel. In the next, Jefferson was silent when a *federal* grand jury indicted Aaron Burr's brother-in-law, Judge Tapping Reeve, for the same crime. Seditious libel, speech unpleasant to the regime, had been a British crime, and much abused by tyrants; it was prohibited to the federal government under the constitution, as Jefferson and Madison had proclaimed in the aftermath of Adams's Alien and Sedition Acts.

Though the suit against Reeve was ultimately dropped, its repressive effect could not be expunged, and *Respublica v. Dennie,* 4 Yeates (Penn.) Reports 267 is famous in our jurisprudence. Since that was not for archaeological reasons, we cannot pause here to recount the tale of how Dennie got off. But in the aftermath of the case, the defendant's drinking became so compulsive that a group of his contributors headed by Nicholas Biddle increasingly assumed responsibility for the magazine in 1811 and 1812, when Dennie died.

Thereafter, Biddle took on the *Port Folio,* while his friend and fellow contributor, Robert Walsh, commenced publication of *The American Review of History and Politics,* a like-minded quarterly.

Biddle and Walsh were a shady lot when viewed from Monticello. They had both been secretaries to James Monroe in Paris, while Monroe was at odds with Jefferson; Monroe was still a competitor to James Madison, who had just won the presidency only because of Jefferson's support. The Biddles had been hosts and constant friends to Aaron Burr during and after his trials. So the president had redoubled reason

---

From Brackenridge's account as transmitted to Thomas Jefferson and published in 1834 in his *Recollections,* as enlarged in the 1868 edition.

to watch what emerged in the *Port Folio* in his final year in office and during the first of Madison's term.

For these reasons there can be little doubt that Jefferson saw the splendid map of the circle-and-square at Hopeton and the description to go with it that appeared in the *Port Folio* in July, 1809, signed "J.C.", which James L. Murphy persuasively attributes to an Ohio writer named John Pogue Campbell, whose rumination on Indian architecture was published posthumously in 1820 in the *Port Folio*. Campbell drew a rough map of the Newark octagon and square in 1812 or 1813, which Dr. Murphy has discovered in the Draper Papers of the Wisconsin Historical Society. It was not, apparently, published; in 1820 Caleb Atwater published his version of the Newark works in the *Archaeologica Americana* of the American Antiquarian Society. It was this, final, printed version to which Jefferson responded in his letter to the Society.[3]

From 1809 onward, in *The Port Folio* and elsewhere, article after article appeared giving the precise shapes of the Ohio geometric works, circles, squares, and octagons.*

---

*A map of the Newark works bearing the inscription "Correct copy—Robert Walsh Jr. Sept. 10th 1815" has recently been discovered in the form of a photostat of an unknown original, in the Licking County Historical Society. Walsh was in the area in May of that year, but does not seem to have published his map. (Bradley Lepper informed me by letter of September 28, 1993, that John Weaver of the Society told him of the map, which had been hanging in the women's rest room of the Society, and Lepper subsequently found a letter in the New-York Historical Society from Walsh to George Ticknor stating that he would cross Ohio in May, 1815.)

WILLIAM DUNBAR ON THE WONDERS OF ARKANSAS

O *ctober 23, 1804:* Such is the situation of a most valuable tract upon which this Frenchman is settled: his house is placed upon an Indian mount with several others in view: there is also a species of rampart surrounding this place and one very elevated mount; all of which I purpose to view and describe on my return, our situation not now admitting delay: the soil here is equal to the best Mississippi bottoms; the proprietor says that this high mount is not less than 80 feet perpendicular . . . the bed of the lake then becomes the residence of immense herds of deer, of turkeys, geese, ducks, cranes, &c &c. . . .

Wednesday the 24th: Vegetation is extremely vigorous along the alluvial banks; the twining vines entangle the branches of the trees and expand themselves along the margin of the river, in the richest and most luxuriant festoons, and often present for a great extent a species of impenetrable curtain variegated and spangled with all possible gradations of color from the splendid orange to the enlivening green down to the purple & blue and interwoven with bright red and russet brown. A carpet of the finest shrubbery overspreads the elevated margin, composed of a variety of elegant vegetables, to many of which probably no names have yet been assigned by the botanist; and in positions where the shade is too deep, the surface is enameled with thousands of humbler plants in full blossom at this late season.

Monday, Nov. 5, 1804: The willow tree pendent over the water, presents a fine deep yellow along the outline of the plant, from whence may be traced a regular gradation, through the admired lemon color down to the soft and delicate summer's green, which last in the shade, retains its full verdure: on other trees may be seen a deep color inclining to black, descending by regular shades to the palest pink mingled with green from these by similar gradation to the usual summer ver-

---

From Dunbar's report on his expedition up the Ouachita, reprinted as "Journal of a Voyage" in Rowland, *Life, Letters and Papers*

dure of the plant. Leaves plucked from the tree at this season and preserved in the shade will retain their beautiful colors for a great length
of time. . . . The water of this river is extremely agreeable to drink and
much cleaner than that of the Ohio; in this respect it is very unlike its
two neighbors the Arkansas and Red rivers; whose waters are extremely charged with earthy matter of a reddish brown color, giving to
the water a chocolate-like appearance; and when those rivers are low
their waters are not potable, being extremely brackish, from the great
number of salt springs flowing into them and very probably from the
beds of rock salt over which (it has been reported) they flow:

Saturday, Nov. 17: The deer is now fat and their skins in perfection;
the bear also is now in his prime with regard to the quality of his fur
and the quantity of fat or oil which he yields, he has been feeding lux-
uriously for some time upon the autumnal fruits of the forest, such as
persimmons, grapes, pawpaws, walnuts, packanaws, hickory—nuts,
chinquapins, beech-mast, a great variety of acorns &c &c.

Monday, Dec. 3, 1804: We arrived at the Chutes: this promontory
presented some appearance at a distance, of the ancient ruined fortifications and castles so frequent in Europe, the effect was greatly heightened by a flock of swans which had taken their stations under the walls
which rose out of the water; as we approached the birds floated about
majestically upon the glassy surface; and in tremulous melancholy ac-
cents seemed to consult each other upon measures of safety, the ensem-
ble produced a truly sublime picture: several masses of the same hard
rock insulated by the river conveyed the idea of redoubts and outworks.

Sunday, the 30th: The sky was most serenely clear this day, its color
over head was that of a dark Prussian blue and during the last night the
stars shone with uncommon lustre—People have conceived an idea
that they see more stars here than any where else, which idea arises
only from the extreme serenity of the atmosphere which causes the
stars to strike the eye with greater brightness, and no doubt some stars
of inferior magnitude will be seen in a pure sky which are invisible in
one replete with vapors. This evening some light clouds appeared
above the Sun setting which is an indication of change of weather.

Monday 21st and Tuesday 22nd, Jan. 1805: At this place are several
Indian mounts being mostly covered by a thick cane brake, it was difficult to examine them with due attention: there are 5 of the usual form
placed within the angle formed by the Black river and the Catahoula,
another lies beyond the Catahoula; those are oblong, about 50 yards
long by 25 wide on the top, with a rapid descent about 12 feet perpendicular; there exists a sixth mount of a very particular construction, the
base is nearly square and consists of three stories; M. Heberd the proprietor thinks the whole is 80 feet high, but I cannot persuade myself

that it exceeds 40 or 45 feet, the ascent of the first story is not very rapid and may be estimated at 15 feet perpendicular; a flat of 5 of 6 feet wide reigns all around the mount, from which arises the second story, the ascent of which is not more rapid than the first and may be about 8 feet perpendicular, a second flat of the same breadth is found above the 2d story passing in like manner around the mount from whence arises the third story, whose ascent is extremely steep, it is necessary to support oneself by the canes, which cover this mount to be able to get to the top. The form of the third story is that of a very regular cone, terminated at the top by a circular flat of about 8 feet diameter, which has probably been less. The perpendicular height of the cone may be about 20 feet. Having brought no instruments with me from the boat and moreover the mount being extremely covered by thick canes I had it not in my power to make an exact survey, which I hope to do upon some future occasion. The proprietor says that the base covers a square of about 180 feet to each side, and at each angle, there is a kind of abutment or projection, from which an imperfect idea may be formed of the curious form at this singular mount; which may have been a temple for the adoration of the Supreme being; or it may have been a monument erected to the honor of some great chief, or it may have been barely a watch tower. The country all around being alluvial, or at least subject to inundation, it is extremely probable that the five [?] oblong mounts were places of residence, composing a considerable village, there is also the appearance of an embankment, which composes two sides of an imperfect square, the black river and the Catahoula forming the other two: this embankment has probably been nearly perpendicular without & in form of a glacis.

MR. BRACKENRIDGE SPEAKS
FOR HIMSELF

The mounds at Grave Creek and Marietta have been minutely described, but in point of magnitude they fall far short of the others [in the St. Louis area].

To form a more correct idea of these, it will be necessary to give the reader some view of the tract of country in which they are situated. The *American Bottom,* is a tract of rich alluvial land, extending on the Mississippi, from the Kaskaskia to the Cahokia River, about eighty miles in length, and five in breadth; several handsome streams meander through it; the soil of the richest kind, and but little subject to the effects of the Mississippi floods. A number of lakes are interspersed through it, with high and fine banks; these abound in fish, and in the autumn are visited by millions of wild fowl.

There is, perhaps, no spot in the western country, capable of being more highly cultivated, or of giving support to a more numerous population than this valley. If any vestige of the ancient population were to be found, this would be the place to search for it—accordingly, this tract, as also the bank of the river on the western side, exhibits proofs of an immense population.

If the city of Philadelphia and its environs were deserted, there would not be more numerous traces of human existence. The great number of mounds, and the astonishing quantity of human bones, everywhere dug up, or found on the surface of the ground, with a thousand other appearances, announce that this valley was at one period, filled with habitations and villages. The whole face of the bluff, or hill which bounds it to the East, appears to have been a continued burial ground.

But the most remarkable appearances, are two groups of mounds or pyramids, the one about ten miles above Cahokia, the other nearly the

From Brackenridge's account as transmitted to Thomas Jefferson and published in 1834 in his *Recollections,* as enlarged in the 1868 edition.

same distance below it, of various sizes. The western side also contains a considerable number.

A more minute description of those above Cahokia, which I visited in the fall of 1811, will give a tolerable idea of them all.

I crossed the Mississippi at St. Louis, and after passing through the wood which borders the river, about a half a mile in width, entered an extensive open plain. In 15 minutes, I found myself in the midst of a group of mounds, mostly of a circular shape, and at a distance resembling enormous haystacks scattered through a meadow. One of the largest which I ascended, was two hundred paces in circumference at the bottom, the form nearly square, though it had evidently undergone considerable alteration from the washing of the rains. The top was level, with an area sufficient to contain several hundred men.

The prospect from this mound is very beautiful; looking towards the bluffs, which are dimly seem at the distance of six or eight miles, the bottom at this place being wide, I had a level plain before me, varied by islets of wood, and a few solitary trees; to the right the prairie is bounded by the horizon. . . . Around me, I counted 45 mounds or pyramids, besides a great number of small artificial elevations; these mounds form something more than a semi-circle, about a mile in extent. . . .

Pursuing my walk along the banks of the Cahokia, I passed eight others in the distance of three miles before I arrived at the largest assemblage. When I reached the foot of the principal mound, I was struck with a degree of astonishment, not unlike that which is experienced in contemplating the Egyptian pyramids. What a stupendous pile of earth! To heap up such a mass must have required years, and the labors of thousands. The shape is that of a parallelogram, standing from north to south; on the south side there is a broad apron or step, about half way down, and from this, another projection into the plain about fifteen feet wide, which was probably intended as an ascent to the mound.

By stepping round the base, I computed the circumference to be at least eight hundred yards and the height of the mound about ninety feet. The step, or apron, has been used as a kitchen garden, by the monks at La Trappe, settled near this, and the top is sowed with wheat. Nearly west there is another of smaller size, and forty others scattered throughout the plain. Two are also seen on the bluff, at the distance of three miles. Several of these mounds are almost conical.

As the sward had been burnt, the earth is perfectly naked, and I could trace with ease, any unevenness of surface, so as to discover whether it is artificial or accidental. I everywhere observed a great number of small elevations of earth, to the height of a few feet, at regular distances from each other, and which appeared to observe some order; near them, I also observed pieces of flint, and fragments of earthen vessels. I concluded that a very populous town had once existed here, similar to those of Mexico, described by the first conquerors.

The mounds were sites of temples, or monuments to the great men. It is evident, this could never have been the work of thinly scattered tribes. If the human species had at any time been permitted in this country to increase freely, and there is every probability of that fact, it must, as in Mexico, have been astonishingly numerous. The same space of ground would have sufficed to maintain fifty times the number of the present inhabitants, with ease; their agriculture having no other object than mere sustenance.

Amongst a numerous population, the power of the chief must necessarily be more absolute, and where there are no laws, degenerates into despotism. This was the case in Mexico, and in the nations of South America; a great number of individuals were at the disposal of the chief, who treated them little better than slaves. The smaller the society, the greater the consequence of each individual. Hence there would not be wanting a sufficient number of hands to erect mounds or pyramids. . . .

I have frequently examined the mounds at St. Louis; they are situated on the second bank just above the town, and disposed in a singular manner; there are nine in all, and form three sides of a parallelogram, the open side towards the country, being protected, however, by three smaller mounds, placed in a circular manner. The space enclosed is about four hundred yards in length, and two hundred in breadth. . . . Below the first mounds, there is a curious work, called the Falling Garden. Advantage is taken of the second bank, nearly fifty feet in height at this place, and three regular stages or steps, are formed by earth brought from a distance. This work is much admired [in 1811—it was destroyed a generation later].

In tracing the origin of institutions or inventions amongst men, we are apt to forget, that nations, however diversified by manners and languages, are yet of the same species, and that the same institutions may originate amongst twenty different people. . . . The American tribes belong to the human race. . . . Men, without any intercourse with each other, will, in innumerable instances, fall upon the same mode of acting. . . . Man is everywhere found in societies, under governments, addicted to war, hunting, or agriculture, and fond of dances, shows and distinction.

Perhaps the first employment of a numerous population when not engaged in war, would be heaping up piles of earth, the rudest and most common species of human labor. We find these mounds in every part of the globe; in the north of Europe, and in Great Britain, they are numerous, and much resemble ours, but less considerable. The pyramids of Egypt are perhaps the oldest monuments of human labor in that country, so favorable to the production of a numerous population. . . .

It has ever been in the mildest climates, gifted by nature with plenty, that civilization has had its origin. Egypt and fruitful Asia, first became possessed of a numerous population, and first cultivated the arts and sciences. In America, civilization first appeared, in similar climates, where nature, with little help from man, produces abundance of food. In both the old and the new world, the celestial spark kindled in those happy climes, would be carried to less favored regions. . . .

In wanderings of fancy, I have sometimes conceived this hemisphere, like the other, to have experienced the genial ray of civilization, and to have been inhabited by a numerous, polite, and enlightened people.

NOTES

Chapter One. The Founders of American Architecture: The Cultures That Nourished Them, and the Great Dying

1. Joe Saunders of Northeast Louisiana University sent confirmation of carbon dates of 6530 and 6309 years ago, with variances in the first case of 230 years and in the second of 140, in a personal communication of October 7, 1992.

   His earlier investigations and those of Reca Jones produced the configuration given in the text (personal communications in July, 1992, from Kathleen Byrd and Saunders).

   The courtesy of recording the specific investigators who are adding to our understanding of these places in the 1980s and 1990s would require a detailed listing of their reports, often in journals only accessible to their peers. Since those peers already know that work, we must content ourselves with the general statement that none of this discussion would be possible without the published work, the private letters received from, and innumerable telephone calls exchanged with Joe Saunders, Jon Gibson, Stephen Williams, Kathleen Byrd, and Dennis LaBatt. Citations to the more accessible sources can be found in the bibliography.

2. The network may have had knotting points at places very distant from Poverty Point, such as settlements in the boot heel of Missouri, at Titterington (in American Bottom across from St. Louis), along the Gulf Coast from Tampa to the Trinity River in Texas, and even the shell-ring settlements of South Carolina and Georgia.

   There is a rapidly increasing store of published material on Poverty Point. I have found that most useful to lay people to be that produced by Jon Gibson, William Haag, Bruce Smith, and Stephen Williams (see Bibliography). Kathleen Byrd has informed me of Saunders's work in letters, and Saunders has discussed its recent disclosures by telephone.

   Gibson, Williams, Smith, and Byrd have patiently explained to me the connections between what appears at Poverty Point and a range of very early architectural remains. For the outliers or knots, see especially Stephen Williams in Byrd et al. 1991.

3. These figures have been revised downward by Jon Gibson from earlier estimates (see Gibson, "Poverty Point Earthworks").

4. No subject is more hotly debated than the magnitude of the population of North America before the Great Dying, though there is no debate among scholars that it occurred and was terrible. After reading many

disparate estimates, I have chosen to follow in general the outline of Dobyns in *Their Number Became Thinned.*

5. Population estimates for Europe, Asia, or America in these pre-census days can only be approximate. I am using those provided by Dobyns in *Columbian Consequences,* Vol. 3, p. 544.

6. Ibid., pp. 543, 550, 544.

Chapter Two.   Albert Gallatin and the Possibility of Understanding

1. Quoted in Walters, *Albert Gallatin,* p. 218.

2. Stevens, *Albert Gallatin,* p. 377.

3. Quoted in H. Adams, *Gallatin,* p. 72.

4. Gallatin, in letters cited by Walters, *Gallatin,* p. 322, n. 32

5. Ibid.

6. Quoted in Walters, *Gallatin,* p. 281.

7. Dangerfield, *The Era of Good Feeling,* p. 5. Lord Bryce and Marcus Cunliffe are Dangerfield's only peers among the innumerable English commentators upon the American experience, and Cunliffe his only equal as a writer.

8. Gallatin and La Perouse discussed the far Northwest both in Maine and subsequently in Boston. See Stevens, *Gallatin,* and for Hearne the wonderful account in De Voto, *Course of Empire,* pp. 252 ff.

9. Jackson, *Thomas Jefferson and the Stony Mountains,* 1981, p. 129.

10. Quoted in Silverberg, *The Mound Builders,* p. 64.

11. James Gallatin, *Diary,* Count Gallatin, ed., (1924), p. 17, cited in Dangerfield, *Good Feeling,* p. 5.

12. Gallatin, *Selected Writings,* pp. 488–89.

13. Ibid.

14. Ibid.

15. Geinapp, *The Origins of the Republican Party,* p. 95.

16. Quoted in Walters, *Gallatin,* pp. 378–89.

17. Quoted in Stevens, *Gallatin,* p. 365.

18. Quoted in Walters, *Gallatin,* p. 377.

19. Mexicans as inferior and dark, Johannsen, *To the Halls of the Montezumas,* pp. 23–24.

20. Johannsen, *Halls of the Montezumas,* pp. 156–57. Though I sense that Johannsen and I do not quite see eye to eye on the justification for the

war, his description of its literary qualities has been essential to my treatment of the subject.

21. Ibid., p. 157.

22. Gallatin, 1845, pp. 180–82.

23. Ibid. p. 206–7.

24. Ibid., p. 208.

25. Ibid., p. 209.

Chapter Three. Bloody Years Amid the Ruins

1. Having earned promotion to a general's rank in the British army, Bouquet was given what turned out to be a poisoned gift, command of the Southern Department based at Pensacola. Soon after he arrived there in the following summer, in his forty-seventh year, he caught a fever. Perhaps he, like the Shawnee and Mingo, had insufficient antibodies to content with certain diseases, for he died eight days later, on September 2nd, 1765. Bouquet's story is magnificently told by Dale Van Every in his *Forth to the Wilderness*.

2. Zeisberger quoted in Henderson, Jobe, and Turnbow, *Indian Occupation*, pp. 184–85.

3. Quoted in T. Smith, *Mapping*, n.p.

4. Ibid.

5. Ibid.

6. Irwine must himself have learned of "Circleville" from someone else, for he had gone "some distance out of his way in his travels through the wilderness on purpose to see it." (Jones in Smith, *Mapping*, n.p.)

   Jones included a map and a precise statement that he was dealing with Circleville in his magazine account. (*Royal American Magazine* for January 1775, pp. 29–30.

   His memories were reprinted for Joseph Sabin, in N.Y. in 1865, with a biographical note by Horatio Gates Jones, as *A Journal of Two Visits to Some Nations*. The original was published in an even smaller edition in Burlington, N.J. (1774). I am following the reprint in Smith.

7. Jones, Ibid.

8. Ibid.

9. Ibid.

10. William F. Romain first drew attention to the Marietta large square (1,510 by 1,510 feet) as the composition of 1,040-foot units.

11. William F. Romain created the nesting diagram, which made these relationships clear, among his other means of clarifying the relationships

among these figures. Romain deserves credit for clustering them in "families" which had eluded previous inquirers.

12. As to the half circle at Hopewell, my statement is based on Clinton Cowen's survey of 1892, as distinguished from that of Squier and Davis, who were, lamentably, frequently in error when they did not themselves actually do the work—see the acerb Cyrus Thomas on Squier, Davis and Liberty Works, p. 482. I am grateful to William Romain for calling my attention to the fact that Cowen resurveyed the Hopewell Square, as well, adding it to the 1,040–1,060 family. See Greber and Ruhl, *The Hopewell Site,* p. 15.

13. The definitive work on Zane's Trace is an unpublished dissertation by John Bernard Ray, *Zane's Trace, 1796–1812.* I am indebted to Richard Francovilia and to the staff of the Ohio Historical Society for this reference and for useful maps of the Trace.

14. Cedar Bank appears as Plate XVIII in Squier and Davis, "Ancient Monuments"; in Fowke's *Archaeological Monuments* on pp. 196–98, and in Cyrus Thomas, *1894 Report,* pp. 474–76.
    Hopeton appears in Squier and Davis as Plate XVII, in Fowke on pp. 190–195, and in Cyrus Thomas *1889 Report,* pp. 23–25.

15. Lepper's views have been communicated to me in a series of letters in 1992 and 1993.

16. Circleville appears in Squier and Davis as Figure 10, Fowke, pp. 208–9; Piketon, also known as Seal and as Barnes Farm, Squier and Davis, Plate XXIV, Cyrus Thomas, *1889 Report,* pp. 14–15; 1894, pp. 489–91.

17. Romain's work appears in a series of articles for the *Ohio Archaeologist* in 1991, 1992, and 1993.
    Romain has done distinguished work in demonstrating the correlations among the sizes of the Hopewell figures, and has suggested a standard unit of measure which might bring them together with the postmold patterns (indications in the earth of the presence of long-decayed posts) of surviving Hopewell burial chambers.
    His contributions to the discussion of the Great Hopewell Road have been in a series of detailed and generous contributions to correspondence among Lepper, Romain, and me in the winter of 1992–93. I trust that his views will have been published by the time these words reach print.

18. My reference to Atwater is from *American Antiquarian* 3, no. 4 (July 1881), p. 265.
    I am indebted to Bradley Lepper for this reference, and equally indebted to my old friend Stephen Williams for warning me not to include with it a further confirmation by Josiah Priest, "a lousy source—he did no field work" (private communication, April 2, 1991).
    What Priest had to say was that from Newark there was a "road running off to the country, which is also walled in the same way; it has been surveyed a few miles, and is supposed to connect other similar works on the Hohocking, thirty miles distance, at some point a few miles north of

Lancaster, as walls of the description connected with this work, of ten or twelve miles in extent, have been discovered." (My quotation from Priest is from *American Antiquities* etc. Albany, N.Y. (1833) p. 158.)

In a letter received at the same time as Williams's, Terry Barnhart of the Ohio Historical Society added useful biographical data on Smucker, and joined in dismissing Priest as "a charlatan," a view extended by Stephen Williams in his rollicking *Fantastic Archaeology.*

Still, Priest may well have been referring, as he often did, not only to Atwater but also to an undisclosed primary source.

No similar dispute surrounds the report of Alexander W. Bradford, in 1843, who wrote of "parallel walls" proceeding "towards the interior of the country" from Newark. "From a careful examination of the adjacent country, and the occupance of similar walls at various intervals, it has been supposed these works were connected with others at Hockhocking River." (Bradford, p. 41.)

Maps of the Newark earthworks published in 1848 and 1866 were limited in scope to the works within the town itself, but all indicated the first two or three miles of Atwater's "parallel walls." The 1848 map was in Squier and Davis. The Wyrick map was published in 1866 in Beer's *Atlas of Licking County, Ohio.*

In 1869 or early 1870, Samuel Park, an antiquarian of Marshall, Illinois, traveling southwest of Newark, encountered an elderly farmer named Jesse Thompson. Thompson testified that sixty years earlier, when he "first settled on Walnut Creek . . . there was a graded road, easily traced in the timber; that it was some thirty or forty feet wide between the ditches, and appeared to be as old as the . . . mounds, and he always thought it to be a road leading from the works near Newark to those at Circleville as it was on a line between those points." (Thompson quoted in Park, *Notes,* p. 41)

Walnut Creek meanders from a point about ten miles from Newark to its intersection, another ten miles away, with the Hocking (or Hohocking) River. The confluence is 3½ miles north of Lancaster.

In 1903, the Reverend Stephen Peet offered an extensive description of the walls and road, apparently based largely upon the testimony of Isaac Smucker (1807–1894) who died in 1894 and whose father had come into the region soon after 1800. According to Peet, Smucker "thinks one set of parallels may have led across Licking Creek to Lancaster. . . . He also says that the works extended from the Raccoon to the Licking and covered the plain." Peet, *The Mound Builders,* pp. 254–55.

Smucker himself was not quite so emphatic, when writing on his own in 1888. "It is not known to the writer, however, that any effort was ever made to follow those parallel walls to ascertain that the space between them did or did not serve the purposes of a road between this point and the Hockhocking." (This quotation is to be found in papers in the Licking County Historical Society.)

19. Simkins's account was found in a Newark newspaper by Lepper. That newspaper is in the Licking County Historical Society.

Simkins's assertion that his map represented the state of knowledge "antedating 1861" was confirmed in 1862 by James Salisbury and his brother Charles, who produced a map of Newark bearing an inscription that they had found traces of the road four miles beyond the farthest point shown on the 1848 map. (Lepper rediscovered the Salisburys' maps and notes in the archives of the American Antiquarian Society, as deposited there in 1862.)

Conceding that maps by Whittlesey, Squier and Davis, and Wyrick all showed a curved beginning, near the octagon at Newark, Lepper correctly points out that the Salisbury map, more correct in other respects than these others (that is to say, better confirmed by archaeological evidence) shows a straight course for that portion of the route.

Furthermore, Lepper points out that the "H" figures and parallel lines lying in this six-mile-long stretch of the road are on a straight course, as indicated in the Salisburys' map, and not on the curves suggested by the others.

20. For Peru, see Von Hagen, *Highway of the Sun,* p. 151, referring to seven stations at intervals of a little over two miles.

21. Lepper has found a letter from Weiant to Emerson F. Greenman of the Ohio Archaeological Society dated June 25, 1931, urging that the Society quickly record the path of the walls which he observed after they "did cross the airport and connect up with the circle and then continue on southwestward in a straight line for Millersport. I traced these parallels while flying, through two fields south of the airport."

This implies that there was another circle south of the airport, as well as the circle "at the Newark airport."

Millersport lies within about a mile of our projected route for the Great Hopewell Road, and about twelve miles along its route toward Chillicothe.

22. Ibid.

23. All references to Lepper hereafter are from private correspondence in 1991, 1992, and 1993.

24. In earlier drafts of this chapter I was equivocal about whether the likeliest pilgrimage route was Newark to Chillicothe or vice versa. I have been persuaded by William F. Romain that the former is the likelier.

Mound City appears in Squier and Davis, "Ancient Monuments," as Plate XIX, and in Fowke, *Archaeological History of Ohio,* on pp. 198–202; the evidence for a ford is to be found in Brose, 1987.

The Dunlap enclosure, parallels and platform mound have been obliterated. They are depicted in Squier and Davis, Plate XXIII, No. 1, and in Fowke, 199–202.

25. Works East appears in Squier and Davis as Plate XXI, no. 3, and in Fowke at p. 190; Highbanks, also known as High Bank, appears in Squier and Davis as Plate XVI, in Fowke on pp. 187–190, and in Cyrus Thomas, *1889 Report,* on pp. 14, 20–23, and in Cyrus Thomas, 1894 *Report,* on pp. 476–479.

26. The Newark works appear in Squier and Davis on Plate XXV, in Fowke on pp. 162–71, in Cyrus Thomas, *1894 Report,* on pp. 459–68.

27. Portsmouth appears in Squier and Davis as Plates XXVII and XXVIII, and in Fowke on pp. 173–79.

28. The "Ancient Excavation, Big Bottom, Pike County" is described by Whittlesey, *Descriptions of Ancient Works in Ohio,* p. 8. Whittlesey's engraving, Number I, is dated October, 1837.

29. Squier and Davis (pp. 66–67) allude to a *herradura*-like figure ("N") a mile north of a circle and square composite at Piketon.

30. The Graded Way at Piketon, actually a mile south of the Piketon (Seal) works, is described, with an engraving, in Squier and Davis, p. 88.

31. For references to this octagon or hexagon, see discussion of the possible octagon on the other side of the river, in Portsmouth itself, below.

32. This group was too far gone even when these earthworks were mapped in the 1840s to be clearly discerned—a millennium and a half is a decent shelf-life for earthen architecture.

    The lunar crescent possibility was suggested in 1933 by Stansbury Hagar, in *Popular Archaeology,* 42(2), pp. 35–50. I am grateful to William F. Romain for this reference.

33. In 1914 and 1915, excavators found in one of its subterranean chambers several hundred Hopewell stone smoking pipes, many broken ritually. There were ninety more, however, that had been carefully repaired with copper; these bore animal effigies—beaver, bears, and ducks carved in a highly realistic and very beautiful style. No better work was created in northern Europe during these centuries, and much that is worse has drawn forth reverential theses by European art historians.

    In 1992, the Tremper mound remains imperiled and on private land.

34. As we will have occasion to observe, it is likely that the Newark, Scioto, and Portsmouth webs functioned in similar ways. Each of them probably connected the same specialized components: Burial mounds, "charnel houses" (mortuaries in which the bodies of the dead were prepared for death), ceremonial geometry, and settlement areas. In format, however, each was distinct from the others.

35. Quoted in Clay Lancaster, *Vestiges* p. 7.

36. Quoted in Kwas and Mainfort, "The Johnston Site."

37. Ibid.

Chapter Four. The Gallatinians: Thomas Worthington and Adena

1. Quotations from Sears, *Thomas Worthington,* pp. 29–33.

2. Latrobe went over the Appalachians and worked in Pittsburgh for a year, in terrain earlier reconnoitered by Washington and Burr. As an historian

of architecture, an inveterate diarist, and respectable painter, he might have left us some account or at least one of his famous watercolors of the earthen ruins he saw. None has so far been found, but his depictions of the western landscape had twofold impact. He showed it as romantically as the Hudson River School later painted their own, before any other first-rate landscapist had emerged in America. And he knew how to show a boom town like Steubenville in the earliest phases of urban sprawl, spreading its grid pattern across the plain in a metaphor of ineluctability before which the very trees retreat.

Latrobe did his work in Pittsburgh amid a mound complex, and passed the group of mounds on the upper Ohio, below Pittsburgh, four times, though he does not seem to have gotten so far as the cones at Grave Creek or Portsmouth.

It may seem finicking to distinguish among the styles of Euramerican architecture which followed each other at intervals of only a few decades, when Ohio offers examples created at millennial distances, but Worthington was among the new, nineteenth century men as Jefferson was among the older, eighteenth century men, and one can see in their houses how rapidly the world was changing as these two generations were in conversation.

At Poplar Forest (see Chapter Seven), Jefferson strung together, on a line, a succession of blocks arranged hierarchically, with the philosopher-builder at the center of all his geometric mazes and outworks. Like any great neo-Palladian country house in England or Ireland, Poplar Forest is baroque in its ambition to organize the landscape around it, to dominate a much larger terrain than its own footprint, as if it were a pinwheel, whirling about at its maximum extension, and making a claim to dominate everything it touched and everything it might touch. Jefferson made those claims even more plain by his system of octagons and circles rippling out across the land in emulation of what he had done in the interior of the room in the center of the house in the center of all this.

Jefferson was a man of the eighteenth century. People of Worthington's generation thought of the Sage of Monticello as an old man, whose taste, they were fond of saying, was "antique," which is fair enough if one counts antiquity in decades rather than millennia. If one pays a call on Jefferson's Monticello or Poplar Forest or to Worthington's Adena, one can easily observe how brief was the shelf-life of style in the opening years of the nineteenth century as tastes moved allegretto from yesterday to tomorrow.

Adena is much less ambitious than Monticello. It is a villa, not a mini-palace. It is one of a family of Latrobian designs of which another (possibly by Latrobe himself) is Huntley, a villa which still survives, though much imperiled, south of Alexandria, Virginia. In both plan and elevation, Adena, completed in 1807, is a clear presentiment of Huntley, built a decade later.

The plans for Huntley have never been found, nor any correspondence tying its design to an architect. But it could easily have been the result of a table-napkin sketch by Latrobe, thinking of Adena or of any of his three other Washington-area villas. As we have had several occasions to note, there was a a cat's cradle of commercial, political, affectionate, and architectural relations between Ohio and Kentucky in the West and the tidewater of Virginia, between those who had crossed the mountains into the Great Valley and those remaining at home.

Huntley was built as a summer house, where Thompson F. Mason, grandson of George Mason of Gunston Hall, might escape the heat and the fevers of Alexandria. From its front porch you can see, beyond the blue smear of Huntley Meadows marsh, speckled with ducks and punctuated occasionally by the rise of a heron, the exhausted lowlands which not long ago were Mason and Washington lands, and on the shore of the Potomac, the white bulk of Mount Vernon.

And if you were Thomas Worthington in 1820, having visited your old dispirited friend Thompson Mason at Huntley, or Mason's cousins at Analostan, now Roosevelt Island, below the once-thriving and now declining port of Georgetown, you might in some complacency take your ease in the courtyard of Adena, looking out across the Scioto over farms fertile for a thousand years, fertile in 1820—and, if you were Adena's curator in 1993, you might be complacent, too, for they are remarkably fertile today.

Much of the land extending from Adena to the blue Ohio horizon had been acquired by exchanging Worthington's title deeds to Virginia's thin soil for the Ohio military scrip owned by S. Thompson Mason, uncle of the builder of Huntley.

3. Gilbert Imlay on Heart, *Topographical Description,* p. 289. Heart's report appears in *Transactions of the American Philosophical Society,* Vol. 3 (read to the Society February 3, 1792), pp. 314–16.

4. Imlay, p. 286.

5. For Sargent, see American Philosophical Society, *Transactions* of 1799, Vol. 4, pp. 177–78.

6. According to what we are told by Charles Whittlesey, writing in 1850, based on research done by Dr. Daniel Drake in the first decade of the century, there may have been a square, as well, to complete the analogy, and there was certainly a 660-foot remnant of a sacred way.

   The parallel sides . . . are forty to forty-six feet asunder. . . . An oblong mound, thirty-five feet high . . . until 1843, was not entirely obliterated. General Wayne, whose army camped near it in 1793, cut off the summit, in order to erect a sentry-box. It was in this mound that the curious stone was found. (Whittlesey, *Descriptions,* pp. 11–12)

   Whittlesey was referring to the mysterious Cincinnati Tablet, the deciphering of which is still a major archaeological puzzle. He went on to ruminate upon the evidence available to him, which was limited to Ohio:

   It is remarkable that the mound-builders of old, and the city builders of our own times, selected a great many of the same sites. Portsmouth, Marietta, Circleville, Chillicothe, Alexandersville, Frankfort, Piketon and Newark, are on or near the sites of ancient cities.

Whittlesey had not had the benefit of tours of ancient St. Louis, Cahokia, New Madrid, Nashville, Natchez, Monroe, or Lexington.

When Arthur St. Clair was appointed governor of the Northwest Territory, he did not join the other Cincinnati at Marietta, but set up his capital within the Symmes Tract, where he changed the name of the hamlet of Losantiville to "Cincinnati," and began sending Indian artifacts to Thomas Jefferson.

Winthrop Sargent moved with the capital; his archaeological interests continued; when the burgeoning town, fattening on hogs and West Virginia salt, widened Main Street in 1794, one of its principal mounds was demolished, and burials were exposed (probably Hopewell).

Sargent's lost map was succeeded by Daniel Drake's, made in 1815, published in 1850 by Charles Whittlesey, appearing as his Plate IV.

The first systematic archaeology was done on the ruins of ancient Cincinnati by Dr. Drake, a physician trained in science in the Philadelphia circle of David Rittenhouse and Benjamin Rush, like so many others (including the best early archaeologist of the Natchez Trace, Dr. Rush Nutt—see Chapter Eight).

Drake has been a well-known figure in the history of Western medicine, but Drake the archaeologist has been restored to us by the researches of Stephen Williams. Drake mapped and explored the earthworks shortly after 1800, and described them in his *Picture of Cincinnati,* published in 1810 and again in 1815.

Drake led the way to the understanding of the epidemiology of malaria. (He treated the two subjects separately, though malaria was a plague in low-lying areas of the prairie around Cincinnati.) (Williams's paper is entitled "The Ohio Valley Circle: An Early Look at Mounds and Meanings.")

7. In Sears, *Thomas Worthington,* 19–20.

8. Ibid., p. 18. Worthington to his wife, quoted in S. W. K. Peter (1882), p. 24.

9. Ibid.

10. Among those so voting were most of the Federalists in the Senate; decades had passed since the party took its risks for Blacks in Virginia, in Louisiana, and in New York. Among those who had lost their antislavery ardor, and could not resist Jefferson's personal charm, was William Plumer of New Hampshire. Plumer left in his diary the only consistently skeptical view of Worthington which appears in the memoirs and letters of the time. It is a prime example of that competition for intimacy with the Great which besets all camps and capitals.

Like all gossips, however public-spirited and grave, Plumer relished his private conversations with Jefferson, and may have resented Worthington's claim to have entered so close as he upon the confidence of the philosopher-president. Plumer implied that Worthington (and possibly Gallatin as well) had turned from Burr to Jefferson because he assessed Jefferson to be the likely winner and would be more likely to protect his own western speculations.

"Worthington," said Plumer, "is a cunning designing man; he has more talent than integrity. Though his talents are not of the first class[,] yet he is effective, industrious and intriguing. I always suspect evil from this man; his disposition is malevolent. . . . He is deeply engaged in land speculations, and owns much unimproved land in the western world." (Plumer, p. 576)

Worthington had come to him with the tale that Jefferson, "with tears running down his face," had sought to increase the armed forces and had been disappointed: "The people expect I shall provide for their defence—but Congress refuse me the means." Plumer, knowing how seldom Jefferson wept for strangers, went on to "note this same Mr. Worthington is a strange man." (Plumer, pp. 475–76)

Worthington had by that time made clear that like most Western politicians, he did speak for the speculators, and also for easy access to settlement in western lands, which is not quite the same thing. Therefore he was a natural leader for those in Ohio who opposed the efforts of the Cincinnatian military government of Marietta to control of the pace of western migration. In the Senate, he did not so frequently oppose the Federalists in debate as he did the intransigent proponents of the expansion of slavery, such as James Jackson of Georgia.

Jackson built a career upon finding Yazooism among his political opponents. Since nearly every politician in Georgia had such a record, Jackson's invidious piety could be sprayed in every direction. Jackson inflamed Worthington by implying that his own advocacy of continued military government for Louisiana, coupled to the protection of slavery, was Jefferson's position. He suggested that unless Westerners were kept under military control, whether in Louisiana or in the Northwest, they would be likely to form breakaway states, and horror of horrors, Burrite, abolitionist refuges. To this Worthington replied:

The gentleman from Georgia talks of a *separation*—Sir, the western lands will not separate unless the *eastern States* by their conduct render it absolutely *necessary*." (Plumer, p. 134.)

By "western lands," Worthington meant the slave-free states north of the old Northwest. "The eastern" were those from Maryland through Jackson's Georgia, Virginia included. Worthington was expressing the widespread view among antislavery northerners that the plantation system would prevail in the Great Valley, forcing those who abhorred slavery to secede.

11. Sears, *Worthington*, p. 185; Mary Ann Brown, curator of Adena, has rescued me from many an error in this chapter. She has admonished me in a letter of late May, 1991, that we do not know that Worthington was, in fact, "portly" at thirty-nine. That is true, but according to contempo-

rary descriptions he was corpulent when observed somewhat later in Washington, so I have retained the mental picture, without being certain it is wholly proven as exact.

12. Gilbert (1989), pp. 240 ff.

13. Ibid.

14. Quoted in Dangerfield, *The Era of Good Feeling,* pp. 335–36.

15. If a generation older, Worthington might have been one of those fierce Virginia Federalists whose record on the question of slavery has been lost in the immense shadow of the genius of Monticello. Lest they be utterly forgotten, and their links to the antislavery Gallatin wing of Jefferson's party overlooked, we should recall that occasion, at the end of the 1780s, when the Three-Fifths clause that gave Virginia's slaveowners their disproportionate power in national elections came up for debate in Virginia's House of Burgesses. All but one of the Virginia Federalists voted *against* it. Furthermore, they voted *against* the confinement of the franchise to white freemen, recalling that free Blacks who held property could vote in Virginia in colonial times (as they could in most colonies). The first Jim Crow period, a century before the second and more familiar one, rolled on, and the Federalists were defeated.

Chapter Five. George Washington: His Land, Its Inhabitants, and the Cincinnatian Solution

1. The encounter in the log cabin comes from the testimony of John Russell Bartlett, quoted in Adams, *Life of Albert Gallatin,* pp. 57–59.

2. Ibid.

3. Ibid.

4. Washington's self-description comes from a letter to his tailor in London in 1763. The proportions given would not have changed much thereafter, though he was certainly less "slender" by 1784. I am indebted to Howard Morrison for this letter, a copy of which is in the files of the National Museum of American History, and to Donald Kloster for the measurements.

5. Gallatin's holdings are detailed in Rice, *The Allegheny Frontier,* p. 139.

6. The description of the mound at Grave Creek is from a letter of May 27, 1819, from "the Rev. Dr. Doddidge" published by Caleb Atwater in the *Transactions* of the American Antiquarian Society, (1820) Vol. I, pp. 186–87. Barton in his *Observations,* p. C 2.

7. Harris, *Journal,* p. 62.

8. William N. Morgan, in his magnificent work of surveying and reconstructing, imaginatively, the *Prehistoric Architecture in the Eastern United States,* has estimated the relative magnitudes of these conical

mounds. The largest seems to have been at Pinson, Tennessee. Then comes Grave Creek, then that at Portsmouth, Kentucky.

I have converted his meters into feet, and added on other Ohio Valley "Adena" cones:

	Diameter at Base	Height
Pinson	334 ft. (102 m.)	73 ft. (22.3 m.)
Grave Creek	319 ft. (97.5 m.)	70 ft. (21.3 m.)
Portsmouth	410 ft. (125 m.)	22 ft. (6.7 m.)
Miamisburg (Butler Cty.)	511 ft. (now 178 ft.)	43 ft. (now 34 ft.)

9. Quotations from Cleland, pp. 260 ff. The sutty bird may have been an American bittern or great blue heron.

10. The note about savages appears in the annotated *Diaries*, p. 416, appended as a footnote to the entry of October 24, 1770.

11. Washington to Chastellux, October 12, 1783, *Writings*, Vol. 27, pp. 188–90.

12. Flexner, *The Forge of Experience*, p. 86.

13. Quoted in Cleland, *George Washington*, p. 237.

14. The petitioners are quoted in Sturdevant, *Quest for Eden*, p. 23; Washington, *Diary*, November 22, 1770.

15. See Flexner, *George Washington*, p. 292.

16. Washington to Chastellux, October 12, 1783, *Writings*, Vol. 27, pp. 189–90.

17. See Sturdevant, *Quest for Eden*, pp. 54, 163, 184.

18. Ibid., p. 69.

19. Ibid., pp. 34, 37.

20. Quoted in ibid., p. 39, and, it seems, in a hundred other works.

21. The extent of Washington's western holdings varied from time to time. By one scrupulous accounting he had only acquired 33,210 acres in what is now West Virginia between 1772 and 1784. See Rice, *The Allegheny Frontier*, p. 139; Washington, *Writings*, Vol. 33, p. 404.

22. James T. Flexner, *The Forge of Experience*, p. 289.

23. George William Fairfax was the son of William Fairfax, son of Lord Thomas Fairfax's uncle Henry of Toulston, Yorkshire; he was the son of a first cousin.

William was the father of several children by a woman he had, quite possibly, married during a tour of duty in the West Indies. It was the "impression" later reported by George William's wife, Sally Cary Fairfax, that she was "Black." (See Cary, *Sally Cary*, pp. 49–50.) That impression is confirmed by the only portrait remaining to us, which, as his father wrote to his English relatives (asking "their indulgences to a poor West India boy"), "has the marks in his visage that will always testify to his parentage." (Fairfax of Cameron manuscripts, cited in Brown, *Virginia Baron*, p. 59.)

Though it has been the custom of Washington's biographers to dismiss as "rumors" Fairfax's African heritage, the testimony of his wife and father, and the behavior of his English relatives gives it as much strength as fact as most history. Unless we had a witness at his conception, we would be unlikely to come much closer than that. For "rumor" see Ketchum, *World of George Washington*, p. 27, on which appears further evidence in the form of an excellent likeness of his "visage."

It is, therefore, somewhat ironic that Washington wrote that during his expedition with Fairfax he was forced to live under such primitive conditions that he slept in his clothes "like a Negro." See *Writings*, Vol. 1, ed. Fitzpatrick, p. 17.

24. Flexner (1984), p. 372.

25. Ibid., p. 392.

26. Ibid.

27. Much of my treatment of Washington on slavery is grounded in Flexner, *Washington, The Indispensable Man*, pp. 390 ff. The discussion with Bernard appears in Bernard, p. 91.

28. Flexner, p. 390.

29. Washington, *Diaries*, Vol. 2, pp. 316 ff.

30. Cyrus Thomas, *Report* p. 414.

31. Washington, *Writings*, Vol. 18, pp. 317–20.

32. Washington to Gilbert Simpson, February 12, 1784, *Writings*, Vol. 17, pp. 329–30. These letters are to be found in context in Rick Sturdevant's thesis, cited elsewhere and, appropriately often, in this text. Sturdevant is fecund in ideas and useful references.

33. Quoted in a draft study for the Mount Vernon Ladies' Association of May, 1991, generously provided me by Dean Norton, horticulturist for the association, and by Barbara McMillan, its librarian.

34. Ibid.

35. Washington's diary entries for March 13, 16, and 18, 1786, and in his letter to Vaughn cited above.

36. Washington, *Diaries*, pp. 139 ff.

37. The Pheasant's description is found on p. 439 of Washington's *Diaries*.

Washington records the estimate that Bull Creek was at that point "at least 30 miles from the mouth but not more than 5 from the mouth of Muddy Creek, in an ESE direction." Everything comports with the possibility that he is referring to Buffalo Creek except the thirty mile guess. There is no creek so long as that running in parallel with the Ohio and five miles away.

38. Quotations from Cleland, *George Washington,* pp. 260 ff.

39. Washington to Lewis, May 5, 1773, *Writings,* Vol. 3, pp. 209–11.

40. Washington to Butler, *Writings,* Vol. 29, pp. 369–70, Jan. 10. 1788.

41. Ibid.

42. These lines, from Washington's copybook, appear on p. 15 of Rick W. Sturdevant's exemplary but so far unpublished thesis, *Quest for Eden: George Washington's Frontier Land Interests.* Sturdevant offers by far the best treatment of his subject in print. It is only fair to say that, on the basis only of the Lewis letter and Sturdevant's "understanding of GW's attitudes and actions" he suggested, though in a "highly conjectural" way, that Washington "anticipated the day when he would be able to travel far into the American interior and lodge regularly at his own lucrative stations" (p. 59 and fn. 12 on p. 83).

   It does not seem to me that we require that Washington have lucre as an inducement. Sturdevant was onto something, but he was too diffident. There is more evidence than that letter, as I have tried to show. The "understanding" is sound, and the conjecture a good one. After all, history is by its nature conjectural—except autobiography, and *it* is prejudiced.

43. Washington to Sally Fairfax, ibid. p. 372. It is scarcely worth the stress, but it will not hurt to add that Washington's reference to the Fairfaxes was in the plural, and so was his reference to the Washingtons, himself and his wife. The notion that he had violated his friendship with George to seduce Sally is too repugnant to sense or sympathy to gain credence. It also would deny to us the pleasure of contemplating the two Washingtons rejoicing in a progression from two friendships of two into a friendship of four.

Chapter Six.   The Cincinnati

1. Gallatin on dining with Washington, quoted in Adams, *Life of Albert Gallatin,* p. 182.

2. Quoted in Flexner, *Washington,* p. 324.

3. Ibid., p. 325.

4. "Charmingly benign" is quoted from Richard Hofstadter by Thomas P. Slaughter; Hofstadter also was the butt of the dismissive "duck soup." See his exemplary *The Whiskey Rebellion,* fn. 5 on p. 233. Slaughter and

I do not agree on some points, especially with reference to George Washington's motivation, but his is by far the best book on the subject.

5. Collot, *Journey in North America,* Vol. 1, p. 29.

6. Quoted in Sturdevant, *Quest for Eden,* p. 153.

7. Washington to John Witherspoon, March 10, 1784, in *Writings,* Vol. 27, pp. 348–52.

8. Quoted in J.P. Dunn, Jr., *Indiana, A Redemption from Slavery,* p. 196.

9. The earthworks as described by Jonathan Heart, in Thomas Smith, *Mapping of Ohio,* n. p.

10. Onuf, *Statehood and Union,* p. 38.

11. Ibid., p. 43.

12. Ibid., p. 71.

13. Ibid., pp. 38–39.

14. Myers, *Liberty Without Anarchy,* p. 53.

15. Sears, *Thomas Worthington,* pp. 52–53.

16. Myers, *Liberty,* p. 107.

17. Onuf, p. 116.

18. The Kentucky Abolition Society proposal appears in an excellent discussion of this subject in Meinig, *The Shaping of America,* Vol. 2, p. 301.

19. In James M. Varnum, *An Oration . . . ,* Newport (July 4, 1788) as reprinted in Samuel P. Hildreth, *Pioneer History . . . ,* p. 515, also quoted in Edith Reiter, *Marietta and the Northwest Territory,* p. 29.

20. Myers, *Liberty,* p. 113.

21. Constable quoted in ibid., p. 119; Varnum in *An Oration . . . ,* as reprinted in Hildreth, *Pioneer History. . . . ,* p. 515.

22. St. Clair's artifacts, *Pennsylvania Magazine of History* 43 (1919, p. 130.

23. Sargent reported the details of one burial in a local newspaper, the *Sentinel of the Northwestern Territory,* and brought the information to the eastern world in the *Massachusetts Magazine* in 1795 and to the American Philosophical Society in 1796. The Society published Sargent's work in 1799. (Stephen Williams in a paper entitled "The Ohio Valley Circle: An Early Look at Mounds and Meanings" for the Mid-South Conference at Pinson Mounds, Tennessee, June 1990.)

24. See the excellent editorial note in Vol. 6 of the Jefferson *Papers,* p. 583 ff.

25. Ibid.

26. Flexner, *George Washington, Anguish and Farewell,* pp. 49–50.

27. Ibid.

28. Ibid.

29. Quoted in Richard Norton Smith, *Patriarch,* p. 286.

Chapter Seven.   Thomas Jefferson and the Persistence of Prejudice

1. Quoted in Egnal, *A Mighty Empire,* p. 101.

2. Ibid.; the lines about India and granary are from the report of a British agent who signed himself P. Allaire, quoted in Slaughter, *The Whiskey Rebellion,* p. 59.

3. The up-country gentleman farmer comes from Lewis, "Jefferson and Virginia's Pioneers," p. 553, though it might be taken from any number of other essays; Claude Bowers has drawn the most familiar picture of Peter Jefferson as yeoman in his *Young Jefferson.* We will take each of the other elements of this brew as we come to them.

4. Bowers, *The Young Jefferson,* p. 9.

5. Bowers, *The Young Jefferson,* p. 8.

6. Henry Adams, *History of the Jefferson Administrations,* pp. 99.

7. Lewis, "Jefferson and Virginia's Pioneers," p. 579.

8. Adams, *History of Jefferson Administration,* p. 99.

9. Ibid., p. 553. It does not seem, however, that Jefferson had any aversion to speculators who were also Virginians, the most spectacular of whom was his own guardian. He wrote that:

    America was conquered, and her settlement made . . . at the expense of individuals, and not of the British public. . . . For themselves they fought, for themselves they conquered, and for themselves alone they have the right to hold. . . . *Each individual* of the society may appropriate to himself such lands as he finds vacant, *and occupancy will give him title* [italics Jefferson's].

    Jefferson's revolutionary rhetoric was conventional for his time: in 1763, it was not unusual for people arguing his side of the Revolutionary dispute thus to sweep aside the deeds, in the war just concluded, in 1763, of the heroic General Wolfe at Quebec, of Forbes at Fort Pitt, and of all the other armies and navies recruited from the "British public" and sustained by their taxes.

    But there is nothing in his record to indicate that squatters would be welcome on land owned by the Greenbrier company, by the Randolphs, Carters, Coles, Cabells, or any of the other squirely speculators based in Virginia. "Occupancy" did not provide "title" in Jeffersonian western Virginia, Kentucky, or Ohio, as many squatting "individuals" found out in conversation with sheriff's shotguns.

10. See Miller, *The Wolf by the Ears,* p. 65; and Nash, *Red, White and Black,* p. 106.

11. Jefferson, *Notes on Virginia,* Answer to Query VI, pp. 182–190.

    Jefferson's lawyerly eloquence about Logan has tended to overshadow his unfairness to Colonel Michael Cresap, whom he charged with being leader of the murderers.

    The true culprit was Daniel Greathouse—at the time, Cresap was fifty miles away, conferring with George Rogers Clark, a fact of which Clark informed Jefferson in writing in 1798. Jefferson never withdrew the charge, never removed the slander from later editions, and never apologized, though in the 1800 edition of the *Notes* he printed an appendix giving a new summary of the matter, indicating that he had been, as his biographer, Dumas Malone put it, "incorrect in detail." (See Malone, *Jefferson the Virginian,* pp. 386–87. I am grateful to George Knepper for identifying Greathouse as the murderer; private communication, March, 1993.)

    Cresap's son-in-law, Luther Martin, did not regard a murder charge as a matter of detail, and became one of the most effective lawyers for Aaron Burr in the trial of 1807, in which Jefferson's charge of treason was found to be insufficiently based upon evidence to go to trial.

12. Ibid.

13. For a more enthusiastic view of Jefferson's attitude toward Indians, see Bowers, *The Young Jefferson,* pp. 294–95.

14. Jefferson, *Notes,* Query VI.

15. Jefferson's precise language is given in the *Notes,* pp. 276–77, and a critical view of his stance in Levy, *Jefferson and Civil Liberties,* p. 10.

16. Levy, p. 10.

17. Jefferson, *Notes,* Answer to Query VI, pp. 182–190.

18. Volney, *View of the Soil and Climate of the United States,* p. 422.

19. Jefferson, *Notes,* Query II, p. 133.

20. *Jefferson Papers,* 9, pp. 476–478. It is puzzling that the editors of the Jefferson papers asserted (*Jefferson Papers,* 17, p. xxxi) that the map they printed as that provided by Parsons to Stiles (and by Stiles to Jefferson) was "actually" the same as that published in the *Columbian Magazine* by Captain Heart. Heart's map was discernibly different from Parsons's.

    The map in the Jefferson *Papers,* received from Parsons, is likely to be what Stiles, a careful scholar, said it was, "taken by General Parsons on the spot." (*Jefferson Papers,* 9, p. 476).

    Parsons's map appeared subsequently twice, first in Stibbons, "Fortifications at Marietta," p. 340. Stibbons wrote that he had copied the map "for president Stiles, more than half a century ago. . . . At this distance of time I cannot recollect who presented the original to president Stiles, but I believe it was either general Putnam or Mr. Lyman."

Stibbons probably meant Parsons, another general "on the spot." *The American Pioneer* reprinted the map in Hildreth, "Pyramids at Marietta," p. 243, together with engravings of the mounds. The first was by Winthrop Sargent, donated in 1787, in his "Plan of an Ancient Fortification at Marietta, Ohio" *Memoirs*, p. 29. There are two other apparently contemporary maps: the first is said to be by Putnam and dated 1788, published in Shetrone, *The Mound Builders*, p. 10. Sargent's account was first published in a letter to Benjamin S. Barton, *Transactions of the American Philosophical Society* (1799), Vol 4, p. 177.

In 1807, Christian Schultz published an account of his *Travels on an Inland Voyage* (New York: Riley) containing yet another map. (This book can be found in the Jewitt Room of the Arts and Industries Building of the Smithsonian Institution.)

21. Jefferson to Stiles, September 1, 1786, *Jefferson Papers*, 10, p. 316; Jefferson to Thomson, September 20, 1787, *Jefferson Papers*, 12. p. 159.

22. Imlay, *Topographical Description*, p. 289.

23. Harris, *Journal of a Tour into the Territory Northwest.*

24. Jefferson to Isaiah Thomas and the American Antiquarian Society, October 14, 1820, Isaiah Thomas Papers, at the Society. I am grateful to Thomas Knoles, Curator of Manuscripts, for this reference.

25. The construction process at Poplar Forest is detailed in Chambers, "Revelations from the Records," and McDonald, "Ghost Stories," from which my quotations are drawn.

26. Quoted in Beebe, "The Rescue and Restoration of Jefferson's Poplar Forest," p. 7.

27. I have tried to explore the very complicated relationships of Jefferson to "Georgian" British tradition and to French neoclassicism and, as well, to the efforts of Major L'Enfant and of Benjamin Henry Latrobe to create a new American architecture in both *Orders from France* and *Greek Revival America.*

28. I am much indebted to C. Allan Brown for his investigations of Poplar Forest, published in part in "The Mathematics of an Ideal Villa." Brown notes that "mounts" had been frequent devices in English Renaissance gardening. These probably were "mottes" inherited from older landscapes, in which these truncated mounds had been capped by palisades for defensive purposes. Some were undoubtedly constructed afresh, romantically or nostalgically, even in America among English settlers. Brown records three instances of single, unintegrated mounts observed by Jefferson, one for "Mr. Meredith's house" in Virginia, another, more familiar one, at Alexander Pope's villa on the Thames, and those at Mount Vernon.

Brown is the first to note Jefferson's instruction and the relationship of the plantings on the mounds and the dimensions of the house. See his p. 126.

In the winter of 1991–92, Michael Strut, an archaeologist working with both conventional excavation techniques and ground radar at Poplar Forest, and his crew discovered three roughly horizontal layers of cobblestones set around one of these mounds which they are excavating. Work is not complete, so they have not determined whether or not these "treaders" were octagonal in outline. But the mounds were *not* casual "dumps" for unneeded earth, nor were they evenly sloped; the earth is compressed in layers, only coming to appear even as these layers come to their exposed and eroded edges. These were architectural elements, not gently-rounded blobs of earth. (Strut's news was communicated by telephone on March 1, 1992.)

The excavations have still to confirm that the original shape of the mounds at Poplar Forest was octagonal or circular. It is not, of course, necessary that they should add a further octagonal element to the Poplar Forest geometry. There were plenty there already.

I am indebted to William Kelso for this piece of incidental intelligence: the first Thomas Jefferson to be recorded as present upon this continent arrived about 1620, and lived at a place called Hopewell, about ten miles southeast of Richmond, where important archaeological sites are now imperiled by industrial expansion.

29. Jefferson was acquainted with the shapes of these constructions and had an inkling that their *size* exceeded anything he had known when he wrote his *Notes*. He had been repeatedly, and sometimes pointedly, informed of "walls, ramparts, and mounds of earth of astonishing magnitude and extent; some of a circular and semicircular form, and others in squares and straight lines." (Harris, *Journal of a Tour into the Territory Northwest of the Allegheny Mountains;* Schultz, *Travels on An Inland Voyage,* p. 147. I have no knowledge that Jefferson did or did not know of this particular account. The language is fairly typical of the genre on the subject.)

The mounds he created for Poplar Forest between 1806 and 1812 were on an Ohioan scale, larger than those he had seen in Virginia, including those he had excavated many years earlier. Jefferson's mounds were closer in scale to the earthen cone at Marietta, which had excited the speculations reported to him in Paris.

Marietta had no octagons. They were provided by the Scioto and Licking complexes. Thomas Jefferson, of all men, needed no octagonal reminders. He was, his friends reported, obsessed with octagons. In his twenties, he had diagrammed simple means to draw octagons within circles and traced plans of octagonal garden pavilions from English pattern books.

Jefferson employed several means of drawing octagons if we are to judge from Kimball's compilation of his sketches in *Thomas Jefferson, Architect,* especially Nos. 24 and 94. His theoretical device (No. 94) seems to me (though I claim no expertise in the matter) roughly similar to the Hopewell procedures deduced from their remaining work by James Marshall, R. Hively, and R. Horn. See Marshall, "American Indian Geometry," "Geometry of the Hopewell Earthworks," and "An Atlas of

American Indian Geometry." See also Hively and Horn, "Geometry and Astronomy in Prehistoric Ohio."

Brown carefully points out in his article cited above that an intention to create the square, while indicated clearly in Jefferson's correspondence, is not born out yet in the archaeology currently being carried out on the site. Nor do we have indications of the octagonal fence in documentation much more than a century old. But my own observation of the site sees confirmation of the circular drive in the massive presence of tulip-poplars which he either planted or left standing where they would confirm such a form.

My hypothesis that Jefferson was responding to his knowledge of Native American architecture in both the forms and materials used at Poplar Forest does not require one *more* octagon in the fence, and one *more* square. He gave us plenty, there, without them.

As to Ohio geometrics, Circleville, Seal, Newark, and Highbanks come to mind. At Frankfort (the Ohio Frankfort, not the Kentucky Frankfort) and Hopeton, the "hyphen" is omitted and the circle and square abut directly. At Marietta the "hyphen" was much extended, running to a circle—the ditch about the conical mound—much smaller in proportion to the square than that at Poplar Forest and those other Ohio sites.

30. Brown, "Poplar Forest," gives the evidence for the fence in his footnote 107, and describes the furniture in footnote 137.

In a letter to me of March 28, 1991, noted above, Brown is emphatic that "ongoing archaeological investigations have yet to confirm conclusively the existence of the circular road or the square kitchen garden as Jefferson intended them. My article attempted to document Jefferson's vision for Poplar Forest, his 'mind's blueprint' of the place, yet much further work is needed to determine the actual configuration as laid out."

Therefore, the sketch included among our illustrations is our own extension of what we think Brown's prose suggests to have been Jefferson's plan. Brown regards it to be "critical that the speculative nature of the 'circle' and 'square' be emphasized." (letter cited above).

Clay Lancaster, the Kentucky historian, once made an inventory of Jefferson's octagonizing and found "over fifty plans, each with some octagonal feature.... Thirty of these have one or more perfectly formed eight-sided rooms or pavilions." "Over fifty" is a goodly proportion of Jefferson's total production. (Lancaster in "Some Octagonal Forms in Southern Architecture," p. 105)

Jefferson's octagons became a joke among the Piedmont gentry. In 1811, Isaac Coles reported to John Hartwell Cocke that he had asked Jefferson for advice to pass along to Cocke to assist in the planning of a house at Bremo. "As you predicted he was for giving you Octagons." (Coles to Cocke, February 23, 1816, Cocke Family Papers at the University of Virginia, cited by Brown in footnote 28).

31. Jefferson to Benjamin Rush, August 17, 1811, unpublished manuscript to be found on microfilm in the Library of Congress, cited in Brown, "Poplar Forest," fn. 133.

32. Quoted in Malone, *The Sage of Monticello,* p. 292. The balance of the report of crowds quoted in Brown, "Poplar Forest," p. 117. Jefferson to William Short, November 24, 1821, in the Massachusetts Historical Society, and to Nathaniel Macon, January 12, 1819, Library of Congress, both cited in Brown, *Poplar Forest,* p. 139.

33. Jaffe, *Man and His Symbols,* p. 273.

34. Gallatin in the Pennsylvania legislature, quoted in Walters, *Gallatin,* p. 376.

35. Berkhofer gives a good treatment of the ebb and flow of events in 1784.

36. Walters, *Gallatin,* p. 181.

37. Miller, *Wolf by the Ears,* p. 241.

38. Jefferson on "other colors of men": writing to Banneker, Writings, pp. 982–983.

39. Jefferson on Wheatley and Gregoire, see Miller, *Wolf by the Ears,* pp. 75–77.

40. Jefferson's views on Indians are given in *Notes on the State of Virginia,* in answer to Query VI, pp. 182 ff.; as to Blacks, in answer to Query XIV, esp. pp. 266–67.

41. Jefferson to Gallatin, August 2, 1823, *The Writings of Albert Gallatin,* Vol. 1, pp. 263–74.

Chapter Eight.   Jefferson's Archaeologists: Part One. The North

1. Jefferson to Isaiah Thomas and the American Antiquarian Society, October 14, 1820, Isaiah Thomas Papers, at the Society. I am grateful to Thomas Knoles, Curator of Manuscripts, for this reference.

2. Brackenridge, *Recollections of Persons and Places in the West,* pp. 10 ff.

3. I am citing a quotation in Kennedy, *Orders from France,* from which this brief account is excerpted, p. 309–310.

4. By far the best treatment of Wilkinson's relationship to Jefferson in exploring the southwestern borders of Louisiana is in Flores, *Jefferson and Southwestern Exploration;* I have used Flores's excellent summary, in a footnote on p. 51, as the base of this paragraph, though with some interjections of my own.

5. The Indian mounds committee circular appears on pp. xxxvii ff. of Vol. 4 of the *Transactions of the American Philosophical Society.*

6. Wilkinson's little services, and the enumeration of scientific services to Jefferson, from Jackson, *Thomas Jefferson,* p. 100.

7. The Elkhorn forts were so interesting to Innes that he showed them, as well, to Collot.

It is possible, though unlikely, that this may be the roughly hexagonal earthwork at the intersection of the Town and South forks of the Elkhorn reported by Squire and Davis (*Smithsonian Contribution,* Plate IX, No. 3, and p. 26) to be seven miles from Lexington.

This last mentioned work appears to have been similar to the "Indian Fort" on Indian Fort Mountain in Madison County, which lies another fifteen miles to the southeast.

The kneeling woman, Harry Innes to Jefferson, July 8, 1790, *Jefferson Papers,* 17, p. 20, illustrated after p. 218, described on p. xxx. TJ, replying to Harry Innes, March 17, 1791, *Jefferson Papers,* 19, p. 521. This statuette is now in the collection of the National Museum of the American Indian, Fitzhugh Collection.

The footnote in the *Jefferson Papers* appearing on p. xxxi of Vol. 17 dates the letter to Jefferson from Harry Innes about the Elkhorn fortifications as "8 July 1779." That is a misprint for 8 July 1790. This same footnote implies that the Parsons map of Marietta was Heart's, which it is not (see p. 316).

8. Brown's letter of October 1, 1799, in the Library of Congress; *Monthly Magazine* of Vol. 24, 1807, p. 74.

The description of the "male and female" busts "plowed up" or "found by laborers digging" (the accounts vary to this extent) in the state of Tennessee comes from a privately published account by John Edwards Caldwell (1808), essentially repeated in *Niles' Weekly Register,* January 4, 1817, pp. 317–18, with the addition that the busts are said to be "sitting in an Indian position . . . considerably defaced."

Brown's letter to Jefferson offering the figurines came from Palmyra, Tennessee. That letter also gives their weight, and says they were "about the size of children of eight or ten years old." *The Monthly Magazine* carried a slightly different account, which was reprinted with a few alterations of words in the Richmond *Enquirer* of July 4, 1808. In this version there are described "several busts carved by the Indians; in these the human form reaches down to the middle of the body, and they are nearly of the natural size . . . found by some laborers digging at a place called Palmyra, *on* the River Tennessee."

Though both versions spoke of Palmyra as being "on" the Tennessee, it is, in fact, "on" the Cumberland River. Jefferson's response to Brown of January 16, 1800 in the Library of Congress quite explicitly refers to "two Indian busts found on the Cumberland."

The *Enquirer* reported "the traits [*The Monthly* said "lineaments"] are strongly marked . . . among others is one of them representing an old Savage, in which the wrinkles in his face, and his whole countenance [are] peculiarly expressive."

9. According to an expert on these matters, James Victor Miller of Lebanon, Tennessee, a third of the known examples of this class of figurines have been found in the Castalian Springs area, while no similar concentrations are to be found elsewhere.

Miller provided us (by letter of April 2, 1991) a detailed analysis of similar figurines at the Smithsonian, the Peabody Museum at Harvard, and the Valentine Museum in Richmond, Virginia, comparing them to another in the Metropolitan Museum (1979.206.1139), and one in the McClung Museum, at the University of Tennessee, Knoxville, and one depicted (but now lost) in Haywood, *Aboriginal History of Tennessee,* pp. 120–121.

This stretch of the Cumberland is full of later history. Gallatin, Tennessee, named and founded in 1802, lies close to Cragfont, the limestone mansion of General James Winchester, who joined with Overton and Jackson in founding Memphis. Wynnewood is there, too, a log complex showing how elegant could be this north European form when extended in modular units, and Rock Castle, the Daniel Smith house begun in 1796, near Hendersonville, named for the North Carolina speculator—excellent browsing for amateur architectural historians working up an appetite for the grandeurs of Nashville, Columbia, and Maury Counties.

10. Jefferson to Wilkinson, January 16, 1800, and Wilkinson to Jefferson, September 1 and November 29 of that year, in Vols. 16, 17, and 18 of the *Jefferson Papers.*

We wish we knew maps of what, for they were accompanied by some meteorological reports prepared, apparently for Wilkinson, by William Dunbar. This is the first recorded association of Dunbar to Wilkinson; the *last* is more dramatic, and, as we shall see, of considerably greater political importance to both Wilkinson and Jefferson.

James R. Jacobs, in his *Tarnished Warrior,* confused William Dunbar, a surveyor employed by Wilkinson, who apparently committed suicide at about this time (p. 181), with William Dunbar of The Forest, the meteorologist. The latter did have occasion to tell one of the merchants with whom he was doing business that there was another William Dunbar in the area with whose mail his might be confused.

11. The hide paintings now in the Peabody Museum collection of Harvard University are there described (1993) as having come from Poplar Forest, by way of the Peale Museum, to which Jefferson himself conveyed other items—animal skins and skeletons—by gift on October 6, 1805 (Letter from Jefferson to Peale that date, Library of Congress). The Peabody was relying upon what was said by Charles Sellers in 1980 in his *Mr. Peale's Museum,* pp. 172–85. But correspondence in the Monticello archives between Sellers, who was determined upon that interpretation, and the staff of Monticello at the time leave considerable doubt that the paintings ever got to Poplar Forest.

See also Jefferson to Meriwether Lewis, October 26, 1806, in Jackson, *Letters of the Lewis and Clark Expedition,* pp. 350–51.

12. Jefferson's response to Brown of January 16, 1800 in the Library of Congress. The baron de Montlezun reported in 1816 only "two busts man

and woman." ("A Frenchman visits Monticello, 1816" tr. and ed. J. M. Carrier and L. G. Moffatt, *Papers of the Albemarle County Historical Society,* Vol. 4 (1943–44), pp. 45–52.

13. Thruston, *The Antiquities of Tennessee,* p. 205.

14. Nutt's observations are to be found in the Park Service Archives, and excerpted in *The Journey of Mississippi History* 9 (January–October 1947) pp. 51–52, 57–58.

15. Brandau, *History of Homes and Gardens of Tennessee,* p. 150.

16. My information on the nobby road, and much else in these paragraphs comes from Harriet Simpson Arnow's magnificent *Seedtime on the Cumberland.* For the quotation, see p. 20.

17. Ibid., p. 20.

18. Green, in *The Spanish Conspiracy,* Peter Smith, Gloucester, Mass. (1967 reprint of the 1891 original edition) p. 40.

19. My quotations about Clark and Nourse are from Abernethy, *Western Lands,* p. 127.

20. Quoted in Skele, *The Great Knob,* p. 17.

21. Van Every, *Ark of the Empire,* p. 176.

22. Collot, *Journey in North America,* Vol. I, p. 115.

23. For Collot on Kentucky fort, Vol. I, p. 115. As indicated in footnote 7, above, Collot and Harry Innes were both interested in the geometric earthforms created by ancient Americans and their sculpture.

    As also noted in footnote 7, above, there seem to have been at least two, and possibly three, fortlike structures in the vicinity of Lexington. There was Collot and Innes's structure, at the intersection of the Town and South Forks of the Elkhorn shown in Squire and Davis (Plate IX, No. 3, and p. 26) and another on Indian Fort Mountain, in Madison County, 15 miles away.

24. Collot, *Journey,* Vol. I, p. 152.

25. Ibid., pp. 128–29, 217.

26. Ibid., Vol. I, pp. 153, 171.

27. Collot, *Journey,* Vol. II, p. 226.

28. Ibid., pp. 144, 248.

29. Van Every, *Ark of Empire,* p. 289.

30. Ibid., p. 290.

31. Osgood, *The Field Notes of Captain William Clark,* pp. 16–17. This site is on the northwest edge of the Cahokia complex, beneath the present town of Mitchell, Madison County, Illinois, about eight miles north of

Cahokia. Three railroad beds driven through the site obliterated the mounds.

32. W. Clark, July 12, 1804; see Osgood, *Field Notes*, p. 76.

33. Ibid., p. 118.

34. I am indebted to F. A. Calabreze of the National Park Service for the information that these two sites are within Van Meter State Park. See also Wood, "Culture Sequence at the Old Fort,"

    Professor Gary Moulton of the University of Nebraska very helpfully corrected several pages of this manuscript in this section of my narrative.

35. Generations of urbane Kentuckian Boones, descended from Daniel, have gracefully reminded us that he was an able memoirist and sophisticated real estate speculator, though like George Rogers Clark, he had acquired a reputation as a bad speller. His most celebrated inscription was placed on a tree: "Dan'l Boon kild a bar." If, in fact, he ever descended to such simplified spelling it is likely that he did so out of calculation rather than orthographic incompetence. Boone was quite capable of calculating that such a slogan would become a billboard no one would forget.

    If that was his purpose, he succeeded, and, borrowing from his celebrity, we may inscribe here the important fact that archaeology along the Missouri owes as great a debt to curiosity about Boone aroused among scientific Englishmen by Lord Byron's version of the Boone myth as to Lewis and Clark. Byron drew upon an account of Boone generated by the frontiersman's partner in complex real estate speculations, Gilbert Imlay.

    Boone was considerably more than the simple-minded, bear hunting, noble White Savage appearing in historical pageants. Byron made him internationally famous in an apostrophe in *Don Juan*, striding alone into Kentucky, the first of his breed. He was, in fact, a brave man, a stout and resourceful leader, and very good company, though seldom the first anywhere, except to the land office at filing time. Boone was a relative latecomer to Kentucky even among Virginians. He was a frontier gentleman, sufficiently politic to gain election to the Virginia legislature, sufficiently bourgeois to enter twice into large-scale real estate speculations in Kentucky and another in Missouri, sufficiently cosmopolitan to procure the services of Gilbert Imlay as a sort of literary agent in London, and sufficiently companionable to consort with John James Audubon, who was not promiscuous in such matters.

    The urbane French painter and the "bar" skinner were frequent hunting companions. Boone was only a little less sophisticated than George Rogers Clark, to whose classical education we have already alluded.

    Imlay is a name known principally to readers of romantic biographies of romantic poets and of their letters. He emigrated to Ireland and then to England from Kentucky in the early 1790s, and became common-law husband of Mary Wollstonecraft. After he deserted her, she wrote him letters so affecting that when her friends had them published he became established in literary circles as the quintessential cad.

Their child was Fanny, who had a misfortune equal to her mother's; she fell in love with Percy Bysshe Shelley after that paragon of virtue had already produced pregnancies in her half sister, Mary Wollstonecraft Godwin, and her childhood companion, Claire Clairmont.

In America, Imlay is generally dismissed as a minor writer of travel books, though sometimes acknowledged to be a contender with Hugh Brackenridge for the honor of being author of the first novel *about* the West. He was more than that, though Americans are likely to find proof of his caddishness in his having been guilty of a full-scale assault upon the reputation of Thomas Jefferson (Imlay's diatribe has recently been republished). Whatever shreds of repute Imlay had left after the just fury of feminist historians had spent itself have been swept away by Jeffersonian scholars. (See Imlay, *Topographical Description;* Jefferson is the subject of Letter IX, pp. 221.)

Imlay appears before us not because of the Shelley connection, nor because we intend to rehearse his merciless dissection of the racism of the *Notes on Virginia,* nor because he represented Daniel Boone's literary interests in London, and thus brought Boone to the attention of Shelley's friend, Lord Byron. He is mentioned here because he was a popular author who brought the monumental architecture of the Ohio Valley Indians for the first time to a large international audience.

Imlay was a marginal man; always at extremes, from the time he appeared on the Kentucky frontier as a prospectus writer for Richard Henderson in the 1780s, as one of the Wilkinson circle, to his ignoble end in London. But he had the pluck to expose the racial views of the Virginia Dynasty when such candor was far from fashionable, and to propose that the intra-racial marriages of which they were so proud when the bride was an Indian princess, might well be extended to include Blacks. And of course, no aristocratic Virginian was ever heard to claim descent from an Indian prince.

Imlay was in London by the time of the publication of his *Topographical Description,* in 1792 and his novel, *The Emigrants,* in 1793. He was also attempting to sell what purported to be a collection of Boone's letters to publishers in London at the time that he was consorting with Wollstonecraft. Shelley and Byron were full of romantic notions of Kentucky and of Boone. They had learned about the West directly from Imlay and from reading the accounts of Brackenridge in *Views of Louisiana.*

John Bradbury, an English botanist, became acquainted with Boone through Byron, and was delighted to have an opportunity to converse with the eighty-four-year-old patriarch in his ultimate frontier-post in Missouri. When Bradbury told Henry Brackenridge of the occasion, Brackenridge hastened up the Missouri to apply his technique in oral history to Boone, but arrived just after the old man's death.

That event would have happened a good deal earlier if James Wilkinson had had his way. In 1804, Wilkinson not only prodded the Spaniards to intercept the Lewis and Clark expedition, but also urged them to go after "an individual named Boone" who, said Wilkinson, was on the

Missouri intending to attack Santa Fe. (In 1913, Isaac Joslyn Fox reported that he had found among the Cuban Papers in the Spanish Archives this document, dated April 10, 1804. See Fox, p. 31.)

Poor old Boone; his time for such exertions was long past. He had been a lion in the 1770s. By 1811, when Bradbury found him, his heroic days were over, but he kept on living. Indeed, he almost outlived Byron; Boone died in 1820 and Byron in 1824.

36. The elder Brackenridge on Indians, in his *Indian Atrocities,* Cincinnati, 1782, p. 62, quoted in *The Savages of America,* p. 54.

Henry Brackenridge distinguished among Indians he knew personally, Indians who might have created monumental architecture in the past, and Indians sunk into barbarism. He defended a murderer in the last category from hanging on grounds that he was "totally deficient on the very ground-work of our social order," and remarked that others he saw on his voyage up the Missouri were so depraved that "the world would lose little, if these people should disappear before civilized communities." (Ibid., p. 65).

37. Ibid., p. 29.

38. Ibid., p. 185.

39. Ibid., pp. 40–2.

40. Wilkinson admitted to setting assassins after John Connolly. See Jacobs, *Tarnished Warrior,* p. 89.

41. Brackenridge, *Recollections,* pp. 11, 12, and 59.

42. Brackenridge's sketches went to Jefferson by way of Richard Walsh of St. Louis, a fact discovered, along with many others deployed in this account, by Brackenridge's only biographer, William F. Keller (see *The Nation's Advocate*).

43. Brackenridge to Jefferson, May 30, 1814, Library of Congress.

44. Brackenridge, *Recollections,* p. 28. He does not give a date, only "about this time" which must have been about 1798.

45. These two documents are to be found among the Jefferson Papers in the Library of Congress, as #35458 and #35698. For them and many other treasures I am indebted to Matthew Mulcahy.

I cannot find any evidence to support the assertion, made by some historians, that Brackenridge was, in effect, reporting back, having toured the Mississippi Valley under a commission from Thomas Jefferson, and the tone of the correspondence between the two makes this unlikely.

46. Ibid.

47. In Fowler, *The Cahokia Atlas,* p. 17. *The Great Knob,* by Mikels Skele, published by the same agency in 1988, is more useful to historians and general readers.

The letter from Brackenridge to Jefferson is to be found in the *Transactions* of the American Philosophical Society for 1813, Vol. 30, pp. 151 ff.

48. Ibid.

49. Ibid.

50. Ibid.

51. Ibid.

52. Ibid., p. 251.

53. Ibid., p. 288.

54. Ibid., p. 292.

55. Ibid., p. 322.

56. Ibid., P. 320.

57. Ibid., p. 363.

58. Brackenridge's letter to Jefferson was read to the American Philosophical Society on October 1, 1813, and printed in the *Transactions* of the Society for 1818, No. 7.

59. Ibid., p. 369.

60. Ibid., p. 372.

61. Ibid., p. 378.

Chapter Nine. Jefferson's Archaeologists: Part Two.

1. Sargent quoted in Abernethy, *South*, pp. 160–61.

2. Dunbar to Sargent, August 10, 1799, Rowland, p. 102.

3. Ker, while at Edinburgh may have known Dr. James Thornton—the architect, poet, patent commissioner, and supporter of Gregor MacGregor—and Dr. James Stevens—American minister to Toussaint Louverture. See Kennedy, *Orders from France.*

4. Nutt's findings of his Natchez Trace explorations went into a series of notebooks lost through unaccountable carelessness by descendants.

   Fortunately, however, those descendants had previously lent some of Nutt's notebooks to members of the National Park Service, who recorded sections from them. Even these remnants offer us the most comprehensive and intelligent anthropological studies made in the region made until well into the twentieth century. We have bits of Nutt's observations of the Chickasaw (Shiloh) mound group in Chickasaw County, Mississippi, about a mile from De Soto's winter camp of 1540–41, of that "stone fort" on the Harpeth River which had also attracted the attention of John Sevier, and those to which we have already referred in discussing the village in which John Overton had built his house.

Nutt went on to reject the idea that architecture had been accomplished with iron tools. Nutt's observations are to be found in the Park Service Archives, and excerpted in *The Journal of Mississippi History,* 9 (January–October 1947): 51–52, 57–58.

5. Flores, *Jefferson and Southwest Exploration,* pp. 39, 47 fn.

6. In an earlier version of this text I said at this point: "possibly that named Anilco by the soldiers of Hernando de Soto, who in early April, 1542, came upon it in the midst of the most populous country they had encountered and the most abounding in maize. They proceeded to massacre its male inhabitants and enslave the women and children."

   This is an appetizing correlation, and one which is permitted by some reconstructions of the route of De Soto. But lamentably it must be relinquished because of the still more powerful arguments to the contrary of Hudson and especially Schambach, "End of the Trail," pp. 9 ff. especially p. 28.

7. Quoted in Flores, *Southwest Exploration,* p. 60.

8. Quoted in Stuart, *Research Report* p. 12.

9. For Rafinesque and the glyphs, see Stuart, ibid.

10. Flores, *Southwest Exploration,* p. 49 fn.

11. Ibid., p. 28.

12. March 3, 1803, Dunbar p. 159.

13. Flores, *Southwest Exploration,* pp. 54, 56, 80, and 86.

14. Ibid., p. 323.

15. Ibid., pp. 199–206.

16. Ibid., p. 313. I am again following Flores' account.

17. Ibid., p. 293.

18. Dunbar to Wilkinson, May 3, 1807, quoted in ibid., p. 312. Flores also notes the end of the Dunbar-Jefferson correspondence in the footnote on the following page.

19. There is a letter dated, but only with question marks attached, September 20, 1809, in Rowland at p. 204. The contents make it clear that the question should be answered in favor of a date no later than 1805.

20. Quoted in Flores, *Southwest Exploration,* p. 208.

21. The sighting of Lafon is recorded in Spanish documents reviewed and cited in detail in Faye, "Privateersmen," pp. 60–61. The best recent account of Lafon is that of Bos, *Barthelemy Lafon.*

22. Ibid., p. 154.

23. Lafon to Dunbar, August 19, 1805, Rowland, *William Dunbar,* pp. 178 ff.

24. The description is by Henry Brackenridge. See Appendix C.

25. Lafon to Dunbar, Rowland, *Dunbar,* pp. 178 ff.

26. *WPA Guide,* p. 478.

27. Ibid.

28. Collins, pp. 200–207.

29. The computation of the value of the estate is my own, based upon the valuation approaching $300,000 in 1819 dollars in Bos, *Lafon.* The inventory of the estate appear in Bos and in sources cited by her.

Chapter Ten.   Evangelism and Amnesia: Explaining Away the Mounds

1. Letter from Jefferson to Benjamin Rush, April 21, 1803, in *Writings,* 10, pp. 379–385.

2. Jefferson to Cooper, November 2, 1822, *Writings,* 15, p. 404.

3. Adams to Jefferson, September 14, 1813, in Wilstach, pp. 82–83.

4. Ibid.

5. Adams to Jefferson, November 4, 1816, quoted in Wilstach, pp. 146–47.

6. Ibid., February 23, 1819, p. 167.

7. There is a wonderful passage describing this resumption of evangelical fervor among the Founders, together with the quotation from Rush, in Gordon Wood, p. 366.

8. The search goes on for these figures (1994). For quotations, see *Sketches of the Moon and Barclay Families etc.* Compiled by Anna Mary Moon (1939) in the Monticello archives.

9. See Bedini, *Thomas Jefferson, Statesman of Science,* pp. 378–79 and citations on p. 582.

   These heads are inventoried as 7 ½ inches tall, so they are unlikely to be the statuettes, discussed earlier, listed as 18.1-inch "busts."

   The hide paintings now in the Peabody Museum collection of Harvard University are there described as having come from Poplar Forest, by way of the Peale Museum, to which Jefferson himself conveyed other items—animal skins and skeletons—by gift on October 6, 1805. (Letter from TJ to Peale that date, Library of Congress.) The Peabody was relying upon Charles Sellers, as conveyed in his *Mr. Peale's Museum,* pp. 172–85.

10. Letters to Secretary Spencer F. Baird of the Smithsonian from Dr. William C. Dabney, of Charlottesville, Virginia (April 29, 1875) and from Alexander Wetmore, Assistant Secretary of the Smithsonian to Miss H. G. McCormack of the Valentine (August 27, 1938), both in the Smithsonian's archives.

11. For Dabney and Stockton, see previous note.

    Randolph insisted, according to what museum curators call the "provenance letter," that it (or they) had been "sent to Mr. Jefferson from 'the West'" through he did not know "by whom or from what point." The Smithsonian's file in the matter is placed under "Tennessee" and the Valentine's accession description also says "dug up in Tennessee," though in neither case is documentation offered. But judging from information provided by James Victor Miller, it seems likely that all five of Jefferson's Indian sculptures came from the Cumberland River Valley as it passes from Tennessee into Kentucky.

    Miller made a detailed analysis of the figurines at the Smithsonian, the Peabody, and the Valentine, comparing them to another in the Metropolitan Museum, one in the McClung Museum at the University of Tennessee, Knoxville, and one depicted (but now lost) in John Haywood's *Aboriginal History of Tennessee* of 1823, pp. 120–21. (Miller by letter of April 2, 1991; the Metropolitan's identification number is (1979.206.1139).

    It is possible that there were *four* lost figures from Tennessee. An inventory of Jefferson's collection made in either 1809 or in 1815 (the date is one or the other, but it is not clear which) spoke of "two busts of Indian figures, male and female by Indians, in hard stone. *18.1. high.* They were dug up at a place called Palmyra, *on* the Tennessee." Eighteen inches high is not "life size" for a human body, even for a child "eight or ten years old." Miller offers an interesting hypothesis to explain the curious fact that Jefferson gave away the figurine from Innes and yet treasured the Brown pair: "Could it be that Innes made no reference to mounds in his letter and Brown did, thus connecting the latter with Indian earthworks? Just wondered." (Miller, letter cited above.)

12. Sanders, pp. 338–39.

13. There is an elegant summation of this tale in Stephen Williams's *Fantastic Archaeology*, pp. 32, 33.

14. My account follows the wonderful tale told by Sanders, pp. 362–65.

15. Ibid.

16. Ibid., pp. 368–69.

17. Ibid., p. 371.

18. Quoted in Gwyn Williams, *Madoc*, p. 11.

19. Ibid., p. 42.

20. I am following Gwyn Williams, who writes with such subtle irony as to

mislead some subsequent scholars, such as Dean DeBolt of the University of West Florida, to think him "a passionate advocate of the Madoc legend." Williams is an eloquent writer and a fine scholar, contriving to tread the line between parody and diffidence while sustaining prose justifying accompaniment by a great Welsh chorus. (DeBolt, fn. 4, p. 16)

21. Carver in DeBolt, p. 12.

22. Filson, *Discovery and Settlement of Kentucky,* p. 96.

23. I am grateful to Stephen Williams for pointing out that Sargent was no Madocian, and that, later, Henry Brackenridge took a similar view.

24. Jefferson on Evans, quoted in DeBolt, p. 13. Stephen Williams points out that Jefferson had a lively interest in Tartars and in trans-Siberian migration, as well as in Welshmen, but insists that the term "mound builders" is misleading as implying that they were a discrete people, instead of a widely dispersed people creating widely variegated architecture of earth. Williams's suggestions appeared as marginalia on one of my final drafts of this chapter, and were written in September, 1993. I hope I have stated his view accurately.

25. Atwater in Silverberg, *The Mound Builders,* p. 51. Silverberg does a good job in reviewing the mound-building myths.

26. Quoted in ibid., p. 129.

27. Foster quoted in Stephen Williams, *Fantastic Archaeology,* p. 73.

28. Cyrus Thomas quoted in Silverberg, p. 162; and as to problems, in Thomas, *Report* p. 21.

29. Ibid., pp. 129 and 132.

30. There was plenty of academic and field work in archaeology during the late nineteenth century, as Stephen Williams points out in *Fantastic Archaeology,* pp. 61–76. But it did not reach the public; Williams himself has done more to catch the attention of a larger audience than all the colleagues to which he gives polite attention in those pages.

31. Atwater, "Antiquities Discovered," pp. 141–45.

32. Buckingham quoted in Reps, *The Making of Urban America,* p. 488.

33. See ibid.

34. For Putnam, see Williams, *Fantastic Archaeology,* p. 30.

35. In 1993, carbon dates were secured in the spine of the Serpent Mound suggesting that it was built about 1060, rather than earlier, at the time when a set of Adena-related objects were found nearby. I have no desire to enter the furious field of fire which has subsequently exploded between those who support one date or another. Besides, the point is not yet proven either way.

Chapter Eleven.   Why Were the Mounds Built?

1. Lincoln, *Speeches and Writings,* pp. 405–6.
2. Washington, *Writings,* Vol. 29, pp. 369–70, January 10, 1788.
3. Jefferson to Isaiah Thomas and the American Antiquarian Society, October 14, 1820, Isaiah Thomas Papers, at the Society.
4. Squier and Davis, *Ancient Monuments,* p. 68.
5. Jund, *Analytical Psychology,* p. 200.
6. Hall, "Ghosts," pp. 360 ff.
    For the moatlike structure at Highbanks, found only in 1972, and therefore beyond tracing throughout the entire perimeter, see Hively and Horn, "Geometry and Astronomy," fn. 7.
7. Park's remarks are printed in *American Antiquities,* of July 4, 1970, available from the Licking County Historical Society, p. 47.
8. Peet, *Mound Builders,* p. 255; the cobble circle at Newark, Smucker, "Mound Builders," p. 269.
9. Peet, Ibid.
10. Romain, "Hopewell Geometric Enclosures."
11. For the reconstruction of the Fairgrounds Circle, I am relying upon authorities collected and upon recent archaeological work conducted by Bradley Lepper, the chatelaine of the Fairgrounds complex.
12. Isaac Smucker, "Mound Builders" p. 266.
13. Lobell, "Special Archetypes," pp. 71 ff.
14. This idea came to me from A. Martin Byers, in his "The Earthwork Enclosures of the Central Ohio valley, etc." I have been urged by many archaeologists to avoid controversy by eschewing citation of Byers, who is not one of them, but his work is exceedingly interesting.
15. Byers brought the idea of purposefully disturbed earth to my attention, though I later found it, as well, in the works of Joseph Campbell, together with much conjecture about the agricultural discoveries and their social impact which I do not find persuasive.
16. The Adena transition toward specialized buildings, and the implication that this arose from increased population, I derive from Clay, "Ritual Spaces," p. 32.
17. Smith, *Floodplain Weed Theory,* p. 117.
18. Smith's tussle with the Gender-Credit Critique is the subject of his "Floodplain Weed Theory" article.
19. Ibid., p. 120.
20. Smith, "Hopewellian Farmers," p. 12.

21. There are some important differences between the Fort Center circle and those in Ohio: it is cut into the earth, upon a boggy savannah, while they are built up upon the earth, with an inner ditch. The last thorough report on the site was in 1971, by Sears, "Food Production and Village Life, etc." I read Sears to say that the circle surrounded a corn field, and that this association of a circle to maize cultivation was complete by A.D. 1, well before the Ohio circles of the same size were constructed and in the absence of maize. It would surprise me if further investigation did not decouple the date and the primary reason for the circle.

22. Edward Edinger, *Anatomy of the Psyche,* as quoted in the *Encyclopedia of Archtypal Symbolism,* p. 216.

23. Ibid.

24. For a comprehensive and comprehendible summary of this work, see Robert Riordan, "Enclosed Hilltops."

25. Riordan, Ibid., p. 10.

26. Ibid., p. 11.

27. Ibid., p. 14.

28. Ibid., pp. 13–14.

29. Ibid., pp. 15–16.

30. Ibid., pp. 11–12.

31. Prufer in *Ohio Hopewell,* p. 69.

32. Dragoo, "Development of Adena Culture," p. 31. In the 1950s, it was hotly debated among archaeologists whether the Adena people, then often said to be physiologically distinct from the Hopewell, came from Illinois eastward or from New York westward. The former scenario still has much to commend it, especially if one adds to it the thought that the band of Fort Ancient hilltop enclosures which lies along the western frontier of the Hopewell heartland along the Scioto, may have been occupied by them first. Thus the Hopewell might have been a second band of westerners pressing eastward into fertile central Ohio.

33. Sullivan, *A System of Architectural Ornament,* p. 124.

34. I am following the admirable work of Hively and Horn, "Geometry and Astronomy."

35. The octagon in Newark is formed by eight lines making manifest in straight earthen walls the patterns one might draw along the earth to record the "pause points" of the moon. (See Hively and Horn.)

36. The term "geomantic" was first applied to these processes by Romain.
    It appears that these enormous earthen constructions were created with these lines to the sky in mind, created to accommodate the observed rising and setting of the moon—one of the few aspects of our human

experience which has a discernable, regular, and even predictable pattern. Hively and Horn have found eighteen or more lunar and solar correspondences between these complementary but distant architectural correspondences between these complementary but distant architectural assemblages. Each of these correspondences falls within a margin of one percent error.

Solar alignments do not seem to have been as important as lunar in the Hopewell architectural lexicon. But they are probably there as well. The first wall one encounters to the left upon emerging into the Highbanks octagon from its sacra via is aligned to the summer solstice rise of the sun. There are solar as well as lunar orientations at Highbanks, and there may also be among the like-sized squares along Paint Creek. (For solar observations at Highbanks, see Hively and Horn.)

N'omi Greber has studied the like-sized squares close to Highbanks and along Paint Creek, has suggested that they may have a solar orientation, though she is exceedingly careful about rushing into any conclusions in a sky-watching field known more for its cranks than for its archaeologists and mathematicians. Greber has been kind enough to discuss with me her tentative hypotheses.

37. *Encyclopedia,* pp. 83–84.

38. Smith, "Hopewell Farmers," p. 65. Smith notes the "stark" contrast between residential and ceremonial life in the Hopewell period. There was, he said, "evidence of strong community scale social integration in the form of corporate labor efforts . . . ceremonial structures, mounds, geometric earthworks," and "the almost total absence of evidence from habitation sites for spacial organization or social integration . . . above the household level . . . combined with the lack of evidence within the domestic sphere for differential status or social ranking." (Ibid.)

On the other hand, David Brose insists that "the burials in mounds and the earthworks themselves are the best possible evidence for social integration above the household level, while the *vast* disparities among Ohio Hopewell grave lots are equally good evidence for differential social status." (Brose in helpful marginalia on my manuscript, April 1991.)

Though several friendly anthropologists have urged that I abandon terms such as "farms," "yeomen," and "Jeffersonians" as "quite inappropriate," I have retained them in order to underline assertions about *both* Ohioans of the geometric period *and* the true believers among Jeffersonians. The underlining about Jeffersonians is necessary, I think, for twentieth century Americans, living long after the shattering of the Jeffersonian equilibrium, brief, narrow in effect, and fragile as it was. It lasted only until its fragility was demonstrated in his presidency, and, even more, by that of his chosen successor, James Madison.

Yet while the dream lasted, it was possible to insist that civic grandeur in assemblages of large, columned buildings (such as the classical complex Jefferson intended for Capitol Hill in Richmond, the University of Virginia, or even smaller civic centers such as the "Acropolis" at Palmyra, Virginia), could be created by a society which eschewed either large government, a hierarchy (except, of course, a distinction between slaves and free), or tightly organized urban centers.

Jefferson's columned architecture was didactic; his ceremonial structures and spaces were intended to instruct; to be, as he put it, "academical villages," with the emphasis upon the adjective, not the noun. The curriculum that was to be taught by these buildings was Jeffersonian civil religion. People were to come together to work on the cathedrals of secular democracy, and then, quickly, lest they stick too close, come apart again.

I wrote *Greek Revival America* in large measure to tell that tale.

39. I am indebted to Bruce Smith for pointing out to me the work of Wesley Cowan dealing with the average height of the dwellers of the central Ohio valley (personal letter of October, 1993)

40. See Sherrod and Rolingson, *Surveyors.*

41. Purrington did offer the possibility of lunar alignments there, and my guess is that others will corroborate his work. (Sherrod and Rolingson, *Surveyors,* p. 132, and Purrington, "Supposed Solar Alignments."

42. Sherrod and Rolingson emphasized that "flat-topped mounds are most often associated with the solstitial positions, when form can be determined." They go on to say that "lineal mounds are generally not a common mound form [as indeed they are not in the years after 1000 B.C. in the Delta, and before 100 B.C. or after A.D. 400 in the Ohio Valley], but in the few instances of these mound shapes they are also in solstitial positions. [They are in lunar positions in Ohio and Kentucky between 100 B.C. and A.D. 400.] Conical mounds are less frequently associated with alignments." (Ibid., p. 132.)

Their results were published in 1987, before Romain's tentative findings of a few solar orientations from the Hopewell period, but after Robert Purrington demolished the notion that there might be solar orientations at Poverty Point.

43. Mimi Lobell instructs us that when people live in this way they may aptly be said to inhabit the World of the Hero. I am following her cross-cultural explorations, and adding a few of my own, probably to the derision of some anthropologists. See Lobell, "Spatial Archetypes," p. 77. Lobell (ibid., pp. 77–78) offers as examples of the quartering heroes the Bronze and Iron Age Indo-Europeans, including the Wessex, Scythian, Celtic, and Viking cultures, and the Aryans of India; the Persians, Hittites, and Phrygians, Etruscans, Aeolians, Ionians, Archaeans, and Dorians; the Hsia, Shang, and Choiu; the Yayoi and Yamato; the Ubaids and the Gerzian dynasts of Egypt; the Israelites before David brought the Ark of the Covenant to Jerusalem; the Plains and Northwest Coast Indians. She suggests as further examples the "pre-pyramid building phases of the Olmec culture in Mexico and the Chavin culture in Peru."

I suggest, in turn, and with far less authority, that we might wish to look into the timing of the supremacy of corn in Mexico, especially its relationship to the quartering of circles in the symbols used at the extremities of the area dominated by Teotihuacan. (See Hedingham, *Early Man*, p. 181.) Maybe the Olmecs belong in this sequence, maybe not.

44. Claude Lévi-Strauss describes the destruction of the spiritual traditions of the Bororo by Salesian missionaries through the forced abolition of the circular village form. I am indebted to Richard Paulson, in his remarkable *The Pure Experience of Order*, pp. 117–118 for this reference and for the quotation from Black Elk.

45. I have used the translation and arrangement of N. D. O'Donoghue, from James P. Mackey, ed., *Introduction to Celtic Christianity*, p. 47.

Appendix A.   Thomas Jefferson and Nicholas Biddle

1. Jefferson to Biddle, Aug. 20, 1813, in the Biddle papers at Andalusia.

2. There is a vast literature of attacks and counter-attacks on Jefferson's record on Civil Liberties. By citing only Jefferson's oft-quoted words, I do not imply that the last word about the matter has been uttered. (See Levy, *Jefferson and Civil Liberties*, especially p. 48.)

3. I am grateful to Dr. Lepper for leading me to Dr. Murphy's work, which has appeared in a number of papers not yet published but presented to a series of meetings from 1985 onward. See also a letter to me dated September 15, 1993, from Dr. Murphy.

BIBLIOGRAPHY

Abernethy, Thomas Perkins. *Western Lands and the American Revolution.* New York: D. Appleton-Century Company, 1937.

———. *The South in the New Nation 1879–1819.* Baton Rouge: Louisiana State University Press, 1976.

Adams, Henry. *The Life of Albert Gallatin.* New York: Peter Smith, 1943.

———. *Second Administration of Thomas Jefferson,* New York: Library of America Edition, 1986.

Adams, John Quincy. *Memoirs.* Edited by Charles Francis Adams. 12 vols. Philadelphia: Lippincott, 1874–77.

Adams, Percy G., ed. *Crevecoeur's Eighteenth-Century Travels in Pennsylvania and New York.* Lexington: University of Kentucky Press, 1961.

———. "Crevecoeur and Franklin." *Pennsylvania History* 14, no. 4 (October, 1947): 273–278.

———. *Travellers and Travel Liars 1660–1800.* Berkeley. University of California Press, 1962.

Agar, Herbert. *The Price of Union.* Boston: Houghton Mifflin, 1950.

Allen, John Logan. *Passage Through the Garden.* Urbana: University of Illinois Press, 1975.

Ambler, Charles. *George Washington and the West.* Chapel Hill: University of North Carolina Press, 1936.

American Philosophical Society. *Documents Relating to the Purchase and Exploration of Louisiana* (Two Reports, one by T. Jefferson and one by William Dunbar). Boston: Houghton Mifflin, 1904.

Andrews, Kenneth. *Trade, Plunder and Settlement: Maritime Enterprise and the Genesis of the British Empire 1480–1630.* New York: Cambridge University Press, 1984.

Atwater, Caleb. "Description of the Antiquities Discovered in the State of Ohio", *Archaeologia Americana* 1 (1820): 105–267.

———. *Description of the Antiquities Discovered in the State of Ohio and Other Western States, Transactions of the American Antiquarian Society* 1 (1820): 186–87. Reprinted in *American Antiquarian* 3, no. 4 (July 1881).

Aubry, Octave. *Napoleon, Soldier and Emperor.* Philadelphia: J. B. Lippincott, 1938.

Bacarisse, Charles A. "Baron de Bastrop," *The Southwestern Historical Quarterly,* 43, no. 3, (January 1955).

Bareis, C. J., and J. W. Porter, "Tittering Phase of the American Bottom Sequence in Illinois," *American Bottom Archaeology.* Urbana: University of Illinois Press, 1984.

Barnhart, Terry A. "Of Mounds and Men: The Early Anthropological Career of Ephraim George Squier." Ph.D. dissertation, Miami University, 1989.

Barton, Benjamin Smith. *Observations on Some Parts of Natural History.* London, 1787.

Bartram, William. *The Travels of William Bartram.* Edited by Mark Van Doren. New York: Dover Publications, 1955.

Bedini, Silvio. *Thomas Jefferson: Statesman of Science.* New York: Macmillan, 1990.

Beebe, Lynn A. "The Rescue and Restoration of Jefferson's Poplar Forest," *Lynch's Ferry* 4, No. 1 (1992).

Berman, Eleanor. *Thomas Jefferson Among the Arts.* New York: New York Philosophical Library, 1947.

Bernard, John. *Retrospections of America.* New York: 1887.

Berns, Walter. "The Constitution and the Migration of Slaves." *The Yale Law Journal* 78, no. 2. (1968): 198–228.

Berthoff, Rowland. *An Unsettled People: Social Order and Disorder in American History.* New York: Harper and Row, 1971.

Bohannan, Paul. Introduction to *Houses and House-Life of American Aborigines* by L. H. Morgan. Chicago: University of Chicago Press, 1965.

Bos, Harriet P. *Barthelemy Lafon.* Masters thesis, Tulane University, 1977.

Bourne, Henry E. "The Travels of Jonathan Carver." *The American Historical Review* 11, no. 2 (January 1906): 287–302.

Bowers, Claude. *The Young Jefferson.* Boston: Houghton Mifflin, 1945.

Boyd, Julian P. *Number 7.* Princeton: Princeton University Press, 1965.

Brackenridge, Henry Marie. *Early Discoveries by Spaniards in New Mexico, Containing an Account of the Ruins of Cibola.* Pittsburgh: Henry Miner, 1857.

_____. *History of the Western Insurrection, 1794.* New York: Arno Press and the New York Times, 1969.

_____. *Recollections of Persons and Places in the West.* Philadelphia: J. B. Lippincott, 1868.

_____. *Views of Louisiana.* Chicago: Quadrangle Books, 1962.

Brackenridge, Hugh Henry. *Modern Chivalry.* New York: American Book Co., 1937.

Bradford, Alexander W. *American Antiquities and Researches into the Origin and History of the Red Race.* New York: Wiley and Putnam, 1843.

Brain, Jeffrey. *La Salle at the Natchez.* Jackson: University of Mississippi Press, 1982.

Brandau, Roberta Seawell, ed. *History of Homes and Gardens in Tennessee.* Nashville: Pantheon Press, 1936.

Brodie, Fawn. *Thomas Jefferson, an Intimate History.* New York: Bantam, 9th printing, 1981.

Brooks, Van Wyck. *The World of Washington Irving.* New York: Dutton, 1950.

Brose, David. "An Historical and Archaeological Evaluation of the Hopeton Works, Ross County, Ohio," Report to the National Park Service, 1976, contract No. PX-6115-6-0141.

_____. *Hopewell Archaeology.* Kent, OH: Kent State University Press, 1979.

_____. *Yesterday's River: The Archaeology of 10,000 Years Along the*

Tennessee-Tombigbee Waterway. Mobile District (Alabama): U.S. Army Corps of Engineers, 1991.

Brose, David, James Brown, and David Penney. *Ancient Art of the American Woodland Indians.* New York: Harry Abrams, 1985.

Brown, C. Allan. "Poplar Forest: The Mathematics of an Ideal Villa," *Journal of Garden History* 10, no. 2 (1990): 117–139.

Brown, Everett Somerville, ed. *William Plumer's Memorandum of Proceedings in the United States Senate 1803–1807,* New York: Macmillan, 1923.

Brown, Lloyd Arnold. *Early Maps of the Ohio Valley.* Pittsburgh: University of Pittsburgh Press, 1959.

Brown, Stuart E. *Virginia Baron.* Berryville, VA: Chesapeake Book Co., 1965.

Buley, R. Carlyle. *The Old Northwest* (2 Vols.). Bloomington: Indiana University Press, 1950.

Burland, Cottie, and Werner Forman. *The Aztecs: Gods and Fate in Ancient Mexico.* London: Orbis, 1975.

Burrows, Edwin. "Notes on Settling America: Albert Gallatin, New England, and the American Revolution," *New England Quarterly* 58, no. 3 (1985).

Byers, A. Martin. "The Earthwork Enclosures of the Central Ohio Valley: A Temporal and Structural Analysis of Woodland Society and Culture." Ph.D. dissertation, State University of New York at Albany, 1987.

Byrd, Kathleen M., ed. "Recent Research at the Poverty Point Site." *Louisiana Archaeology* 13 (Louisiana Archaeological Society, 1986).

Caldwell, Joseph R., and Robert L. Hall, eds. *Hopewellian Studies.* Springfield: Illinois State Museum Scientific Papers, 1964.

Carlson, J. B. "Prehistoric America's Golden Age," *Early Man,* Winter 1979.

Carson, Gary et al. "Impermanent Architecture in the Southern American Colonies," *Winterthur Portfolio,*

Carver, Jonathan. *Travels Through the Interior Parts of North America in the Years 1766–68.* Minneapolis: Ross and Haynes, 1956.

Cary, Wilson Miles. *Sally Cary.* New York: De Vinne Press, 1916.

Cherry, P. P. *The Grave Creek-Mound: Its History, and Its Inscribed Stone, with Its Vindication,* Wadsworth, OH: Steam Printing House, 1877.

Clay, R. Berle. "Adena Ritual Spaces." In *Early Woodland Archaeology,* Vol. 2. Kenneth B. Farnsworth and Thomas E. Emerson, pp. 581–95. Kampsville, IL: Center for American Archaeology Press, 1986.

_____. "Adena Ritual Development." In *The Human Landscape in Kentucky's Past,* Charles Stout and Christine K. Kensley. Frankfort: Kentucky Heritage Council, 1991.

Cleland, Hugh. *George Washington in the Ohio Valley.* Pittsburgh: University of Pittsburgh Press, 1955.

Coe, Michael, Dean Snow, and Elizabeth Benson. *Atlas of Ancient America.* New York: Facts on File Publications, 1986.

Cole, Frank. "Thomas Worthington of Ohio," *The Old Northwest Genealogical Quarterly,* April 1902.

Collins, Henry B. *Archaeological Work.* Washington, DC: Smithsonian Institution, 1927–29.

Collot, George-Henri-Victor. *A Journey in North America,* 3 vols. New York: AMS Reprint, 1974.

Coming, Alexander. "Travels." *Tennessee Historical Magazine* 5 (1919): 125–26.

Corlew, Robert. *Tennessee.* Knoxville: University of Tennessee Press, 1981.

Count, Earl W. "The Earth-Diver and the Rival Twins," In *Indian Tribes of Aboriginal America,* ed. Sol Tax. Chicago: University of Chicago Press, 1952.

Cox, Isaac Joslin. "The Louisiana-Texas Frontier," *The Southwestern Historical Quarterly* 10 (1913): 1–75; 17 (1913): 1–44.

———. *The West Florida Controversy: A Study in American Diplomacy.* Gloucester, MA: Peter Smith, 1967.

Crane, Verner. *The Southern Frontier,* New York: W. W. Norton, 1981.

Cronon, William. *Changes in the Land.* New York: Hill and Wang, 1983.

Crosby, Alfred. *The Columbian Exchange: Biological and Cultural Consequences of 1492.* Westport, CT: Greenwood Publishers, 1972.

———. *Ecological Imperialism and the Biological Expansion of Europe 900–1900,* New York: Cambridge University Press, 1986.

Dangerfield, George. *The Era of Good Feeling.* New York: Harcourt Brace, 1952.

Daniel-Hartung, Ann L. "Archaeoastronomy at a Selection of Mississippian Sites in the Southeastern United States." In *Archaeoastronomy in the Americas,* ed. Ray A. Williamson, pp. 101–110. Los Altos, CA: Ballena Press, 1981.

Davis, Hester, ed. *Archaeological and Historical Resources of the Red River Basin.* Little Rock: Arkansas Archaeological Survey Research Series No. 1, 1970.

Davis, Robert, Jr. "Fort and Blood Mountains: Secrets of the North Georgia Indians." *North Georgia Journal* 4 (December 1987).

Davis, William C. *Breckenridge: Statesman, Soldier, Symbol.*

De Voto, Bernard. *The Course of Empire.* Cambridge, MA: Riverside, 1952.

DeWitt, John. "Journal of John Sevier." *Tennessee Historical Magazine* 5, no. 3 (1919).

Diehl, Richard. *Tula: The Toltec Capital of Ancient Mexico.* London: Thames and Hudson, 1983.

Dobyns, Henry F. *Their Numbers Became Thinned.* Knoxville: University of Tennessee Press, 1983.

Dowd, Gregory Evans. *A Spirited Resistance.* Baltimore: Johns Hopkins Press, 1992.

Dragoo, Don W. "The Development of Adena Culture and Its Role in the Formation of Hopewell Culture." *Illinois State Museum Scientific Papers* 7, no. 1: 3–34.

Drinnon, Richard. *Facing West: The Metaphysics of Indian-Hating and Empire Building.* New York: Meridian, 1980.

Duel, Thorne, ed. *Hopewellian Communities in Illinois.* Springfield: Illinois State Museum Scientific Papers, No. 5, 1952.

Dunn, J. P. *Indiana: A Redemption From Slavery.* Boston: Houghton Mifflin, 1905.

Dye, David, and Cheryl Cox. *Towns and Temples Along the Mississippi.* Tuscaloosa: University of Alabama Press, 1990.

Early, James. *Romanticism in American Architecture.* New York: Barnes, 1965.

Eddy, J. A. "Archaeoastronomy of North American: Cliffs, Mounds and Medicine Wheels." In *In Search of Ancient Astronomies,* ed. E. C. Krupp, pp. 133–163. Garden City, NY: Doubleday, 1978.

Edwards, J.H. "Ancient Fortifications." *Ohio Archaeologist* 6, no. 3 (July 1956):102–104.

Egnal, Marc. *A Mighty Empire: Origins of the American Revolution.* Ithaca: Cornell University Press, 1988.

Emerson, Thomas, and Barry Lewis, eds. *Cahokia and Its Hinterlands: Middle Mississippian Cultures of the Midwest.* Urbana: University of Illinois Press, 1991.

Encyclopedia of Archetypal Symbolism, ed. Beverly Moon. Boston: Shambala Publications, 1991.

"Environmental Assessment Hopewell Sites Study," Department of the Interior, National Park Service, Midwest Region, July 1987.

Faulkner, Charles. *The Old Stone Fort.* Knoxville: University of Tennessee Press, 1968.

Fay, Bernard. *The Revolutionary Spirit in France and America.* New York: Cooper Square Publishers, 1966.

Faye, Stanley. "Privateersmen of the Gulf and Their Prizes," *Louisiana Historical Quarterly* 22, no. 4 (October 1939).

Fehrenbacher, Don E. *Slavery, Law, and Politics, The Dred Scott Case in Historical Perspective.* New York: Oxford University Press, 1981.

Filson, John. *The Discovery and Settlement of Kentucke,* available from Ann Arbor: University Microfilms, 1966.

Finley, Moses, ed. *The Legacy of Greece.* New York: Oxford University Press, 1984.

Fitzhugh, William. *Crossroads of Continents: Cultures of Siberia and Alaska.* Washington, DC: Smithsonian Institution Press, 1988.

Flaherty, Carolyn. "The Domestic Architecture of Downing," *The Old House Journal,* no. 10 (October 1974).

Flexner, James. *George Washington: The Forge of Experience.* Boston: Little, Brown, 1965.

_____. *George Washington and the New Nation.* Boston: Little, Brown, 1969.

_____. *George Washington: Anguish and Farewell.* Boston: Little, Brown, 1972.

_____. *Washington: The Indispensible Man.* New York: Signet, 1984.

Flores, Dan, ed. *Jefferson and Southwest Exploration: The Freeman and Curtis Accounts of the Red River Expedition.* Norman: University of Oklahoma Press, 1984.

Foote, Shelby. *The Civil War.* New York: Random House, Vintage Edition, 1986.

Ford, J. A., and C. H. Webb. "Poverty Point, a Late Archaic Site in Louisiana," *American Museum of Natural History* 46, Part 1 (1956).

Ford, R. I. "Northeastern Archaeology: Past and Future Directions." *Annual Review of Anthropology* 3 (1974):384–413.

_____. "Gathering and Gardening: Trends and Consequences of Hopewell Subsistence Strategies." In *Hopewell Archaeology: The Chillicothe Confer-*

ence, ed. D. Brose and N. Greber. Kent, OH: Kent State University Press, 1979.

Formwalt, Lee. "Benjamin Henry Latrobe and the Revival of the Gallatin Plan of 1808." *Pennsylvania History* 48, no. 2 (1981).

Fowke, G. *Archaeological History of Ohio.* Columbus: Ohio State Archaeological and Historical Society, 1902.

———. *Notes on Ohio Archaeology.* Norwalk, OH: Langing Printers, 1893.

Fowler, Melvin. *The Cahokia Atlas: A Historical Atlas of Cahokia Archaeology,* no. 6. Springfield: Illinois Historic Preservation Office, 1989.

Fox, Isaac J. *The Louisiana-Texas Frontier,* 2 vols. Austin: University of Texas Press (1906–1913).

Franklin, Benjamin. *The Writings.* Edited by Albert Henry Smith. New York: Haskell House, 1970.

———. *William B. Willcox, et al.* New Haven: Yale University Press, 1966–76.

Gabriel, Kathryn. *Roads to Center Place. A Cultural Atlas of Chaco Canyon and the Anasazi.* Boulder: Johnson Books, 1991.

Gallatin, Albert. *Correspondence of Jean Badollet and Albert Gallatin.* Edited by Gayle Thornbrough. Indiana Historical Society Publication, Vol. 22. Indianapolis: Indiana University Press, 1963.

———. *The Papers of Albert Gallatin.* Edited by Carl E. Prince and Helene W. Fineman. Philadelphia: Historic Publications, 1969; 46 reels of microfilm, with *Guide* by Prince, 1970.

———. "Synopsis." *Proceedings of the American Antiquarian Society* 2 (1838).

———. *The Writings of Albert Gallatin.* Edited by Henry Adams, 3 vols. Philadelphia: Lippincott, 1879; reprint New York: Antiquarian Society, 1960.

Galloway, W.A. *Old Chillicothe.* Xenia, OH: Buckeye Press, 1934.

Garland, Elizabeth Baldwin. *The Obion Site, an Early Mississippian Center in Western Tennessee.* Mississippi State University: The Cobb Institute of Archaeology, 1992.

Garraty, John, ed. *Quarrels That Have Shaped the Constitution.* New York: Harper and Row, 1962.

Geinapp, William E. *The Origins of the Republican Party.* New York: Oxford University Press, 1987.

Gibson, J. L., "Poverty Point: The First North American Chiefdom," *Archaeology* 27, no. 2 (1974).

———. "The Earthen Face of Civilization: Mapping and Testing at Poverty Point, 1983," Report submitted to the Louisiana Division of Archaeology, Baton Rouge, LA, 1984.

Gibson, Jon. "Earth Sitting: Architectual Masses at Poverty Point, Northeastern Louisiana," *Louisiana Archaeology Society,* 1986.

———. "The Poverty Point Earthworks Reconsidered," *Mississippi Archaeology* 22, No. 2 (December 1987): 14 ff.

———. "The Prehistory of the Ouachita River Valley, Louisiana and Arkansas." *Louisiana Archaeology Society,* no. 10, 1983.

———, with J. Richard Shenkel. "Louisiana Earthworks: Middle Woodlands and Predecessors." *Archaeological Report,* no. 22, (1988).

Gilbert, Bil. *God Gave Us This Country: Tekamthe and the First America Civil War.* New York: Doubleday, 1989.

Gilman, Roger. "The Romantic Interior." In *Romanticism in America,* ed. George Boas. New York: Russell and Russell, 1961.

Graham, James. *The Life of General Daniel Morgan.* New York: Derby and Jackson, 1856.

Gratz, Simon. "Thomas Rodney." *The Pennsylvania Magazine of History and Biography* 43–45 (1919–1921).

Green, John. *American Science in the Age of Jefferson.* Ames: Iowa State University Press, 1984.

Gregory, Hiram F. and Webb, Clarence, *The Caddo Indians of Louisiana,* Baton Rouge, La. Department of Culture, Recreation and Tourism, anthropological Study, No. 2, 1990.

Hall, Robert, "Ghosts, Water Barriers, Corn and Sacred Enclosures in the Eastern Woodlands," *American Antiquity* 41, no. 3 (July 1976).

Harris, T. M. *Journal of a Tour into the Territory Northwest of the Allegheny Mountains: Made in the Spring of the Year 1803.* Boston: Manning and Loring, 1805.

Harrison, W. H. "A Discourse on the Aborigines of the Valley of the Ohio," *Transactions of the Historical and Philosophical Society of Ohio* 1 (1839):217–267.

Haven, Samuel F. Report of the Librarian, *Proceedings of the American Antiquarian Society,* April 29, 1863, pp. 19–33.

———. "Archaeology of the United States," *Smithsonian Contributions to Knowledge* 8 (1855).

Hawke, David. *Franklin.* New York: Harper and Row, 1976.

Hawkes, Jacquetta. *Atlas of Ancient Archaeology.* New York: McGraw Hill, 1974.

Hay, Robert. "The Pillorying of Albert Gallatin," *Western Pennsylvania Historical Magazine* 65, no. 3 (1982).

Hay, Thomas, and M. R. Werner. *The Admirable Trumpeter: A Biography of James Wilkinson.* Garden City, NY: Doubleday, Doran and Co., 1941.

Haywood, John. *The Natural and Aboriginal History of Tennessee.* Nashville: George Wilson Co., 1823.

Hedingham, Evan. *Early Man and the Cosmos.* Norman: University of Oklahoma Press, 1984.

Hedrick, Basil C., with J. Charles Kelley and Carroll L. Riley. *The Mesoamerican West: Readings in Archaeology, Ethnohistory, and Ethnology.* Carbondale: Southern Illinois University Press, 1974.

Hemmings, E. Thomas. "Investigations at Grave Creek Mound 1975–76: A Sequence of Mound and Moat Construction," *West Virginia Archaeologist* 36, no. 2, 1984.

Hempstead, Giles. *Antiquities of Portsmouth and Vicinity.* Portsmouth, OH, 1875.

Henderson, Gwynn A., with Cynthia E. Jobe and Christopher A. Turnbow. *Indian Occupation and Use in Northern and Eastern Kentucky During the Contact Period (1540–1795): An Initial Investigation.* Lexington: University of Kentucky, 1986.

Hesslink, George K. *Black Neighbors: Negros in a Northern Rural Community.* Indianapolis: Bobs-Merrill, 1968.

Higginbotham, A. Leon, Jr. *In the Matter of Color, Race and the American Legal Process, The Colonial Period.* New York: Oxford University Press, 1978.

Hildreth, S.P. "Pyramids at Marietta." *The American Pioneer* 2, no. 6 (June 1843).

Hildreth, Samuel P. *Pioneer History.* Cincinnati, 1848.

Hively, R., and R. Horn. "Geometry and Astronomy in Prehistoric Ohio." *Journal for the History of Astronomy,* 13, supplement, *Archaeoastronomy* (1982) 4:S1–S20.

Holmes, W. H. "Notes upon Some Geometric Earthworks, with Contour Maps." *American Anthropologist* 5 (1892): 363–373.

Horsman, Reginald. *Diplomatic History,* Vol. 15. 1991, 115–124.

Hudson, Charles. *The Southeastern Indians.* Knoxville: University of Tennessee Press, 1976.

Hunington, David. *Art and the Excited Spirit: America in the Romantic Period.* Ann Arbor: The University of Michigan Museum of Art, 1972.

Hunter, George. "The Western Journals of Dr. George Hunter." Edited by J. F. McDermott. *Transactions of the American Philosophical Society,* New Series, 53, part 4 (1963).

Imlay, Gilbert. *Topographical Description of the Western Territory of North America.* New York: Johnson Reprint, 1968.

Jackson, Donald, ed. *Letters of the Lewis and Clark Expedition,* Urbana: University of Illinois Press, 1978.

———. *Thomas Jefferson and the Stony Mountains: Exploring the West from Monticello.* Urbana: University of Illinois Press, 1981.

Jacobs, James. *Tarnished Warrior.* New York: Macmillan, 1938.

Jacobs, Wilbur. *Dispossessing the American Indian,* Norman: University of Oklahoma Press, 1972.

Jaffe, Aniela. "Symbolism in the Visual Arts." In *Man and His Symbols.* New York: Dell, 1974.

James, James A. *The Life of George Rogers Clark,* Chicago, 1928. Reprint. New York: AMS, 1970.

Jefferson, Thomas. *The Thomas Jefferson Papers.* Edited by Julian Boyd. Princeton: Princeton University Press, 1950–1982.

———. "Notes on the State of Virginia," *The Complete Jefferson.* Edited by Saul K. Padover. New York: Duell, Sloan and Pearce, 1943.

Jefferson, Thomas. *Autobiography.* In *Thomas Jefferson, Writings.* New York: Library of America, 1984.

———. *Writings,* ed. A. A. Lipscomb and A. E. Bergh. Washington, DC, 1903–4.

Jenkins, Ned J. "Archaeology of the Gainesville Lake Area: Synthesis," *Archaeological Investigations in the Gainesville Lake Area of the Tennessee-Tombigbee Waterway,* Vol. 5, 1982.

Jennings, Francis. *The Invasion of America: Indians, Colonialism and the Cant of Conquest.* New York: Norton, 1975.

Jennings, Jesse, ed. *Ancient North Americans.* New York: W. H. Freeman and Company, 1983.

———. "Nutt's trip to the Chickasaw Country," *Journal of Mississippi History* 9 (1947).

Johannsen, Robert W. *To the Halls of the Montezumas.* New York, Oxford University Press, 1985.

Johnston, Henry P. *The Correspondence and Public Papers of John Jay 1763–1826.* New York: Da Capo Press, 1971.

Jones, David. A Journal of Two Visits to Some Nations of Indians, Burlington, NJ 1774.

Jones, R. B. "Archaeological Investigations in the Ouachita River Valley, Bayou Bartholomew to Riverton, Louisiana," *Louisiana Archaeology* 10 (1983). (Also in *The Prehistory of the Ouachita River Valley, Louisiana and Arkansas,* ed., Jon Gibson. Lafayette: The University of Southwestern Louisiana, 1985).

Jung, Carl. *Analytical Psychology; Its Theory and Practice,* The Tavistock Lectures. New York: Vintage Paperbacks, 1970.

_____. *Psychology and Alchemy.* New York: Pantheon Books, 1953.

Kelemen, Pal. *Medieval American Art.* New York: Macmillan, 1943.

Keller, William. *The Nation's Advocate: Henry Marie Brackenridge and Young America.* Pittsburgh: University of Pittsburgh Press, 1956.

Kelsay, Isabel Thompson. *Joseph Brant 1743–1807, Man of Two Worlds,* Syracuse: Syracuse University Press, 1984.

Kenin, Richard, and Wintle, Justin, eds. *The Dictionary of Biographical Quotation.* New York: Knopf, 1978.

Kennedy, Roger. *Greek Revival America.* New York: Stewart, Tabori and Chang, 1989.

_____. *Orders from France: The Americans and French in a Revolutionary World.* Philadelphia: University of Pennsylvania Press, 1990.

_____. *Rediscovering America; Journeys Through Our Forgotten Past,* Boston: Houghton Mifflin, 1990.

_____. "Jefferson and the Indians." *The Winterthur Portfolio* 27, no. 2/3 (Summer/Autumn 1992).

Kerber, Linda K. *Federalists in Dissent, Imagery and Ideology in Jeffersonian America.* Ithica: Cornell University Press, 1970.

Ketchum, Richard. *The World of George Washington.* New York: American Heritage Press, 1974.

Kimball, Fiske. *Thomas Jefferson, Architect.* New York; Da Capo, 1968.

King, Mary E., and Joan S. Gardner. "The Analysis of Textiles from Spiro Mound, Oklahoma." In *The Research Potential of Anthropological Museum Collections,* eds. A. M. Cantwell, J. B. Griffin and N. A. Rothschild. New York: Annals of the New York Academy of Sciences, 1981.

Kirk, Russell. *John Randolph of Roanoke.* Indianapolis: Liberty Press, 1951.

Knepper, George W. *Ohio and Its People.* Kent: Kent State University Press, 1989.

Kongas, Elli Kaija. "The Earth-Diver." *Ethnohistory* 7, no. 2 (1960).

Kubler, George. *The Art and Architecture of Ancient America.* New York, Penguin Books, 1962.

Kwas, Mary L., and Robert C. Mainfort, Jr. "The Johnston Site: Precursor to Pinson Mounds?" *Tennessee Anthropologist* 11, no. 1 (1986).

Lancaster, Clay. "Some Octagonal Forms in Southern Architecture," *The Art Bulletin* 28, no. 2 (June 1946).

_____. *Vestiges of the Venerable City, A Chronicle of Lexington, Kentucky.*
Lexington: Lexington-Fayette County Historic Commission, 1978.

Lange, Frederick. *Cortez Crossroads: A Guide to the Anasazi Heritage and
Scenic Beauty of the Four Corners Region.* Boulder: Johnson Books, 1989.

Langhorne, Elizabeth, K. E. Lang, and W. D. Rieley. *A Virginia Family and
Its Plantation Houses.* Charlottesville: University of Virginia Press, 1987.

Latrobe, Benjamin Henry. *The Correspondence and Miscellaneous Papers of
Benjamin Henry Latrobe,* 3 vols. Edited by John C. Van Horne and others.
New Haven: Yale University Press, and Baltimore: Maryland Historical
Society, 1984–1988.

Lepper, B. T. "A Historical Review of Archaeological Research at the Newark Earthworks," *Journal of the Steward Anthropological Society* 18, nos.
1 and 2 (1989): 118–140.

_____. "New Discoveries at the Newark Earthworks: James H. Salisburys
1862 'Survey & Description of the Earthworks at Newark, Ohio.'" Paper
presented at "Vanishing Heritage: Planning for the Future of Ohio's Past,"
Ohio State University, Newark, Ohio, 1989.

_____. "The Newark Earthworks: A New Look at the Lost Grandeur." Paper
presented at the ESAF Annual Meeting, Columbus, Ohio, November 10,
1990.

Levy, Leonard. *Jefferson and Civil Liberties.* Cambridge, MA: Harvard University Press, 1963.

Lewis, Anthony Marc, "Jefferson and Virginia's Pioneers" in *The Mississippi
Valley Historical Review,* Vol. XXXIV, No. 4, March, 1948, pp. 551 ff.

Lewis, Thomas A. *For King and Country.* New York: Harper Collins, 1993.

Lincoln, Abraham, *Speeches and Writings,* New York; Library of America,
1989.

Lobell, Mimi. "Spacial Archetypes." *Revision* 6, no. 2 (Fall 1983): 69 ff.

Logan, Marie. *Mississippi-Louisiana Border Country: A History of Rodney,
Miss., St. Joseph, La., and Environs.* Baton Rouge: Claitor's Publishing,
1970.

Lomask, Milton. *Aaron Burr: The Years from Princeton to Vice President.*
New York: Farrar, Straus and Giroux, 1979.

"Louisiana-Texas Frontier," *Quarterly of the Texas State Historical Association* 10 and 17, (July and October, 1913).

Lynd, Straughton. *Class Conflict, Slavery, and the United States Constitution.*
Indianapolis: Bobbs-Merrill, 1968.

Mackey, James P. ed. *An Introduction to Celtic Christianity.* Edinburgh: T. T.
Clark, 1989.

MacLean, J. P. *The Mound Builders: Archaeology of Butler Country, Ohio.*
Cincinnati: Robert Clarke and Company, 1879.

Mainfort, Robert C., Jr. "Pinson Mounds: A Middle Woodland Ceremonial
Center." *Tennessee Department of Conservation, Division of Archaeology
Research Series,* no. 7, 1986.

_____. "Middle Woodland Ceremonialism at Pinson Mounds." *American An-
tiquity* 52, no. 1: 158–173.

_____. "Excavations at Pinson Mounds: Ozier Mound." *Midcontinential
Journal of Archaeology* 17, no. 1: 112–136.

Mainfort, Robert C., and Kenneth C. Carstens. "A Middle Woodland Embankment and Mound Complex in Western Kentucky," *Southeastern Archaeology* (1987):57–61.

Malone, Dumas, ed. *The Dictionary of American Biography,* Vol. 13. New York: Charles Scribner's and Sons, 1934.

Malone, Dumas. *Jefferson the Virginian.* Boston: Little, Brown, 1948.

———. *The Sage of Monticello.* Boston: Little Brown, 1981.

Malville, J. McKim, and Claudia Putnam. *Prehistoric Astronomy in the Southwest.* Boulder: Johnson Books, 1989.

Mannix, Richard. "Albert Gallatin and the Movement for Peace With Mexico." *Social Studies* 60, no. 7 (1969):310–318.

Marshall, J. "American Indian Geometry." *Ohio Archaeologist* 28, no. 1 (1978): 29–33.

———. "Geometry of the Hopewell Earthworks." *Ohio Archaeologist* 30, no. 2 (1980): 8–12.

———. "An Atlas of American Indian Geometry." *Ohio Archaeologist* 37, no. 2 (1987): 36–49.

Martin, Lawerence, ed. *The George Washington Atlas.* Washington, DC: United States George Washington Bicentennial Commission, 1932.

McColley, Robert. *Slavery and Jeffersonian Virginia.* Urbana: University of Illinois Press, 1973.

McCullough, Niall, and Valerie Mulvin. *A Lost Tradition: The Nature of Architecture in Ireland.* Dublin: Grandon Editions, 1987.

McDermott, John Francis, ed. *The French in the Mississippi Valley.* Urbana: University of Illinois Press, 1965.

McDonald, Jerry, and Susan Woodward, *Indian Mounds of the Atlantic Coast.* Blacksburg, WV: McDonald and Woodward, 1987.

———. *Indian Mounds of the Middle Ohio Valley.* Blacksburg, WV: McDonald and Woodward, 1986.

McDonald, Travis C. "Ghost Stories." *Lynch's Ferry,* Spring/Summer, 1991.

McFaul, John. "Expediency vs. Morality: Jacksonian Politics and Slavery." *Journal of American History,* 62, no. 1 (June 1975).

Meggers, Betty. *Prehistoric America: An Ecological Perspective.* New York: Aldine Publishing, 1979.

Meinig, D. W. *The Shaping of America, Vol. 2, Continental America, 1800–1867.* New Haven: Yale University Press, 1993.

Merck, Frederick. *History of the Westward Movement.* New York: Knopf, 1980.

Mereness, Newton. *Travels in the American Colonies.* New York: Antiquarian Press, 1961.

Miller, John Chester. *The Wolf by the Ears.* New York: Macmillan, 1977.

Mitchell, Jeannie, and Robert Calhoun. "The Marquis de Maison Rouge, the Baron de Bastrop and Colonel Abraham Morehouse—Three Ouachita Valley Soldiers of Fortune/The Maison Rouge and Bastrop Spanish Land 'Grants,'" *The Louisiana Historical Quarterly* 20, no. 2 (April 1937).

Monette, John Wesley. *History of the Discovery and Settlement of the Mississippi Valley.* New York, 1846.

Moore, Clarence B. "Certain Sand Mounds of the St. John's River, Florida."

Journal of the Academy of Natural Sciences of Philadelphia, 2nd series, vol. 10 (1896).

———. "Some Aboriginal Sites in Louisiana and in Arkansas." *Journal of the Academy of Natural Sciences of Philadelphia,* 2nd series, Vol. 16 (1913).

Morgan, Lewis. "Houses and House-life of American Aborigines." *Contributions to North American Ethnology,* Washington D.C.: Government Printing Office, 1881.

Morgan, William. *Prehistoric Architecture in the Eastern United States.* Cambridge, MA: MIT Press, 1980.

Myers, Minor. *Liberty Without Anarchy.* Charlottesville: University of Virginia Press, 1983.

Nabokov, Peter, and Robert Easton. *Native American Architecture.* New York: Oxford University Press, 1990.

Nash, Gary. *Red, White and Black: The Peoples of Early America,* Englewood Cliffs, NJ: Prentice Hall, 1974.

Nevins, Allan. *The Emergence of Lincoln.* New York: Scribners, 1950.

Neuman, Robert. *An Introduction to Louisiana Archaeology.* Baton Rouge: Louisiana State University Press, 1984.

———. *Melanges: An Archaeological Assessment of Coastal Louisiana.* Baton Rouge: Museum of Geoscience, LSU, 1977.

Newcomb, Rexford. *Architecture in Old Kentucky.* Urbana: University of Illinois Press, 1953.

Noble, David. *Ancient Ruins of the Southwest.* Flagstaff, AZ: Northland Publishing, 1981 and 1991.

———, ed. *The Hohokam: Ancient People of the Desert.* Santa Fe: School of American Research Press, 1991.

Norona, Delf. *Moundsville Mammoth Mound.* Moundsville: West Virginia Archaeological Society, 1954.

Norwich, John Julius. *Byzantium, The Early Centuries.* New York: Knopf, 1989.

Nuttall, Thomas. *A Journal of Travels into the Arkansas Territory During the Year 1819,* ed. Savoie Lottinville. Norman: University of Oklahoma Press, 1980.

Officer, James E. *Hispanic Arizona: 1536–1856,* Tuscon: University of Arizona Press, 1987.

Onuf, Peter S. *Statehood and Union.* Bloomington: Indiana University Press, 1987.

Osgood, E. S., ed. *The field Notes of Captain William Clark.* New Haven: Yale University Press, 1964.

Oszuscik, Philippe. *Louisiana's Gothic Revival Architecture.* Baton Rouge: Claitor's Publishing Division, 1973.

Park, Samuel. "Notes of the Early History of Union Township." O. J. Smith, Terra Haute, 1870, printed in *American Antiquities,* July 4, 1970, available from the Licking County Historical Society.

Parkman, Francis. *LaSalle and the Discovery of the Great West.* New York: Modern Library, 1985.

Patterson, Richard S., and Richardson Dougall. *The Eagle and the Shield.* Washington, DC: Department of State, 1976.

Paulson, Richard. *The Pure Experience of Order.* Albuquerque: University of New Mexico Press, 1982.

Pearce, Roy. *The Savages of America: A Study of the Indian and the Idea of Civilization.* Baltimore: Johns Hopkins University Press, 1953.

Peet, Stephen. *The Mound Builders; Their Works and Relics.* Chicago: Office of American Antiquarian, 1903.

Peter, S. W. K. *Private Memoir of Thomas Worthington, Esq.* Cincinnati: Robert Clarke and Co., 1882.

Peterson, Jeanette F. "Garden Frescoes of Malinalco: Utopia, Imperial Policy and the Acculuration in 16th Century Mexico." Ph.D. dissertation, University of California, Los Angeles, 1985.

Pfeiffer, John. "Indian City on the Mississippi." *Time/Life Nature Science Annual,* Alexandria, VA, 1974.

Phillips, Phillip. *Archaeological Survey of the Lower Yazoo Basin, Mississippi, 1949–1955,* 2 vols. Cambridge, MA: Peabody Museum, 1970.

Pitt, Arthur. "Franklin and the Quaker Movement Against Slavery," *Friends Historical Association Bulletin* 32, no. 1 (spring 1943): 16, 17.

Porter, Eliot. *American Places.* New York: Crown Publishers, 1983.

Priest, Josiah. *American Antiquities and Discoveries in the West,* 2nd Edition. Albany, NY, 1933.

Proskouriakoff, Tatiana. *An Album of Maya Architecture.* Norman: University of Oklahoma Press, 1963.

Prufer, Olaf H. "The Hopewell Complex in Ohio." *Illinois State Museum Scientific Papers* 12, no. 2: 35–83.

_____. "The Hopewell Cult," *New World Archaeology,* eds. E. Zubrow, M. C. Fritz, and J. M. Fritz, pp. 222–230. San Francisco: W. H. Freeman, 1974.

Prussing, Eugene. *The Estate of George Washington, Deceased.* Boston: Little, Brown, 1927.

Purrington, Robert D. "Supposed Solar Alignments at Poverty Point," *American Antiquity* 48, pp. 157–161.

Quinn, David. *North America from Earliest Discovery to First Settlements.* New York: Harper and Row, 1977.

Rafferty, Janet. "A New Map of the Ingomar Mounds Site." *Mississippi Archaeology* 18, no. 2 (1983).

Railey, Jimmy A. "Woodland Settlement Trends and Symbolic Architecture in the Bluegrass." In *Early Woodland Archaeology,* ed. Kenneth B. Farnsworth and Thomas E. Emerson, 2, pp. 581–595. Kampsville, IL: Center for American Archaeology Press, 1991.

Randall, E. O. "Washington's Ohio Lands." *Ohio Archaeological and Historical Quarterly* 19 (July 1990).

Randall, Henry S. *The Life of Thomas Jefferson.* Philadelphia: Lippincott, 1865.

Reeves, D. M. "A Newly Discovered Extension of the Newark Earthworks," *Ohio State Archaeological and Historical Quarterly* 45 (1936):187–193.

Reiter, Edith. *Marietta and the Northwest Territory 1788*. Marietta, OH: Hyde Brothers Printing Co., Ninth Printing, 1986.

Reps, John. *The Making of Urban America: A History of City Planning in the United States*. Princeton, NJ: Princeton University Press, 1965.

Rice, Otis. *The Allegheny Frontier*. Lexington: University of Kentucky Press, 1970.

Riley, Carroll. *The Frontier People*. Albuquerque: University of New Mexico Press, 1987.

Riordan, Robert V. *The Enclosed Hilltops of Southern Ohio*. Presented at Ohio Archaeological Conference, Chillicothe, Ohio, November 19, 1993. Available from Professor Riordan, Wayne State University.

Rodney, Thomas. "Arthur St. Clair." *Pennsylvania Magazine of History and Biography* 43 (1919).

_____. "Cincinatti and Marietta." *Pennsylvania Magazine of History and Biography* 43 (1919).

_____. "Natchez." *Pennsylvania Magazine of History and Biography* 44 (1920).

Rogers, Richard, Larry Martin, and T. Dale Nicklas. "Ice-Age Geography and the Distribution of Native North American Languages." *Journal of Biogeography* 17 (1990).

Rogin, Paul. *Fathers and Children: Andrew Jackson and the Subjugation of the American Indian*. New York: Vintage, 1975.

Romain, William F. "Possible Astronomical Alignments at Hopewell Sites in Ohio." *Ohio Archaeologist* 41 (1991).

_____. "Evidence for a Basic Hopewell Unite of Measure", *Ohio Archaeologist* 41, no. 4 (Fall 1991): 28 ff.

_____. "Hopewellian Concepts in Geometry," *Ohio Archaeologist* 42 (1992).

_____. "More Astronomical Alignments at Hopewell Sites in Ohio", *Ohio Archaeologist* 42, no. 1 (Winter 1992): 38ff.

_____. "Hopewell Ceremonial Centers and Geomantic Influences", *Ohio Archaeologist* 43, no. 1 (Winter 1993): 35 ff.

_____. "Hopewell Geometric Enclosures: Symbols of an Ancient World View." Unpublished manuscript, January 28, 1994.

Rorabaugh, W. J. *The Alcoholic Republic: An American Tradition*. New York: Oxford University Press, 1981.

Rowland, Mrs. Dunbar, *Life, Letters and Papers of William Dunbar,* Jackson, MS; Press of the Mississippi Historical Society, 1930.

Sabloff, Jeremy, *The New Archaeology and the Ancient Maya,* New York: Scientific American Library, 1990.

Salisbury, J. H., and C. B. Salisbury. "Accurate Surveys and Descriptions of the Ancient Earthworks at Newark Ohio." Manuscript on file, Worcester, MA, American Antiquarian Society, 1862.

Salmoral, Manuel. *America 1492: Portrait of a Continent 500 Years Ago*. New York: Facts on File Publications, 1990.

Sandberg, Carl. *Abraham Lincoln: The Prairie Years*. New York: Harcourt Brace, 1926.

Sargent, Winthrop. "Plan of an Ancient Fortification at Marietta, Ohio," *Memoirs of the American Academy of Arts and Sciences,* New Series, 5 (1853).

Sauer, Carl. *Sixteenth Century North America*. Berkeley: University of California Press, 1971.

Saum, Lewis. *The Fur Trade and the Indian.* Seattle: University of Washington Press, 1965.

Savelle, Max. *George Morgan; Colony Builder.* New York: Columbia University Press, 1932.

Schachner, Nathan. *Aaron Burr.* New York: A. S. Barnes. 1961.

Schambach, Frank F. "An Outline of Fourche Maline Culture in Southwest Arkansas." *Arkansas Archaeological Research Series,* No. 15, 1982.

———. "The End of the Trail: The Route of Hernando De Soto's Army Through Southwest Arkansas and East Texas." *Arkansas Archaeologist* (Arkansas Archaeological Society) 27 (1986).

———. "Some New Interpretations of Spiroan History." In *Archaeology of Eastern North America: Papers in Honor of Stephen Williams,* ed. James B. Stoltman. Jackson: Mississippi Department of Archives and History, Archaeological Report No. 25, 1993.

Schambach, Frank, and Frank Rackerby, eds. "The Archaeological Background," from *Contributions to the Archaeology of the Great Bend Region.* Fayetteville: Arkansas Archaeological Survey Research Series, 22 (1982).

Schelbert, Leo. "Albert Gallatin 1761–1899." *Swiss American Historical Society Newsletter* 18 no. 1 (1982).

Schlesinger, Arthur, Jr. *The Age of Jackson.* Boston: Little Brown, 1947.

Schoolcraft, Henry R. "Observations Respecting the Grave Creek Mound," *Transactions of the American Ethnological Society* 1, (1845): 369 ff.

Schultz, Christian. *Travels on an Inland Voyage . . . in 1807 and 1808,* New York: Isaac Riley, 1810.

Sears, Alfred. *Thomas Worthington: Father of Ohio Statehood,* Columbus: Ohio Historical Society, 1958.

Sears, William. *Fort Center: An Archaeological Site in the Lake Okeechobee.* Gainesville: University of Florida Press, 1982.

———. "Food Production and Village Life." *Archaeology* 24, no. 4 (1971).

Seeman, M. F. *The Hopewell Interaction Sphere: The Evidence for Interregional Trade and Structural Complexity,* Prehistory Research Series 5(2). Indianapolis: Indiana Historical Society, 1979.

———. "Feasting with the Dead: Ohio Hopewell Charnel House Ritual as a Context for Redistribution." In *Hopewell Archaeology: The Chillicothe Conference,* ed. D. S. Brose and N. Gerber. Kent, Ohio: Kent State University Press, 1979, pp. 39–46.

Sellers, Charles. *Mr. Peale's Museum: Charles Wilson Peale and the First Popular Museum of Natural Science and Art.* New York: W. W. Norton, 1980.

Shepard, Henry. *Antiquities of the State of Ohio.* Cincinnati: John Yorkston, 1887.

Sherrod, P. Clay, and Martha Ann Rolingson. *Surveyors of the Ancient Mississippi Valley.* Fayetteville: Arkansas Archaeological Survey Research Series No. 28, 1987.

Shetrone, H. C. *the Mound Builders: A Reconstruction of the Life of a Prehistoric American Race.* New York: D. Appleton and Company, 1930.

Showalter, Joseph. "The Travels of George Washington." *National Geographic,* 61 no. 1 (January, 1932).

Sibley, William. *The French Five Hundred*. Gallipolis, OH: published privately, 1933.

Silverberg, R. *The Mound Builders*. Athens: Ohio University Press, 1986.

Simons, M. Laird, ed. *Cyclopaedia of American Literature*, Vol. 1. Philadelphia: Wm. Rutter & Company, 1856.

Skele, Mikels. *The Great Knob: Interpretations of Monks Mound*. Studies in Illinois Archaeology No. 4, Springfield, IL: Illinois Historic Preservation Office, 1988.

Slaughter, Thomas. *The Whiskey Rebellion*. New York: Oxford University Press, 1986.

Smith, Bruce. "The Archaeology of the Southeastern United States." In *Advances in World Archaeology*. Fred Wendorf and Angela E. Close ed., Vol. 5. Orlando: Academic Press (1986).

_____. "Harvest of Prehistory: Ancient Seeds Yield Insight into Early American Agriculture." *The Sciences*, May/June 1991.

_____. "Hopewellian Farmers of North America," paper presented at Plenary Session, Eleventh Congress, International Union of Prehistoric and Protohistoric Sciences, September 1987, Mainz, Germany.

_____. *The Mississippian Emergence*. Washington, DC: Smithsonian Institution, 1990.

_____. "Reconciling the Gender-Credit Critique and The Floodplain Weed Theory of Plant Domestication." *In Archaeology in Eastern North America; Papers in Honor of Stephen Williams*. Ed. James B. Stoltman. Jackson: Mississippi Department of Archives and History (1993).

Smith, Henry. *Virgin Land: The American West as Symbol and Myth*. Cambridge: Harvard University Press, 1978.

Smith, Page. *John Adams*. Garden City: Doubleday, 1962.

Smith, Richard Norton. *Patriarch*. Boston: Houghton Mifflin, 1993.

Smith, Thomas. *The Mapping of Ohio*. Ohio: Kent State University Press, 1977.

Smucker, I. *Issac Smucker Scrap Book*. (Two volumes of newspaper clippings and notes, on file at the Granville Public Library, Granville, OH.) 1875.

_____. "Mound Builders' Works Near Newark, Ohio," *American Antiquarian* 3 no. 4 (1881):261–270.

Sparks, William H. *The Memories of Fifty Years*. Philadelphia: Claxton, Remsen and Haffelinger, 1870.

Sprague, Marshall. *So Vast, So Beautiful A Land: Louisiana and the Purchase*. Boston: Little Brown, 1974.

Squier, E. G., and E. H. Davis. *Ancient Monuments of the Mississippi Valley*. Washington, DC: Smithsonian Institution, 1848.

Stagg, J. C. *Mr. Madison's War*. Princeton: Princeton University Press, 1983.

Stanton, Phoebe B., *Gothic Revival and American Church Architecture*. Baltimore: Johns Hopkins University Press, 1962.

Stanley, Samuel. "The End of the Natchez Indians," *History Today*, 28 (1978).

Stegmaier, Mark, "Zachary Taylor Versus the South." *Civil War History* 33, no. 3 (September, 1987).

Stephens, A. Ray, and William Holmes. *Historical Atlas of Texas*. Norman: University of Oklahoma Press, 1989.

Stevens, John A. *Albert Gallatin*. Boston: Houghton Mifflin & Co., 1884.

Stibbons, Daniel. "Fortifications at Marietta." *The American Pioneer* 1, no. 10 (October 1842).

Stoddard, Amos. *Sketches, Historical and Descriptive, of Louisiana*. Philadelphia: Mathew Carey, 1812.

Stuart, George E. "The Beginning of Maya Hieroglyphic Study: Contributions of Constantine S. Rafinesque and James H. McCulloh, Jr." *Research Reports on Ancient Maya Writing*, 28 (November 1989).

Sturdevant, Rick. "Quest for Eden: George Washington's Frontier Land Interests." Ph.D. dissertation, Santa Barbara, University of California, 1982.

Sullivan, Louis. *A System of Architectural Ornament* (facsimile edition). New York: Rizzoli, 1990.

Syrett, Herald C., ed. *The Papers of Alexander Hamilton*. New York: Columbia University Press, 1977.

Tanner, Helen. *Atlas of the Great Lakes Indian History*, Norman: University of Oklahoma Press, 1987.

Tavernor, Robert. *Palladio and Palladianism*. London: Thames and Hudson, 1991.

Thomas, Cyrus. *Report on the Mound Explorations of the Bureau of Ethnology, Twelfth Annual Report of the Bureau of Ethnology, 1890–91*. Washington, DC: Government Printing Office, 1894. (This is the great Thomas Report, but under his leadership the Bureau issued a preliminary report in 1889, which was largely superseded in the 1890–91 report, but in a few instances had information unique to itself, and is thus cited as "1889 Report.")

Thomas, David Hurst, ed. *Columbian Consequences*. Washington: Smithsonian Institution Press, 1990.

Thruston, Gates P. *The Antiquities of Tennessee*. Cincinnati: Robert Clarke, 1890.

Thwaites, Reuben, ed. *Travels and Explorations of the Jesuit Missionaries in New France: The Voyages of Marquette*. Cleveland: Burrows Bothers Publishers, 1966.

Truettner, William H., ed. *The West as America, Reinterpreting Images of the Frontier, 1820–1920*. Washington, DC: Smithsonian Institution Press, 1991.

Turner, Frederick Jackson. *The Frontier in American History*. Edited by Ray Billington. New York: Holt, Rinehart and Winston, 1962.

Twain, Mark. *Life on the Mississippi*. Boston: Osgood, 1883.

Usner, Daniel H., Jr. *Indians, Settlers, and Slaves in a Frontier Exchange Economy*. Chapel Hill: University of North Carolina Press, for The Institute of Early American History and Culture, Williamsburg, VA, 1990.

Van Every, Dale. *Forth to the Wilderness*. New York: Morrow, 1961.

_____. *Ark of the Empire, The American Frontier 1784–1803*. New York: Quill, 1963.

Viola, Herman. *After Columbus: The Smithsonian Chronicle of North American Indians*. Washington, DC: Smithsonian Institution Press, 1990.

_____, and Carolyn Margolis. *Seeds of Change: Five Hundred Years Since Columbus*. Washington, DC: Smithsonian Institution Press, 1991.

Volney, Constantin Francois Chasseboeuf, compte de. *A View of the Soil and*

Climate of the United States of America, Philadelphia Edition (facsimile). Edited by George W. White. New York: Hafner, 1968.

Von Hagen, Victor W. *Highway of the Sun.* London: Gollancz, 1956.

von Simson, Otto. *The Gothic Cathedral.* Princeton: Princeton University Press, 1962.

Walker, Winslow M. "The Troyville Mounds Catahoula Parish, La." *Smithsonian Institution Bureau of American Ethnology Bulletin 13,* Washington, DC: U.S. Government Printing Office, 1936.

Walters, Raymond Jr. *Albert Gallatin.* Pittsburgh: University of Pittsburgh Press (1957).

Washington, George. *The Diaries of George Washington.* Edited by John Fitzpatrick. Boston: Houghton Mifflin, 1925.

Webb, Clarence, and Hiram Gregory. *The Caddo Indians of Louisiana.* Baton Rouge: Louisiana Archaeological Survey, Anthropological Study, No. 2, 1986.

Wellman, Paul. *The Indian Wars of the West.* New York: Doubleday, 1956.

White, L. "Indian Intermound Orientations in Ohio." *Ohio Archaeologist 35,* no. 3 (1985):8–10.

Whittlesey, Charles. *Descriptions of Ancient Works in Ohio,* Vol. 3. Washington, D.C.: Smithsonian Publications, May 1850.

Wicke, Charles. "Pyramids and Temple Mounds." *American Antiquity 34,* no. 4 (1965).

Williams, Edward G. "A Survey of Bouquet's Road, 1764." *The Western Pennsylvania Historical Magazine* 66 and 67 (1983 and 1984).

Williams, Gwyn. *Madoc: The Legend of the Welsh Discovery of America.* New York: Oxford University Press, 1987.

Williams, Stephen. "Aboriginal Location of the Kadohadacho and Related Tribes," in *Explorations in Cultural Anthropology,* Ward Goodenough, ed. 1965.

———. *Fantastic Archaeology: The Wild Side of North American Prehistory.* Philadelphia: University of Pennsylvania Press, 1991.

———. "Nineteenth Century Perceptions of Cahokia and its Meaning," paper read at the Cahokia Symposium, Society of American Archaeology, Meetings, April 26, 1991.

Williams, Stephen, and Jeffrey Brain. *Excavations at the Lake George Site, Yazoo County, Mississippi.* Cambridge, MA: Peabody Museum Papers, Vol. 74, 1983.

Wills, Garry. *Cincinnatus: George Washington and the Enlightenment; Images of Power in Early America.* New York: Doubleday, 1984.

Wittkower, Rudolph. "English Neoclassicism and Palladio's 'Quatro Libri,'" in *Palladio and English Palladianism,* London: Thames and Hudson, 1974.

Wood, Gordon S. *The Radicalism of the American Revolution.* New York: Knopf (1992 [original publisher]); Random House (1993).

Wood, Peter, Gregory Waselkov, and M. Thomas Hatley, eds. *Powhatan's Mantle: Indians in the Colonial Southeast.* Lincoln: University of Nebraska Press, 1989.

Wood, W. Raymond. "Culture Sequence at the Old Fort, Saline County, Missouri." *American Antiquity 38,* no. 1 (1973).

ACKNOWLEDGMENTS

As I have read through this manuscript for the last time, I have noted with pleasure the scores of occasions in which individual scholars have helped me at specific points in the text. In all those cases in which that help came in writing I have made reference to it in the notes. Michael Zuckerman, Bruce Smith, and Stephen Williams read large sections of this text in its many earlier drafts, and other scholars read great chunks of material which have been removed from this book, to be saved for later volumes, and they will be thanked then. Other assistance has come in person or by telephone from Kathleen Bird, David Brose, C. Allan Brown, Martin Byers, Berle Clay, Jon Gibson, N'omi Greber, George W. Knepper, Bradley Lepper, Ray Luce, Donald Meinig, Gerald Milanich, James L. Murphy, Ken P'Pool, Robert V. Riordan, William F. Romain, Mike Russo, Joe Saunders, Frank Schambach, Michael Taylor, and my colleagues in the Smithsonian Institution. Naomi Glass and Joyce Ramey served to manage my time and my office life at the National Museum of American History during the years in which this book distracted that life, and Mathew Mulcahey, Timothy Deal, and Stephen Ostrander helped during my Smithsonian years with research on this book.

Bruce Nichols and Celia Knight of the Free Press worked to bring coherence to the work, and to prune from it many of my detours and obscurities. Their energy, tolerance, and intelligence have been essential to its arrival at its present state, a considerable distance from that at which it first arrived upon their doorstep. I wish to thank them, and thank as well C. Vann Woodward, who told me years ago that he thought there might be a book in all this.

INDEX

Winchester, James, 322*n*
Winthrop, John, 225
Wollstonecraft, Mary, 324*n*–325*n*
Works East, 51, 57, 247*n*, 304*n*
World of George Washington, The
 (Ketchum), 312*n*
Worthington, Thomas, 70–72, 74–81,
 117, 119, 120, 142, 143, 148*n*–
 149*n*, 182*n*, 306*n*–310*n*
Wright, Frank Lloyd, 247*n*, 268, 285
Wynnewood, 322*n*

Yakima Indians, 250–251
York, Duke of, 118*n*
Young, Bennet H., 61*n*
Young, Brigham, 230

Zane, Ebenezer, 52–53, 302*n*
Zane's Trace (Ray), 302*n*
Zeisberger, David, 46–48
Zinzendorf, Nicholas Ludwig, 46*n*
Zumarraga, Juan de, 224

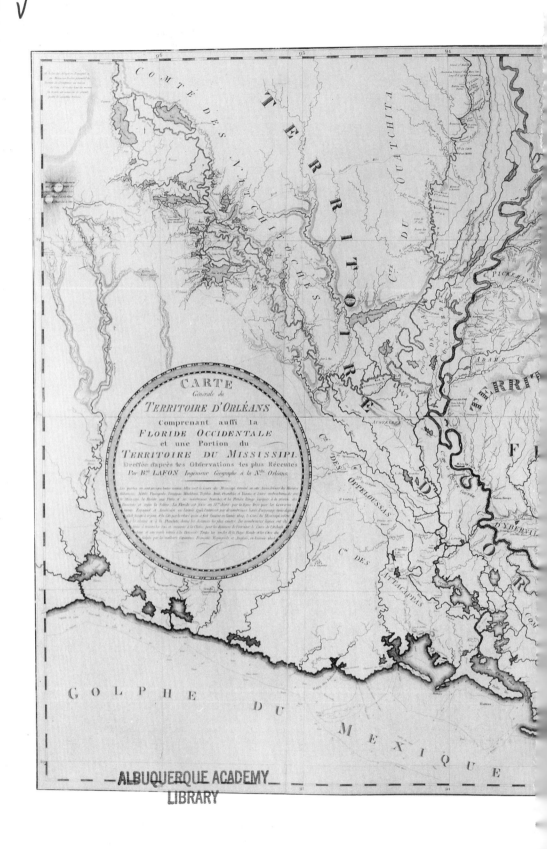

CARTE
Générale du
TERRITOIRE D'ORLÉANS
Comprenant auffi la
FLORIDE OCCIDENTALE
et une Portion du
TERRITOIRE DU MISSISSIPI.
Dreffée d'après les Obfervations les plus Récentes
Par Bon LAFON Ingénieur Géographe à la N^lle Orléans.